The Handbook of
Knowledge-Based Coaching

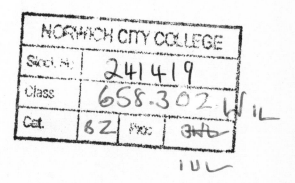

The Handbook of Knowledge-Based Coaching

FROM THEORY TO PRACTICE

Leni Wildflower
and
Diane Brennan

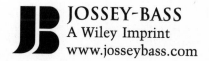

JOSSEY-BASS
A Wiley Imprint
www.josseybass.com

Published by Jossey-Bass
A Wiley Imprint
989 Market Street, San Francisco, CA 94103-1741—www.josseybass.com

Readers should be aware that Internet Web sites offered as citations and/or sources for further information may have changed or disappeared between the time this was written and when it is read.

Limit of Liability/Disclaimer of Warranty: While the publisher and author have used their best efforts in
preparing this book, they make no representations or warranties with respect to the accuracy or completeness of the contents of this book and specifically disclaim any implied warranties of merchantability
or fitness for a particular purpose. No warranty may be created or extended by sales representatives or
written sales materials. The advice and strategies contained herein may not be suitable for your situation.
You should consult with a professional where appropriate. Neither the publisher nor author shall be liable
for any loss of profit or any other commercial damages, including but not limited to special, incidental,
consequential, or other damages.

Jossey-Bass books and products are available through most bookstores. To contact Jossey-Bass directly
call our Customer Care Department within the U.S. at 800-956-7739, outside the U.S. at 317-572-3986,
or fax 317-572-4002.

Jossey-Bass also publishes its books in a variety of electronic formats. Some content that appears in print
may not be available in electronic books.

Library of Congress Cataloging-in-Publication Data

The handbook of knowledge-based coaching: from theory to practice / [edited by] Leni Wildflower
and Diane Brennan.
    p. cm.
  Includes bibliographical references and index.
  ISBN 978-0-470-62444-9 (hardback); ISBN 978-1-118-03336-4 (ebk); 978-1-118-03337-1 (ebk);
978-1-118-03338-8 (ebk)
  1. Executive coaching. I. Wildflower, Leni. II. Brennan, Diane.
  HD30.4.H3497 2011
  658.3'124—dc22

                                                   2011011134

Printed in the United States of America
FIRST EDITION
HB Printing   10 9 8 7 6 5 4 3 2 1

CONTENTS

The Jossey-Bass
Business & Management Series

To all those who take the risk of changing their careers
to be of service to others through coaching

PREFACE
FROM THEORY TO PRACTICE

As coaches we have responsibilities: to master the skills of our trade, to work on the issues in ourselves that might obstruct or distort our dealings with clients, to be ethical, to acknowledge limitations and recognize boundaries, to justify the trust clients put in us. We also have a responsibility to understand the intellectual underpinnings of our fledgling profession.

Some of us have an instinctive ability to draw people toward greater insight; some of us have to work at it. But we all need to understand what we do when we coach, to recognize that coaching has not sprung fully formed from the protocols of our coaching schools or the minds of individuals, however dynamic and innovative, but has grown from a rich tilth of wisdom and study.

Some of this knowledge is the direct history of coaching. Much of it could be thought of as coaching's prehistory—ideas developed in entirely independent fields before coaching in its modern sense was conceived of. But far from dry or dutiful, these explorations have the power to continually reignite our sense of coaching as a living practice.

In each of the chapters that follow there is a progression from theory to application, studying first a model or a set of findings in the context of a particular discipline and then identifying the implications for the practicing coach. There is a mind-opening diversity in this, but also a striking unanimity. Coaching may derive from the confluence of many rivers, but it flows with its own powerful current.

Leni Wildflower
Diane Brennan

ACKNOWLEDGMENTS

To the students and alumni of the Fielding Graduate University Evidence-Based Coaching Certificate Program: your enthusiasm for our program—the curiosity and idealism with which you responded to its mix of theory and practice—inspired us to take this book forward.

To the Fielding Graduate University Human and Organizational Development Program (HOD), particularly Judy Stevens-Long, who championed the Coaching Certificate Program in the crucial planning stage, and Dean Charles McClintock and Associate Dean Katrina Rogers, who oversaw its inception and continue to nurture it: you gave us the support and encouragement to make this book possible.

To our Wiley publishers and especially senior editor Kathe Sweeney: we owe much to you for believing in us.

To our many contributing authors: thank you for your time, your energy, and your patience, and for the wonderful range of knowledge and insight you have brought to this project.

To our husbands and kids—Joe, Jesse, Bill, and Ashley: thank you for putting up with our late nights, early mornings, and endless phone calls, and our long preoccupation with this enterprise.

To Joe Treasure, our writing coach: you challenged and inspired us to keep working toward greater clarity of thought and expression, and to discover a way to create a unique coaching book.

The Handbook of
Knowledge-Based Coaching

PART ONE

Human Behavior and Coaching

In its adolescent phase, coaching was sometimes reluctant to acknowledge its parents.

There was a concern to establish the independence of this new activity, to assert the particular limits and possibilities of what we were doing, which expressed itself in a tendency to define coaching by what it was not—obviously not consulting and not exactly mentoring either, but above all not therapy or counseling or any form of psychology-in-practice.

No doubt there was an element of insecurity in these negative definitions, a fear of being overshadowed or subsumed, a suspicion that the connection was, at times, too close for comfort. But there was also a legitimate concern. Coaching did have something new and distinct to offer, and it was important to establish its separateness.

Now, from a position of relative maturity, the profession can more freely recognize and embrace its origins. It is clear that coaching draws on and fulfills some of the essential premises of humanistic and positive psychology, beginning with an assumption not of sickness but of well-being and aspiring not merely to remedy but to transform. It leans on the concept of adult development. It builds on the idea that there is a cyclical relationship between cognition and behavior.

These connections are not merely historical. The relationship between coaching and psychology is dynamic. We continue to draw on research from psychology, neuroscience, and other related fields; such knowledge is not the exclusive territory of the specialist, any more than mathematical knowledge is to be used only by mathematicians.

As coaches, we take from psychology the essential understanding that we humans are more alike than not, with similar needs and fears and impulses, and we find this recognition liberating and life-enhancing. And we recognize that while our work with clients is pragmatic and forward looking, we should not be frightened of the kinds of personal issues that have traditionally been considered the domain of psychologists.

chapter ONE

Humanistic and Transpersonal Psychology

Alison Whybrow and Leni Wildflower

Psychology provides the primary theoretical underpinning to the theory and practice of coaching. The theories of humanistic psychology and Carl Rogers (1961) have formed the basis for many of the skills and assumptions used today in the coaching engagement. Coaching has also been significantly influenced by the psychological theories of Fritz Perls (Perls, Hefferline, & Goodman, 1994) and Gestalt therapy; Abraham Maslow's work on self-actualization and peak experiences (1968); and Stanislav Grof (2000), Roberto Assagioli (2007), and transpersonal psychology.

CARL ROGERS AND THE CLIENT-CENTERED APPROACH

There is probably no single person more responsible for shifting psychology from a pathological, childhood-focused Freudian orientation to a present-day, positive orientation than Carl Rogers. A clinical psychologist with a PhD from Columbia University, Rogers began developing client-centered or nondirective therapy in the 1940s. He opposed the assumption that the therapist knows more than the client or has a more informed understanding of the client's problem, and should therefore direct the progress of the therapeutic engagement. He objected not only to explicit forms of direction, such as offering a diagnosis or giving advice, but also to more subtle forms of control, such as asking direct questions.

Rogers took issue with the psychoanalytic and behaviorist approaches that were dominant at the time. Neither seemed to offer a particularly optimistic or noble vision of the human predicament. Both could be seen to fragment and diminish the wholeness of the individual. Freud, the founder of psychoanalysis, had emphasized unconscious motivation, often destructive or antisocial in nature; the inevitability of deep internal conflict; and the search for early trauma as an explanation of adult dysfunction. Behaviorism, which had grown out of Ivan Pavlov's study of the conditioned reflex, also put the focus on impulses and patterns of behavior beyond conscious control. From these perspectives, the individual is a stranger to herself. Certainly Jung, Freud's chosen successor, had allotted a more positive and creative role to the hidden regions of the mind, envisioning in the collective unconscious and the archetypes that inhabit it an ancient repository of shared wisdom. But the dominant view among Rogers's contemporaries was of the unconscious as a dangerous and disturbing terrain to be explored only with the guidance of a professional.

In contrast, Rogers argued that given a healthy therapeutic environment, people can be trusted to understand and resolve their own problems, that they are naturally inclined toward what is good for them, and that they have a huge capacity for positive growth. Rogers's work rested on several critical principles. To establish the right kind of environment, the therapist must first of all be genuine in his relationship with the client. In a word favored by the existentialists (a significant influence on Rogers's thinking), the therapist must be *authentic*. Rogers saw no place for the kind of professional façade designed to preserve the therapist's detachment, anonymity, or authority. It follows that the therapist might find it appropriate at times to disclose thoughts or feelings of his own. Just as important, there is no place for judgment. The therapist must communicate unconditional positive regard for the client, who should feel genuinely accepted and valued.

Within this relationship, the essential work of the therapist is to listen attentively to the client to understand the world as the client experiences it. This listening must be not only empathetic but accurate: the therapist should be willing to check that he has understood correctly. He must be sensitive to implied meanings as well as explicit ones, and to feelings and thoughts not fully grasped by the client. The purpose of client-centered therapy is to enable the client to become more open to experience, to develop greater trust in herself, and to continue to grow, pursuing goals of her own choosing. This development of a stronger and healthier sense of self is sometimes referred to as "self-actualization." Rogerian therapy imposes no particular structure and is not based on a set of techniques, but is highly dependent on the nature of the relationship the therapist establishes with the client, a relationship in which the therapist must be present in the most profound sense.

In the late 1950s, Rogers began working with other theorists and practitioners interested in promoting a more holistic approach to psychology, including Abraham Maslow. This led to the formation in 1961 of the Association for Humanistic Psychology, and it became possible for humanistic psychology to be identified as a "third force" in psychology after psychoanalysis and behaviorism.

Coaching clearly owes a great deal to client-centered therapy in its emphasis on treating the client with respect, trusting her instinct for what she needs, and allowing her to take the lead in shaping the purpose and direction of the process. It was important in its time as a corrective to what some have experienced as the disempowering experience of more traditional forms of psychotherapy. Perhaps its major drawback is that it does not allow any mechanism for feedback to assist the essentially healthy client in correcting unhelpful or dysfunctional behaviors.

Coaching Applications

- **Establish collaboration as the basis for the coaching relationship.** It is your responsibility to actively engage your client in dialogue with such questions as *What would you like to work on today?*

- **Practice empathetic listening.** Attend carefully to your client's experience, imagine that you are in her shoes, ask for clarification, and communicate to her your understanding of her situation.

- **Communicate to the client that he has the knowledge, emotional strength, and personal power to make the changes he desires.** Use his experience and understanding as the basis for your work together.

- **Work to create a relationship with your client that is caring and mutually respectful.** This relationship is fundamental to the success of the coaching endeavor. Metastudies in psychotherapy have demonstrated that it is the relationship, not necessarily the type of therapeutic intervention used, that produces a positive experience and growth. The same is almost certainly true of coaching.

- **Be authentic in the coaching relationship.** Be yourself. Give open and honest feedback to the client to support her exploration and learning. At the same time, value her without judgment wherever she finds herself in life. This is what it means to hold her in "unconditional positive regard" and is fundamental to your role in empowering her to change.

FRITZ PERLS AND GESTALT THERAPY

Approximately translated, *gestalt* is German for "form." Gestalt therapy was founded in the 1940s by Fritz and Laura Perls. Rooted in the idea that the mind has a capacity to see things in their wholeness and to construct forms out of fragmentary information, it is concerned with helping the individual observe herself in the broader context of a web, or field, of relationships. It can be seen as a process of experimentation and observation. In contrast to a tradition of experimental psychology that has tended, on the model of the physical sciences, to break things down into their component parts, the Gestalt approach is essentially holistic.

The philosophy underlying Gestalt therapy is existentialist in its view that most people live in a state of self-deception, accepting conventional notions that obscure the reality of how the world is; that this leads to feelings of anxiety and guilt; and that to live authentically, people must continually rediscover and reinvent themselves. Therapists and clients engage in dialogue, with the aim of observing the process rather than its content. Dialogue is understood to include all forms of communication, such as body language and movement as well as speech. Perceptions, feelings, and actions are considered to be more reliable kinds of data than explanations or interpretations. Relationships experienced in the present moment, including that between therapist and client, are more immediately revealing as objects of study than what is merely reported, but external relationships can be effectively brought into the room and reexperienced.

During the session, the client will show behavior patterns that occur outside the session. Noticing these patterns will increase the client's awareness of how she behaves in the world. This will enable her not only to accept and value herself as she is but also to change and grow and become more fully responsible. The role of the therapist is not to lead or direct the process and not to put theory or interpretation in the way, but to be present without judgment, modeling authentic dialogue.

Coaching Applications

- **Encourage self-observation so that your client is both *being* in the moment and *seeing* himself being in the moment.** Create greater awareness by helping him notice any disconnect between what he is saying and the behavior he is exhibiting. Be conscious of subtleties of body language, tone of voice, and other nonverbal indicators.

- **Be aware of the importance of cocreating a safe, open, and honest relationship with your client.** A feeling of profound trust is essential if she is to feel safe exploring unacknowledged or unrecognized truths.

- **In working with groups or teams, encourage awareness of what is *happening* in the group as opposed to what is spoken.** In other words, shift the focus from the content of the conversation to the process.

ABRAHAM MASLOW AND SELF-ACTUALIZATION

Abraham Maslow, along with Rogers and Perls, is considered one of the founders of the humanistic psychology movement. Among the contributions for which he is best known are his Hierarchy of Needs model and the concept of peak experiences. The needs Maslow identifies, starting with the most basic, are physiological needs (food, shelter, water, sleep, sex); need for safety and security; need for love and belonging; need for self-esteem and esteem by others; and self-actualization needs. Maslow defines self-actualization as a sense of knowing exactly who you are and where you are going, and the ability to enjoy a state of completeness and wholeness in life. According to Maslow, a self-actualized individual experiences play and work as similar, has an increased capacity for spontaneity, and an acceptance and expression of the inner core of self.

Self-actualization can be achieved intermittently in what Maslow calls peak experiences. These transient moments of self-actualization can occur at any time in life, though Maslow felt they were more likely to occur during adulthood. Peak experiences take us beyond our ordinary perceptions and provide a moment of transcendence. They are nonreligious, quasi-mystical experiences that might encompass a sudden feeling of intense happiness and well-being, a sense of wonder and awe, or fleeting moments of enlightenment.

At one point Maslow developed a set of qualities that characterized a self-actualized individual. Some of the qualities he posited included

An ability to see problems in terms of challenges and situations requiring solutions

A need for privacy; being comfortable with being alone

The reliance on one's own judgment and experiences; not being influenced by social pressures

The ability to accept others as they are and not attempt to change people

Being comfortable with oneself, with a sense of humor about oneself and an ability to see others as completely separate from oneself

A sense of excitement and interest in everything

The capacity to be creative, inventive, and original

Coaching Applications

- **If appropriate, use Maslow's Hierarchy of Needs model to help your client understand himself in terms of his needs, desires, and aspirations.** Like the balance wheel (see Chapter Twenty-Five), Maslow's hierarchical pyramid and definition of a self-actualized individual can be used as templates to give structure to an exploration of issues in your client's life.

- **Invite your client to consider the moments in her life when she has felt self-actualized.** Think about appropriate ways of asking this question. When has she experienced a sense of acceptance, wholeness, or fulfillment; been at her most creative; realized her full potential? When has she been at one with herself, at peace with her work and her life? There are times when focusing on a peak experience from the past may help create a sense of possibility.

STANISLAV GROF, ROBERTO ASSAGIOLI, AND TRANSPERSONAL PSYCHOLOGY

In the 1960s, Maslow's study of peak experiences made a significant contribution to the emerging field of transpersonal psychology. Another leading figure was Stanislav Grof, who directed research at the Maryland Psychiatric Research Center and went on to become scholar-in-residence at the Esalen Institute in Big Sur, California (see Chapter Twenty). Grof became interested in what he identified as nonordinary states of consciousness, studying the impact of LSD on the mind, and later developing breathing techniques to achieve similar effects.

Transpersonal psychology explores states of consciousness that have been traditionally associated with mystical and spiritual experiences. Proponents of transpersonal psychology state that if these experiences can be accessed, they offer the potential for joy, insight, and healing. Whereas mainstream psychology has tended to marginalize these experiences or identify them as symptoms of mental illness, transpersonal psychology sees them as glimpses of a greater reality.

To this extent, the roots of transpersonal psychology can be traced to various religious traditions, particularly to eastern traditions that emphasize meditation and mindfulness. More immediate influences include Carl Jung, who envisaged a collective unconscious in which reside the archetypes of shared human experience. In addition, Roberto Assagioli, a friend and colleague of Carl Jung, worked on the concept, proposed by Jung, of psychosynthesis—a coming together of personal growth, personality integration, and self-actualization. His goal was a direct experience of the pure self at a spiritual level. Like Grof and Maslow, Assagioli researched the higher levels of human awareness.

The application of transpersonal psychology to coaching is less well established, although there are strong philosophical links between Gestalt and transpersonal approaches. In fact, Gestalt is often viewed as a transpersonal approach.

Coaching Applications

- **Listen to your client.** What needs does he express? What needs is he not yet able to identify or ready to acknowledge?

- **Be open to a view of life's mystical dimension that you don't happen to share.** Your client may feel attuned to the transpersonal and the transcendent, or may think of herself as a rationalist and a skeptic. Whatever your own view, be responsive to hers.

Additional Reading

Assagioli, R. (2007). *Transpersonal development: The dimension beyond psychosynthesis.* Findhorn, Scotland: Smiling Wisdom.

The most recently published book by Assagioli discussing his research into altered states.

Boeree, G. *Personality theories: Abraham Maslow*. Available on the Web at www.ship .edu/~cgboeree/maslow.html.

Good and thorough introduction to Maslow's theories and the concept of self-actualization and peak experiences.

Cox, E., Bachkirova, T., & Clutterbuck, D. (2010). *The complete handbook of coaching*. London: Sage.

An excellent overview of coaching theories in a more academic context, including a theoretical essay on transpersonal psychology.

Grof, S. (2000). *Psychology of the future: Lessons from modern consciousness research*. Albany: State University of New York Press.

Grof's most recent book describing his research into consciousness. Helpful reading in this area.

Kirschenbaum, H., & Henderson, V. L. (Eds.). (1989). *The Carl Rogers reader: Selections from the lifetime work of America's preeminent psychologist, author of* On Becoming a Person *and* A Way of Being. Boston: Houghton-Mifflin.

An excellent overview of Rogers's life and work.

Leary-Joyce, J., & Allen, M. (2010). *The Gestalt coaching handbook*. Available on the Web at www.aoec.com.

An online publication that supports coaches in understanding the application of Gestalt to coaching.

Maslow, A. H. (1999). *Toward a psychology of being* (3rd. ed.). Hoboken, NJ: Wiley.

Maslow's most well-known book on his theories and their application.

Perls, F. S. (1992). *Gestalt therapy verbatim*. Gouldsboro, ME: Gestalt Journal Press.

A collection of talks by Perls, originally published in 1969, with commentary. Gives a good sense of his dynamic personality.

Rogers, C. R. (1980). *A way of being*. Boston: Houghton-Mifflin.

Rogers's classic text on self-actualization and how to facilitate this process.

chapter TWO

Cognitive Behavioral Therapy and Related Theories

Leni Wildflower

There is nothing either good or bad, but thinking makes it so.

—Hamlet, act 2 scene 2

Assume a virtue if you have it not. . . .
For use almost can change the stamp of nature.

—Hamlet, act 3 scene 4

In the midtwentieth century, mainstream therapeutic assumptions—that behavior is governed by feeling and that extensive reflection on the past is necessary for healing—were challenged by new cognitive and behavioral approaches. Cognitive behavioral therapy and the theories related to it can readily be adapted to certain coaching situations. They share with coaching an emphasis on attending cognitively to the issue at hand, a pragmatic interest in overcoming present and future limitations, and an immediate engagement with the world as a testing ground for better ways of functioning.

COGNITIVE BEHAVIORAL THERAPY AND AARON BECK

Aaron Beck trained as a psychoanalyst, but in the 1960s repudiated the Freudian emphasis on unconscious processes and developed cognitive therapy. He is considered the father of cognitive behavioral therapy (CBT). Instead of exploring the unconscious and delving into childhood experience to find the sources of unhappiness and dysfunction, CBT focuses on changing behavior. It is goal oriented and focused on the here and now. It emphasizes the role of thinking in the treatment of emotional and behavioral disorders, and operates on the premise that present-day changes in thoughts or behaviors can be highly effective in solving deep-seated emotional problems:

> For a good part of their waking life, people monitor their thoughts, wishes, feelings and actions. Sometimes there is an internal debate as the individual weighs alternatives and courses of action and makes decisions. . . . Cognitive therapy consists of all the approaches that alleviate psychological distress through the medium of correcting faulty conceptions and self-signals. . . . By correcting erroneous beliefs, we can damp down or alter excessive, inappropriate emotional reactions. (Beck, 1976)

CBT grew out of a merging of two rival approaches. Behavior therapy, popular in the 1950s, was rooted in research by John B. Watson and B. F. Skinner into behavior modification and in Ivan Pavlov's work on conditioned stimulus response. It was challenged by cognitive psychologists, including Aaron Beck and Albert Ellis. For the behaviorists, the key factor in learning was the environment. Cognitive theory, in contrast, focused on the way the brain processes information—particularly in sorting it into long-term and short-term memory—and attributed more control to the individual learner. Behaviorism asserts that a change in behavior will alter one's thinking, whereas in cognitive therapy the emphasis is on changing one's thought patterns to bring about a change in behavior. In reality, thought and behavior influence each other, so that it is difficult to distinguish which comes first. Recent research indicates that maximum effectiveness in this approach is achieved when there are both cognitive and behavioral shifts.

Currently, CBT is used primarily in treatment of panic disorder and agoraphobia, obsessive-compulsive disorder, posttraumatic stress disorder, depression, eating disorders, psychotic symptoms, and generalized health anxiety. Research has demonstrated the effectiveness of this type of therapy (Reinecke & Clark, 2004).

A central feature of CBT is the behavioral experiment. In Beck's early publication (1976), he likens CBT to a scientific investigation. Therapist and patient are encouraged to view the patient's beliefs as hypotheses and to develop experiments to test and challenge these hypotheses empirically. Therapist and patient first select the assumption they want to test. A task is then identified that allows an experimental test of the assumption. Once the experiment has been completed, therapist and patient evaluate the results of the experiment to determine whether the experiment has altered the patient's original assumption. Although behavioral experiments (known as BEs) are not the only therapeutic procedure in CBT, they are a key component of this type of treatment.

Additional Characteristics of Cognitive Behavioral Therapy

- CBT is brief and time limited. Contributing to its brevity is its instructional nature and the fact that it makes use of homework assignments. CBT therapists assign reading and experiments to test assumptions, and encourage their clients to practice the techniques learned.

- CBT is a collaborative effort between the therapist and the client. CBT therapists seek to learn what their clients want out of life, and then help their clients achieve those goals.

- CBT does not tell people how they should feel. Most people seeking therapy, however, want to escape from a current state of feeling. CBT teaches the benefits of remaining *calm* when confronted with undesirable situations, emphasizing that such situations will continue to exist whether we are upset about them or not.

- CBT therapists often encourage their clients to ask questions of themselves—for example: "How do I really know that those people are laughing at me? Could they be laughing about something else?"

- CBT is based on an educational model. CBT therapists focus on teaching rational self-counseling skills. The goal is to help clients *unlearn* their unwanted reactions and learn a new way of reacting. The educational emphasis of CBT has long-term results. When people understand how and why they are doing well, they can continue doing what they are doing to make themselves well.

A Practical Application of CBT: Christine Padesky

Psychologist Christine Padesky and her associates, working in the United States, have applied CBT methods to a variety of mental health conditions (Padesky & Greenberger, 1995). Partly driven by the limitations of medical insurance payments for therapy in the United States, they constructed a clear, time-limited protocol for increasing client involvement in the therapeutic process. They have had considerable success in treating highly dysfunctional people over a short period of time; however, many of their procedures are directly applicable also to coaching work with high-functioning, healthy individuals.

Coaching Applications

- **Make sure assignments are relevant and interesting to your client.** Work with her to devise tasks that are suited to her level of skill and that require manageable changes of behavior. Be sure she is engaged in the process and understands fully what she has agreed to do before the next session.

- **Emphasize the learning component of any exercise.** Getting it right in the short term is less important than gaining long-term insight. Striving for perfection can be a trap.

- **Work with your client to set goals that are concrete and measurable.** Questions that might help him define his goal include the following:

  What small steps would show that you were inching toward the goal?

  What do you need to do first before the final goal is possible?

  How many weeks or months do you think it will take to reach your goal?

  What one or two things should you do first?

  What would be the first sign that you are making progress?

  If this were a friend's goal, what would you advise him or her to do to get started?

  Are there one or two smaller changes that would make you feel better and let you know you are on the right track?

  How might you break your goal into a number of smaller steps?

  Are your specific goals achievable, and can they be observed?

How will you know if you are making progress? What will be different in your life?

CBT APPLIED TO THE CONCEPT OF FEELING GOOD: DAVID BURNS

In his best-selling book *Feeling Good: The New Mood Therapy,* David Burns (1980) has provided the general public with a practical guide to understanding CBT concepts and reversing unhelpful thinking. Burns summarizes ten definitions of cognitive distortions:

1. *All-or-nothing thinking.* You see things in black-and-white categories. If your performance falls short of perfect, you see yourself as a total failure.

2. *Overgeneralization.* You see a single negative event as a never-ending pattern of defeat.

3. *Mental filter.* You pick out a single negative detail and dwell on it exclusively so that your vision of all reality becomes darkened.

4. *Disqualifying the positive.* You reject positive experiences by insisting they "don't count."

5. *Jumping to conclusions.* You make a negative interpretation even though there are no definite facts that convincingly support your conclusion. For example, you arbitrarily conclude that someone is reacting negatively to you, or you are convinced that something will turn out badly when you have not yet experienced it.

6. *Magnification (catastrophizing) or minimization.* You exaggerate the importance of such things as your errors or someone else's achievement. Conversely, you inappropriately shrink such things as your own desirable qualities or someone else's imperfections.

7. *Emotional reasoning.* You assume that your negative emotions necessarily reflect the way things really are.

8. *"Should" statements.* You try to motivate yourself with *shoulds* and *should nots* and as a result often feel guilt, anger, frustration, or resentment toward others.

9. *Labeling and mislabeling.* Instead of accepting accountability and describing an error you have made, you attach a negative label to yourself or others—"I'm a loser" or "He's a terrible person."

10. *Personalization.* You see yourself as the cause of some negative external event, for which in fact you were not primarily responsible.

Coaching Applications

- **Where appropriate, show your client David Burns's list of the ten cognitive distortions.** Ask her to choose any that apply to her and write down personal examples.

- **Help your client recognize that another person's behavior might have nothing to do with anything your client has done.** For the client, reframing the situation in this way can be one step toward changing his own role in it.

- **Raise awareness around the client's use of language that might increase her feelings of guilt or resentment.** Words such as *should* and *shouldn't* can reinforce her sense of judgment about her own behavior or other people's. Ask her to track her use of such words, recognizing the way they limit her thinking.

- **Be aware of your client's progress or lack of progress as he navigates the process of behavior change.** Acknowledge his accomplishment in taking on assignments and experiments. Notice and address resistance or stalled efforts. Help him be accountable for his work toward the goal.

RATIONAL EMOTIVE BEHAVIORAL THERAPY AND ALBERT ELLIS

Rational emotive behavioral therapy (REBT) is similar to CBT but stresses humanistic principles, including the importance of offering the client unconditional positive regard, and strives for more long-term changes in behavior through desensitization, positive reinforcement, and working directly on emotions. In reality, many of the irrational thought patterns that Beck and Ellis presented as bases for dysfunction are very similar (Peltier, 2001). However, Ellis concentrated more on what can be termed absolutist thinking and used a somewhat broader approach in his treatment (Ellis & Dryden, 1997). Ellis saw three core beliefs or philosophies destructive to human well-being:

1. One must perform well under all conditions and at all times to get and keep the love and approval one needs.

2. It is critical to one's well-being that others behave nicely, are considerate, and treat one fairly.

3. The conditions under which one lives must at all times be favorable, safe, and enjoyable.

According to Ellis, people engage in absolutist thinking when they believe that if any of these conditions are not present, terrible things will occur and life will not be worth living. Therapy involves modifying thinking and behavior patterns and developing self-acceptance, other-acceptance, and life-acceptance as precepts of mental health.

Coaching Applications

- **If a client wants to change some behavior, encourage her not to spend time and energy feeling bad about it or analyzing what in her past might have caused it.** Help her acknowledge her current feeling, then work with her to devise exercises or experiments that will help shift her behavior.

- **Help your client in the process of behavior change by having him record and measure his progress.** A client who loses his temper, for example, might keep a tally of how often this happens and aim to reduce the number from one week to the next.

- **Help your client become aware of an unhelpful belief and encourage her to put it to the test.** A client who says or thinks *If I admit to making a mistake, my colleagues will despise me* could decide to acknowledge an error and observe what effect this has.

- **Devise activities with your client that will help him change a behavior or attitude.** For example, have him interview someone he admires to find out how that person copes with problems, or keep a self-observation journal to record his own behavior and feelings.

SOCIAL LEARNING THEORY: ALBERT BANDURA

Beginning in the early 1970s, psychologist and therapist Albert Bandura (1977) developed what he termed social learning theory, which asserts that cognition, behavior, and the environment interact with each other to produce the human condition. This interaction is continuous and reciprocal. Bandura emphasized the importance of individuals observing and modeling the behaviors, attitudes, and emotional reactions of others. Because modeling encompasses attention, memory, and motivation, social learning theory spans both cognitive and behavioral frameworks. The principles of social learning are as follows:

- Learning can occur without a change in behavior. People do not have to actually change. They can learn by observation alone, not only performance.

- Cognition plays a critical role in learning. Awareness and expectations of future reinforcements or punishments can have a major effect on the behaviors that people exhibit.

- People are reinforced for imitating the behavior of others and conforming to the social environment.

- People are more likely to engage in certain behaviors when they believe they are capable of executing those behaviors successfully.

- Individuals who experience increased self-efficacy are capable of self-monitoring and self-reinforcement. They can monitor and observe their own behavior. They are also able to change their behavior by reinforcing themselves.

Coaching Applications

- **Ask your client to identify an individual she admires and to write down that person's qualities.** Such an exercise in attention, as Bandura would call it, is a way to begin the process of modeling desired behaviors. Encouraging her to be specific about what she admires in the other person will help her focus on behaviors she would like to practice herself.

- **Be aware of the environment in which your client lives or works.** Help him observe ways in which the people around him might be either pressuring him into unskillful behavior or supporting him in becoming more effective.

COGNITIVE BEHAVIORAL COACHING

Several schools of coaching techniques derived from CBT thinking have grown up since the 1990s. Cognitive behavioral coaching (CBC) has been defined as "an integrative approach which combines the use of cognitive, behavioral, imaginal and problem solving techniques and strategies within a cognitive behavioral framework to enable coaches to achieve their realistic goals" (Palmer & Szymanska, 2007, p. 86). Like CBT, CBC works to help clients correct distorted thinking patterns, accept themselves, and experiment with new behaviors. According to Williams, Edgerton, and Palmer (2010), the main goals of CBC are to

- Facilitate clients in achieving their realistic goals
- Facilitate self-awareness of underlying cognitive and emotional barriers to goal attainment
- Equip the individual with more effective thinking and behavioral skills
- Build internal resources, stability, and self-acceptance in order to mobilize the individual toward a choice of action
- Enable clients to become their own coaches

Coaching Applications

- **Help your client notice how her thinking supports or limits her in achieving a desired outcome.** Encourage her to distinguish between performance interfering thoughts (PITs) and performance enhancing thoughts (PETs) (Williams et al., 2010).

- **Introduce a problem-solving framework to assist your client as he begins to reframe his thinking.** Two examples are the PRACTICE model (Williams et al., 2010) and the Context Shifting Worksheet (Pellerin, 2009). Having a structured process to work through will support him in expanding his thinking, gaining perspective, and defining next steps.

Additional Reading

Burns, D. (1999). *The feeling good handbook*. New York: Penguin Putnam.
A popular handbook based on Burns's original book, *Feeling Good*. The handbook is useful in applying CBT methods to depression and anxiety, and to experiencing greater intimacy in relationships.
Padesky, C. A., & Greenberger, D. (1995). *Clinician's guide to mind over mood*. New York: Guilford Press.
A clearly written manual on CBT techniques and practices.

Pellerin, C. (2009). *How NASA builds teams.* Hoboken, NJ: Wiley.

A book written about Dr. Pellerin's firsthand experience working within NASA. His Context Shifting Worksheet is a particularly useful tool for aiding individuals and teams to move from problem situation to solution.

Williams, H., Edgerton, N., & Palmer, S. (2010). Cognitive behavioral coaching. In E. Cox, T. Bachkirova, & D. Clutterbuck (Eds.), *The complete handbook of coaching* (pp. 37–51). London: Sage.

The authors provide a thorough look at CBC and examine several models and their application in practice.

Positive Psychology

chapter THREE

Kate Hefferon

Over the last decade, the integration of positive psychology into the coaching world has increased significantly (Grant, in press; Grant & Spence, in press; Kauffman & Scouler, 2004). Although this is an obvious pairing, it is only recently that the publication of accessible and scientifically supported literature in positive psychology has enabled coaches to access existing validated positive psychology interventions (known as PPIs). These offer a wealth of innovative and invigorating exercises for coaches to use in their client sessions.

Major areas in the field of positive psychology include positive emotions, resilience, strengths, and flow. What follows is by no means an exhaustive review of the discipline; however, these are the theories that have proven most useful to coaches.

POSITIVE PSYCHOLOGY AND MARTIN SELIGMAN

Positive psychology is the science of well-being and optimal functioning (Seligman & Csikszentmihalyi, 2000). It focuses on a way of thinking that differs crucially from mainstream psychology. Instead of concentrating on pathology, positive psychology begins by examining the individual's positive qualities, including success, contentment, and fulfillment. As a result, the center of attention is the study and fostering of *flourishing* within the normal population. The areas of supported research concentrate on positive emotions, resilience, strengths, optimism, hope, goals, meaning, and flow. Seligman and Csikszentmihalyi claim that the experience of happiness is derived from essentially three sources: experiencing pleasure, having meaning in one's life, and experiencing flow while at work or play.

Plotting levels of function on a scale that runs from −8 to +8, the health model framework aims to shift people from +3 (languishing) to +8 (flourishing). This contrasts with the more familiar medical model, which focuses on shifting significantly depressed people to only moderately depressed levels of functioning, from −8 to −3.

Where the traditional medical model treats depression, the health model studies *well-being*. A concern with psychopathology is replaced with an interest in *flourishing*. In place of repairing and reducing deficiencies, the health model puts the emphasis on *growing and building strengths*. Attention shifts from removing pain to *adding pleasure*.

While acknowledging the validity of negative emotions, positive psychologists Seligman and Csikszentmihalyi (2000) demonstrated the importance of well-being for physically, emotionally, and psychologically healthy individuals. For example, research has shown that people who report high levels of happiness have been found to outlive their more unhappy peers; they tend to get married and stay married longer; they excel in work, achieving higher wages, evaluations, and status; have better social relationships; and are more altruistic and creative (Biswas-Diener & Dean, 2007).

The good news is that, as individuals, we have a lot of say in becoming more happy. Researchers postulate that we have control over approximately 40 percent of our happiness. (Genetics are responsible for 50 percent; life circumstances, 10 percent.) Lyubomirsky (2006, 2008) calls this the *40% solution*. Positive psychology researchers and practitioners have focused on developing this 40 percent as one of the keys to flourishing. In order to harness the power of the 40% solution, positive psychology interventions (PPIs) have been found to have a significant positive effect on well-being (Seligman, Steen, Park, & Peterson, 2005; Sin & Lyubomirsky, 2009).

Coaching Applications

- **Work with your client to increase her feeling of well-being.** Because the ability to experience happiness is such a crucial element in life, you can attend to this in conjunction with almost any of the issues that come up in the coaching engagement.

- **Offer to administer one of the positive psychology instruments to your client.** Make sure the tool fits with his personal, social, and environmental circumstances. You might start with the Personality Fit questionnaire (Lyubomirsky, 2008), which will assess whether or not an activity fits with his source of happiness, strengths, and lifestyle (Sheldon & Elliot, 1999).

- **Encourage your client to list activities that might enhance her level of happiness.** Include sources of pleasure, activities that would contribute to her sense of meaning in life, and ways of experiencing flow.

- **Help your client focus on the positive aspects of his life.** Be aware of where he is in relation to happiness and his desired outcome. Activities that increase the client's happiness might include exercise, meditation, writing, savoring, spending time in a beautiful setting, concentrating on a relationship, and, in general, appreciating what he has in his life.

THE BROADEN-AND-BUILD THEORY AND BARBARA FREDRICKSON

Until recently, researchers were unaware of the extent to which positive emotions are an integral component of our success and well-being. Barbara Fredrickson's broaden-and-build theory of positive emotions (Fredrickson, 2004; Fredrickson, Tugade, Waugh, & Larkin, 2003) posits that the experience of positive emotions broadens people's momentary thought-action repertoires, which in turn serves to build their enduring personal resources, ranging from the physical and intellectual to the social and psychological. Fredrickson's findings suggest that the capacity to experience positive emotions may be a fundamental human strength central to the study of human flourishing. Fredrickson and Losada (2005) built on Fredrickson's research and concluded that the optimal positive-to-negative emotional ratio for flourishing is three to one. It appears that people who experience this key ratio express and demonstrate higher levels of well-being and success (Fredrickson, 2009).

Coaching Applications

- **Ask your client to identify her positivity ratio and work with her toward a healthy ratio of three to one.** Monitor this ratio daily, over a one-month period, to identify her true emotional picture. Use Fredrickson's site, www.positivityratio.org, for questionnaires and a daily diary of positive emotions.

- **Ask your client to write out three things that went well for him during the day and the role that he played in bringing them about.** Ask him to do this every night for one week. One source of happiness is gratitude. Another is focusing on positive experiences. Attending to the day's successes and achievements will contribute to his sense of well-being.

- **Ask your client to put aside twenty minutes for each of three consecutive days to write about an intensely positive experience (IPE) in her past, an occasion on which she felt intense happiness, joy, wonder, or awe.** The key is to get her to write about the experience, not just think about it.

- **Ask your client to perform five helpful acts toward others, one day a week, and reflect on how he felt as well as how the recipient of the act of kindness reacted.** Positive emotions can also come from helping others, especially when they are acts that go beyond what one would do in normal circumstances.

REIVICH, SHATTE, AND RESILIENCE

Resilience is widely regarded as the ability to persevere in the face of stressors and to bounce back from setbacks (Reivich & Shatte, 2002). It is connected to psychological well-being, development, success, and happiness. People who are not born resilient can become so. When faced with a difficult situation, people may revert to pessimistic beliefs and behavior. They may engage in one of several thinking traps, such as jumping to conclusions, having tunnel vision, magnifying the negative and minimizing the positive, personalizing or externalizing blame, overgeneralizing small setbacks, engaging in mind reading, and using unhelpful emotional reasoning (Reivich & Shatte, 2002). One of the main pathways to resilience in these situations is developing an "optimistic explanatory style" (Reivich & Shatte, 2002; Seligman, 2002). Becoming optimistic in the face of challenging situations involves rethinking and renaming the situation so that resilience is increased. Because pessimistic rumination is the precursor and maintainer of depression (Papageorgiou & Wells, 2003), this technique is imperative for challenging destructive thoughts and creating more resilient individuals.

- **Work with your client to identify her destructive thinking patterns and traps.** Challenge these disparaging and pessimistic thoughts, and help her construct a more realistic view of adversity.

- **Explore with your client past situations in which he displayed resilient qualities.** By recalling previously resilient behaviors, he may gain confidence as well as insight into how he can solve current challenges.

- **Work with your client to identify small-scale goals and execute them.** One aspect of resilience is the ability to break down problems and challenges into reasonable, attainable mini-goals.

- **Ask your client to think of herself in the future, when current situations have been overcome and goals achieved.**

STRENGTHS THROUGH VIA (VALUES IN ACTION)

Among the biggest contributions of positive psychology to the coaching discipline are the scientific data surrounding the area of strengths (Linley & Harrington, 2006). Although there are now several schools of thought surrounding strengths, this section will focus solely on the influence of strengths-based coaching underpinned by the Values in Action (VIA) approach (www.via.org). The VIA is a strengths measurement tool; it consists of twenty-four character strengths that are divided into six values: wisdom and knowledge, courage, humanity, justice, temperance, and transcendence (for a detailed review, see Peterson & Seligman, 2004). These strengths constitute what the authors would consider globally valued morals and virtues. The research suggests that using a strengths-based approach in work, parenting, life, and relationships can build resilience and promote flourishing, insight, confidence, vitality, perspective, and optimism (Boniwell, 2006; Hodges & Clifton, 2004; Park, Peterson, & Seligman, 2004).

Studies have also found that when people simply identify their top five signature strengths, their happiness levels rise significantly (Seligman et al., 2005). Furthermore, people who use their top five strengths in their life, work, and play tend to be more successful, fulfilled, and happier than those who don't (Linley & Harrington, 2006).

- **Ask your client to take the VIA online and bring the results to the session.** Once she knows her top five signature strengths, you can work with her to create a plan as to how she can incorporate these strengths into her daily life.

- **Ask your client to remember and describe a time when he was at his best.** Ask him to use examples of how his strengths got displayed. What did this look like? What was achieved? What did he do, think, and feel?

- **Work with your client to help her use her top five strengths to create solutions and reach desired goals.** Assign her homework in which she describes how to use her top five strengths in a new way. You can also have her examine her bottom five strengths, or challenges, and discuss her reaction to these qualities.

CSIKSZENTMIHALYI AND THE CONCEPT OF FLOW

Flow, or "being in the zone," is the intense psychological experience of being fully immersed in an activity. According to Csikszentmihalyi (1990), flow is a transcendent experience of everyday life. It is best understood as the experience of being so caught up in an activity that time becomes irrelevant. Flow-inducing activities tend to be structured, to provide a balance of challenges and skills, to offer clear goals and immediate feedback, to provide a sense of control, and to produce complete concentration and loss of awareness of oneself. People report an intrinsic motivation for participating in flow activities as well as heightened levels of well-being following engagement with the activity (Csikszentmihalyi, 2009). Research has shown that when people are in flow, they function at higher levels of performance.

Coaching Applications

- **Talk with your client about flow—what it is, how it works, and why it is desirable.** If the experience is unfamiliar, work with him to discover what prevents him from experiencing flow in his life.

- **Design homework to raise your client's awareness of flow.** Encourage her to notice when it occurs and what situations strengthen or diminish the feeling.

- **Remember that each client is unique and will have his own experience and perspective on flow.** These may change according to circumstances and life situations.

Additional Reading

Boniwell, I. (2006). *Positive psychology in a nutshell.* London: Personal Well-Being Centre.
A quick, easy-to-read overview of the subject, theories, and critiques.

Buckingham, M., & Clifton, D. O. (2001). *Now, discover your strengths: How to develop your talents and those of the people you manage.* New York: Free Press.
This book reviews the "talent"-based strengths approach. Log on to www.strengthsfinder.com for more information.

Csikszentmihalyi, M. (1990). *Flow: The psychology of optimal experience.* New York: HarperCollins.
Research and theory on how people experience peak states. An early work in the area of positive psychology.

Fredrickson, B. (2009). *Positivity: Groundbreaking research reveals how to embrace the hidden strength of positive emotions, overcome negativity, and thrive.* New York: Crown.
A comprehensive overview of Fredrickson's research findings.

Linley, P. A., & Joseph, S. (Eds.). (2004). *Positive psychology in practice.* Hoboken, NJ: Wiley.
An excellent overview of how positive psychology is being applied across several settings.

Lopez, S. (2009). *The encyclopedia of positive psychology.* London: Wiley.
This encyclopedia is the most up-to-date reference book and excellent for those wanting a snapshot of the areas within positive psychology.

Pennebaker, J. W. (2004). *Writing to heal: A guided journal for recovering from trauma and emotional upheaval.* Oakland, CA: New Harbinger Press.
Pennebaker's writing approach has yielded fantastic results in building resilience and enhancing health during stressful or adverse times. This book may be appropriate for clients who are currently experiencing difficult circumstances.

Peterson, C., & Seligman, M. (2004). *Character strengths and virtues: A handbook and classification.* New York: Oxford University Press.
A giant textbook manual, this book has been called the un-DSM in positive psychology circles!

Positive Psychology Services LLC, at: http://www.intentionalhappiness.com.
This site provides examples of excellent workbooks.

Reivich, K., & Shatte, A. (2002). *The resilience factor: 7 keys to finding your inner strength and overcoming life's hurdles.* New York: Broadway Books.
This is an excellent book based on years of resilience research by the authors.

Transactional Analysis

Jenny Rogers

A s a philosophy and therapeutic methodology, Transactional Analysis (TA) was developed in the 1960s and 1970s by Eric Berne, a Canadian psychiatrist and psychoanalyst. TA draws on humanistic, psychoanalytic, and cognitive approaches. Berne had huge popular success with his book *Games People Play,* and such concepts as *assertiveness, win-win, I'm OK/You're OK,* and *victim-thinking* have passed into popular language without people necessarily knowing their origin. TA has been one of the main strands of theory contributing to the development of coaching as a profession.

TA is founded on these assumptions and principles:

- People are OK. You're OK and I'm OK. I might not always like what you do, but I accept what you are. We are equals, regardless of the normal human markers of difference and status.

- Everyone has the capacity to think. Everyone except the severely brain damaged has this capacity. You are responsible for yourself, and you live with the consequences of what you have decided.

- You can decide to change. You cannot be made to feel anything or to behave in a particular way. You have autonomy even though others may exert strong pressures on you to do what they want. You are not doomed to live out the consequences of an unsatisfactory upbringing.

- Practitioner-client relationships are based on equality. We work as equals. The practitioner does not do things to the client, and the client does not expect to have things done for him or her. There is clear contracting at every stage about what each side's role is.
- There is open and transparent communication. The entire process is transparent; notes are available to the client, and the client is taught TA terms and concepts as part of this commitment to openness.

The aims of TA are for the client to achieve autonomy through consciously choosing mindfulness, openly sharing feelings, and getting free of the defensive thinking we develop in childhood.

EGO STATES

Ego states are the core concept in TA. There are three main behavioral modes, one of which usually predominates at any one time. According to TA, the *Parent* state is our *taught* concept of life and is how we replay behavior, thoughts, and feelings we have learned from someone in our past, most usually parents and teachers. This is what provides us with discipline. It is characterized by guilt and "shoulds." The Parent state has two variants: Controlling and Nurturing.

The *Adult* state is our *thought* concept of life. Operating in the here and now, processing information rationally, and making decisions about how to act, it results in the most rational, mature, nonjudgmental, and logical behavior of the three ego states.

In the *Child* state, we are in our *felt* concept of life, replaying the behavior, thoughts, and feelings from our past that we still carry with us. We experience strong emotions and desires—for example, fear, anger, delight, joy, and sexual arousal. The Child ego state should not be confused with "childish" or "immature" behavior. The Child can be either Adapted (compliant, sulky, obedient) or Natural (spontaneous and playful).

We all need all of these ego states to be complete.

TRANSACTIONS

Social interaction is conducted via what Berne called *transactions*. A *transactional stimulus* from one person results in a *transactional response* from another. In *complementary* transactions, needs are expressed and met, such as in problem solving (Adult-Adult), in mutual play (Child-Child or Parent-Child), or when two people gossip (Parent-Parent). Problems arise when a crossed transaction occurs. Take, for example, the stimulus "Do you know where my glasses are?" The response "Why don't you look after your own things instead of always relying on me?" represents a controlling Parent response to an Adult stimulus.

STROKES

A stroke in TA is a unit of recognition from another person. It may be verbal or nonverbal, positive or negative. TA assumes that we are recognition hungry and that any stroke is better than none. There is a *stroke economy* in which stroking is limited by unspoken rules—for instance, that you shouldn't *ask* for strokes. Restricting strokes is a way of trying to control others.

LIFE SCRIPTS

Another central concept in TA is that we develop an idea of our lives as a story in which we are the central character; it is a specific plan for life, rather than a general view of the world, and it is made at an unconscious level. We don't *decide* in the adult sense on our life script; the script is developed from feelings and depends on a different kind of reality testing from that used by adults; it's a means of survival in a hostile and confusing world, and its aim is to achieve the unconditional love of the adults around us. To that extent it represents magical thinking. TA suggests that we tend to redefine reality to justify our script, so the script causes a distortion of reality.

LIFE POSITIONS

TA suggests that as children we create convictions about ourselves and that these are likely to have long-lasting impact. These are well described by Thomas Harris in his *I'm OK, You're OK* (1967), an early contribution to TA. Harris describes four possible life positions based on two axes: "*I'm OK—I'm not OK*" and "*You're OK—You're not OK*" (see Figure 4.1).

I'm OK—You're not OK

You have learned as a child that by striking back you can survive. You have probably been at the receiving end of authoritarian parenting, so you know

Figure 4.1.
The Four Life Positions

	You're not OK	You're OK
I'm OK	I'm OK–You're not OK	I'm OK–You're OK
I'm not OK	I'm not OK–You're not OK	I'm not OK–You're OK

how to be tough, and it becomes a life position to bully and threaten. This comes out of the energy created by fear. The best form of defense is to attack. Those around you are likely to perceive you as overbearing, aggressive, and insensitive.

I'm not OK—You're not OK

This life position is born out of profound pessimism and fear of conflict. You take a gloomy view of the human race, believing that others are hopeless cases, that our life paths are predetermined and choice impossible. Events have made you their victim. Living your life from such a position of powerlessness makes you doomed to failure. If you believe that you are a failure, then you will be proved right.

You're OK—I'm not OK

You believe others are cleverer, more resourceful, and more important than you are. You have never grown out of the feeling that most of what you did was wrong as far as one or both parents were concerned, or you learned that whatever you did would be ignored. Either you seek to get away from people because they always know or do better than you, or you perpetually play the "Mine is better than yours" game: accumulating honors, possessions, money; overworking; or attaching yourself to people who lend you some of their own power and glamour.

I'm OK—You're OK (the ideal)

You see yourself and others as equals, regardless of gender, race, nationality, age, hierarchical position, social status, or intelligence. You assume that your life will be successful as defined by you, not by others. You will be able to receive feedback without defensiveness as well as able to give it skillfully. This can be a risky position. To be in it you make yourself vulnerable, but it is the vulnerability that comes from strength and self-confidence.

Most of us will dip in and out of all four positions during a typical day or week, but there will most probably be one that we adopt as our default.

INJUNCTIONS

TA identifies twelve basic instructions about how *not* to be—most probably nonverbal messages we receive as children. Many of us will have experienced at least one and possibly several of these, not necessarily in their malign form and mostly not from parents who consciously wished us any harm. They include such messages as *Don't be who you are, Don't change, Don't be a child, Don't grow up, Don't make it in your life, Don't think,* and *Don't feel.*

COUNTERINJUNCTIONS AND DRIVERS

From among the many different instructions, or *counterinjunctions,* people receive in childhood—for example, *Work hard, Be my little princess, Be good, Tell the truth*—TA identifies five *drivers* that are especially powerful; these are ways we defend ourselves against the negatives of the injunctions. They can have the force of superstition. Hearing *You're only OK if . . . ,* we believe that disaster will follow if we don't obey.

Be Perfect. Demanding perfection of ourselves, we may also expect it of others, which can be hard on those around us.

Be Strong. Remaining calm, aloof, and controlled, we may stand apart from playful activities fearing we'll look stupid.

Try Hard. We love new projects. When stressed, we may start too many things but not finish them.

Please Others. We like to please people, but rather than ask them how, we prefer to guess. We worry about changing our behavior in case others won't like us.

Hurry Up. We get a great deal done but at cost of overload. We may overlook important aspects of tasks, and are likely to be impatient with others, even finishing their sentences for them.

FITTING THE WORLD TO OUR SCRIPT: DISCOUNTING

Discounting is a useful TA concept that elegantly codifies the many ways in which we can deny reality and resist change. Discounting represents distorted perception, and it happens outside conscious awareness. The ferocity with which we cling to a discount is directly related to the intensity of the perceived threat. Discounting may occur at four levels: discounting the existence of a problem, discounting the significance of the problem, discounting the solvability of the problem, and discounting one's ability to change.

One of the reasons we stay fixed in a problem is that there is some payoff for doing so. When we feel stuck, however miserable we are about it, there is always some benefit. The prison of misery may be horrible, but at least it's familiar. The following are some typical payoffs:

Controlling and manipulating others by engendering guilt

Creating some personal space and "reward" for yourself

Protecting yourself from failing by not even trying

Forcing others to take responsibility for you, so that you don't have to blame yourself if things go wrong

Avoiding facing up to actual weaknesses

JUSTIFYING OUR SCRIPT: GAMES

Games in TA terms are repetitive patterns of behavior in which you and the other person end up feeling equally bad. A game is a psychological exchange played according to predetermined rules at an unconscious level. Games are about negative feelings, and they end with both parties blaming each other. By definition, a game never resolves the discomfort of the underlying feelings but allows us to luxuriate in anger, self-righteousness, or self-pity. Games allow us to further our life script without any inconvenient interruption from perspective or reality. We get a payoff: pompous anger, the drama and excitement of the fight. We save up grudges to use next time. Games create pseudo-intimacy and in the short term may get us what we want.

In the Drama Triangle, for example, an idea first developed by Stephen Karpman (1968), there are three roles:

Victim. *It's all terrible; whatever I do is wrong; I am helpless; others—or the system—are always against me.* The victim role is essentially manipulative. Its purpose is to force others to be responsible for the victim's happiness—something that is literally impossible.

Persecutor. *I have the power; it's my right to tell you what to do; you are inferior.* The persecutor role is about win-lose. You have to be right at all costs. Decisions are black or white; there are no shades of grey. People are either on your side or totally against you.

Rescuer. *It's my role to be the helper; I care about you; I can come to your aid.* Rescuing is underpinned by pity and disrespect based on the patronizing assumption that the person you are rescuing cannot make choices for himself or herself.

In common with other games, the Drama Triangle invariably involves a switch. The victim may turn on the persecutor, attacking him or her, thus becoming the persecutor. The persecutor may turn on the rescuer ("This is none of your business; why don't you keep out of it") so that the rescuer becomes the victim. Or the persecutor may break down in self-pity, becoming the victim. There are no winners in the Drama Triangle. In fact, it is common for people who typically play persecutor and rescuer to say they feel like victims themselves.

Other common games identified by TA include the following:

Wooden Leg. *I could be successful if only I didn't have this handicap.* When the handicap is removed, the person simply looks to another route to avoid success.

See What You Made Me Do. *If something dreadful happens to me, it's all your fault.*

I'm Only Trying to Help You. A compulsive rescuer gets upset when unwanted help is rejected.

Yes But. Offered a solution, the person finds another obstacle. In its extreme form, this game conveys *You can't help me—I am unhelpable.*

Coaching Applications

- **Be aware of the different ego states present in a coaching session, both in yourself and in the client.** Changes in ego state are appropriate. When using creativity techniques, such as brainstorming, you could both be in Natural Child. For logical problem solving you could both be in Adult, but it is wise to avoid being in Adult—or too detached—for the entire session. Be alert also to a client's overvaluing the Adult state. She may have difficulty accessing the other ego states. You could get sucked in to a cool, rational exchange that gets nowhere near the underlying difficulties.

- **When a client is upset and angry about something that has happened to him, be aware that he is likely to be replaying Adapted Child.** It is useful to invite him to get some perspective from his Adult. You might ask, *How will it look in a year's time?* or *What theories could explain this?*

- **Remember that people are commonly stroke starved.** Getting through the stroke barrier may be difficult for clients who have absorbed the idea that they shouldn't ask for feedback or that all feedback is conditional—on whether or not you respect the person or whether you feel you "deserve" the stroke—or believe that stroking is only ever done for malign reasons (negative comments to punish, positive ones to manipulate).

- **When you hear a client's account of her early life, be conscious that you are hearing a script.** Ask her for her reflections on the themes it reveals; look out for and discuss how self-limiting beliefs were formed. Ask the client, *If this account of your life were a film, what title would you give it? What kind of film would it be—comedy, melodrama, tragedy, romance? Who would watch it, and how would they react?*

- **Introduce the four life positions and ask the client which quadrant most accurately describes his position.** Remember that few people are in one position permanently. Ask the client to review his response to a particular problem through this lens. Where is he when inhabiting this problem? What would it be like to assume that the top-right quadrant is the only one in which a genuine resolution will be found? What behaviors would accompany this assumption? How might these new behaviors be tested?

- **Work with your clients to disprove the superstitious underpinnings of their injunctions and counterinjunctions.** Encourage them to "step out of script" by behaving differently, even though this will feel uncomfortable. For a client whose driver is Be Perfect, encourage a little deliberate imperfection. A client driven to please should learn to say no. Help a client with a Hurry Up style to slow down and acquire some listening skills.

- **Notice when a client discounts a problem.** Remind her of her overall goals. Encourage her to look at the facts, challenge the fantasies that lie behind the defense, and work with her to identify the payoff for staying stuck.

- **Listen for evidence that the client has become caught up in a game.** Most games are about the quest for strokes, or recognition. Ask the client what strokes he was seeking. Suggest that he name the game with the other person and refuse to play. Encourage him to be authentic about his needs with the other person and actually ask for what he really wants instead of playing the game.

Additional Reading

Berne, E. (1964). *Games people play*. New York: Grove Press.
> The book that brought TA to the general public. An excellent, clear explanation of how TA works.

Stewart, I., & Joines, V. (1987). *TA today: A new introduction to Transactional Analysis*. Nottingham, UK, and Chapel Hill, NC: Lifespace.
> An excellent update on concepts of TA and how to use them. It includes concrete exercises that apply to coaching as well as therapy.

Adult Development

chapter FIVE

Leni Wildflower

The idea that human lives follow a progression of stages, with different impulses and challenges appropriate to each, is deeply embedded in many cultures. Stages are enumerated in Hinduism and in Native American traditions. When Shakespeare wrote Jacques's celebrated "seven ages of man" speech in *As You Like It* ("At first the infant / Mewling and puking in the nurse's arms . . ."), he was elaborating on an idea familiar to his audience.

Studying the question from a scientific rather than a poetic perspective, adult development theory has taken two approaches. One group of theories focuses on an age or phase in the life cycle marked by certain characteristics, ways of being, or issues one faces (Erikson, 1980; Jung, 1961; Loevinger & Blasi, 1976; Levinson, 1978; Vaillant, 1993). In contrast, the constructive development theories are defined by the assumption that the ways an individual makes meaning become more complex over time and that generally, though not always, this happens as people get older (Kegan, 1982, 1994; Belenky, Clinchy, Goldberger, & Tarule, 1986; Fisher & Torbert, 2000). Separate from these two groups is Wilbur (1973/1993), who explores an expanded vision of what constitutes consciousness.

THE MIDLIFE EXPERIENCE AND CARL JUNG

Jung was the first theorist and practitioner to write extensively on the experience of midlife (1961). Although Jung didn't coin the term *midlife crisis,* his contribution to this concept cannot be underestimated. He described his own midlife experience as an "inner journey" and, in a phrase borrowed from the sixteenth-century mystic John of the Cross, a "dark night of the soul." According to later researchers and therapists, the age at which people go through this experience varies widely—from late thirties to midfifties. In Jungian terms, "finding one's soul" or "self" involves confronting the unconscious and integrating its elements into one's consciousness. For Jung, this was a spiritual journey. He conceptualized the stages of the midlife transition as (1) a breakdown of the personal (or identity); (2) the release of the shadow consisting of those aspects of oneself that are repressed, denied, rejected; and (3) facing the part of oneself that embodies the other sex—the anima or inner feminine aspect of a man and the animus or inner masculine aspect of a woman. Jung used the term *liminality* to describe the experience of being suspended during this period. Jungian psychologist Murray Stein (1983) describes liminality in the following manner:

> In the state I call psychological liminality a person's sense of identity is hung in suspension. You are no longer fixed to particular mental images and contents of yourself or others. The "I" is caught up in a field that it cannot control, whose patterns it does not recognize as "me." While the sense of "I-ness" and some of its continuities remain during liminality, the prevailing feeling is one of alienation, marginality, and drift. (p. 8)

Coaching Applications

- **Be alert to the possibility that your client may be going through a midlife transition.** She may be experiencing some of these feelings: a yearning for an undefined dream or goal, a sense of remorse for goals not accomplished, a desire to reclaim a sense of youthfulness, an urge to spend more time alone or with particular peers. If she is open to it, offer her something to read on the midlife experience. Reading the narratives of others who have gone through it will help her know that she isn't alone, and relieve her of feelings of anger or shame.

- **Work with your client to help normalize feelings of dislocation, disorientation, and grief, which may accompany the process of midlife transition.** Encourage him to let close friends and family members know what he is going through. Remind him that midlife transition is a process, not a permanent state of being.

ADULT DEVELOPMENT AS A SERIES OF STAGES CHARACTERIZED BY TASKS AND CONTRADICTIONS: ERIC ERIKSON AND GEORGE VAILLANT

Erikson, a student of Freud, developed an eight-stage model, the earlier of which is based in part on Freud's phases of childhood. Erikson, who introduced the concept of the identity crisis, finds the individual faced at each stage with a basic human contradiction, crisis, or primary task. The resolution of this contradiction, the accomplishment of the task, signals a move to the next stage of development (1980). Erikson was one of the first theorists to construct a complete stage theory of human development, and his work is still highly regarded. The last three stages are relevant to adult life.

Intimacy versus isolation. The young adult's task is to build a primary relationship, establish a family, become established in work, and form mature adult friendships and involvement with others.

Generativity versus stagnation. The stage of middle adulthood is characterized by a generative impulse, a desire to give back. Erikson called it "minding the store" and relates it to what Hindus call "the maintenance of the world" (Erikson, 1982, p. 66). The major commitment at this level is to take care of the persons, products, and ideals one has learned to value.

Integrity versus despair. At this final stage, the individual has developed mature ideas about the meaning of life and death. The key task is to review one's life and to feel that goals have been accomplished and that one has lived an authentic life.

Life expectancy in the developed world has increased significantly since Erikson developed his model. People are working longer. Furthermore, Erikson's adult stages are quite broad. George Vaillant, another developmental theorist, added two intermediate stages (1993, p. 145) to create a more nuanced picture of adult development and the many tasks involved.

Career consolidation versus self-absorption. In the latter half of the middle years, there is a search for a resolution of the tension between creating a fulfilling career and tending to one's family and personal life.

Keeper of the meaning versus rigidity. The latter half of adulthood brings a capacity to look forward to the second half of life with openness and flexibility.

With Vaillant's two stages added to the three of Erikson's that are relevant to adult life, there are five stages of adult development.

1. Intimacy versus isolation
2. Career consolidation versus self-absorption
3. Generativity versus stagnation
4. Keeper of the meaning versus rigidity
5. Integrity versus despair

Coaching Applications

- **Be aware of the ways in which a particular issue your client is dealing with might be characteristic of her developmental stage.** An understanding of Erikson's adult development stages can provide a valuable framework for you, and might be enlightening and relieving for her. At the same time, however, it can never be a substitute for tuning in to her unique circumstance and perspective.

- **Remember that a young adult may need to deal with a relationship issue before he can get to the work issue.** Keep in mind the distinction between therapy and coaching when working in this area.

- **Be ready to work with a younger client on building self-esteem.** She may, for example, be too dependent on the recognition of a boss or older peers, or simply think too little of herself. Help her build internal resources of self-praise and self-acknowledgment. Be aware that she might become reliant on you for praise. The work for both of you is to build her sense of self-worth and her capacity to feel confident in the absence of another person's approval.

STAGE DEVELOPMENT AND MIDLIFE ISSUES: DANIEL LEVINSON

Daniel Levinson wrote a groundbreaking and highly popular book titled *The Seasons of a Man's Life* (1978), which he followed with *The Seasons of a Woman's Life* (1997). Each was based on a series of intensive interviews. Levinson divides life into four seasons or eras, the last three being early, middle, and late adulthood. These eras are subdivided, and linked by periods of transition. Early adulthood, for example, is characterized by entering the adult world, settling down, consolidating one's identity, creating a stable life structure, and establishing one's niche in society. Late adulthood involves coming to terms with oneself and one's achievements and failures in life.

Like Erikson, Levinson defines the tasks that need to be accomplished during different stages. Central to his model is the need of the individual to find something that gives shape and meaning to life at each stage. What this might be is shaped by the social environment, but often includes family and work. As an individual matures, the ability to create, revise, and re-create satisfying life structures—ways of living that are suitable for the self and viable in the world (Levinson, 1978)—depends on the person's increasing individuation over time. In Levinson's framework, this means knowing one's strengths, weaknesses, desires, and values well enough to make good choices for oneself, as well as seeing who other people really are, undistorted by projections of self. Individuation enriches one's capacities to find both meaningful work and mutually enhancing relationships.

The midlife transition at age forty to fifty has particular significance, and is characterized by what Levinson calls the resolution of individuation polarities: young-old, destruction-creation, masculine-feminine, attachment-separateness. In other words, it is in midlife that people are able to resolve these contradictory impulses. They are able to contain youthful and elderly aspects of themselves. Destructive and creative impulses are integrated. Both men and women are more able to take on qualities of the opposite sex. The conflicting fears of abandonment and engulfment recede.

Levinson contrasts the male and female experience at midlife, which is often harder for men than for women. When children leave home, for example, many men seem to have a harder time than women in coping with the change. Although women may mourn the loss of full-time motherhood, for many there is a feeling of emancipation.

Coaching Applications

- **Be prepared for issues of work-life balance to surface with clients at midlife and beyond.** As Levinson describes, the search for a satisfying balance between work and life may take on greater meaning and urgency as people get older.

- **Be prepared to help an older client who is struggling to define underlying dissatisfactions and unease.** Working with an individual in the middle years may involve some soul searching. The goal that has brought him to see you—the desire to make a big career change, for example—might be redefined or replaced with something significantly different during the coaching engagement. Simply identifying the real issue is sometimes an excellent outcome.

INCREASED COMPLEXITY OF MEANING MAKING: ROBERT KEGAN

Robert Kegan, one of the best known and most esteemed developmental theorists, builds on constructivist theory in observing that individuals construct meaning throughout their lives. The individual can own only his or her construction of reality, which is created in language. According to Kegan, this construction is centered on the particular meaning-making stage of each individual person rather than on age or a phase in life (1982). As people grow and develop, the content of their ideas may not necessarily change, but the form of their understanding is likely to develop. The way an individual makes meaning changes over time to become more complex and multifaceted (1994). In Robert Kegan and Lisa Lahey's latest work, *Immunity to Change* (2009), they outline three levels of mental complexity that they and their researchers have found in adults:

1. **Socialized mind.** I am shaped by the definitions and expectations of my personal environment. Whatever I identify with, I align with and am loyal to. I am a faithful follower who seeks direction.

2. **Self-authoring mind.** I am an agenda-driven person who is able to step back enough from the social environment to generate an internal "seat of judgment" (p. 17). I maintain my own belief system, ideology, or personal code, which allows me to self-direct, take stands, set limits, and create and regulate personal boundaries. My capacity to solve problems is independent of other people's influence.

3. **Self-transforming mind.** I am able to step back from and reflect on the limits of my own ideology or personal authority. Having a capacity for multiframe thinking, I seek to hold on to multiple systems rather than projecting one over another. I align with the dialectic of more than one way of thinking.

What is interesting, and hopeful, about Kegan's theory is that the capacity to increase our mental complexity is always with us, regardless of our age. Kegan is passionate both about this theoretical analysis and about the need for people to become more aware—to develop more complex thinking: "The problem is the inability to close the gap between what we genuinely, even passionately, want and what we are actually able to do. Closing this gap is the central learning problem of the twenty-first century" (Kegan & Lahey, 2009, p. 2).

According to Kegan, as a person moves up to a higher level of mental complexity, lower-level thinking is still present. One can perform at both the lower and higher levels of mental complexity. Kegan and Lahey have conducted behavior studies of different cultures, particularly cultures where "groupthink" is more prevalent. They found that the capacity for independent thinking, and greater complexity, exists throughout the world. "It is a phenomenon that owes its origin not to culture, but to complexity of mind" (2009, p. 18).

Kegan and Lahey have developed a process for revealing the reasons why it is difficult to make changes in one's life. The Immunity to Change process involves an exercise that helps identify what Kegan and Lahey term "competing commitments" and ultimately to uncover one's "big assumption" (Kegan & Lahey, 2001). This illuminating exercise can be invaluable in helping clients see what is keeping them from moving forward. It also offers the possibility of teaching clients to think in a more complex fashion.

Coaching Applications

- **Help the client through the Immunity to Change process by working with her to fill in her four-column map.** First you will need to master the process yourself and gain personal experience in how it functions. *How We Talk Can Change the Way We Work* (Kegan & Lahey, 2001) provides the clearest guide for doing this.

- **Be aware that one client may be less able than another to self-reflect or to recognize and understand another person's point of view.** In accommodating this, you will inevitably find it necessary to modify the way you engage with this client. But always remain alert for openings that might lead him toward a greater awareness of himself and others.

DEVELOPMENT AND AWARENESS: STEVEN AXELROD

According to Steven Axelrod (2005), the ability to function at a higher level of awareness, whether by virtue of one's age (Erikson and Levinson) or an increased understanding and consciousness (Kegan), might result in any or all of the following qualities in executives:

A longer time frame and increased capacity for strategic thinking

An increased propensity for reflective thinking

An increased ability to acknowledge, understand, and integrate the meaning of personal and career failures

An increased tolerance of ambiguity and paradox

An increased ability to listen to and appreciate different points of view

An increased ability to reconcile differences based on an understanding of underlying trends and causes

A shift from a work style based on brute strength or endurance to one based on prioritizing and leading broad efforts

An increased ability to look broadly across the organization and identify with the larger mission

These qualities can be used as benchmarks in measuring improvements in levels of consciousness and understanding among leaders.

Coaching Applications

- **Remember that these models offer broad and general categories.** Individuals are complex and multifaceted. A client who seems dependent on explicit rules and clear direction in some areas might reveal a surprising capacity for self-belief and independent judgment in others. Allow the client space to be her most subtle and developed self.

- **Be prepared to serve as a "translator" when working with a client who has difficulty intuiting other people's motives and reading their signals.** Your work may include helping him become aware that other people's perspectives are different but understandable.

- **Support your client's sense of self-efficacy and her ability to make judgments.** Reinforce her capacity to observe and understand a range of different viewpoints and to use that understanding as a launching pad for her own ideas.

- **Remember that every client presents a different challenge.** A client with a highly developed capacity for self-reflection and a capacity to contain multiple perspectives might seem capable of coaching himself, and may do so a lot of the time, but there will still be areas where he needs to be stretched or confronted.

DEVELOPMENT, CONSCIOUSNESS, AND INTEGRAL STUDIES: KEN WILBER

Wilber's approach to the study of consciousness has been to research eclectically, seeking coherent patterns across disparate and sometimes mutually hostile fields of study. This process of constructing a unified picture out of a diverse range of elements he calls "integral studies" (1973/1993). Drawing on an extensive range of disciplines and traditions, both eastern and western, he has developed a model that divides existence into four quadrants: intentional, behavioral, cultural, and social.

Each quadrant contains a branching hierarchy of elements. The *behavioral* quadrant, for example, contains the building blocks of material evolution, from atoms up through molecules and cells to the higher functions of the human brain. These are the elements of existence most readily identified and measured by western science. The *intentional* quadrant contains the elements more conventionally associated with human consciousness, including sensation, perception, impulse, emotion, and so on. Both these quadrants relate to aspects of the individual.

The remaining two quadrants describe collective states. The *cultural* quadrant contains the stages of societal development, such as the magic, the mythic, and the rational; the *social* quadrant contains units of organization, from galaxies and planets to families and so on.

Dividing the model another way, the intentional and cultural quadrants describe aspects of interior reality, as experienced by the individual or the culture; the behavioral and social quadrants describe aspects that lend themselves to external observation.

Wilber identifies the elements within these quadrants, using a term he takes from Koestler (1967), as *holons,* a holon being a whole that is at the same time part of a greater whole, as an atom is whole in itself but might also be part of a molecule. He postulates that there are at least ten major levels within each quadrant. And he argues that we can only begin to understand consciousness when we recognize that it exists in every one of these quadrants and at every level. He calls this the "all-quadrant, all-level approach." Consciousness, in other words, is a collective as well as an individual attribute. It exists inside and also outside the neural system. We should conceive of it as an attribute not only of the individual but also of the molecule and of the planet.

Further study of integral theory is accessible through such programs as Fielding Graduate University (www.fielding.edu/programs/hod/isC). More information on the teachings and applications of integral theory can be found on the Integral Institute Web site (www.integralinstitute.org).

Coaching Applications

- **Help your client understand herself within a context that includes biological, psychological, cultural, and spiritual dimensions.** Where appropriate, use the Wilber framework to introduce the possibility that consciousness may not be bounded by the individual's neural system, encouraging the client to see her thoughts, troubles, and ambitions as a part of a large continuum.

Additional Reading

Axelrod, S. D. (2005, Spring). Executive growth along the adult development curve. *Consulting Psychology Journal: Practice and Research*, pp. 118–125.
  Axelrod's study of the outcomes of higher levels of awareness.
Erikson, E. (1997). *The life cycle completed.* New York: Norton.
  A very readable description of Erikson's theory, with an elaboration on adult development by his wife, Joan Erikson.
Hollis, J. (2005). *Finding meaning in the second half of life: How to finally, really grow up.* New York: Gotham Books.
  A great primer for understanding the experience of midlife.
Kegan, R. (1995). *In over our heads: The mental demands of modern life.* Cambridge, MA: Harvard University Press.
  A dense but fascinating book describing Kegan's model of adult development and its application to modern society.
Kegan, R., & Lahey, L. (2009). *Immunity to change: How to overcome it and unlock the potential in yourself and your organization.* Boston: Harvard Business School Press.
  The most recent book on the subject. This simplifies the developmental model and offers concrete ways to use the Immunity to Change model in organizations.
Levinson, D. J. (1978). *The seasons of a man's life.* New York: Random House.
  A very readable book about changes men go through throughout their lives. This is particularly good reading material for male clients.

Richo, D. (1991). *How to be an adult: A handbook on psychological and spiritual integration.* Mahwah, NJ: Paulist Press.

A wonderful handbook for anyone, at any point in life.

Sheehy, G. (1995). *New passages: Mapping your life across time.* New York: Ballantine Books.

More popular than Levinson's book on women, this is easy to read and has been helpful to many women.

Stein, M. (1983). *In midlife: A Jungian perspective.* Dallas, TX: Spring.

A brilliant book on midlife, incorporating Jungian and mythological archetypes into the narrative.

Vaillant, G. E. (1993). *The wisdom of the ego.* Cambridge, MA: Harvard University Press.

Elaboration on Erikson's model, with special emphasis on adult transitions.

Wilber, K. (1998). *The essential Ken Wilber: An introductory reader.* Boston: Shambhala.

A good introduction to the thinking and explorations of Wilber's work and integral studies.

Wilber, K., Patten, R., Leonard, A., & Morelli, M. (2008). *Integral life practices: A 21st-century blueprint for physical health, emotional balance, mental clarity and spiritual awakening.* Boston: Shambhala.

A complex topic presented in a readable and organized manner.

chapter SIX

Theories of Intelligence

Jonathan Passmore, Chloé Tong, and Leni Wildflower

From its beginnings in 1904, when psychologist Alfred Binet was asked by the French government to find a way of distinguishing between children who could benefit from regular public education and children who would need additional help, the concept of a singular numerical measure of intelligence has lent itself to simplistic interpretation and discriminatory uses. In spite of Binet's warnings, the Binet Scale and the concept of a general mental ability were taken up by psychologists and educators in America and around the world. Further tests were developed to determine an individual's intelligence quotient, or IQ.

Later theorists added more complexity. Thurstone (1931) confirmed general intelligence, or g, as the singular dominant factor, but included second-order factors, such as spatial reasoning and memory. Cattell (1963) distinguished between *fluid* intelligence (gf), the biologically determined underlying capacity for reasoning, and *crystallized* intelligence (gc), the more accidental environmental aspects of skills, knowledge, and experience. Carroll's three-stratum model (1993) incorporated the earlier theories and reinforced the hierarchy common to all of them, with a singular g at the apex of a pyramid. The middle stratum contains broad memory, retrieval, and learning abilities. The lowest stratum has a large number of more narrowly defined abilities. Tests based on these models are still widely used. Examples include the Wechsler Adult Intelligence Scale and Raven's Progressive Matrices, which result in a singular IQ score.

Cognitive ability tests differ in that they target particular facets of ability—usually numerical, verbal, and spatial, or abstract reasoning—and result in more than one score.

Use of cognitive ability tests is widespread as a method of differentiating between individuals. In occupational settings, the trend in larger firms in western cultures tends toward the use of ability tests in selection and recruitment processes and during individual development programs.

Several difficulties are reported in literature as inherent to IQ measurement tools. Empirical research suggests a bias toward nonminority individuals; gender effects have been reported; and scores tend to improve with practice. From the testing of newly arrived immigrants at Ellis Island in the early twentieth century with questions and puzzles for which nothing had prepared them (Gould, 1981) to the suggestion in *The Bell Curve* (Herrnstein & Murray, 1994) that genes probably contribute to racial variations in intelligence, IQ tests have been used to support notions of racial difference that are more readily explained by cultural and environmental factors. The fact that IQ test results have exhibited a gradual inflation since they were first introduced is perhaps the clearest indication that the ability to get a good score is an acquired skill, not an inherent attribute. The famous assertion by experimental psychologist Edwin Boring (1923) that "intelligence is what the tests test" remains one of the most succinct observations on the circularity of IQ testing.

More recent research has tended to focus on breaking down the notion of a unitary measure and exploring multiple and alternative intelligences.

THEORY OF MULTIPLE INTELLIGENCES: HOWARD GARDNER

Gardner (1983) asserted that from birth, human beings possess seven relatively autonomous areas of cognition or intelligence. Although the concept of the existence of more than one area of intelligence or cognition was not new (Thurstone, 1931), Gardner's work was unique in that he identified a specific number of intelligences and described their relationship to one another. He began with seven types.

Linguistic intelligence involves being sensitive to spoken and written language, having an aptitude for learning other languages, and being able to effectively express oneself rhetorically or poetically. Someone with linguistic intelligence is more likely to use a verbal component in remembering information.

Logical-mathematical intelligence is associated with ability in mathematics and science, and is characterized by the capacity to use logic and reason in analyzing problems, to understand and manipulate numbers, and to detect abstract patterns.

Musical intelligence involves the ability to hear rhythms, harmonies, and notes of different pitch; to make music, through playing or composition; and to respond to music aesthetically.

Bodily-kinesthetic intelligence allows one to use one's body in solving problems and in such processes as learning and remembering. It involves the ability to coordinate physical movements for expressive or practical purposes.

Spatial intelligence enables one to think in three dimensions, to be aware of space, and to envision the spatial relationships between objects. This capacity is essential for activities as diverse as architecture and parallel parking.

Interpersonal intelligence is what enables us to understand other people—to read their intentions; to intuit their unstated motivations, fears, and desires; and to respond to implicit signals.

Intrapersonal intelligence enables us to be aware of our own feelings and responses and to understand what causes and connects them. It allows us to achieve a sense of identity.

Gardner has subsequently conjectured that there might be further kinds of intelligence, such as naturalist intelligence, which would be concerned with recognizing, categorizing, and responding to aspects of the environment; and spiritual and existential intelligences, though he reports that his findings on these are so far inconclusive.

Coaching Applications

- **Explain to your client the theory of multiple intelligences to help her understand herself, people she works with, or family members.** Any framework that explains or contextualizes differences in the way people think can promote acceptance and accommodation of others.

- **Help your client look at where his strengths are as he considers the seven types of intelligence.** This allows him to gain understanding and insight into his own thinking and learning. He may also want to experiment with other types of intelligence to expand his perspective and to strengthen his learning capacity.

- **Be aware that your client's way of thinking, learning, and interacting with the world may be different from yours.** He may be less or more comfortable than you are with words or movement or abstract formulations. Be open to his particular forms of intelligence.

EMOTIONAL INTELLIGENCE: DANIEL GOLEMAN

Emotional intelligence refers to the ability to recognize, understand, and appropriately use emotions to guide one's thoughts and behaviors (Salovey & Mayer, 1990). Gardner was one of the pioneers of this concept. Two of his seven kinds of intelligence, inter- and intrapersonal, could be viewed as a single "personal" intelligence, containing the ability to understand one's own and other people's emotions, needs, and intentions. Interest in emotional and social intelligence as alternatives to traditional cognitive ability has exploded in recent years. Its popularity has been linked to psychological research and media coverage suggesting that a high degree of emotional intelligence can increase success in all areas of life (see, for example, Gibbs, 1995; Goleman, 1995). In occupational settings, for example, it is suggested that the concept of emotional intelligence may be used to inform development and selection procedures, understand management styles, and assess the behaviors and attitudes of individuals. There are three major models of emotional intelligence. Mayer and Salovey's ability model (1997) breaks down emotional intelligence into three component abilities: to perceive emotions, to use them to facilitate thought, and to understand and manage them (Mayer, Caruso, & Salovey, 2000). Bar-On's model (1997) groups skills under five headings: intrapersonal skills, interpersonal skills, adaptability, stress-management ability, and general mood. Goleman's model (1995) is based on five core concepts:

1. Emotions play a far greater role in thought, decision making, and success in life than is commonly acknowledged.

2. Emotional intelligence is an innate human capacity. We are all born with varying degrees of emotional intelligence.

3. Emotional intelligence involves the ability to be self-aware and aware of others, to empathize with others and understand their point of view, and to be able to communicate effectively, given one's understanding of others.

4. Emotional intelligence can grow and strengthen with nurturing and training.

5. Emotional intelligence has become an increasingly important human quality for people working in whatever capacity, but particularly in leadership, in today's world.

In subsequent work, Goleman (1998/2004) defined two major areas of emotional intelligence: personal capacities and social capacities:

Personal capacities: emotional self-awareness, accurate self-assessment, self-confidence, empathy, organizational awareness, and service orientation

Social capacities: self-control, trustworthiness, conscientiousness, adaptability, achievement orientation, initiative, developing others, inspirational leadership, influence, communication, catalyzing change, building bonds, teamwork and collaboration

Coaching Applications

- **Engage your client in "what if" situations.** Talking about an imagined scenario can allow him to imagine how he might feel and to rehearse different ways of reacting. It can help him anticipate possible situations and explore a range of emotional responses.

- **When you are working with a client on developing self-awareness and awareness of others, consider some of these activities:** invite her to ask her boss, a peer, and a direct report to give feedback on her strengths and weaknesses; have her list the most important people in her working life and describe their strengths, their weaknesses, and what they need from her; ask her to focus on an emotion that she struggles with—depression, anger, anxiety—and record it at regular intervals during the day, together with any cause or content associated with it, as a basis for later coaching discussion.

- **Recognize that organizations may still test for IQ or cognitive ability rather than emotional intelligence (EQ) and other intelligences.** Reassure a client who faces an IQ or cognitive ability test as part of a job interview that he can prepare for this, just as for any other part of the assessment process. There is plenty of evidence that practice improves results.

SOCIAL INTELLIGENCE: KARL ALBRECHT

Social intelligence is a concept built on the theories of Gardner and Goleman. According to Albrecht (2006), social intelligence, simply put, is "the ability to get along well with others and to get them to cooperate with you" (p. xiii). Albrecht's theory describes the components of externally oriented competencies, differing in this from Goleman's early work, which focused more on internally oriented competencies. Five dimensions or categories of competence make up Albrecht's theory of social intelligence (p. 29):

1. **Situational awareness:** our ability to read situations, to interpret the behaviors of other people in these situations and discern their possible intentions and emotional states, and to interact with others

2. **Presence:** a range of verbal and nonverbal indicators, including appearance, posture, voice, and subtle movements that communicate who we are

3. **Authenticity:** signals others pick up from us that help them judge whether or not we are honest, open, ethical, trustworthy, and well intentioned

4. **Clarity:** our competence in explaining ourselves, illuminating ideas, articulating our views, and so on, in an effort to get others to cooperate with us

5. **Empathy:** an emotion beyond sympathy; a shared feeling between ourselves and others that creates a connectedness with another person

Albrecht (2006) proposes a series of situational skills exercises to develop social intelligence:

- Study the proxemic contexts in which you find yourself. How does the physical arrangement of space and structure influence the way people behave? Who sits where in the business meeting? How does the arrangement of someone's office communicate status or authority?

- Study the nonverbal signals people use to define and reinforce their relationships. How does the boss convey authority or approachability? How do people signal deference toward others in authority or of higher status?

- Ask one or more close friends, preferably individually, to share with you the impressions they got when meeting you for the first time. This might also be a way to gently invite them to share with you any aspects of your interaction they feel could be improved.

- Keep track of situations in which others try to induce you to act in ways that contradict your personal values. How did you react? How did you, or didn't you, assert your right to behave authentically?

- Write a personal mission statement that explains to yourself why you think you're on the planet, what your priorities are, and what you want to do to make your life meaningful. Keep revising it until it expresses what your life is all about. Then type it and print it out; put it up on your wall or on your refrigerator and read it every day. Ask yourself: *Am I living the mission I want to live?*

- Study a person who seems to connect with others easily; make a list of specific behaviors you observe that seem to attract others and invite them to connect on a personal level.

Coaching Applications

- **To help a client raise situational awareness, have him describe in writing his boss, coworkers, and direct reports.** Have him consider these questions: *What are these people like? What motivates them? What brings them satisfaction? What do they need from me?* The process of reflecting on these questions will help him become more aware of the people he comes into contact with every day.

- **Ask your client to describe what people think of her.** Encourage her to see herself from the point of view of an observer.

- **Have your client interview the individual with whom he has the most problems.** Work with him on compiling a list of interview questions that will help him understand the individual better.

- **Suggest any one of Albrecht's situational skills exercises to your client.**

TRIARCHIC THEORY OF INTELLIGENCE: ROBERT STERNBERG

Sternberg (1985) defines intelligence in terms of the ability to achieve success in life based on one's personal standards and within one's sociocultural context.

Achieving success involves capitalizing on one's strengths and correcting or compensating for one's weaknesses.

Culture determines what characteristics constitute intelligence. Solutions to problems that are considered intelligent in one culture may be different from those considered intelligent in another. However, the mental processes needed to reach these solutions are the same.

According to triarchic theory, a balance of analytical, creative, and practical abilities enables the individual to adapt to, shape, and select his environment. With our analytical intelligence, we analyze, evaluate, judge, compare, and contrast. It helps us with problems of a more abstract kind, for which some level of detachment is appropriate. IQ tests and other conventional tests of cognitive ability focus on this capacity. Creative intelligence involves the ability to respond with insight to novel situations and stimuli. It enables us to make connections between our internal world and external reality. Compared to analytical intelligence, creative intelligence is more specific to particular areas of activity. You might be significantly more creative in one area than in another. With our practical intelligence, we tackle the kinds of problems that confront us in daily life, at home or at work. The capacities involved in such activities are described by Sternberg as tacit knowledge—things we know even though we have never been explicitly taught or have even heard verbalized. Practical intelligence tends to increase with age, depending on how effectively we are able to learn from experience. Sternberg's Multidimensional Abilities Test measures all three intelligences on separate scales.

Coaching Applications

- **Encourage your client to value her own kind of intelligence.** It can be reassuring to know that intelligence is multifaceted and can vary from one culture to another. Ask her to write down the particular kinds of intelligence in which she excels.

- **Challenge your client to recognize the various kinds of intelligence exhibited by others.** We can be impatient with people who have difficulty with tasks that seem simple to us, and can overlook abilities that we're not used to valuing.

Additional Reading

Albrecht, K. (2006). *Social intelligence: The new science of success*. San Francisco: Jossey-Bass.

A thorough introduction to the understanding and emergence of social intelligence, presented in practical and interesting terms.

Caruso, D. R., & Mayer, P. (2008). Coaching for emotional intelligence: *MSCEIT*. In J. Passmore (Ed.), *Psychometrics in coaching* (pp. 153–170). London: Kogan Page.

An excellent chapter on emotional intelligence in a book focusing on the use of psychometrics in coaching and developmental conversations. The book describes the model and discusses how it can be applied.

Gardner, H. (1983). *Frames of mind: Theory of multiple intelligences*. New York: Basic Books.

A good source for more on Gardner's work. Another good source explaining Gardner's theory and its application to education is the Web site www.education-world.com/a_curr/curr054.shtml.

Goleman, D. (1995). *Emotional intelligence: Why it can matter more than IQ*. New York: Bantam.

The basic text on emotional intelligence is easy to read, though perhaps Goleman overstates the evidence concerning the impact of emotional intelligence.

Goleman, D. (2004, January). What makes a leader? *Harvard Business Review*, *82*(1), 82–91.

Reprint of Goleman's article originally published in 1998. A very accessible read with an easy-to-understand description of emotional intelligence, what it is, and how to improve it.

Sternberg, R. J., & Sternberg, R. (1997). *Thinking styles*. Cambridge, England: Cambridge University Press.

This book is a highly respected resource in understanding how people think and learn. It is insightful and provocative for the coach or client.

Neuroscience

chapter
SEVEN

Linda J. Page

New discoveries in neuroscience, the scientific study of the brain and nervous system, are reported almost daily in the media. Shirley Tilghman, biochemist and president of Princeton University, claims that neuroscience will dominate scientific endeavor in the first half of the twenty-first century, much as physics dominated the first half of the twentieth century and molecular biology the second half (Ollwerther, 2010). Coaches want to know what is useful to take from neuroscience research, but we must be cautious about implementing every new finding. Media reports are often presented in sound bites and headlines that have more to do with spin than with accuracy. It is difficult to know whether a particular finding may apply outside the laboratory and, if so, how. Original reports outlining details and limitations are often written in highly technical language and buried in various journal databases that are difficult to access. Furthermore, science works by questioning, testing, retesting, and working through many iterations before drawing reliable conclusions. Nonetheless, neuroscience research yields several practical applications for coaches.

PEOPLE HAVE CHOICES: HENRY STAPP

The claim that human beings have the capacity to make choices is generally unquestioned among coaches. However, this assumption has been opposed by a substantial portion of the scientific community (see, for example, Dennett, 1991), which defends a mechanistic paradigm which assumes that material causes

61

determine all that happens, and that causality operates in only one direction. In this view, choice is an illusion. The new systemic paradigm offers a different view, one that draws on quantum theory to validate our subjective experience of making real choices.

At the level of physical objects in our daily lives, we are familiar with mechanistic cause-effect relationships. Physicist Henry Stapp (2007) explains that the rules of engagement are different at the tiny quantum scale of our brain's connections. Here, different effects are produced by the same causes, different causes are followed by the same effects, prediction is a matter of probabilities, and the very identity of what is observed can be affected by whether there is an observer. By asking a question and carefully observing the answer, we tend to find what we are looking for. Although the relationship of quantum physics to neuroscience is still hotly debated, this perspective provides the possibility of squaring our subjective experience of free will, choice, and volition with everyday physical reality (Schwartz, Stapp, & Beauregard, 2004).

Coaching Applications

- **Remember that "anything can be different," no matter how often a client forgets** (Zander & Zander, 2000). From a brain perspective, it is true that connections become stronger the more they are activated, yielding habitual behaviors. It is also true that we are not built with an immediate delete button for those connections. It may be useful to explain to the client that the brain has an effective process called *pruning,* in which unused connections wither and die. It may be that the best way to get rid of unwanted impulses is to ignore them and do something else (Schwartz & Begley, 2002).

- **Build "veto power."** Becoming conscious of an impulse, perhaps a habit we want to change, is a choice point. Scientists have discovered that, in that moment, our brains are capable of shifting what was previously thought to be outside our control (Libet, 1985). We have a choice to "veto" that impulse and not engage in a particular behavior, even in extreme cases that seem neurologically fixed, such as for clients with obsessive-compulsive disorder (Schwartz & Begley, 2002).

- **Encourage the learner mind-set.** It is important not only for the coach to ask powerful questions of the client but for the client to ask questions of herself. People ask themselves questions that open their minds to new possibilities for learning, or they ask questions that leave them wallowing in self-limiting judgment (Adams, 2004). When the client recognizes her own underlying questions, she is able to choose which mind-set to practice.

ATTENTION CHANGES THE BRAIN—AT ANY AGE

The principle of *neuroplasticity*, which is supported by robust neuroscience research results, opens a world of possibilities. The idea that adults can change both the function and structure of their brains was considered heretical a little over a decade ago. Orthodox science accepted that infants' brains grow and develop at an enormous pace, but become fixed at a young age. Beyond making connections required for establishing new memories, and allowing for inevitable decline, disease, and accident, adult brains were thought to be largely set in stone—not at all "plastic."

The series of experiments in the late twentieth and early twenty-first centuries that overturned this assumption is described by Sharon Begley (2007). Research with amputees, stroke victims, and other adults who engage in simple exercise showed that concentrated physical practice stimulates brains to rewire themselves. Scientists continue to apply this principle in new circumstances and with different populations, and there seems to be no age limit. The weight of evidence for neuroplasticity has overcome resistance to the idea (see "Michael M. Merzenich Award," 2001).

It was even more difficult to accept a further discovery that directly connects neuroplasticity to coaching: measurable changes in the brain did not result from mere passive exercise—from someone else moving a stroke victim's limb, for instance. In order for neurostructural reorganization to take place, the person in question had to *intend* to make the movement and had to *attend* to the process. That is, deliberate mental activity is required for the physical effects of rewiring to result. This was an even more radical idea. In a mechanistic universe, as traditionally conceived, only the physical can affect the physical, and what causes something cannot also be caused by it. If the mind is a mere reflection of the physical brain, it cannot have any causal effect on the brain that causes it.

Elements of a systemic paradigm, including quantum theory and the rediscovery of volition, explain the results of experiments in which people's mental efforts have a measurable effect on their brain structure. When a coach asks a question that invites the client to intentionally pay attention to some area of his or her life, activation increases in the part of the brain that processes that information. Concentrated attention over a long period stimulates increases in the number of neurons, their connections, and the expanse of their neural real estate, leading to increased processing capacity. We can know more, do more, and sense more complex and subtle signals—that is, enhance whatever part of the brain is being stimulated. Clients who believe they are too old or too set in their ways to change are simply ignoring the evidence that neuroscience has accumulated. To paraphrase Daniel Siegel (2007), at any age, our minds are using our brains to create themselves. In short, attention changes the brain.

Coaching Applications

- **Pay attention to attention.** If attention changes our brains, it follows that you can predict where a client is headed by noticing what he pays attention to. This requires pattern recognition and "listening with the third eye" (Kopp, 1995) to the stories and metaphors he uses, to changes in energy levels and how they relate to topics being discussed, to signs of being stuck, and to unconscious and nonverbal signals.

- **Communicate so as to maximize limited working memory.** Our ability to pay attention is severely limited (Rock & Page, 2009). You can help your client arrange her surroundings and reduce distractions so as to be able to pay better attention to what matters. And keep your questions brief. Generally, the fewer words in a question, the better the client will be able to focus on it.

- **Shift attention to solutions rather than problems.** A corollary of the claim that attention changes the brain is that paying attention to what we do *not* want shifts the brain in that negative direction. Research on positivity (Frederickson, 2009) underscores the efficacy of nurturing gratitude, hope, and other positive emotions. Paying relatively more attention to the positive without ignoring the negative (in a three-to-one ratio) can result in a mutually reinforcing beneficial spiral.

- **Nurture "mindsight," or the ability to reflect on one's own thinking.** The capacity to selectively pay attention can be nurtured (Siegel, 2010). In addition to asking questions that help the client become more aware, you may recommend mindfulness training (Begley, 2007). Enhanced quality and quantity of attention is the real benefit of such training, whatever form it takes. If the client wants more of something in his life, paying more attention to it can enhance his capacity to perceive it and reduce his tendency to be distracted from it.

THE SOCIAL BRAIN: LESLIE BROTHERS

Neuroscientist Leslie Brothers (2001, 1997) has marshaled considerable evidence showing that our brains are fundamentally designed to participate in social life. In the early 1990s, a group of neuroscientists at the University of Parma in Italy discovered what they called "mirror neurons" in the brains of primates (Rizzolatti & Sinigaglia, 2008). Brain cells in a monkey's motor cortex respond to movements of others just as they do to similar movements of the monkey itself. The existence of mirror neurons in the brains of humans is a controversial topic, but may help explain the capacity of people to feel what others feel, to imitate their behavior, and to experience some part of what they experience. When you observe someone moving his arm to pick up a coffee cup, it may be that neurons fire in your brain that would fire if you yourself picked up a coffee cup.

But that is not the whole story. Apparently, it is only when the other person *intends* to pick up that cup that your brain reacts as though you were actually performing the action. If he moves his arm in what appears to be the same gesture but without intending to grasp the cup, your mirror neurons do not fire. If this is so, it means we are connected with one another at a level of intentions, motivations, and emotions. Our brains are indeed constructed for social participation. It is little wonder that emotions are contagious (Ochsner & Lieberman, 2001; Lieberman, 2007).

Research and experience, however, show that successful construction of a socially adept brain is not automatic. Since attachment theory was first introduced by John Bowlby (1951, 1969), research has shown the consequences of different caregiver relationships on children's mental health, on the mental health of those children as adults, and on the capacity of those adults to nurture their own children. People who have never experienced nurturing relationships are limited in their ability to participate socially with others. Looking at these studies from a neuroscience perspective, Siegel (1999) makes a claim that is of major consequence for coaches: certain kinds of relationships make our brains grow.

Fortunately, the principle of neuroplasticity applies to anyone who experienced nurturing deficits in childhood. We now know that the capacity to grow new brain functions and structure does not end with childhood. Some adults who themselves had difficult attachment histories nonetheless developed healthy relationships with their own children. How did they achieve this? By engaging in the same kinds of relationships, as adults, that they had missed out on as children.

Coaching Applications

• **Engage in collaborative, contingent conversations with clients.** When parents engage in games such as peek-a-boo with their preverbal infants, they are not being silly (or not *only* being silly). Even before children can speak, they engage with caretakers in conversation, each taking turns, leading and responding to the other's signals, the parent ratcheting the intensity up or down so as not to lose the child's interest or cause alarm. Siegel (1999) characterizes these conversations as *contingent* and *collaborative.* These conversations stimulate the development of a child's ability to tune in to the inner lives of others. This attuned interaction provides a model for future verbal conversations and, eventually, for healthy adult relationships. One person serves the conversational ball, and the other returns, back and forth, neither determining what will happen but each making a contribution that is both self-expressive and cognizant of the other. Although coaching tools and techniques may be useful, especially in assuring coaches that they are "doing something," coaches should never underestimate the value of a simple, mutually attuned conversation.

• **Experience others directly, through the senses, in the moment.** Collaborative, contingent conversations require that both parties be present in the present (Senge, Scharmer, Jaworski, & Flowers, 2005). We have the capacity to slip into past or future stories or assumptions about ourselves or people we are talking with. Mindfulness training helps us recognize this slippage and consciously refocus our attention on the person in front of us. Because our clients are high functioning, they have the capacity to respond to our present orientation by becoming more present themselves. In this way, both coach and client grow their social brains.

• **Recognize and balance the needs of physical brain and body, mind, and relationships.** The part of the brain that particularly benefits from collaborative, contingent conversations is the prefrontal cortex (PFC), the area of the brain behind our forehead that supports many of the qualities considered to be markers of health and wellness: physically, to marshal the energy and motivation to work and play effectively, productively, enjoyably, and also to be able to relax and recover; mentally, to analyze situations, see the big picture, set reasonable targets, hold to plans, and also to shift quickly when necessary; socially, to empathize and connect with others, understand something of their inner lives, go along with them and be part of the team, and also do the right thing even when it is not popular. These qualities characterize people whose PFC is well developed enough to orchestrate an integrated brain, a self-reflective mind, and attuned relationships. These are proposed by Siegel (2007) as the three necessary components of health beyond mere absence of disease or dysfunction. Thus, an attuned coaching relationship itself contributes to a healthful, holistic life balance.

- **Help clients recognize and sidestep threats to effective social participation.** Why have a brain? Ultimately, in order to anticipate and either pursue reward or avoid danger. To do its primary job, the brain is constantly scanning and comparing what is happening with what it predicts, based on past experience. Anything unexpected sets off an error response, and the alarm for a threat is much more compelling than a signal of a possible reward. Signals of a threat response are fed into the amygdala, located conveniently in the center of the brain. Its central place means that it can communicate effectively with other parts of the brain, particularly the PFC. When the amygdala is in a state of threat—Daniel Goleman (1995) referred to this as an "amygdala hijack"—it is difficult for the PFC to maintain such functions as seeing the big picture and understanding other people's perspectives.

- **Help clients to identify their particular ways of reacting to threat.** David Rock (2008) catalogued brain reactions to types of threats that show up particularly in workplaces, and devised the SCARF model, an acronym for *status, certainty, autonomy, relatedness,* and *fairness.* Understanding your own typical SCARF reactions can help with self-management, for both you and the client. If clients know they are less effective when their relatedness has been threatened—for instance, when losing a favorite coworker to restructuring—they can give themselves time to recover before expecting peak performance. As a coach, you may find yourself overidentifying with clients whose SCARF reactions match your own, or not understanding why clients react differently from you. Understanding one's SCARF profile and being able to sort out whose issues belong to whom is an important competency for coaches.

Additional Reading

Adams, M. (2004). *Change your questions, change your life: 7 powerful tools for life and work*. San Francisco: Berrett-Koehler. (Web site: www.inquiryinstitute.com)
The effects of asking questions from a "learner" rather than a "judger" mind-set are illustrated by one man's story of personal and professional transformation.

Begley, S. (2007). *Train your mind, change your brain: How a new science reveals our extraordinary potential to transform ourselves*. New York: Ballantine Books.
A gifted storyteller explains the series of experiments that established neuroplasticity.

Brothers, L. (1997). *Friday's footprint: How society shapes the human mind*. New York: Oxford University Press.
A neuropsychiatrist presents a cogent argument for the inherently social nature of our brains.

Doidge, N. (2007). *The brain that changes itself: Stories of personal triumph from the frontiers of brain science*. New York: Viking.
A psychiatrist inspires all of us with stories of people who overcame challenges once thought to be beyond repair.

Fredrickson, B. L. (2009). *Positivity: Top-notch research reveals the 3-to-1 ratio that will change your life*. New York: Three Rivers Press.
Clients will benefit from reading these convincing results of a well-thought-out and ongoing research program.

Schwartz, J. M., & Begley, S. (2002). *The mind and the brain: Neuroplasticity and the power of mental force*. New York: ReganBooks.
This book introduces groundbreaking methods that even severely disturbed patients can use to improve brain dysfunction.

Senge, P., Scharmer, C. O., Jaworski, J., & Flowers, B. S. (2005). *Presence: An exploration of profound change in people, organizations, and society*. New York: Doubleday/Society for Organizational Learning.
Colleagues describe a mutually reinforcing discovery of where to find passion and purpose and their relationship to personal and social transformation.

Siegel, D. J. (2007). *The mindful brain: Reflection and attunement in the cultivation of well-being*. New York: Norton.
A personal journey of self-reflection and exploration of mindfulness practices is presented through the eyes of the neuropsychiatrist who developed interpersonal neurobiology.

Siegel, D. J. (2010). *Mindsight: The new science of personal transformation*. New York: Bantam.

A leader in the field of interpersonal neurobiology describes eight types of integration that define mental health and well-being.

Stapp, H. P. (2007). *Mindful universe: Quantum mechanics and the participating observer.* Berlin: Springer-Verlag.

A physicist writes a surprisingly accessible and exceedingly humane explanation of the relation of quantum physics to our mental processes.

PART TWO

Human Interaction and Coaching

I t's not easy being human, and sometimes it seems that the worst part of it is all the other humans we have to deal with. We are, however, essentially social beings. We function in relation to each other. Extended isolation, when not embraced as a spiritual discipline, is generally considered a cruel punishment.

It makes sense to study humans in a social context: how we communicate (or not), how we resolve conflict (or not). Most of us are born into family systems, and the groups in which we find ourselves working are sometimes susceptible to similar patterns. We are at the mercy of changes over which we have little control, and that demand all our resources of patience and adaptability. Even our individual learning is contextual—a necessary back-and-forth between study and experience, between knowing and doing—and most effective when incorporated into our dealings with others.

For the coach, theories of adult learning, conflict management, communication, and systems are rich sources of insight.

Theories of Adult Learning

chapter EIGHT

John Leary-Joyce and Leni Wildflower

Adult learning, as a distinct branch of education theory, is a development of the later twentieth century. Earlier pioneers of education reform, whose influence can be felt in these newer concepts, include John Dewey and Paulo Freire.

Dewey (1916) was an American philosopher, psychologist, and educator, who played a major role in education reform in the early decades of the twentieth century. He believed in education both as a process of personal development and as a means of creating the informed and educated populace that is essential to a fully functioning democracy. A proponent of hands-on education, he advocated an approach that allowed students to make connections between classroom learning and their own experiences.

Brazilian educator Paulo Freire (1969) studied law and philosophy and taught Portuguese in Brazilian public schools. His own experience of growing up in poverty led to radically experimental approaches to teaching and a deep political engagement in the importance of universal education. He worked with illiterate adults, as well as children, at a time when literacy was a requirement for voting in Brazil. He argued that education must be related to the needs and experiences of students, and that teachers learn from students as well as students from teachers.

The influence of these reformers can be seen in the concepts of adult learning. Four theories are particularly applicable to the coaching engagement: the concept of andragogy pioneered by Malcolm Knowles (Knowles, Holton, & Swanson,

2005); Jack Mezirow's transformational learning (1991, 2000); David Kolb's Learning Cycle and his Learning Styles Inventory (1984); and Gillie Bolton's concept of reflective learning (2004).

ANDRAGOGY: MALCOLM KNOWLES

Malcolm Knowles's andragogy has stood as a core concept in adult learning for over thirty years. In his book *The Adult Learner,* Knowles defined andragogy as "the process of adults gaining knowledge and expertise" (Knowles et al., 2005, p. 174). He saw andragogy as sharply differentiated from pedagogy, which relates to children.

According to Knowles et al. (2005), six assumptions characterize adult learning:

1. Adults learn best if they know why they need to learn. Learning must be relevant and goal oriented.

2. Because adults have a formed self-concept, they prefer to be self-directing and to feel in control of their learning.

3. Adults' own life experiences are a rich resource for learning.

4. Adults generally learn to solve real-life problems. They tend to come to learning when they need it.

5. Adults are interested in the practical application of the learning. They tend to be life centered, task centered, or problem centered in their approach to learning rather than subject or content centered.

6. Adults are motivated by an internal sense of purpose—a desire to grow, develop, and make progress.

Coaching Applications

- **Whatever the subject of the coaching engagement, incorporate concepts of adult learning into your coaching plan.** Effective coaching involves developing a plan of learning and behavior change that honors the principles of andragogy and creates a foundation for mutual respect and clear agreement between coach and client.

- **Remember that the issues addressed in the coaching engagement must be relevant and tailored to your client.** In alignment with principles of adult learning, she should be a voluntary participant in the process with an intrinsic motivation to be engaged. Even in situations where coaching has been suggested by the organization, your first responsibility is to help the client see it as an opportunity to learn.

- **Remember that your client is an expert in his own life.** Remain aware of his needs and responses. Using adult learning principles reinforces the importance of the client's agenda rather than your own.

- **Acknowledge life experiences as a source of knowledge.** Encourage your client to use her own experiences in exploring her coaching issues. Her knowledge is the primary source of information on which to base the coaching engagement.

TRANSFORMATIONAL LEARNING: JACK MEZIROW

Mezirow's cognitive-rational approach to transformational learning is based, in part, on the work of Paulo Freire. According to Mezirow (2000), adult education should lead to empowerment. Knowledge is created from interpretations and reinterpretations in light of new experiences. Mezirow (p. 7) states

> [T]ransformative learning refers to the process by which we transform our taken-for-granted frames of reference (meaning perspectives, habits of mind, mind-sets) to make them more inclusive, discriminating, open, emotionally capable of change, and reflective. . . . Transformative learning involves participation in constructive discourse to use the experience of others to assess reasons justifying these assumptions, and making an action decision based on the resulting insight.

Transformational learning involves not only receiving information or ideas but acting on them and being fundamentally changed by them:

1. The process begins with a "disorienting dilemma" (Mezirow, 1991, p. 168), which is often a personal crisis. Subsequent transformational researchers have found that this process is often fluid, is not necessarily linear, may occur in a cumulative fashion over a long period of time, and often involves feelings and emotions (Merriam, 2001, p. 18).

2. As a result, a person engages in critical reflection and reevaluates the assumptions she has made about herself and her world.

3. She then engages in "reflective discourse" (Mezirow, 2000, p. 11). She talks about her new perspective to test its validity and to gain validation from others.

4. She undertakes action on the new perspective. This is essential. Transformational learning involves not only discovering a new perspective but also living this new perspective.

Coaching Applications

- **Encourage your client to learn from his mistakes and explore the elements of his successes.** Useful techniques for promoting transformational learning include critical incident analysis, role-play, journaling, and biography. In reviewing experiences, help the client come to terms with negative feelings and view past behavior with understanding and empathy.

- **Help your client uncover assumptions and beliefs that keep her from functioning at a more skillful level.** The process of reflective discourse, central to Mezirow's theory, is precisely what coaches talk about when they recall outstanding coaching conversations.

LEARNING STYLES: DAVID KOLB, PETER HONEY, AND ALAN MUMFORD

Building on the work of John Dewey (1938) and Kurt Lewin (1997), psychologist David Kolb (1984), along with his associate Roger Fry, introduced a model to explain how adults learn from experience and process their experience in different ways. Kolb asserted that adults learn by doing, so experiential learning involves a direct encounter with the topic being studied—what is happening in the present—and adapting to the situation as it unfolds, rather than merely thinking about it. His cyclical process involves four elements:

1. **Concrete experience (CE):** direct experience; action

2. **Reflective observation (RO):** reflecting on the effects of the action

3. **Abstract conceptualization (AC):** understanding the principles that affect the action

4. Active experimentation (AE): testing, adjusting, and planning a new course of action

Kolb argued that the learner may enter this learning cycle at any one of the four points, depending on her learning style preference (discussed later in this chapter). However, it most often begins with a particular action; the person reflects on it, forms theories about it, and tests those theories. Learning and development occur as the cycle is completed, provided that each stage of the cycle is experienced. Kolb asserts the importance of fully engaging with each stage of the cycle, wherever the entry point is, in order to make the most of any learning experience. Therefore, when the same experience is encountered again, the responses will be different and better developed. The process is then repeated. In this way, the experiential learning cycle is really more like a spiral, with greater ability to reflectively observe, conceptualize, adjust, and experiment with each turn. In practice, few learners spend enough time on each stage, generally favoring one of the four, commonly the RO stage, though this will depend to some extent on their learning preference.

As coaches, coaching teachers, and researchers have pointed out (among them, Elaine Cox in a lecture at Oxford Brooks Coaching School in the United Kingdom), the Kolb Experiential Learning Model can often guide the coaching process. For instance, the GROW model (Whitmore, 2009) maps directly onto the cycle as depicted by Kolb (1984). Whitmore's "goal setting" equates to an actual or proposed concrete experience; the exploration of "reality" is equivalent to reflective observation; "options" involves abstract conceptualization; and "What will you do?" suggests active experimentation. For a more detailed summary of the GROW model, see Chapter Twenty-Nine.

Learning Styles Inventory

Building on the experiential learning cycle, Kolb developed the Learning Styles Inventory, a model of learning style preferences, which recognizes that people favor particular stages of the learning cycle. This does not place learners in rigid categories; people can develop other styles. Kolb takes the four elements of the learning cycle and pairs them up in four different combinations to create four poles on a two-dimensional map. The four poles, each representing the combination of two preferred styles, create the following learner preferences:

Diverger/reflector (CE/RO). Strong in imaginative ability, good at generating ideas and seeing things from different perspectives, the person with this preferred style is interested in people and has broad cultural interests.

Assimilator/theorist (AC/RO). The person with this preferred learning style has a strong ability to create theoretical models, excels in inductive reasoning, and is concerned with abstract concepts rather than people.

Converger/pragmatist (AC/AE). Strong in practical application of ideas, the person with this learning preference can focus on deductive reasoning on specific problems. He or she is likely to be unemotional, with limited but often very focused interests.

Accommodator/activist (CE/AE). The greatest strength of someone with this preferred learning style is finding out by doing things. He or she is a risk taker and performs well when required to react to immediate circumstances, solving problems intuitively.

Honey and Mumford Learning Styles

Honey and Mumford (1992) adapted Kolb's learning styles to relate more directly to managerial functions and the business community. Honey and Mumford's Learning Styles Questionnaire (LSQ) is a self-development tool and differs from Kolb's Learning Styles Inventory by inviting managers to complete a checklist of work-related behaviors without directly asking managers how they learn. Honey and Mumford's model includes four types: the *Activist,* who prefers doing and experiencing; the *Reflector,* who likes to observe and reflect; the *Theorist,* who wants to understand reasons, concepts, and relationships; and the *Pragmatist,* who likes to try things out to see if they work.

Coaching Applications

- **Become familiar with the different learning styles.** Depending on your client's learning style and interest, it may be useful to share more about the experiential learning process with him. Simply explaining the learning styles can help him understand the way he both learns and works through problems. Assessments for determining learning styles such as Kolb's or Honey and Mumford's may also be a good resource.

- **Help your client expand her learning toolkit.** Encourage her to use a range of strategies in coping with personal or professional situations and in considering next steps. If she is an accommodator, for example, and inclined to engage mainly with the concrete experience stage, she can work on ways to become more of an assimilator.

- **Encourage your client to reflect on an experience as a source of learning.** Ask him to describe his experience and its effects in detail with such questions as *What actually happened? What went well? What did not go so well? What was the outcome? What do you think was really going on? What else? What are you learning about yourself, about the situation, about others?*

- **At the abstract conceptualization stage, help your client identify the process and interpret the event:** *What was the process and how did it play out? What did you want the outcome to be? Was the outcome what you expected or wanted?*

- **At the active experimentation stage, ask more speculative questions:** *Could you have done it differently? What might you have done? If you were to act in this way, what would be the likely outcome?*

REFLECTIVE LEARNING: GILLIE BOLTON

Reflective learning is the capacity to learn through self-examination and self-correction. One of the pioneers in advancing the concepts of the reflective learner and the reflective practitioner was Donald Schön (1983). Bolton (2004, p. 31) further develops an understanding of reflective practice as "one of constant reflexive self-examination—actions, thoughts, feelings, motives, assumptions." Educationally and developmentally, reflective learning and self-awareness are vital to increased capacity for learning and change. Bolton states that reflective learning can enable us to (1) study our own decision-making processes, (2) be constructively critical of our relationships with our colleagues, (3) analyze problematic and painful episodes, and (4) identify learning needs.

Coaching Applications

- **Use list making as a tool for prompting self-reflection.** Suggest that your client list his fears, goals, dreams, desires, reasons to take action, and reasons not to take action. Writing these lists begins to enable him to understand how he thinks.

- **Ask your client to write a description of her boss, a coworker, a direct report, or a family member.** Prompt her with such questions as *What motivates that person? What makes that person happy? What is upsetting or frightening to that person?* Self-reflection involves not only understanding oneself but also understanding oneself as separate.

- **Work with your client on the issue of self-judgment.** Ask him to list the qualities that he considers positive about himself from the point of view of his boss, his spouse, and a colleague. A critical element of reflective learning is for the client to be able to observe himself without judgment.

Additional Reading

Honey, P., & Mumford, A. (1992). *The manual of learning styles* (3rd ed.). Maidenhead, England: Peter Honey.

The definitive book on the Honey and Mumford work-oriented learning styles.

Knowles, M., Holton, E. F., & Swanson, R. (2005). *The adult learner: The definitive classic in adult education and human resource development* (6th ed.). Boston: Elsevier.

First published in 1973, this is the definitive classic in adult education and human resource development.

Merriam, S. (2001). *The new update on adult learning theory*. San Francisco: Jossey-Bass.

A concise, easy-to-read compendium of new thoughts on adult learning theories.

Schön, D. A. (1983). *The reflective practitioner: How professionals think in action*. New York: Basic Books.

In this well-known book, Schön demonstrates the value and meaning of reflective practice.

www.businessballs.com/kolblearningstyles.htm or www.nwlink.com/~donclark/hrd/history/kolb.html.

Books by Kolb and associates tend to be abstract and expensive. The best resources for learning about Kolb's experiential learning model and Learning Styles Inventory can be found on the Internet.

Social Constructionism

chapter NINE

Sherry Harsch-Porter

Social constructionism is not a single, unified theory. Rather it describes a broad set of ideas, characteristics, and conversations. Some of these conversations overlap, and some are unique among social construction scholars (Gergen & Gergen, 2003; Burr, 2003). To date, not much has been written about social constructionism and coaching, but its focus on relationship, language, meaning-making, and narrative make it particularly relevant to coaching theory and practice. A social constructionist approach to coaching is a philosophy, a stance, and a way of experiencing the world.

Social constructionism is considered a postmodern philosophy. Postmodernism rejects the idea that there are grand theories (metanarratives) that can adequately explain or describe our world. Further, it holds that there is no "ultimate truth." Instead, there is a belief in the coexistence of multiple valid ways of life (Anderson, 1997; Burr 2003; Gergen, 1999). In addition, Gergen (1973) argues that all knowledge, including psychological knowledge, is a product of the historical era in which it is advanced and the culture in which it originated. Social constructionism makes relationship and relational practices the central theme of what it means to be human. It challenges the idea of society as a collection of individual entities "acting on" one another. Rather, there is "I" allowing for an "other" and the overlapping "space" where meaning and relationship are created. Philosopher and theologian Martin Buber calls this "the between" (1970, p. 63). He writes that we can relate to another person as an impersonal subject-object (I-It), or we can relate to the other as a personal presence (I-Thou), which creates the between.

This between space plays a central role in social constructionist coaching, as it is where relationship, meaning-making, and the possibility of change exist.

Theories of social constructionism share certain characteristics that have particular relevance to coaching:

- Knowledge is communally created.

- Personhood (self and identity) is created within relationship.

- Language creates our world.

SOCIAL CONSTRUCTIONISM AND COMMUNALLY CREATED KNOWLEDGE

We are born into a social world that already exists. Our particular world comes with boundaries—embedded language forms, social practices, customs, myths, fables, conceptual frameworks, and categories. These particulars are passed on through the ordinary conversations we have with the people in our lives and are habitualized into systems of thought, belief, and patterns of action (Gergen, 1999; Hosking & McNamee, 2006; Cooperrider, Whitney, & Stavros, 2005). People both create knowledge and are shaped by the knowledge created.

To say that people construct knowledge does not imply that things and events are not real or that there is no physical world. Children fall down. Friends die. People get fired from jobs they like. But the meaning, one person's particular belief about these things, is constructed within the individual's social groupings and expressed in language. Social constructionism accepts that there are multiple, equally valid truths operating simultaneously.

Coaching Applications

- **Be conscious of the assigned labels or categories the client gives or has been given—*not good enough*, for example, or *too aggressive*.** Help her understand the social circumstances and norms that helped create this self-understanding. This relocates the label or category away from the individual, places it instead within the processes that created it, and allows the client to examine which labels are more, or less, useful.

- **Help your client look at how society has constructed the meaning of certain qualities or characteristics.** Shift the conversation away from labels constructed by others. Instead, help your client look at the processes by which some characteristics are given value and others disparaged.

- **In a coaching conversation, focus less on the client's "wants"** (*I want to be a more effective leader*) **and more on the processes that create the client's understanding of that "want."** Questions you might ask include *How do you define being an effective leader? How is this defined in your organization? Could it be defined differently in other organizations or other parts of your organization? Who will evaluate and decide? How will it be measured? How have others gone about becoming viewed as more effective leaders? What or who might resist your being an effective leader?* These conversations focus less on the "truth" (a single, definable, knowable version of an effective leader) and more on the ways in which a particular version of the truth is created and sustained. Working with multiple truths opens up a space for creating multiple possibilities and multiple paths to success.

- **Encourage your client to invite others into the coaching conversation.** Particularly in work and family situations, the relationship between the coach and client is a fundamental source of knowledge creation, but it is not the only one. Inviting others into the coaching relationship can create the space for greater understanding and generation of knowledge. Others (coworkers, friends, relatives) normally have different versions of reality than that of your client. By hearing other voices and other views, your client can directly experience multiple truths and multiple realities.

IDENTITY, RELATIONSHIP, AND SOCIAL CONSTRUCTIONISM

Social constructionism rejects the essentialist belief that a set of biologically determined characteristics make you the person you are. Rather, "self" is constructed from within the cultural conversations that surround you. Personal identity is woven from a broad array of factors: age, gender, class, race, education, occupation, income, sexual orientation, physical agility, marital and parenting status, and so on. There are as many potential identities as are created by, and embedded in, our conversations (Burr, 2003; Anderson, 1997).

There are multiple identity-constructing conversations at work within any society. Some serve to create and sustain particular identities; others work to limit the identities that are available or acceptable. For example, for a fifty-year-old woman living in the midwestern United States in 2010, the identities of wife, mother, gardener, and income-earner are culturally available. None of these identities pose conflicts with the dominant, prevailing conversations surrounding femininity or age in this western society or at this point in history. However, this woman's decision to start a construction company or become a doctor would likely create conflict or confusion if the culturally available identities do not include women in the construction industry or middle-aged medical students.

There are risks and repercussions for individuals who choose identities that are outside the boundaries of what is culturally available to them. They may be labeled abnormal, incompetent, or wrong. They may lose privilege, power, or access to the respected or socially accepted group.

Further, in our modern, complex, fast-paced society, there is a demand for the individual to move from one identity to another based on a set of expectations that surround particular identities. Within any given day, all of us automatically assume a range of identities, from mother to student to friend to housekeeper to lover. Each identity demands a different set of norms and a different mode of communication.

For instance, the conversation that surrounds age includes an array of identities ranging from young innocence to youthful virility to decrepit old age. The individual is expected to "act into" the appropriate identity based on the prevailing beliefs and expectations that surround the *number* that is defined as age. There are, of course, alternative ways to view aging. Rather than constructing old age as memory decline, weakness, and disease, we can construct it as wisdom, respect, and serenity.

The research of Ellen Langer and Becca Levy indicates that the link between age and memory loss is socially constructed and does not exist in the two cultures they studied in mainland China and in the American Deaf community where it is not expected to occur (Langer, 1997).

Coaching Applications

• **Work with your client to explore the social processes through which she has acquired a particular identity.** Remind her that identity is not fixed, nor is it a quality acquired through genetics, parental determination, or self-understanding.

- **When they are "stuck," invite your clients to test their facts and assumptions.** Examining new information or an old issue from a slightly different perspective may help move them away from either-or dichotomies into the realm of multiple possibilities.

- **If it is appropriate, introduce your client to the concept of social constructionism.** This will enhance his understanding of the social processes that create and sustain identity and help him move beyond self-blame.

LANGUAGE, NARRATIVE, AND SOCIAL CONSTRUCTIONISM

Social constructionism recognizes language as a core process. It is the vehicle through which we communicate with others and ourselves. Of particular interest are how people use language in everyday interactions, how they build accounts of events, and how they use language when performing functions (Burr, 2003). Words are by-products of social relationships and do not exist independent of the people who use them (McNamee & Gergen, 1999; Anderson, 1997).

Social constructionism sees language as

Central to the human experience. Language is what distinguishes us from other species. Other animals communicate through scent, sound, and body posture, but they are incapable of using language as humans do.

Performative. Language brings about effects in the world—it *does* things of consequence. Dramatic examples: *You're fired. I pronounce you man and wife. The jury finds you guilty.*

Embodied acts. These include words, deeds, gestures, artifacts, rituals, and metaphors.

Dependent on embedded use. The meaning of words is dependent on their placement—both what comes before and after. *Yellow* makes no sense as a response to *What's for dinner?*

Having an afterlife. Our words live on in the memories of those who are affected by them and are *re-membered* in other situations.

Although there are many theories about the function and role of language and communication, perhaps the most congenial to the view of social constructionism comes from communication scholar W. Barnett Pearce. Pearce (2007) encourages us to ask such questions as *What are we making together? How are we making it? How can we make it better?* This positions communication as a process of making meaning and coordinating actions. He calls these "speech acts" (which can be verbal and nonverbal), and they include many familiar language forms, such as arguments, compliments, insults, promises, and so on.

This approach to communication has implications for coaching from a social constructionist perspective. It relocates an unwanted outcome (such as conflict) away from the individual and focuses instead on the process that creates it. This shift allows us to examine the joint action that we call "conflict" and moves us to a place of inquiry that creates the possibility for different choices. If "conflict" is something we do well, are there other speech acts—"curiosity," for instance—that might lead us to a different outcome? How might changing the ratio of different speech acts—using less conflict and more curiosity, for instance—affect the outcome? What might happen if we rearrange the order of our speech acts by starting with curiosity before we move to conflict?

Reflecting on these questions may allow us to draw on our inner wisdom at crucial moments and better understand how language practices have an impact on both relationships and outcomes.

People do many things with language including the creation of narrative and story. Social constructionism considers stories as collective rather than individual events. Socially constructed narratives organize and give meaning to events, experiences, and relationships. These include stories about individuals that serve to shape personal identity.

Stories organize experience—people, places, events—into a cohesive whole. These stories are often retrospective and selectively include some people, places, and events while ignoring others. Narrative accounts of the same event are often constructed differently depending on who is doing the telling. Stories are also malleable and changing.

Harlene Anderson (1997), a psychologist and narrative therapist, cautions that those working with individuals to re-author narrative have a special responsibility for the way they position themselves in the "hearing and creating" process—for instance, how they talk *with and about* the individual, which topics are selected for conversation and which are ignored, and how the therapist (or coach) participates in the telling.

Lastly, coaches working from this stance will find ways to incorporate other "tellers" into the re-storying process as a way to create "end points" that may be more useful and productive to their client.

- **Help your client understand her story from the perspective of the influences and characters that create narrative.** One helpful exercise is to separate the "story" from the experience by creating a life map or biographical sketch for review and reflection.

- **Encourage your client to narrate from other perspectives.** These variations may generate new understanding and allow the creation of more useful stories (for example, of a hero overcoming obstacles rather than a loser beset with tragedy).

- **Remind clients that stories can be edited and rewritten.** The way we describe our lives is connected to the way we live them. Help your client understand that he can choose to diminish or edit out elements or characters that no longer serve him well. And he can highlight or include new ones that will serve him better or create more positive and useful end points.

- **As a coach, remember that your words create consequences and have an afterlife.** Pay attention to what encourages or discourages possibility in the coaching engagement.

- **Remember to watch for what you notice and address and what you leave silent.** The questions we as coaches ask our clients also say something about us.

Additional Reading

Aftel, M. (1997). *The story of your life: Becoming the author of your experience*. New York: Fireside.

Includes both theory on the role and importance of narrative and practical exercises that will help coaches listen for stories and help clients "re-story" in useful ways.

Begley, S. (2007). *Train your mind, change your brain: How a new science reveals our extraordinary potential to transform ourselves*. New York: Ballantine Books.

Supported by an interesting mix of scientific research and conversations with the Dalai Lama, this book makes the case that thoughts and experiences can cause physical changes to the brain. Of particular interest to coaches may be the research on memory and aging, compassion, and the happiness set-point.

Burr, V. (2003). *Social constructionism* (2nd ed.). New York: Routledge.

For those interested in a deeper understanding of social constructionism, this scholarly work is a good place to start.

Gergen, K. (2000). *The saturated self: Dilemmas of identity in contemporary life*. New York: Basic Books.

Gergen is a central figure in social constructionist thinking, and this book is his most accessible. He provides historical perspective on the social construction of self through history and shows how the boundaries of a single self are challenged by pluralism, globalization, and the technology-accelerated diversity of ideas.

Goleman, D. (2006). *Social intelligence: The new science of human relationships*. New York: Bantam Dell.

Builds on emotional intelligence as a capacity contained within us to include the notion that, through relationship, we create one another. Of particular interest to coaches will be research on the social brain and contagious emotions, and findings on achievement.

Isaacs, W. (1999). *Dialogue and the art of thinking together*. New York: Doubleday.

A handbook on how to create conversations that are focused on finding new ways of thinking and acting. Particularly useful for coaches will be the discussion of the ladder of inference and the art of listening.

Langer, E. J. (1997). *The power of mindful learning*. Cambridge, MA: Perseus Books.

Dispels many widely held beliefs about how people acquire knowledge and includes practical ideas for becoming more mindful.

Nisbett, R. (2003). *The geography of thought*. New York: Free Press.

A cross-cultural look at how knowledge acquisition is affected by geography and culture, including what we are able to "see," how we categorize things and concepts, and the nature of thought itself.

Pearce, W. B. (2007). *Making social worlds: A communication perspective*. Malden, MA: Blackwell.

A clear departure from the transmission theory of communication, this book makes clear and understandable social constructionism's model of communication as *making* the social world rather than simply talking about it. Of particular interest to coaches will be the concepts of conversational turns, critical moments, and ways to "act into" crucial moments.

chapter TEN

Theories of Change

Leni Wildflower and Diane Brennan

Change is often the impetus for an individual to begin work with a coach. Whether planned for and desired, as in a marriage or promotion, or unexpected and forced, as in the loss of a job, change is challenging. As coaches, we work with people to help them navigate change. This chapter provides an overview of the research around change, tools for working with clients, and an introduction to more recent findings to better understand why there is resistance.

THE TRANSTHEORETICAL MODEL OF CHANGE: PROCHASKA AND DICLEMENTE

> Probably the most obvious and direct implication of our research is the need to assess the stage of the client's readiness for change and to tailor interventions accordingly. (Prochaska, DiClemente, & Norcross, 1992, p. 1110)

Researchers James Prochaska, Carlo DiClemente, and John Norcross conducted a study over several years to examine the process of change in human behavior (1992). They arrived at six stages involved in the change process:

1. *Precontemplation.* This is the stage at which the individual is not aware that change needs to happen or that he desires change.

2. *Contemplation.* The individual is aware that a problem exists and is seriously thinking about overcoming it, but has not yet made a commitment to take action.

3. *Preparation.* This stage combines intention with contemplation of a change in behavior.

4. *Action.* In order to overcome his problem, the individual modifies his behavior, his environment, or how he experiences the situation.

5. *Maintenance.* This is the stage at which the individual works to prevent relapse and consolidate the gains made during the action stage.

6. *Recycling.* The individual learns how to handle the experience of relapse and begin again.

Underlying this model is the research finding that progress through these stages cannot be forced. As Hamlet puts it, "The readiness is all" (act 5, scene 2). The success of any change process depends on an accurate assessment of the individual's readiness for change. Insight (the knowledge that change needs to happen) does not necessarily bring about behavior change. Furthermore, action without insight is likely to lead to only temporary change. Successful change involves full progression through each of the six stages.

Coaching Applications

- **Pay close attention to the extent of your client's readiness to change**. One way to assess this might be to have her write down her thoughts and behaviors as she considers her desire for professional or personal progress. Together you can explore and examine these in light of her desire to change.

- **Help your client understand the importance of completing the first three stages of the change process before he moves into stage four**. Understanding where he is in the change process allows him to celebrate his progress or to notice and address any resistance.

- **Support your client if relapse occurs.** Prochaska et al. (1992) claim that people *rarely* overcome problems their first time around the cycle. Forgiving oneself and beginning again are important ingredients of this process.

MOTIVATIONAL INTERVIEWING: WILLIAM MILLER

Motivational interviewing evolved from the experience of counselors treating people with addictions, particularly people with drinking problems, although it has also been used successfully with people having problems with drugs, diet, and exercise. The theory has been tested widely, and motivational interviewing has been found to produce a positive outcome in all of these areas, with the exception of smoking cessation (Burke, Arkowitz, & Menchola, 2003).

Motivational interviewing techniques have been adapted for use in corporate environments, particularly as a part of the persuasion process in selling. But this is not to be confused with true motivational interviewing, which is a therapeutic technique designed to foster personal change.

Rollnick and Miller (1995) define motivational interviewing as "a directive, client-centered counseling style for eliciting behavior change by helping clients to explore and resolve ambivalence" (p. 325). At the heart of motivational interviewing is the understanding that change must be a choice and that there is no value judgment placed on not changing as opposed to changing. Major assumptions of Miller and Rollnick's model include the following:

- Motivation to change is elicited from the client, and not imposed from without.

- It is the client's task, not the counselor's, to articulate and resolve his or her ambivalence about changing.

- Direct persuasion is not an effective method for resolving ambivalence about change. The counselor should be directive only in helping the client examine and resolve ambivalence.

- Readiness to change is not a client trait, but a fluctuating product of interpersonal interaction between the client and therapist. Resistance to change is often a signal that the counselor is assuming greater readiness to change than the client is actually feeling.

- The therapist interacts with the client as a partner or companion in the change process, not as an expert.

The role of the counselor is, first, to express empathy with the client; second, to support the client's sense of self-efficacy in order to enable the client to believe that change is possible; third, to view the client's resistance to change as natural rather than pathological; and fourth, to help the client examine the discrepancy between his current behavior and his future goals.

On the face of it, the initial process in motivational interviewing is simple. The client is asked to write down the advantages and disadvantages of changing her behavior and the advantages and disadvantages of *not* changing. Then the counselor asks the client to discuss each of these reasons, both on the "change" side of the equation and on the "no change" side. It is in the process of exploring the reasons for no change that the client can be led to a deeper examination of her motives. Other elements of the process can involve a consideration of the dangers or drawbacks of not changing, and an envisioning of a future in which the change has been accomplished.

The four ways in which the counselor interacts with the client—open-ended questions, affirmations, reflective listening, and summaries (or OARS, for short)— are reminiscent of what happens in coaching:

Open-ended questions recognize that the client is more apt to reflect and will be more engaged when asked this type of question compared with questions that elicit a yes-no response.

Affirmations build rapport and authentically acknowledge the client's positive attributes and work along the way. This allows real-time practice in helping the client notice what is working rather than continuing to focus on what is not.

Reflective listening is crucial for noticing the subtleties of what is occurring for the client.

Summaries provide a mirror for the client and demonstrate the counselor's attention and interest. In motivational interviewing, summaries are used frequently to reflect what is heard and to keep the client on track.

It should be remembered that the major application of motivational interviewing as a therapeutic technique has been in dealing with addiction. However, the approach can be effectively applied to anyone desiring to make changes. The emphasis in coaching will be on a positive exploration toward shifts in priorities and focus in order to achieve enhanced levels of freedom.

Coaching Applications

- **Consider using the OARS model as a framework for exploring the pros and cons of a behavior and desired change with your client.** Modify the approach to reflect the equality between coach and client to provide greater freedom for exploration and choice.

- **Raise your own awareness around change and your role in it, as you support the client in his process.** Stay focused on the client's goals and be careful to avoid attachment to the outcome.

- **Remember that any persuasion at all on your part will automatically shift the responsibility for change to you, the coach, and away from the client.** Clients who want to change can often unconsciously be very persuasive in eliciting your support. Once you are "helping" them, the change issue becomes yours, not theirs. Indeed, you may be joining a line of friends, colleagues, or family members "supporting" her in her desire to change. Consider making a point of not being invested in any way in whether she changes or not.

WILLIAM BRIDGES: TRANSITIONS IN ADULTHOOD

According to William Bridges (2003), transition is a process that people go through as they come to terms with a new situation. Change is external; transition is internal. Understanding the process of change allows individuals experiencing it to place themselves in a context that both names and explains what they are going through. Bridges's model illustrates three phases of transition: ending, losing, or letting go; the neutral zone; and the new beginning.

There is no clear demarcation between these phases. Each blends into the others. Feelings accompanying endings, for example, can continue well into the phase when the individual is constructing a new beginning.

Stage 1: Ending. This phase is typically characterized by confusion about what has ended and what hasn't. It resembles the early stages of the Kübler-Ross cycle, so your client can expect, and needs to be prepared to accept, signs of grieving: anger, bargaining, anxiety, sadness, disorientation, and depression (adapted from Kübler-Ross, 1973). Here are some ways to support an individual in the ending stage:

Define what is over . . . and what isn't.

Identify what is being lost . . . and who is losing.

Understand that experiencing an ending can create heightened emotional sensitivity and overreaction.

Acknowledge loss openly and with sympathy.

Communicate what is known about the change, giving people information . . . over and over again, even if it seems repetitive.

Treat the past with respect.

Stage 2: The Neutral Zone. Bridges describes this phase as a "nowhere between
two somewheres" (2003, p. 40). The old has not quite ended, and the new has not
quite begun. One may have feelings of uncertainty, anxiety, and fear. Here are
some ways to support an individual in the neutral zone:

Acknowledge that this is a very difficult but also potentially creative time.

Help "normalize" the experience of being in the neutral zone.

Create temporary systems for managing the neutral zone.

Strengthen intragroup connections.

Remind people that this is an important phase when an inner "sorting" process
occurs . . . letting go of the old and getting ready for the new.

Stage 3: The New Beginning. The new life is starting, but just as it was unclear
what has really ended, it might be equally unclear what has really begun. Starting
a new job may feel unsettling. Questions may arise around the decision, the
environment, or one's own qualifications or competence. There may be a longing
for what was lost with former colleagues and friends and the connection to the
old organization. Here are some ways to support an individual in the new
beginning:

Acknowledge that there is always ambivalence toward the new beginning.

Be aware of the crucial importance of timing for establishing a new
beginning.

Clarify and communicate the purpose of the new beginning.

Help create a purposeful plan with roles for everyone.

Create a symbol of the new identity associated with the process of
beginning.

Bridges (2003) suggests four guiding principles to remember about transition:

1. When you're in transition, you find yourself coming back in new ways to
   old activities.

2. Every transition begins with an ending. We have to let go of an old thing before we can pick up a new one.

3. Although it is advantageous to understand your own style of endings, some part of you will resist that understanding as though your life depended on it.

4. First there is an ending, then a beginning, with a necessary fallow time in between.

In working with individuals going through transitions, Bridges advises professionals to describe and explain each phase in order to normalize it, and then to explore any specific and significant emotions, events, or information associated with each.

Coaching Applications

- **Help your client realize that change is not a linear process.** She may experience all the stages of Bridges's model, and just when she is concentrating on new beginnings, she is overcome by feelings of loss and anger, associated with endings. This is normal.

- **Use Bridges's model as a guide in helping your client manage and make meaning of a personal or professional transition.** Help him understand where he is in the process and know that it is normal to feel uncertain or challenged at times.

- **Remember that the model's purpose is to outline the process of transition, not to expedite the journey through each stage.** Its value is in helping both the client and the coach understand, explore, and reflect on learning as the process unfolds at its own pace.

- **Use this model when working with a client either on planned and wished-for transitions or on unanticipated transitions in her life.** The stages apply to both.

- **Help your client expect and accept that he may experience emotional volatility when navigating change.** Framing change using Bridges's model allows your client to acknowledge emotions at each stage without blaming himself for being angry or confused or for seeming to lack direction. This is especially important if the transition is the result of a planned change. If the client expected everything to go smoothly, he may find his own anger, confusion, or apparent lack of direction particularly hard to accept.

- **Help your client acknowledge the endings phase and notice what she has lost and the impact this has had on her**. Expect and acknowledge signs of grieving with the client: anger, bargaining, anxiety, sadness, disorientation, or depression (adapted from Elizabeth Kübler-Ross, 1973).

- **When everything is "up in the air" and uncomfortable, help your client understand that she is in the neutral zone and that this experience is normal.** As the coach, you need to trust the process. Be patient, manage the ambiguity, and stay with the "stuckness" of the client's situation without reaching for a "remedy" or activity to stave off feelings of "doing nothing."

- **Be prepared for the beginning phase.** Help your client notice and acknowledge feelings of ambivalence. Encourage him to explore and be open to the experience.

IMMUNITY TO CHANGE: ROBERT KEGAN AND LISA LAHEY

> The change challenge today . . . is not a problem of lack of will. The problem is the inability to close the gap between what we genuinely, even passionately, *want* and what we are actually *able* to do. Closing this gap is the central learning problem of the twenty-first century. (Kegan & Lahey, 2009, p. 2)

As the understanding of adult development has matured, Robert Kegan and Lisa Lahey (educators and coaches) have developed a unique process for overcoming the blocks that interfere with people's ability to make changes in their lives. The process, called Immunity to Change, involves the construction of a personal map that outlines one's desired commitment to change and what Kegan and Lahey term one's competing commitments and assumptions that make change difficult, if not impossible. More recently, Kegan and Lahey have developed a set of coaching applications to accompany the map-making process. Both the process and its applications are best taught by Immunity to Change instructors. Information on their programs can be found at www.mindsatwork.com. *Immunity to Change* (2009) is both inspiring and practical on the obstacles and how to overcome them.

Additional Reading

Bridges, W. (2003). *Managing transitions: Making the most of change (2nd ed.).* Cambridge, MA: Da Capo Press.

A highly readable and useable book.

Kegan, R., & Lahey, L. (2001). *How we talk can change the way we work: Seven languages for transformation.* San Francisco: Jossey-Bass.

An accessible book that describes the steps involved in the Immunity to Change process.

Maurer, R. (2010) *Beyond the wall of resistance: Why 70 percent of all changes still fail—and what you can do about it.* Austin, TX: Bard Press.

An excellent review of the kinds of resistance to change, and how to overcome them.

Miller, W. R., & Rollnick, S. (2002). *Motivational interviewing: Preparing people for change.* New York: Guilford Press.

The foundational book from the creators of motivational interviewing.

Prochaska, J. O., DiClemente, C. C., & Norcross, J. C. (2002). *Changing for good: A revolutionary six-stage program for overcoming bad habits and moving your life positively forward.* New York: Quill.

A popular, easy-to-read book on the change process and how it works.

Rosengren, D. B. (2009). *Building motivational interviewing skills: A practitioner workbook.* New York: Guilford Press.

A practical guide to motivational interviewing techniques.

Communication Theory

chapter ELEVEN

Irene F. Stein and Reinhard Stelter

Communication theory covers a wide variety of theories related to the communication process (Littlejohn, 1999). Communication is not simply an exchange of information, in which we have a sender and a receiver. This very technical concept of communication is clearly outdated; a human being is not a data-processing device.

In this chapter, communication is understood as a process of shared meaning-making (Bruner, 1990). Human beings *interpret* their environment, other people, and themselves on the basis of their dynamic interaction with the surrounding world. Meaning is essential because people ascribe specific meanings to their experiences, their actions in life or work, and their interactions. Meaning is reshaped, adapted, and transformed in every communication encounter. Furthermore, meaning is cocreated in dialogues or in communities of practice, such as in teams at a workplace or in school classes (Stelter, 2007).

In the coaching dialogue, meaning-making becomes a process in which, by fostering an open mind, different perspectives and positions meet and can be further developed. The client often comes to the coaching session with the intention that something should change, be different, in his or her life. Having this intention in mind, the coach is asked to *challenge* some of the assumptions, understandings, and meanings that the client has in regard to particular events, situations, tasks, or contexts. This challenge should be issued with sensitivity and empathy and with an intention to sense and grasp the situation from the client's perspective, while also nudging the client to perhaps shift that perspective. By

99

engaging in the coaching session dialogue, coach and client cocreate insights and understanding. Together they shape meaning and develop new or alternative stories about the particular events, situations, tasks, or contexts that the client brought up in the beginning of the session. This description of a cooperative process makes clear that communication in this sense has nothing to do with transferring information. Instead, coach and client are intertwined in a process of cocreated meaning-making with the result that, by talking with each other, both parties change position and move forward toward new understandings and insights.

Anderson, Cissna, and Arnett (1994, p. 2) regard dialogue as "a dimension of communication quality that keeps communicators more focused on mutuality and relationship than on self-interest, more concerned with discovering than with disclosing, more interested in access than in domination." Although there are a variety of theories of dialogue and communication, the four outlined here are most useful in a coaching context: Martin Buber's view of dialogue; Harlene Anderson's collaborative language systems approach; W. Barnett Pearce's dialogue from a communication perspective; and Deborah Tannen's theory of communication styles in conversation.

DIALOGUE: MARTIN BUBER

Martin Buber (1970) saw dialogue as a form of human meeting with an orientation toward connection and relationship.

> There is genuine dialogue—no matter whether spoken or silent— where each of the participants really has in mind the other or others in their present and particular beings and turns to them with the intention of establishing a living mutual relation between himself and them. (Buber, 1965, p. 19)

One of the ways Buber explained his view of dialogue was by using examples of what it is not. He describes three basic forms of communication between individuals: monologue disguised as dialogue, technical dialogue, and genuine dialogue. *Monologue disguised as dialogue* occurs when someone who is talking appears more intent on hearing his or her own voice than on making contact or sharing information of value. *Technical dialogue* is prompted solely by the need for objective understanding or information. It is an impersonal way to communicate, but is the type of communication used most often in the world. In *genuine dialogue*, according to Buber, each of the participants has the other in mind, and the intention is on establishing a living mutual relationship.

In his book *I and Thou* (1970), Buber called genuine dialogue an *I-Thou* relationship, whereas the others are *I-It* relationships. He highlights the importance of the intention of the speaker by pointing out that the "I" of "I-Thou" is not the same "I" as the "I" of "I-It." The combined relationship, which Buber calls "the between," is what is most important in the communication.

Coaching Applications

Though not all coaches may think of their coach-client conversations as dialogue, when those conversations are conducted in a Buberian spirit, new ideas appear in "the between" that neither coach nor client had considered before. Table 11.1 illustrates how other characteristics of Buberian dialogue are applied in a coaching context.

COLLABORATIVE LANGUAGE SYSTEMS: HARLENE ANDERSON

Harlene Anderson, with the late Harold Goolishian, has developed a dialogic process for therapy that she has called either a *collaborative language systems approach* (Anderson, 1993, 1995) or just a *collaborative approach* (Anderson, 1997). She describes this postmodern approach to therapy as "a language system and a linguistic event in which people are engaged in a collaborative relationship and conversation—a mutual endeavor toward possibility" (Anderson, 1997, p. 2). The conceptual underpinnings of her work stem from "the postmodern premises of contemporary hermeneutics and social constructionism, with its emphasis on the interrelated relational nature of knowledge and the notion of self as linguistically constructed and transformed through dialogue" (1997, p. 44). She sees a dialogical conversation as a shared inquiry, one that a therapist and client can explore together, forming a *conversational partnership*.

The philosophical stance Anderson (2007) described for her therapy work can also be applied as the foundation for the collaborative practice in coaching: both coach and client are seen as experts and conversational partners who participate in the joint production of meaning and knowledge as part of the continuous

Table 11.1.
Application of Buberian Dialogue to a Coaching Context

Characteristics of Buberian Dialogue (from Anderson et al., 1994)	Application to Coaching
Immediacy of presence: "To be present is simply to be available and to be relatively uninterested in orchestrating specific outcomes" (p. 13).	Don't try to orchestrate specific outcomes.
Emergent unanticipated consequences: "Fundamentally improvisational and independent of the will of any participant" (p. 14).	Expect the conversation to take on a life of its own.
Recognition of "strange otherness": "Participants refuse to assume that they already know the thoughts, feelings, intentions, or best behaviors of the other" (p. 14).	Don't assume that you know your client's thoughts without checking them out.
Collaborative orientation: "One must stand up for one's self and one must care about the other" (p. 14).	Balance what you as the coach know with what the client needs.
Vulnerability: "Participants . . . open themselves to the other's ideas and hence to the possibility of being changed" (p. 14).	Both you and the client may be changed through the process.
Mutual implication: "Each speaker anticipates a listener or respondent and incorporates him or her into one's utterances" (p. 14). Likewise, the listener "will 'find,' in addition to 'other' and 'message,' something of self as well" (pp. 14–15).	Speak in a way that the client will understand.
Temporal flow: "Presumes an historical continuity. . . . A process, within which segments cannot be entirely isolated and separately analyzed" (p. 15).	Know that the coaching conversation takes place within a historical context.
Genuineness and authenticity: "Significant and persistent thoughts and feelings relevant to the relationship are not deliberately hidden" (p. 15). *Being,* rather than *seeming,* means giving oneself to the other spontaneously without thinking about one's image in the eyes of the beholder.	Be authentic.

process of development, learning, and transformation. The coach is a "generous listener" who tries to base his or her own dialogical input on the client's contributions to the dialogue. For us as coaches to be generous listeners, it might be helpful to be *naively wondering,* to be fluid in regard to our own positions and open minded to new interpretations of the different issues that come up in the dialogue.

Coaching Applications

- **When applying Anderson's model in coaching, remember the following:**
  - You and the client are engaging in an external dialogue with each other.
  - Simultaneously, the client is engaging in an internal dialogue with himself or herself.
  - You, as the coach, are also engaging in and maintaining an internal dialogic space within yourself.
  - Your client will engage in internal and external dialogue outside the coaching session with others, continuing the conversation and possibly the transformation process.
- **Talk with your client about the various components of dialogue.** Consciously observing the dialogue as it emerges within the coaching experience can be very illuminating.
- **Be constantly aware of and manage your own internal dialogue.**

DIALOGUE FROM A COMMUNICATION PERSPECTIVE: PEARCE AND CRONEN

Communication is considered by some as central in understanding much of what happens to and between individuals, families, groups, and societies, and as such should be of interest to all those in the helping professions. *Coordinated management of meaning (CMM)* helps explain how people coordinate their interactions and, as a consequence, create meaning and action. CMM provides a framework for coaches to understand their client's world from a communication perspective. Initially developed by W. Barnett Pearce and Vernon Cronen (1980), both professors of communication, CMM has evolved since the mid-1970s. The basic premise of CMM is that people are *doing* something each time they are communicating and coordinating with others. Instead of merely looking at communication as a transfer of information, CMM focuses on three questions: *What are we making together? How are we making it? How can we make it better?* Pearce (2005) emphasizes *coordination, coherence,* and *mystery* as the three central constructions of meaning-making in communication:

Coordination. Our actions are intertwined with each other, creating patterns. What we see as events and objects in our social world are the product of our coordinated action.

Coherence. Narratives and stories shape meaning and understanding about events in our life. Coherence is the result of this process and forms the basis of individual and collective identity.

Mystery. The world contains more than just what we can see and talk about and can always be approached and understood in different and new ways.

Drawing from Buber, Pearce and Pearce (2000) characterize the practice of dialogic communication as "remaining in the tension between holding one's own position and listening while being profoundly open to the other" (p. 168).

Coaching Applications

- **In a dialogic conversation, pay attention to three levels at once:** yourself, your relationship with the client, and the client's agenda.

- **Be conscious of balancing your attention**—between the client's wants and needs, your own knowledge and experience, and the demands of the situation.

- **Stay focused on the client's agenda,** but also disclose something about yourself when it will further the dialogue.

CONVERSATIONAL STYLE THEORIES: DEBORAH TANNEN

In everyday life we are familiar with conversations that go really well and conversations in which problems occur. Sometimes we attribute the difference to the intentions of the people involved, but often even well-intentioned conversants experience misunderstandings. Deborah Tannen is a sociolinguist who has spent decades studying how people use language in their everyday lives, and how gender, culture, and circumstances affect the use of language (1984, 1986, 1990,

1994a, 1994b). Some of Tannen's concepts can be especially helpful in understanding the intricacies of conversation.

Information and Politeness

When they talk, people are concerned not only with passing information but also with the effect of their talk on the other person. They want to maintain camaraderie, to avoid imposing, and to give the other person some choice in the matter being discussed. Different people have different ways they think are best to deal with these often conflicting goals (Tannen, 1986).

Borrowing from Lakoff, Tannen (1986) asserts that there are four, often contradictory considerations people have when they talk:

1. *Distance* creates privacy and is least intrusive.

2. *Deference* to the other person avoids imposition.

3. *Camaraderie* is created by expressing feelings and being open.

4. *Clarity* of information is most important.

People unknowingly place differing levels of importance on each consideration. It's not hard to see that a person who regards giving privacy (*distance*) as being most polite could easily be misunderstood by someone who grew up thinking that being friendly (*camaraderie*) is most polite. This misunderstanding arises quite often in intercultural exchanges between strangers who are both using their own code of politeness and are perceived by the other as being impolite. Likewise, as often happens in close interpersonal relationships, if one person is looking for *clarity* and the other is being polite by *deferring*, frustration occurs, as in this example of two people traveling together in a car:

Person 1: Are you hungry? *(wants clarity)*

Person 2: We can stop if you want to. *(is deferring)*

Person 1: Why didn't you just answer my question? *(is frustrated due to not getting clarity)*

Power and Solidarity

Contrary to some other popular and academic opinions, Tannen's research has shown that the language strategies for showing power and for creating solidarity are often the same. That is not to say that there is no such thing as power imbalance, but that it is difficult to know from only the language used whether the intended effect is to show power or to show solidarity or both.

One of Tannen's examples (1994a, p. 24) involves two women walking together in the cold from one building to another to attend a meeting. They are joined by a third colleague, a man. One woman greets the man with, "Where's your coat?" to which the man replies, "Thanks, Mom." The woman might have intended a friendly show of solidarity, but the man has heard it as though she is telling him what to do, exerting power. This ambiguity appears often and can be seen especially in the use of particular linguistic strategies of *indirectness* and *interruption*.

Directness and Indirectness

Competent communicators have access to both direct and indirect methods of communication. If information sharing is the sole purpose of an interaction, then clear, direct language is appropriate. There is no need for someone giving a lecture or a presentation to be indirect for the sake of politeness, when clarity is what matters. Indirectness may be used as a hedge to avoid the responsibility of going on record with an idea in case it meets a negative response. This form of indirectness has been deemed *powerless* and has been associated, in some research, with women's language. However, indirectness may also be used as a solidarity strategy, encouraging voluntary cooperation rather than unconditional compliance.

Indirectness may also be a form of politeness. It is the preferred mode of interaction for women in many societies, either under all circumstances or only when talking to men. It is too easy for someone to lose face if the conversation is conducted directly, so western businesses dealing with Japanese companies, for example, must learn what types of *yes* really mean *no*.

Interruption and Overlap

Conventional wisdom, as well as much research, has assumed that interruption is a sign of dominance. One frequently cited finding is that men dominate women by interrupting them in conversation. Tannen (1994a), however, reports that other research does not find a clear pattern of males interrupting females. What she points out is the need to distinguish linguistic strategies by their interactional purpose. Might an interruption be, in fact, an *overlap* that shows support for the speaker, rather than contradicting or changing the topic?

It may very well be a matter of style as to whether overlap is perceived to show enthusiasm or solidarity or whether any particular overlap is considered an imposition on the speaker's rights. If both speakers have the same style, more balance will be achieved in the conversation. A greater amount of overlap (or interruption) may indicate an attempt to dominate or may just be the use of a different style—what Tannen (1984) calls a "high-involvement style." In any case, the intent may not be what is perceived either by the participants or by observers.

Coaching Applications

- **In interactions with clients, be aware of the possibility of each having a different conversational style.** Intention may be different from effect.

- **Be aware of differing perceptions of the words you use.** Though you may use language intended to show solidarity with the client, given the context of the helper-helpee relationship, the client may still think of you as having more power in the relationship. It will take time, and learning how to interact equally, for you and the client to create a symmetrical relationship.

- **Become aware of your own preferences in terms of conversational style.** Is your preference to use language to infer *distance, deference, camaraderie,* or *clarity*? Become familiar with these language styles and how you might use different styles for different purposes in a coaching engagement.

- **Become equally aware of your client's conversational style.** In doing so, you may want to shift your own style to make the coaching conversation match the client's style, and thus increase the client's effectiveness in the interaction.

- **Be aware that your client may experience the frustration associated with differing conversational styles when interacting with others.** Sometimes problems that clients talk about can be framed in terms of different conversational styles.

Additional Reading

Anderson, H. (1997). *Conversation, language, and possibilities: A postmodern approach to therapy*. New York: Basic Books.
  A good introduction to Anderson's theory.

Flick, D. L. (1998). *From debate to dialogue: Using the understanding process to transform our conversations*. Boulder, CO: Orchid.

This is a great "how-to" book that coaches can use to develop their own dialogic skills. Flick's Understanding Process can be directly applied to coaching conversations.

Holmgren, A. (2004). Saying, doing and making: Teaching CMM theory. *Human Systems, 15*(2), 89–100.

Introduces the main ideas of the CMM theory and gives examples of how the different aspects of the CMM theory can be taught, exemplified, and used.

Isaacs, W. (1999). *Dialogue and the art of thinking together: A pioneering approach to communication in business and in life*. New York: Doubleday.

Isaacs is the founder of the Dialogue Project at MIT. Mostly written for a corporate context, this practical book is often cited as foundational for understanding the dialogic process.

Pearce, W. B. (2005). The coordinated management of meaning (CMM). In W. B. Gudykunst (Ed.), *Theorizing about intercultural communication* (pp. 35–54). Thousand Oaks, CA: Sage.

A good introduction to CMM. This can be also be accessed electronically at www.pearceassociates.com/essays/cmm_pearce.pdf or in a special issue of *Human Systems Journal* (www.pearceassociates.com/essays/documents/ContentsCMMExtensionsandApplications.htm).

Pearce, W. B., & Pearce, K. A. (2000). Combining passions and abilities: Toward dialogic virtuosity. *Southern Communication Journal, 65*, 161–171.

An excellent overview of different ways the concept of dialogue has been used by scholars and practitioners. Also presents a model to guide facilitators of dialogue—quite useful for coaches.

Stein, I. F. (2004). The "coach-approach" as dialogic discourse. In I. F. Stein & L. A. Belsten (Eds.), *Proceedings of the first ICF coaching research symposium* (pp. 130–139). Mooresville, NC: Paw Print Press.

Drawing from traditional dialogic traditions and from Pearce and Pearce (2000), this article applies dialogic concepts to the coaching conversation. In particular, it applies the three levels of context (self, relationship, and episode) to the coaching relationship.

Tannen, D. (1986). *That's not what I meant! How conversational style makes or breaks relationships*. New York: Ballantine Books.

Tannen's first book for a popular audience, it struck a chord and explained the basis of her work on conversational style.

Tannen, D. (1994). *Talking from 9 to 5: How women's and men's conversational styles affect who gets heard, who gets credit, and what gets done at work*. New York: Morrow.

An excellent balance of readability and tremendous insight rooted in Tannen's conversational style research. This book applies conversational style to the workplace—a must-read.

chapter TWELVE

Conflict Management

Cinnie Noble, Edward G. Modell, and Diane Brennan

I nterpersonal conflict is inevitable. How we manage conflict depends on our perspective and experience and how well we understand the particular dynamic we're dealing with. Whereas for some, conflict is to be avoided, and even the thought of it evokes negative emotion, others view it as an opportunity or an adventure. The truth is that conflict impedes communication and can result in serious disagreement, deterioration of the relationship, legal action, and possibly violence.

UNDERSTANDING CONFLICT

Conflict is a human dynamic that causes us to become entrenched in emotion. Once we enter an emotional state, such as anxiety, anger, or resentment, we lose perspective and get caught up in the emotion rather than the issue.

According to Ken Cloke and Joan Goldsmith, when we are in conflict, what is at stake is not the trivial issue that first ignites the dispute, but "our capacity for mutual respect, integrity, inner truth, and honest relationships with others" (2000, p. 113). They use the image of an iceberg to suggest the unseen depths that might underlie the apparent issue. As the iceberg of conflict graphically demonstrates, the issue is simply what is visible at the surface. It may have little or no connection to what is really at stake for the individual. To understand these deeper concerns, one has to delve deeper into the iceberg. Cloke and Goldsmith identify seven layers.

109

1. *Issues*: What issues appear on the surface?

2. *Personalities*: Are personality differences contributing to misunderstandings and tension? If so, can you identify them and understand how they operate?

3. *Emotions*: What emotions are contributing to your reactions? What is their impact? Do you think you are communicating your emotions responsibly or suppressing them?

4. *Interests, needs, and desires*: Have you proposed a solution to the conflict? What deep concerns are driving the conflict? What are your interests, needs, and desires, and why are they important?

5. *Self-perceptions and self-esteem:* How do you feel about yourself and your behaviors as you continue the conflict? What do you identify as your strengths and weaknesses?

6. *Hidden expectations*: What are your primary expectations and those of your opponent? Have you clearly communicated your expectations? What would happen if you did? How might you let go of false expectations?

7. *Unresolved issues from the past:* Does this conflict revisit elements from past relationships?

The escalation of emotion that occurs in conflict produces the physiological fight-or-flight response. As described in *Crucial Conversations: Tools for Talking When Stakes Are High* (Patterson, Grenny, McMillan, & Switzler, 2002), the result is either "silence" or "violence." Silence can be perceived as weakness; violence results in domination or bullying. Neither position is helpful in managing conflict constructively. Our challenge is to remember that we have the ability to consciously choose our response. Patterson et al. propose seven principles.

1. *Start with heart.* Focus on what you really want in the conversation.

2. *Learn to look.* Be alert to emotion around the subject.

3. *Make it safe.* Take responsibility for what your role is in the process.

4. *Master my stories.* Understand that you have a story around the situation, and separate fact from story.

5. *State my path.* Express yourself—sharing your facts, telling your story, and asking for others' views. Make it safe for others to express themselves in the process.

6. *Explore others' paths.* Engage with others so that you can listen, learn, and grow in understanding.

7. *Move to actions.* Decide how you will decide together. Establish clear expectations, accountability, and feedback in the process.

When we find ourselves in conflict, both the iceberg of conflict and the principles of crucial conversations can help build appreciation and understanding for ourselves and for others. They can bring perspective and the ability to discover the real issue and focus on it.

Coaching Applications

- **Introduce your client to the iceberg of conflict.** Ask her to consider each of the levels. Ask what she has learned in the process. Is the issue the same or is there a change? Are there any obstacles or new opportunities?

- **Use the principles of crucial conversations as a framework to help your client prepare for a potentially emotional conversation.** These strategies may help him manage his response and recognize that he has a choice in how he deals with conflict.

- **Help your client find a way to center or ground herself.** The ancient martial arts teach the importance of centeredness. Finding that grounding can be just as important in a difficult conversation, allowing you to be at your best and limiting the opportunity for being thrown off balance.

- **Strengthen your own understanding of conflict management whether or not this is your specialty.** Conflict is a normal part of people's lives. It's not uncommon for a client to come to coaching with an interpersonal conflict or with a desire to strengthen her skills and confidence in conflict management. Be ready for this issue to come up.

PRINCIPLED NEGOTIATION AND ALTERNATIVE DISPUTE RESOLUTION

Alternative dispute resolution (ADR) is an umbrella term for a range of methods designed to help people resolve disputes without having to take legal action. It has grown partly out of a need to reduce pressure on the courts, and partly in response to a general desire to find more conciliatory ways to resolve conflicts at work, in communities, and in families. ADR includes such processes as arbitration, mediation, facilitation, and negotiation.

In mediation, one of the most common ADR techniques, a neutral person mediates a discussion among two or more parties in a dispute. The mediator focuses on assisting all parties to identify their interests and to work toward a resolution of their differences. Although mediators may provide some form of coaching in premediation meetings or in breakout meetings during the process (known as caucuses), they must always maintain their neutrality and not champion one party over another.

Some mediators and other practitioners in the field of ADR also train specifically as conflict management coaches, but training and experience in mediation or arbitration are not prerequisites for conflict coaching.

Prominent in the field of conflict resolution, the Harvard Negotiation Project, founded in 1979, established the concept of *principled negotiation*. The idea was to move beyond a contest between winners and losers, creating instead a process that is both objective and exploratory. The negotiator doesn't have to choose between being *hard*, bargaining back and forth in a give-and-take exchange in order to bring the parties to an agreement, or *soft*, working to build a relationship between the parties, but can consider a range of possible outcomes that might have benefits for both sides. This process, which can be used with individuals or groups, involves four key elements:

1. Separating the people from the problem

2. Focusing on interests, not positions

3. Generating a variety of possibilities before deciding what to do

4. Insisting that the result be based on some objective standard

Out of the Harvard Negotiation Project came the groundbreaking book *Getting to Yes* (Fisher & Ury, 1991). The art of negotiation had generally been seen as an esoteric skill, but *Getting to Yes* gave everyone access to a process that supports a positive outcome for all parties.

Coaching Applications

- **Encourage your client involved in a dispute to prepare for mediation.** Help her identify and clarify her interests, discuss strategies, and rehearse saying things she finds difficult to express. Work with her to expand her thinking on possible outcomes and options for settlement that she might want to propose or that might be presented to her.

- **Support your client in the postmediation stage.** Coaching after mediation is a chance to address any unmet or unresolved matters—about the person with whom your client was in conflict, for example, or about the issues under dispute. The client may want support in improving her relationship with the other party, if it remains strained, or in achieving other goals that have emerged from the mediation process.

- **If you work as a mediator as well as a coach, be aware of potential conflicts of interest.** It's usually inappropriate to act as mediator in a dispute in which a coaching client of yours is involved. If your client is happy for you to coach the other party, and the other party is willing to work with you as both coach and mediator, this arrangement might be acceptable. The duration and strength of your existing coach-client relationship would be major considerations here. If you agree to proceed as mediator, you would have to be absolutely and transparently free of bias.

CONFLICT COACHING

There have long been people in the workplace—such as organizational ombudsmen, HR professionals, employee assistance counselors, managers, and union representatives—who have seen it as part of their job to help individuals and teams manage conflict. But conflict coaching, sometimes called conflict management coaching, did not emerge as a distinct activity until the 1990s, when practitioners began drawing on what had been learned from the application of coaching techniques in the field of ADR.

History and Purpose

In 1993, mediators at Macquarie University in Australia found themselves dealing with instances in which only one party appeared for mediation. Mediation is a process of resolving disputes between two or more parties and therefore could not take place with only one party present. The facilitators at Macquarie University recognized the need for a one-on-one conflict resolution process (Tidwell, 1997). But it was at Temple University in Philadelphia in 1996, where the campus conflict resolution program was experiencing a low demand for its mediation services, that the term "conflict coaching" was reportedly first used (Brinkert, 1999).

During the same period, ADR practitioners increasingly came to realize that there was a gap in the services they offered, in that individualized processes were not available except where there were ombudsmen. Meanwhile the coaching profession was developing, and conflict coaching began to emerge as a new specialty.

Since 1996, training in conflict coaching has spread to large corporations, such as IBM, and several government organizations in the United Kingdom and the United States (Jones & Brinkert, 2008). In 2004, for instance, the Transportation Security Administration (TSA) of the U.S. Department of Homeland Security incorporated a conflict management coaching program into its Integrated Conflict Management System, and in 2009, the Maryland Mediation and Conflict Resolution Office (MACRO) funded a pilot project to determine the value of offering conflict coaching through community mediation centers in the state.

In Australia, the Department of Defence uses conflict coaching widely, primarily to prepare parties for mediation. Other private and public sector organizations in Australia and in Ireland also use conflict coaching both as a distinct one-on-one mechanism and in tandem with mediation. In Canada in the 1990s, the Canadian federal government enacted a statute called the Public Service Modernization Act, requiring core agencies and departments to establish "informal" conflict management systems. Early in 2000, conflict coaching was added to the various methods available to staff members who aim to manage their conflicts independently. As with integrated conflict management systems in other organizations, the goal is to provide all staff with a range of methods and access points for managing conflict, along a continuum from self-help to third-party intervention.

Clients seek conflict coaching for various reasons:

- To resolve a dispute from the past, one currently in progress, or one anticipated in the future
- To learn different ways of conducting themselves in conflict
- To gain the skills to initiate or respond to challenging communications
- To prepare for participation in mediation, group facilitation, or another dispute resolution process

Whatever the particular concern, the focus of conflict coaching is to help the client gain the competence and confidence to manage his interpersonal disputes. Someone in a dispute generally has a stated *position*, an expression of the outcome he would prefer. Underlying this position is probably a cluster of needs, hopes, wants, expectations, and objectives, known collectively in the language of conflict management as *interests*, and it's likely to be these interests that give the dispute its emotional intensity. In exploring these deeper or more long-standing concerns, the coach might help the client toward a more creative resolution.

Use of Assessment Tools in Conflict Coaching

Conflict coaching can be done without the use of assessments, but assessments can be helpful. One might be used, for example, to support a client who struggles to articulate the way he responds to conflict or has limited awareness of how his response is perceived by others. An organization using conflict coaching may use an assessment tool as a benchmark to assess the client's shift in conflict styles and responses, repeating the assessment over a period of time. Two common assessments are the Conflict Dynamics Profile (www.conflictdynamics.org) and the Thomas-Kilmann Conflict Mode Instrument (www.kilmann.com).

The Conflict Dynamics Profile (CDP). This instrument assesses conflict behaviors in the workplace, providing a way for clients to improve their self-awareness in understanding what triggers conflict for them and how they respond. The CDP-I is for individual assessment only. The CDP-360 is available as a multi-rater or individual version. Both include a self-assessment of the client's "hot buttons." The 360-degree assessment produces a complete "conflict profile" that provides feedback on

- How an individual perceives the way he or she typically responds to conflict
- How others view that individual responding to conflict
- How the individual responds before, during, and after conflict
- Which responses to conflict have the potential to harm the individual's position in a particular organization

The CDP is psychometrically sound, and the rating scales are straightforward. The respondents indicate the frequency of occurrence of a particular response to conflict along a five-point rating scale continuum from "never" to "always." Training and certification are required to use this instrument.

The Thomas-Kilmann Instrument (TKI).   This instrument pre-dated the CDP and was derived from theoretical models that postulate that the way we deal with conflict results from where we stand on two underlying dimensions: the desire to satisfy our own needs and the desire to satisfy the other person's needs. Respondents answer questions designed to reveal their conflict style: avoidance, accommodation, compromise, collaboration, or competition. There is no certification process for the TKI.

Coaching Applications

- **Help your client identify the "interests" underlying her stated position.** Encourage her to explore the needs, wants, hopes, expectations, and objectives that make this issue important for her. Work with her to consider fresh approaches to furthering these interests.

- **Be aware that a client might not be able to work constructively toward his objectives until he has had the opportunity to vent.** There's usually an emotional dimension to a conflict. It is important that, as a coach, you respond appropriately to the client's feelings before helping him find ways to regulate and manage them.

- **Help your client gain self-awareness about her own reactions and what they might be contributing to the conflict.** Might there be ways of responding rather than reacting that would deflect or diminish the conflict? Give her space to rehearse new ways of interacting, and be prepared to offer feedback on her body language and style of expression.

- **Be aware of the cultural context in which your client lives or works.** It's important to recognize and understand that the way people interact in conflict or react to it might be influenced by ethnicity, gender, race, corporate culture, and other variables.

- **Encourage clients to be alert to signs of interpersonal discord and to seek early assistance with conflict management.** People tend to wait until a conflict has broken out before dealing with it. Organizations also react slowly. If you work with an organization, anticipate conflicts that might occur during periods of downsizing and other systemic changes, and institute conflict management coaching ahead of time.

Additional Reading

Cloke, K., & Goldsmith, J. (2000). *Resolving conflicts at work*. San Francisco: Jossey-Bass.
   Presents a useful model for getting to the real issues.
Crum, T. (1987). *The magic of conflict*. New York: Simon & Schuster.
   A practical guide for understanding conflict and gaining insight and skill in managing oneself.
Fisher, R. & Ury, W. (1991). *Getting to yes: Negotiating agreement without giving in*. New York: Penguin Books.
   A clear and concise strategy for managing conflict, whether personal or professional.
Mayer, B. S. (2004). *Beyond neutrality: Confronting the crisis in conflict resolution*. San Francisco: Jossey-Bass.
   This book offers a critique of the ADR profession and its focus on resolving conflict. The author argues that practitioners must become conflict engagement specialists to be a more powerful force for changing the way conflict is conducted.
Noble, C. (2008). Conflict coaching: A new ADR technique. *Alternative Dispute Resolution*, *17*(1), 5–7.
   This article outlines the development, application, and expectations of conflict coaching as it emerged under ADR and within the coaching community.
Patterson, K., Grenny, J., McMillan, R., & Switzler, A. (2002). *Crucial conversations: Tools for talking when stakes are high*. New York: McGraw-Hill.
   An easy read with stories that anyone can relate to. The authors provide a framework to support people in managing challenging conversations that could easily erupt into confrontation and conflict.
Ury, W. (1991). *Getting past no: Negotiating with difficult people*. New York: Bantam Books.
   A practical model that addresses the most challenging negotiations and offers perspective on how to achieve the best results.

chapter THIRTEEN

Systems Theory and Family Systems Therapy

Leni Wildflower and Diane Brennan

*Family therapists have learned that they don't have to make families
change. Indeed, therapists are finding that when they don't even try to
make families change but instead create a climate in which problems can
be explored in less defensive or polarized ways, families are able to
change themselves.*

—Nichols and Schwartz, 1995, p. 474

If we complain that our workplace is "like a dysfunctional family," we assume some shared understanding, at a nonspecialist level, of what constitutes a healthy or unhealthy family system. Whether the connection we have in mind is principally metaphorical (family as an image or analogy for other human systems) or instrumental (in the sense that individuals are replicating aspects of their actual family roles in the work environment), we express an acknowledgment of the family as a primal structure that informs the way we interact with others. To that extent, the concept of the family system, in all its interconnected psychological complexity, has entered the mainstream.

The modern study of systems has its roots in the 1920s and 1930s with the work of Ludwig von Bertalanffy (1968). Building on insights into biological systems, Bertalanffy analyzed the workings of open systems in general—an open system being one that has both internal coherence and connections with the larger structure of which it forms a part, as the ecosystem of a pond, for example, is part of the wider natural environment. This interdisciplinary analysis, called general systems theory, has influenced work in fields as diverse as engineering and anthropology.

In the realm of human experience, empirical evidence suggests that it is the family system that exerts the greatest influence on the individual, followed by other systems, such as school, church, and work (Becvar & Becvar, 1999). In the view of Salvador Minuchin (1974), the identity of the individual is profoundly and continuously shaped by the family.

> When I see families I have a clear ideology. I don't believe that parents are cruel and children are helpless, or that husbands are logical and wives emotional, or that mothers are sensitive and fathers are not. I see a mosaic—a puzzle in which each individual self defines the others and the whole defines the self, like an Escher painting in which the end is also the beginning. The parts enrich the whole, and the whole enriches the parts. (Minuchin, 1993, p. 286)

Family systems therapy grows out of an attempt to better understand, and more successfully treat, the problems of the individual. The family is of interest as a context for those problems. But study of the family system also opens the possibility that the person seeking help, or for whom help is sought, might not be the one most in need of it.

In its origins, family systems thinking owes much to the work of Gregory Bateson. Conducting ethnographic fieldwork in New Guinea and Bali (where he worked alongside his wife, anthropologist Margaret Meade), Bateson (1972) developed his "synchronic" approach, focusing on the system as it exists in the present, rather than how it has evolved over time.

Later, while studying schizophrenia with psychiatric colleagues in Palo Alto, he developed the concept of the *double bind*. In this circumstance, a child receives from her parents a "double" message in the form of contradictory injunctions— to speak freely and to keep her thoughts to herself, for example. The injunctions are delivered on different levels; for example, one is expressed in words, the other in action. For failing to fulfill either, the child is punished. Unable to leave the family system and yet barred from making explicit reference to the contradiction, the child is caught in a bind. Although developed originally in the context of schizophrenia, this model has been applied to problems of communication in a wider context, and clearly the existence of unspoken rules and unacknowledged expectations that run counter to explicit goals is a feature of many families and organizations (Bateson, Jackson, Haley, & Weakland, 1956).

Later family system therapists, influenced by postmodern thinking, have tended to emphasize the extent to which any family is socially constructed, and that the way each member conceives of the family is a separate construction based on his or her own experience and perspective. Therapeutic approaches have been further influenced by the work of social psychologist Kenneth Gergen and his study of the power of interactions to generate meaning for people (1985).

ASSUMPTIONS OF FAMILY SYSTEMS THERAPY

There are several basic principles associated with family systems thinking:

- Everyone involved in a family system both influences the others and is influenced by them. Relationships are interdependent.

- Systems have boundaries and can be either open or closed. If a system is too closed, it won't let in enough new information or influences to allow it to modify and adapt. If a system is too open, it runs the risk of chaos. Ideally, family systems need to be somewhat permeable. No family system is completely closed or completely open.

- Families develop and change over time. The family system is essentially dynamic.

- The family is greater than the sum of its parts. Behaviors can be ascribed to the whole family that do not necessarily describe any of its individual members.

- Family systems include messages and rules. These are relationship agreements, usually not explicit or written. Reinforced by repetition, they prescribe and limit the behavior of individual members. They are the assumptions about life that we often carry with us into adulthood, long after we are physically separated from our family of origin.

- All family systems have subsystems, coalitions, and alliances. Each subsystem has its own rules, boundaries, and unique characteristics. Membership of subsystems can change over time.

- Family systems therapists look to change behavior, not principally to increase understanding by family members. Understanding is not necessary for change to occur in the family.

- Family systems therapists recognize that it is impossible to make an observation without affecting the thing observed. The involvement of a therapist creates a new system in which the therapist is an active participant.

If a useful analogy can be drawn between the family system and aspects of the work environment, then the closest a coach will come to working with a system as a whole will be in team coaching (see Chapter Seventeen). One-on-one coaching often involves helping the individual understand and accommodate to a system of which he is a relatively small part; however, depending on the size of the system and the hierarchical or personal status of the individual within it, the system can be significantly shifted by a change in that person's behavior or attitude.

MURRAY BOWEN AND BOWENIAN FAMILY THERAPY

Named after its originator, Bowenian family therapy has been a dominant force in the family therapy movement since the 1950s. It is both a theoretical model and a method of treatment. As a practitioner, Bowen was thoroughly trained in Freudian psychoanalysis, but, whereas psychoanalytic theory emphasizes the individual, Bowen became interested in the system of relationships that constitutes the family. Bowen saw the family as an emotional unit. Any change in the emotional functioning of one member of the family is automatically compensated for by changes in the emotional functioning of the others. Interestingly, he seldom met with the entire family, preferring to work with individuals and couples. He encouraged clients to step back from the immediate family dynamics and reflect on the broader patterns, including patterns played out from one generation to the next. His observation that if one member of the family can improve his or her emotional functioning within the family, the whole family will change in response is both optimistic and exciting in the possibility it offers for individuals to have an impact on their family systems (Bowen, 1978).

For Bowen, family members function in reciprocity with each other. This centers on two counterbalancing forces: the drive toward fusion and the drive toward differentiation. The central challenge for the individual within a family is to achieve a healthy degree of differentiation. Differentiation can be intrapsychic and interpersonal. Intrapsychic differentiation is the ability of an individual to separate feeling from thinking. Undifferentiated people have difficulty separating thoughts from feelings and function with others through emotional attachment or rejection. At the interpersonal level, undifferentiated people have little autonomous identity. They react emotionally—positively or negatively—to the dictates of family members or other authority figures (Bowen in Nichols & Schwartz, 1995).

The basic unit of any family system is the triangle. On the one hand, the triangle is more stable than a two-person relationship or dyad, because it allows the tension that would exist within a single relationship to be shifted around among three relationships. On the other hand, it achieves this stability by the process of two members at any one time colluding against the third. The outsider will commonly feel rejected. But if conflict breaks out between the insiders, the outsider position will feel relatively comfortable. Each of the insiders will then typically compete to form a new alliance with the existing outsider. "The average person is about as able to resist emotional triangles as the average cat is able to resist birds" (Nichols & Schwartz, 1995, p. 372).

Other key concepts in Bowenian family theory include the following:

- *Nuclear family emotional process.* This refers to the marital emotional forces in families that operate over the years in recurrent patterns, such as reactive emotional distance between the spouses, physical or emotional dysfunction in one spouse, overt marital conflict, or a projection of the problem onto one or more children.

- *Emotional cutoff.* This describes the response of an individual to the emotional intensity within the family. It can occur over time and between generations, when, for example, an adult child leaves home and refuses to have contact with the parents. The greater the emotional fusion between generations, the greater the likelihood of cutoff.

- *Family projection process.* This happens when parents transmit to the next generation their immaturity, lack of differentiation, and inability to separate from their children. According to Bowen, the emotional fusion between parent and child may take the form of a warm, dependent bond or an angry conflictual struggle. Children caught in this pattern have a high need for attention and approval, difficulty dealing with expectations, a feeling of responsibility for the parent, and difficulty in forming healthy adult relationships.

- *Multigenerational transmission process.* Bowen described how family patterns can be transmitted from one generation to the next. Some Bowenian therapists use a form of family tree known as a genogram to illustrate the way a family pattern is transmitted and replicated (Gerson, McGlodrick, & Petry, 2008).

Although Bowen's original work was in studying families with a schizophrenic family member, he later worked extensively with a broad range of families. He saw no discontinuity between "normal" and "abnormal" family systems. All families are more alike than not, and they function on a continuum from emotional fusion to differentiation (Bowen, 1975).

Coaching Applications

- **Listen for how your client describes himself in relation to others in his environment.** What is the context? How does he describe himself in distinction to others? Where does he place himself in the system? Encourage him to become more conscious of his perceptions and responses within the system so as to expand his thinking and enable him to make more conscious choices of action and behavior.

- **Help your client distinguish her feelings from her thoughts.** Noticing emotional reactions, hers or others', and separating herself from these allow the client to expand her perspective, strengthen her identity and confidence, and become less judgmental of herself and others.

- **Where appropriate, work with your client to raise his awareness of the mechanisms of triangulation.** It can be a useful way of studying the shifting allegiances in a working or social environment, and gaining greater detachment.

STRUCTURAL FAMILY SYSTEMS MODEL: SALVADOR MINUCHIN

> Systemic thinking does not look inside the individual . . . to explain behavior. Rather, internal feeling states are seen as the individual's response to his or her own behavior and to the behavior of others in the social environment. (Schultz, 1984, p. 74)

Structural theory family therapy was developed by Salvador Minuchin and became very influential in the 1970s. In contrast with Bowen, who focused on emotional interactions within a family system, Minuchin observed family interactions from a structural perspective. The family structure is the organized pattern in which family members interact. It is a set of covert rules that governs transactions in the family. Family structures are typically hierarchical, with parents and children having different degrees of authority. Within the family there are subsystems, in which members join to perform various functions. Every member plays significant roles in several different subsystems.

Within the family or its subsystems, roles can adapt. Family members will compensate for one another. If one parent is organized, for example, and inclined to take the lead, the other will be less so, but if the organizing parent becomes ill, the other one will take over (Minuchin, 1993).

Boundaries serve to protect the integrity of the family and its various subsystems. The purpose of boundaries is to manage *proximity*, how emotionally close family members are allowed to become, and *hierarchy*, the allocation of authority. If the boundaries are too rigid, the result is *disengagement*, emotional distancing on the part of certain family members. If they are too weak, the result is *enmeshment*, a fusing of roles and a tendency for some family members to become unduly dependent on others. Among the many levels of boundaries functioning in any given family, Minuchin suggests that the generational boundary is the single most important one.

Minuchin was innovative in incorporating the wider socioeconomic context into his therapeutic model. The larger system within which the family system operates determines to some extent the norms and standards of behavior for the family. Although he has been criticized for being too hierarchical in his approach to the family and somewhat insensitive to issues of gender, Minuchin was unusually aware of the impact of cultural and social forces, and incorporated this knowledge into his practice.

> During the late sixties and seventies, we began to explore not just family therapy but the social context in which families are embedded. This was, of course, a natural development for a systemic thinker who is continually pushed to look at connections with larger systems, but it also seemed a natural continuity in my life. . . . The impact of

multiple social contexts had shaped me, and I was aware of being different in different cultures. (Minuchin, 1993, p. 33)

Coaching Applications

- **As a coach, recognize that you have an impact on the family or team system of which your client is a part.** From a systems perspective, the coach is part of the system, and your behavior affects the system either positively or negatively.

- **Work with your client to identify boundaries that allow her to stay at her best in her personal and professional roles.** Weak or nonexistent boundaries can result in poor interactions, drama, emotional upset, and blame.

- **Raise your client's awareness of the way roles and responsibilities are informally negotiated and adjusted within any system.** There's a natural tendency for one member to step back from the decision-making process in response to a more assertive voice, or to compensate for another person's inadequate contribution. A client's experience of being overwhelmed with work or responsibility or of being insufficiently heard might usefully be understood as a systems issue.

INTERNAL FAMILY SYSTEMS MODEL: RICHARD C. SCHWARTZ

Influenced by the work of Minuchin and Bowen as well as by observations and learning from his clients through his extensive work as a family systems therapist, Richard Schwartz (1997) developed the internal family systems (IFS) model. In IFS, Schwartz built on systems thinking, adding the concept of the multiplicity of the mind—the idea that each of us contains many different beings. He acknowledged the influence of both Carl Jung and Roberto Assagioli, an Italian psychiatrist who helped people get to know their individual subpersonalities. Other influences included Virginia Satir, who did radical work on increasing clients' self-esteem through self-awareness, and Sandra Watanabe, a therapist who developed a method resembling voice dialogue for working with internal characters. There are also recognizable elements of Gestalt and Transactional Analysis in Schwartz's approach.

Schwartz took a systems approach to understanding how an individual's inner thoughts and feelings relate to her overall view of herself. He introduced the concept of self-leadership and the need to connect the individual to her inner team. The IFS model describes the different "personalities" Schwartz saw emerge within his clients as he studied this phenomenon. He categorizes these into three types (2001):

Managers. These personalities are protectors of the individual's system and show up to keep him or her from feeling hurt or rejected.

Exiles. These are deep and burdensome emotions, such as dependency, shame, worthlessness, fear, loss, loneliness, neediness, and pain.

Firefighters. Like managers, firefighters protect the individual's system, but they come into play after an exile is activated. Firefighters distract the individual from working through the issue, showing up as self-destructive behaviors, such as distraction, rage, obsession, addiction, violence, and self-harm. The purpose of a firefighter is to isolate the exile to protect the individual from additional pain.

Understanding that we each have multiple selves or "parts," along with a "Self"—the clear, nonjudgmental perspective, which is the center of our strength as a being—allows us to achieve greater clarity, awareness, purpose, potential, and happiness in our lives. IFS addresses a person's parts in relation to the whole and encourages him to bring more Self into his life.

Schwartz describes the characteristics of a stronger Self as the eight C's: calmness, clarity, curiosity, compassion, confidence, courage, creativity, and connectedness. Strengthening our Self allows us to access more of each of these characteristics and in turn build a capability to bring more of our Self into the present.

Coaching Applications

- **Notice any reference your client makes to different aspects of his inner self.** Use this opportunity to raise his awareness of how his internal team influences his behavior and actions. Help him acknowledge these different parts from the perspective of a strong Self, calmly, curiously, and without judgment.

- **Don't be afraid of working with emotion.** IFS provides a framework that allows you as the coach to assist your client in understanding and appreciating her emotions. Using this framework can open the client up to new awareness and learning.

- **Recognize that exiles, in Schwartz's sense, may surface.** It is always possible for deep and uncomfortable emotions to come up during a coaching conversation. Properly identifying and working through exiles, however, requires skill and expertise that go beyond a surface understanding of IFS. A coach may gain these skills through intensive work and experience with IFS or may refer a client to a qualified IFS therapist.

Additional Reading

Earley, J. (2009). *Self-therapy: A step-by-step guide to creating wholeness and healing your inner child using IFS, a new, cutting-edge psychotherapy.* Minneapolis, MN: Mill City Press.

Earley provides a clear explanation of IFS and outlines a simple model for using the process.

Gerson, R., McGoldrick, M., & Petry, S.(2008). *Genograms: Assessment and intervention.* New York: Norton.

If you like to play with diagrams, you can use this book (aimed at family dysfunction over time) on any organizational system.

Minuchin, S. (1993). *Family healing: Strategies for hope and understanding.* New York: Free Press.

An enlightening and accessible book on structural family systems.

Schwartz, R. C. (2001). *Introduction to the internal family systems model.* Oak Park, IL: Trailheads.

A very practical resource for understanding IFS. Schwartz's explanations and exercises allow you to grasp how one's parts affect the whole.

chapter FOURTEEN

Transition and Career Management

Jenny Rogers

S ooner or later, every coach will meet the client who needs coaching on his or her career, even if, as often happens, the career issues appear unexpectedly in a program that started with a different agenda. Companies are reshaping more frequently, recession creates fierce competition for jobs, more people are interspersing periods of consultancy with stretches of conventional employment, and the average length of job tenure is steadily diminishing. It is no longer unusual for senior clients to change jobs every two-and-a-half years.

Transition management and career coaching involve a rigorous process of reviewing where clients currently are in their private and work lives, identifying their aspirations, assessing their personal "brand" and how they express it through résumés and interviews, supporting them in job searching, and preparing them for the selection process and then for entering the new role. Virtually all transition and career coaching is enhanced by allowing enough time for exploration. Clients who ask "What do I do for the rest of my life?" are unlikely to find the answer in a single session. Similarly, despondent clients who ask, "Who will employ me?" are starting in the wrong place; "What do I really want?" is a far better question.

129

THE NEED FOR CHANGE

In Ana's late thirties, her fast-track career in a glamorous PR agency had suddenly derailed. Ana's question was less about finding another job than about whether or not she wanted to continue working in a world she was increasingly finding "trivial." "Why would I want to promote perfume, or protect some celebrity from the consequences of his own stupidity?"

Bonnie was a highly paid retailer and a new mother reluctantly returning to full-time work. She missed her baby and found her coworkers competitive and surly. But she had a husband who depended on her income, so how could she give it all up?

Carol was a career diplomat. At the age of fifty she was questioning everything about her career: the frequent moves, the domestic upheaval, and what she began to see as "boring" work.

Don, age forty-five, an information technology graduate, had been an early casualty of the recession and unemployed for two years. Married, with a wife with disabilities, he was desperate and considering training as a bus driver.

Edward was a sixty-year-old CEO running a large hospital. Unexpectedly he was approached about taking on a yet more senior job running an even larger hospital. His question was, "At this late stage in my career, can I be bothered?"

Frank was twenty-two and wanted interview coaching for a graduate-level job. When he was offered the job, he was in a frenzy of indecision about whether to take it and requested another session to help him decide.

Gayle was forty-one, a star performer in her department and the most likely successor to her boss. Gayle's HR director recommended coaching because she felt that Gayle could easily compromise her chances through reckless behavior and lack of self-awareness.

Floyd was a thirty-two-year-old research scientist. His pharmaceutical company believed that coaching would help him decide whether he wanted to make the move into management.

At fifty-two, Gerald chose voluntary early retirement from a large corporation and wanted coaching to check out the viability of his long-standing wish to become a freelance consultant.

These clients show both the span of issues that appear in career coaching and the wide age range involved. In people's search for a new job, their levels of urgency and intensity can vary. At one end of the spectrum is the relative calm of the client who knows decisions are coming up at some point but has no immediate need to make any of them. At the other end—when the client experiences the shock of a sudden job loss, for example—the emotional intensity is high, and so is the level of urgency. The following range of statements illustrates the interplay between the contextual and emotional climates.

I should be planning to move some time in the next year.

I'm coming up to retirement.

I'm vaguely unsatisfied with my current job.

There's a merger or restructuring likely.

I can't stand the new boss—I've got to get out.

I've got a job interview next week.

Help! I've been fired.

Career coaching typically benefits from following a path of activities and processes, varied of course according to the needs and wishes of each client.

The Coaching Road to a New Role

Assessing: Where am I now? What's the current reality? What's my psychological state?

Identity and purpose: Who am I really? What's my life purpose? How do others see me?

Skills: What are they? Which are marketable?

Personal brand: What's my image? What do I promise?

Gaps: What are the gaps between where I am and where I want to be?

Job searching: formal, informal; résumés.

Selection: preparing for assessments and interviews.

Negotiating: salary; contracts.

Starting the new role: preparation and the first hundred days.

- **Remind your client that it is important to think of the career coaching process as a complete cycle.** More than a one-off transaction, such as coaching a client for a job interview, it is a transformational process.

- **Be prepared to challenge a client whose panic about getting employment is clouding her thinking.** Keep her focused on the central question: *What do I really want from work?*

- **Encourage your client to take a whole-life perspective.** No one ever makes a career decision in a vacuum.

- **Make sure that your own knowledge is fully up-to-date.** Stay current with job-search techniques, for example, and be aware of the increasing importance of social networking.

ELIZABETH KÜBLER-ROSS AND CHANGE

The more unexpected and brutal the career challenge, the more the client will benefit from understanding the typical psychological responses to change and transition. There are two classic theories: Elizabeth Kübler Ross's ideas about loss and bereavement and William Bridges's framework about transition.

Kübler-Ross developed her theory in the mid-1960s out of work with people who had terminal illnesses (1960/1997). Initially it was also used to negotiate bereavement, but is now just as valuable in exploring any change that involves loss—which most changes do, even those that are eagerly sought. Now sometimes referred to as the *change cycle,* it's a repeating pattern with stages that may be short or prolonged.

1. *Anticipatory grief.* The client knows that change is coming and does some mourning in advance. In a work setting, for example, a client may have heard announcements about downsizing or has been informed that his own job is at risk.

2. *Denial.* The change is too difficult to take in, so the client refuses to look at the facts but behaves as if life were just going on as usual.

3. *Anger.* The client springs to life. Someone or something should be blamed, often an immediate boss or the senior leaders in the organization. Many clients will also guiltily blame themselves at this stage.

4. *Bargaining.* The client believes that she may be able to stave off the inevitable by trying to prolong her notice period, negotiate herself a better deal, or start a grievance procedure.

5. *Depression.* This stage is sometimes referred to as "paralysis"; the client feels numbed. Some may tell you that they fear they will never work again or have no energy for job hunting.

6. *Acceptance.* The client has faced up to the change and is beginning to adjust. There is a return of energy and optimism.

THEORY OF TRANSITION: WILLIAM BRIDGES

William Bridges offers a second useful theory to describe the human response to change. In describing the change cycle, Bridges's theory (1991) maps neatly onto the Kübler-Ross framework. He makes the point that there is a difference between the formal or external change and the psychological or internal change. The psychological change always takes longer. For example, a client may be told on a particular date that his job will be going, but it may take him some weeks, or longer, to accept that this is the reality. Bridges defines three phases of transition: ending, the neutral zone, and the new beginning. Each is inevitable and necessary, though the time taken to pass through them may vary.

Ending. This stage is typically characterized by confusion about what is really over, who has the power, and what has not ended. This resembles the early stages of the Kübler-Ross cycle. Clients may find it hard to imagine life without the old role. If, for instance, they are having to compete for what they regard as their "own" jobs in a reorganization, they may feel sadness and anxiety about what the future holds. If they are leaving, they may feel panic about whether they will ever get another job.

The neutral zone. Bridges describes this as feeling like being "in continuous whitewater." The old has not quite ended, but the new has not quite begun. As well as noting the feelings of being buffeted and directionless, Bridges emphasizes that the neutral zone can also be a time of creative renewal.

The new beginning. The new life is starting, but just as it was unclear psychologically what had really ended, so it might be equally unclear what has really begun. Clients starting new jobs may, for instance, feel deeply unsettled: Did they make the right decision? They may still miss former colleagues and friends or yearn for gossip about the old organization. The new role or organization feels provisional.

Coaching Applications

- **Use the Kübler-Ross and Bridges frameworks to normalize what your client may otherwise find overwhelming.** It is a relief for her to know that these troublesome emotions are to some extent what everyone feels and that eventual adjustment is possible. By helping her see that she is not unique in her anger or confusion, you stand a chance of being able to help shorten the periods of anxiety and get back to the resourceful state in which she can once again take control of her life.

- **Draw the frameworks for your client.** Explain each phase and ask him where he sees himself. Invite him to elaborate on the specifics of his feelings.

- **Discuss tactics for shortening the misery.** For instance, getting involved in the proposed changes short-circuits helplessness; coaching itself helps the client in taking charge of her career; a party with speeches and presents is a graceful ceremonial way of exiting from an organization.

- **Depending on the circumstances, discourage your client from filing a grievance or going to a tribunal.** Ask him to look squarely at the likely results; martyrdom is rarely worth the hassle.

- **Ask your client how she can make maximum use of the neutral zone**—for instance, by retraining, reading, or enjoying a much-needed holiday.

- **Work with your client on a plan for the new life.** Help him anticipate and then manage the entry phase.

- **Take a whole-life perspective.** For instance, financial and physical health, family issues, or the state of personal relationships are all likely to be influential factors. Here you may like to use such well-known tools as the balance wheel— a pie chart with eight wedges representing work, health, money, friends and family, partner, personal growth, fun and leisure, and physical environment. The client scores her satisfaction on each wedge by rating it on a 1–10 scale. This exercise allows her to share important data about her circumstances with you, many of which may have limiting effects on her freedom.

- **Ask your client to talk you through his career so far.** Ask him, *What were the deciding factors in choosing that job at that point in your life? What were the* *pluses of that job? What were the minuses? What were your reasons for moving on to another role?*

- **Remember that it is the client's job rather than yours to identify the threads of motivation and circumstance that link her career choices.** Offer your own suggestions tentatively. You can never know as much about the client as the client knows about herself.

IDENTIFYING LIFE PURPOSE: VIKTOR FRANKL

No one made a better case for asking and answering the question *Who am I?* than Viktor Frankl, a prisoner at Auschwitz during World War II. His moving book *Man's Search for Meaning* (1959) describes how he survived by visualizing his life after the war, teaching and writing about his experiences. He concluded that the human species can endure almost anything as long as we believe we have a meaningful purpose, quoting Nietzsche: "He who has a *why* to live can bear with almost any *how*." As a coach, you have access to innumerable ways in which to work with clients to answer the life purpose question.

Coaching Applications

- **Help your client identify life purpose.** This cuts through waffle and indecision. Once your client is clear about her values, beliefs, and purpose, it is easy to assess any proposed career move against a psychometric template by asking how far it meets these deeply held needs.

- **Encourage the client to answer the question *What do people think of me?*** Here, a 360-degree feedback survey is essential. It has become commonplace in organizations, and chances are that your clients will have been the subject of a 360 review at some relatively recent point. Ask your client to bring along his most recent assessment or invite him to commission one, using one of the many commercially available questionnaires. Some clients may naively imagine that "everyone" thinks and behaves as they do, so it can be a revelation to discover that this is not so. Psychometrics give coach and client a shared vocabulary.

- **Invite the client to take psychometric assessments.** These can accelerate intimacy and trust between coach and client, thus offering a way of cutting to the heart of the career choices that the client needs to make. The value in using such instruments is in the conversations they create rather than in the results themselves. Assessments that are particularly useful in career coaching include the Myers-Briggs Type Indicator, the Strong Interest Inventory, Career Anchors, the Hogan suite of instruments, and FIRO-B. (See Chapter Thirty-Two for more information on assessments.)

THE USE OF "FLOW": CSIKSZENTMIHALYI

Mihalyi Csikszentmihalyi (2003) described being "in flow" as an occasion when time passes seamlessly; there is a sense of using all your innate skills with no self-doubt present; the activity entails some stretch, but it is not overwhelming; there is tangibility in the reward and a feeling of pure pleasure.

Coaching Applications

- **Describe "flow" characteristics to your client and ask her to identify three or four such moments in her life and career.** Ask, *What made this such a satisfying moment? What was the context? Who else was there? What was your own role?*

- **Listen to your client's description of peak experiences in his career and write down all his key words without editing.** Hand him this list and let him highlight the most important words and then work with him to assemble the themes that emerge.

CREATING YOUR PERSONAL BRAND

Let's assume you've done all the activities described so far in this chapter: looked at the client's life through such tools as the balance wheel, given her a sense of where she is in the change cycle, conducted 360 feedback and performance appraisals and gathered the output from several psychometric questionnaires, and analyzed her "peak moments." You might like to summarize all this information visually on a single flip-chart sheet, inviting the client to review it and asking

What does this tell you about what you must have to be satisfied at work?

Where are your strengths? Where can you add real value?

Where are your weaknesses? What do you need to avoid?

What gaps do you see between where you would like to be and where you currently are?

What are the must-have criteria for the next stages of your career?

How does your current (or last) job rate against these criteria?

What do you want people to say about you?

What does all of this suggest about you and your life purpose?

What are the implications for your current or next step?

By answering these questions, the client is in effect creating a personal brand. Arruda and Dixson (2007) emphasize the value of this in career management, pointing out that a candidate for a job needs to present a clear and attractively differentiated "brand identity" rather than trying to be all things to all people.

Coaching Applications

- **Help your client identify and amplify her "brand identity."** What are the key aspects of who she is and what she will bring to a job, around which she can build her application?

- **Help your client identify resources he needs to draft a résumé or find a job.** Some clients have never written a résumé, and few seem aware that skilled networking is how the majority of jobs are obtained rather than through posts that are formally advertised. Make sure you are well informed yourself about these processes. The most comprehensive source of up-to-date, practical information is in Richard Bolles's book *What Color Is Your Parachute?* (2010). There are also dozens of other excellent books on all aspects of finding a job, including Lynn Williams's book on being interviewed (2008).

- **Be prepared to review your client's draft résumé.** Put yourself in the position of an employer reading it for the first time and use the following list to offer the client objective feedback. Don't hold back. You might be the client's best hope of getting honest advice. The most common mistakes are

    Creating an all-purpose résumé not tailored to the specific job, one that is more than three pages long, or one with a dull first page with lists of qualifications and contact details

    Using weak vocabulary—for example, "did" rather than "led," "made" rather than "directed"

Describing jobs in terms of responsibilities rather than achievements

Failing to include tangible proof of achievements—percentages, money, numbers

Including irrelevant information—for instance, listing education before the age of eleven

Lying or "improving" job titles, salary, or length of tenure

- **Encourage your client to research what form of interview procedures and assessments potential employers use.** The most common are simple: verbal and numerical reasoning tests, personality questionnaire, and a presentation.

- **Have your client practice her presentation with you.** Look out for the most common weaknesses: going on too long, trying to impress through the immense sophistication of her analysis, overdoing facts and figures. The presentation part of the selection process is normally designed to be an exercise in persuasion rather than intellectual brilliance. Offer the client feedback on this basis. You do not need to know anything about the job or the organization in order to do this.

- **Encourage your client to do a practice interview with you.** Practicing will greatly increase his chances of success. Remind yourself of the common mistakes made by interviewees:

Failing to research the job and the organization

Doing the wrong kind of research, typically into the background factors—for instance legislation—rather than the skills the jobs needs and the problems the jobholder will be expected to solve

Letting nervousness get in the way

Dressing inappropriately; having a disastrous handshake

Failing to anticipate the obvious questions; overrehearsing answers to questions that are unlikely to be asked

Having a feeble answer to the "Why do you want the job?" question

Giving vague answers; offering opinions and assertions rather than hard evidence of skill and experience

- **Ask your client to come dressed as if for the interview.** Many clients have never received image advice, so if there is something noticeably amiss with how the client looks, you might want to suggest a specialist coach. Rather than attempting to role-play a complete interview, it is a better use of the time to concentrate on improving general skill—for instance, in using storytelling technique to demonstrate experience and competency, learning effective methods of managing nervousness, getting feedback on handshake, practicing a strong answer to the vital question of why the client wants the job. Trust your own responses to her efforts and offer straightforward feedback.

- **Don't think your role is finished once the client has got the job.** You've already made a significant contribution. It is satisfying for you both. However, the work does not stop there. You can be immensely helpful by offering the client coaching on their first hundred days in the new role. This is too big a subject to deal with here, but you should read Michael Watkins's book (2003) if the subject is new to you—and recommend that your client do the same.

Additional Reading

Arruda, W., & Dixon, K. (2007). *Career distinction: Stand out by building your brand.* Hoboken, NJ: Wiley.

This is a very good resource with practical tools for building a personal brand.

Bolles, R. (2010). *What color is your parachute?* Berkeley, CA: Ten Speed Press.

This book, revised annually, is a comprehensive source of practical advice on all aspects of job search, from identifying skills to résumés, networking, researching jobs, and preparing for interviews. The companion Web site, www.JobHuntersBible.com, is also invaluable.

Bridges, W. (1991). *Managing transitions: Making the most of change.* Reading, MA: Addison-Wesley.

A classic in understanding transition, this book provides simple resources that are useful when working with clients.

Csikszentmihalyi, M. (1990). *Flow: The psychology of optimal experience.* New York: HarperCollins.

A foundational book to understanding flow. Useful in helping a client notice and create her own moments of peak experience.

Rogers, J. (2010). *Job interview success: Be your own coach.* London: McGraw-Hill.

A practical guide for anyone considering or in the midst of a job search.

Watkins, M. (2003). *The first 90 days: Critical strategies for new leaders at all levels.* Boston: Harvard Business School Press.

An excellent resource for new leaders at any level. It provides useful information for coaches and clients.

PART THREE Organizations, Leadership, and Coaching

To an outsider, an organization can feel like a foreign country, with its own language and form of government, its explicit rules shadowed by unwritten conventions. For an executive or for a coach, having a framework for decoding organizational structures can mean the difference between floundering and flourishing.

Specifically we need some insight into the range of options for leaders and the extent to which more or less successful approaches to leadership can make the workplace either dynamic or dysfunctional.

We also need an appreciation of the complexity and potential of teamwork. Whatever the size of the enterprise, for most people, work is a cooperative process. Incompatible approaches to a given task can lead to mutual bafflement and personal conflict. But these same contrasts, viewed as complementary work styles, can be harnessed to achieve an outcome that none of the participants, working alone, could have hoped for.

Given the number of our clients who work in organizations, an understanding of how organizations function and of the intense and sometimes conflicting demands they make on individuals is essential.

Leadership

chapter FIFTEEN

Diane Brennan

We live in a complex fast-paced world full of challenge and opportunity. Global media stories remind us almost daily of organizations in crisis and of leaders throughout the world with culpability in scandals resulting in ethical, financial, and economic disaster. Leaders, whatever their title, are key to the success of any organization or system. This is not because the leader has all the answers or all the control, but rather because the leader's impact and influence on others will help determine the culture of the organization and the performance of the employees.

Leadership coaching is a way to build capacity, complexity, and capability with leaders and managers in organizations and business. Many of the theories and applications related to leadership, including adult development, communication, theories of intelligence, psychology, adult learning, social constructionism, and mindfulness, are found in other chapters of this book. Each of these contributes to the foundation that supports an individual's development as a leader. Leadership is not about personality, but it *is* about the person. This chapter focuses on how the study of leadership has contributed to our understanding of what it takes to be a leader, and how this understanding can be translated into action.

Although studies of leadership have focused on people in positions of particular authority, the insights that have emerged can be applied throughout the workplace and beyond. Everyone, whatever his or her title or role, has the potential to lead in work and in life.

CHARACTERISTICS AND ROLE MODELS FOR LEADERSHIP: DRUCKER, BENNIS, COLLINS, AND WHEATLEY

Early studies of leadership were heavily influenced by behavioral psychology. Researchers sought to find the qualities necessary for leadership by studying leadership as a set of behaviors and attempting to differentiate leaders from followers and, later, leaders from managers. While some characteristics were found to be more consistent with a leadership role, there was also evidence to suggest that one's success or failure as a leader would be influenced by the situation. What has emerged over the years is a range of leadership theories that variously emphasize situation (social psychology), personal traits (human behavior and adult development), and cultural influences (organization development).

Peter Drucker, often called the father of modern management, focused on the need for the leader to think through and define the organization's mission, to energize others with vision and integrity, and to establish an environment that fosters trust so that the individual and the team might thrive. Because integrity and trust are foundational to a leader's success, the leader must demonstrate congruency between beliefs, words, and actions. Drucker's work spanned more than sixty years, from the 1940s to 2005. He witnessed and influenced the evolution of business, industries, workers, managers, and leaders. The power of Drucker's work is not in the complexity of his thoughts but rather in the process of his thinking. "Drucker's real contribution lies in his integrative, holistic thinking; fair-mindedness; and dispassionate objectivity. One can learn more—and more deeply—from observing the discipline of his mind than from studying the content of his thought" (Kantrow, 2009, p. 74). To manage and lead well, one needs to manage oneself, deeply understand one's own strengths as well as weaknesses, assess performance, understand how one learns, and articulate and honor one's values.

Warren Bennis said, "becoming a leader is synonymous with becoming yourself. It is precisely that simple, and it is also that difficult" (1994, p. 9). Because change and uncertainty are constants in today's world, being a successful leader involves creating a context that supports and generates creativity, learning, and intellectual capital. A leader has followers and therefore a responsibility to establish a vision, build trust, and authentically inspire others with passion and hope. So what is it that makes a leader? Bennis and Robert Thomas (2008) conclude that an individual's response to adversity is a critical factor. The ability to find meaning, opportunity, and learning in even the most challenging times is one of the most reliable indicators of true leadership.

Jim Collins's research to find what differentiated a good company from a great company led to the findings that produced the Level 5 leadership hierarchy of executive capabilities (2001). The study was not about attributing a company's greatness or lack thereof to leadership, yet what Collins found supported the belief that leadership makes a difference in transforming organizations from good to great. Stated as a formula, Humility + Will = Level 5. Level 5 leaders don't go out expecting to make a name for themselves. They are, as Collins describes, a study in duality: modest and willful, humble and fearless. Level 5 is an empirical finding, not merely a conjecture based on philosophical preference.

In *Finding Our Way,* Margaret Wheatley (2007, p. 2) observes that

> Leaders incite primitive emotions of fear, scarcity, and self-interest to get people to do their work, rather than the more noble human traits of cooperation, caring, and generosity. This has led to this difficult time, when nothing seems to work as we want it to, when too many of us feel frustrated, disengaged, and anxious.

Although her comments may sound despairing, Wheatley encourages us to draw on hope, curiosity, wisdom, and courage; to allow leaders to emerge from the bottom up; to build real-time learning; and meanwhile to accept this state of uncertainty.

Coaching Applications

- **Encourage your client to explore his strengths and weaknesses and to consider whether there are areas where he might benefit from support.** Be sure to establish his agreement to be open, honest, and real in his relationship with you as coach, and be prepared for the possibility that he may be reluctant to consider support.

- **Ask your client to describe the roles she has taken on, and challenge her to consider whether some of these roles may be more appropriate for others on her team.** Consciously or unconsciously, leaders may see themselves as indispensible. They may project a superhero persona to command respect within the organization. Being superhuman is a heavy burden, even where there is a substantial ego.

- **Work with your client to raise awareness of how he handles delegation.** Leaders are frequently labeled micromanagers, wanting to control processes or results. The leader is ultimately accountable, and may have difficulty trusting that the work will be done to an appropriate standard. Explore what systems your client might need to support her in ensuring accountability and quality without having to control everything.

- **Encourage your client to build trust by engaging in clear, open, and honest communication.** Leaders may not be as clear with their team on expectations and accountability as they think they are. If the client complains about a particular team member or work product, encourage him to reflect on his own role in the situation. What direction did he provide? How clear was the communication between them?

- **Where appropriate, discuss with your client the relationship between her personal qualities, positive and negative, and her leadership role.** Leaders are seldom different at home than they are in the workplace. Working on your client's personal attributes is a gift you, as a coach, can give her as a leader.

LEADERSHIP STYLES AND GETTING RESULTS: GOLEMAN

Daniel Goleman's book *Emotional Intelligence: Why It Can Matter More Than IQ* (1995) brought the theory of emotional intelligence into the mainstream. Emotional intelligence, the ability to manage oneself and one's relationships, draws on four fundamental capabilities: self-awareness, self-management, social awareness, and social skill (Goleman, 2000). The concept identifies the "right stuff" to be a leader and recognizes that leadership is more of an art than a science (2004). Each emotional intelligence capability includes traits and competencies that allow for measurement and ongoing development. The following list shows the capabilities and competencies.

Characteristics of Emotional Intelligence

Self-Awareness	Self-Management	Social Awareness	Social Skill
Emotional self-awareness	Self-control	Empathy	Visionary leadership
Accurate self-assessment	Trustworthiness	Organizational awareness	Influence
Self-confidence	Conscientiousness	Service orientation	Developing others
	Adaptability		Communication
	Achievement orientation		Change catalyst
	Initiative		Conflict management
			Building bonds
			Teamwork and collaboration

In "What Makes a Leader?" Goleman asserts that "the leader's singular job is to get results" (2004, p. 1). The question is how to achieve this. Research with the Hay McBer consulting firm named six distinct leadership styles that draw on different components of emotional intelligence. Goleman's research demonstrated that the leaders with the best results draw on elements of the different styles depending on the situation. The six styles are as follows:

1. *Coercive:* leaders who demand immediate compliance

2. *Authoritative:* leaders who move people toward a vision

3. *Affiliative:* leaders who create emotional bonds and harmony

4. *Democratic:* leaders who build consensus through participation

5. *Pacesetting:* leaders who expect excellence and self-direction

6. *Coaching:* leaders who develop people for the future

Leaders who are most successful integrate multiple styles seamlessly into their leadership approach. Each style has its strengths and limitations. Some, like the coercive and pacesetting styles, are recommended only in certain circumstances, on a short-term basis and with caution. This is not about memorizing or switching from one style to the next. It is about observing and growing one's emotional intelligence to develop a range of styles, depending on the task, the situation, and the organizational culture.

Coaching Applications

- **Encourage your client to explore her leadership style and approach.** Use Goleman's six leadership styles as a teaching tool and an opportunity for self-assessment. You might also have the client participate in an assessment that measures leadership or behavior, or a 360-degree multirater assessment that provides feedback and insight into how others perceive her leadership skills. Explore the findings with the client to help her interpret them, process their implications, and gain perspective. Identify goals around what she wants to achieve, and measures for monitoring progress.

- **Help your client build awareness and understanding of emotional intelligence.** Develop experiential exercises with the client to strengthen self-awareness, self-management, social awareness, and social skill. For example, ask him to describe his direct reports in terms of their strengths and challenges. Encourage him to develop skill as a reflective practitioner, becoming an observer of his own actions and interactions—noticing what works, what others perceive, and what he might do differently another time.

- **Challenge the client to develop those areas where she is not comfortable.** These may be around what leaders sometimes consider softer skills, such as listening, clear communication, and relating to others.

- **Challenge the client to listen for understanding without trying to fix a problem.** This is a beginning step in allowing him to engage in open and honest dialogue and to establish or clarify mutual expectations.

BEST PRACTICES OF EXEMPLARY LEADERSHIP: KOUZES AND POSNER

James Kouzes and Barry Posner have spent more than twenty-five years on the study and research of leadership. They began their work with a survey, the

Leadership Practices Inventory, that asked people to select from a list of common characteristics of leaders, rate their experiences of being led by others, and identify the seven top things they look for and appreciate in a leader. Over seventy-five thousand responses over the years yielded a list of characteristics that includes *honest, forward-looking, inspiring, intelligent, fair-minded, broad-minded, supportive, straightforward, dependable, cooperative, determined, imaginative, ambitious, courageous, caring, mature, loyal, self-controlled,* and *independent.* From this work, Kouzes and Posner developed the Five Practices of Exemplary Leadership model (2007). The exemplary leader is expected to (1) model the way, (2) inspire a shared vision, (3) challenge the process, (4) enable others to act, and (5) encourage the heart. Kouzes and Posner validated this model in a survey with over sixty-six thousand responses from employees or followers. The more frequently leaders exhibited the five practices, the more the respondents experienced feelings of personal effectiveness, pride in the organization, team spirit, and trust in management.

Coaching Applications

- **Work with your client to clarify beliefs, values, and vision.** Help her notice any areas where there may be inconsistency in thought, words, or action.

- **Encourage the client to gather feedback from direct reports, peers, supervisor, or board, in order to expand his perspective.** The organization may use assessments as part of its leadership development process (see Chapter Thirty-Two for more on assessments) or, as part of the coaching process, you may be asked to assist in conducting interviews, facilitating conversations, or reviewing assessment reports and feedback with the leader. Kouzes and Posner's Five Practices model offers an opportunity for increased understanding of what it takes to be an exemplary leader and can serve as a guide to establish goals and measures of success.

- **Work with your client to raise awareness about herself and others.** One activity for raising awareness is to ask the client to be an observer between now and the next time you meet. Ask her to notice how she interacts with others, to notice their reactions to her, and to see what she learns as an observer without judging herself or others. Developing the self as an objective observer is a step toward developing one's learning as a reflective practitioner.

LEADERSHIP FROM THE BALCONY: HEIFETZ AND LINSKY

In *Leadership on the Line,* Heifetz and Linsky (2002) discuss the dangers of leadership. Every time a leader tells people what they need to hear rather what they want to hear, he puts himself on the line.

People in organizations encounter problems every day. Some of these problems are technical and can be resolved with a phone call to an authority or an expert, but many are more complicated. They may involve several areas of the organization, or an outside contractor. Heifetz and Linsky call these "adaptive challenges," meaning they require experiments, new discoveries, adjustments, or information from other sources. Such challenges cannot be resolved without attention and effort. The individuals concerned have to work and learn with others. The payoff is that the organization and the people within it build the capacity to adapt in response to new needs.

A key skill for the leader is to maintain perspective in the midst of all these demands. A good leader takes personal responsibility for the organization. He cares about outcomes, results, and performance. As the glue holding all the pieces together, he can find himself stuck in the situation, being dragged further into it, or holding others back.

In this context, Heifetz and Linsky (2002) use the metaphor of a dance floor, advising the leader to "get on the balcony" so that she can see what's really happening. Building reflective capacity allows the leader not only to gain a larger perspective but also to separate herself from the situation, experiencing it as "object" rather than "subject" (Kegan, 1994). Getting on the balcony allows the leader the freedom to look objectively at her role and actions within the situation. This skill is effective for individual learning and also fosters learning within the organization.

Collins (2001) speaks of conducting an "autopsy without blame" in which leaders take responsibility for their part in a failure without blaming anyone. The organizational leaders and team members participate in a critical incident review to elicit maximum learning from the event. "When you conduct autopsies without blame, you go a long way toward creating a climate where the truth is heard" (p. 78).

Coaching Applications

- **Assist the leader in looking for learning rather than blame.** Failure is difficult for anyone and especially a "superhero" leader driven by results. A leader who encourages the kind of review that supports learning rather than blame encourages a culture of truth, trust, and respect within the organization and achieves greater results.

- **"Get on the balcony" with the client.** Help her find perspective. You might invite her to "take a thirty-thousand-foot view" or to "go to the top of a mountain." Which metaphor you choose isn't important, as long as it helps her see the larger context.

- **Use metaphors to enhance your client's learning as a leader.** Effective metaphors often emerge from the coaching conversation. Metaphors are most effective when they resonate with the client. For example, a leader left work a few hours early for a special family activity. Excited about the event and enjoying the novelty of taking time away from work, he forgot about an important meeting the following morning. He'd thoroughly prepared his team, and they carried out the meeting with ease, for which he expressed sincere appreciation. Privately, though, he was devastated that he had forgotten this meeting. Speaking with his coach later in the day, he expressed disappointment in himself and resisted the coach's suggestion that he view the team's performance as a tribute to his preparation and leadership. Then the coach asked him if he thought of himself as human. The client laughed and started talking about basketball. When a shooter goes to the foul line and misses, the client said, he doesn't stop shooting. He doesn't wallow in the miss. He keeps going to the line and shooting again. Creating this metaphor allowed the client to find perspective and turn his mistake into an opportunity for learning.

Additional Reading

Collins, J. (2001). *Good to great.* New York: HarperCollins.

   A useful book for coaches and clients. Collins provides real-world data and insights about leadership, organizational challenges, and what it takes to be a Level 5 leader.

Drucker, P. (2005, January). Managing oneself. *Harvard Business Review*, 100–109.

   Originally published in 1999, this classic article articulates the key elements of self-assessment and the importance of ongoing learning as a leader.

Goleman, D. (2000, March-April). Leadership that gets results. *Harvard Business Review*, pp. 78–89.

   A primer in emotional intelligence and its importance in leadership. The article also presents research findings around leadership style and the impact on organizational climate and performance. It includes nice charts that are useful for clients.

Goleman, D. (2004, January). What makes a leader? *Harvard Business Review*, pp. 82–91.

Reprint of Goleman's article originally published in 1998. A good overview of emotional intelligence that presents Goleman's early findings.

Heifetz, R. A., & Linsky, M. (2002). *Leadership on the line: Staying alive through the dangers of leading*. Boston: Harvard Business School Press.

A "how-to" guide for executives, using real-world examples from work and life. Practical concepts and tools that clients appreciate.

Heifetz, R. A., & Linsky, M. (2008). A survival guide for leaders. In J. V. Gallos (Ed.), *Business leadership: A Jossey-Bass reader* (2nd ed., pp. 447–462). San Francisco: Jossey-Bass.

This book is a great resource that includes Heifetz and Linsky's work as well as many other relevant theorists and writers on leadership, business, and organizations.

Kouzes, J. M., & Posner, B. Z. (2006). *A leader's legacy*. San Francisco: Jossey-Bass.

This book reviews the best practices of exemplary leaders. Linking evidence-based research to practice, the authors provide insight into what it takes to make a difference and leave a lasting legacy.

Kouzes, J. M., & Posner, B. Z. (2010). *The leadership challenge activities book*. San Francisco: Pfeiffer.

A good resource for a coach, trainer, facilitator, or organizational consultant. This book provides activities and ideas that are easy to use and effective.

Wheatley, M. J. (2006). *Leadership and the new science: Discovering order in a chaotic world*. San Francisco: Berrett-Koehler.

A thought-provoking look at what it will take to create harmony and sustainability in the world and ourselves.

chapter SIXTEEN

Organizations and Organizational Culture

Mary Wayne Bush, Tony Latimer, and Leni Wildflower

Organizations are becoming increasingly complex. They are becoming both flatter, with more responsibility at lower levels, and more hierarchical, with tighter financial control at the top. The tension between these two poles presents challenges for employees at every level. Any generalization about an organization is not going to be true for all. However, there are some critical principles that can provide helpful insights.

Organizational theorists in the early twentieth century (Taylor, 1911; Weber, 1922/1968) saw organizations as mechanistic, rational, and bureaucratic. Later theorists focused on the influence of human behavior (McGregor, 1967; Likert, 1967; Burns, 1978). For some recent theorists, the determining factor is organizational culture (Schein, 1988). Others view the organization as a complex system (Senge, 1990; Wheatley, 1994; Morgan, 1997) or as an arena of learning, driven by the tension between organizational goals and individual self-realization (Argyris & Schön, 1974; Nonaka & Takeuchi, 1995). This last set of theorists describe organizational strategies as "organizational learning."

All these elements—organizational structure, systems, and culture—are embedded in position descriptions, depicted graphically as relationships shown on organizational charts, and revealed in distribution of authority and communication channels within the organization. Although coaches are not often asked to address larger organizational factors, issues related to these factors often surface in the course of working with individual contributors and leaders alike. According to the theories of organizational systems noted above, our behaviors are shaped by the context in which we work. There is a dialectical relationship between our environment and our actions, our identity as self-perceived and as socially constructed. To be effective as a coach or an employee requires attentiveness to these systemic forces. Skillful coaching within an organizational context requires

- An understanding of the conscious and unconscious aspects of the organization's culture and systems

- An understanding of the dynamics and definitions of success and efficacy within the organization

- An awareness of the degree to which change in an individual will be supported by the organization

ORGANIZATIONAL STRUCTURE

Organizations are structured differently depending on the product. The most appropriate structure is the one that meets the objectives of the organization. Organizational structures range along a continuum from a functional orientation to a product orientation. A functional organizational structure, for example, arranges departments according to technical discipline—research and development, supply chain, human resources, manufacturing, sales, finance, and so on. Functional structures are usually instituted to support companies whose products are too complex for one person or team to oversee or produce alone.

In a project structure, in contrast, departments are set up to align with the product they produce, not their function or technical specialty. For instance, a large food company may have divisions that produce breakfast cereals, organic snacks, and a range of dinner entrees. Each of these divisions is focused on the product line and will have its own support staff consisting of functions (research and development, supply chain, human resources, manufacturing, sales, finance, and so on).

A matrix organization is a hybrid of both functional and project structures. With a matrix approach, organizations have the ability to select a form that attempts to achieve the benefits of both; however, the matrix structure has inherent difficulties of its own. The "one employee, two bosses" effect can create priority clashes for subordinates and can tend to push decision making down the organization, sometimes to a level where the competence to make the decision is inhibited by a lack of skills, knowledge, or perceived authority.

Coaching Applications

- **Ask the client to describe the structure of her organization, to identify which organizational model it follows, and to say where she fits within it.** If appropriate, talk with her about organizational structures and explore opportunities and challenges within her given structure.

- **Ask the client what he is accountable for at work, at what level his authority stops, and which other individuals or parts of the organization influence his work.** Notice any gaps and challenge his assumptions. Work with the client to help him become more aware of the conscious and unconscious aspects of the organization's culture and systems, to clarify expectations (his own and the organization's), and to determine what support he needs to be successful.

- **Be alert to structures or processes within the organization that may derail the client.** For example, within technology-related firms engaged in product development, you may find what are known as *scrum* or *agility* principles. These are rapid development processes that result in shifts in who leads a team for short periods. Common issues resulting from these situations are peers being led by peers, and nonmanagers having short-term project delivery responsibilities. Be in communication with the leader or HR representative within the organization. Building good relationships allows you to stay current on organizational issues, gain insight into the context individuals operate within, and best serve both the client and the organization.

- **Notice a client's hesitation to take action when she knows it is what is needed.** Recognize that lack of clarity in expectations for the individual or the supervisor can cause fear and underperformance. Help the client determine what she needs to support accountability and forward movement for herself and others.

ORGANIZATIONAL CULTURE: SCHEIN

An organization's culture is a significant factor in understanding a client's current and desired behaviors. There is often a mutual attraction between people and organizations that can be characterized by the notion of *fit*. We often find ourselves feeling more satisfied and successful in certain types of environments and roles than in others.

Schein (2004) defines *culture* as "A pattern of shared basic assumptions that was learned by a group as it solved its problems of external adaptation and internal integration, that has worked well enough to be considered valid and, therefore, to be taught to new members as the correct way you perceive, think, and feel in relation to those problems" (p. 17); others characterize it more informally as "the way things get done around here" (Deal & Kennedy, 2005, p. 4). Each culture has its own normative values that exert influence over individual and group behaviors. Cameron and Quinn (2005) assess culture using a four-quadrant model: one axis maps whether an organization has a predominant internal or external focus; the other indicates whether it strives for flexibility and individuality or stability and control.

1. The *clan* culture has a sense of cohesion, with goals that are strongly shared. Inside, the organization may feel more "family-like" than "business-like." It is internally focused with flexibility and discretion.

2. The *adhocracy* culture is open to change and oriented to the outside world; it is a culture in which innovation can thrive (but sometimes can be disruptive). It is externally focused with flexibility and discretion.

3. The *hierarchy* culture often relies on formal structures, policies, and procedures to keep things running. It is internally focused with stability and control.

4. The *market* culture is concerned with productivity, consistency, results, and the bottom line. The organization is very clear about its customers and has a clear sense of mission. It is externally focused with stability and control.

Schein (2004) also identifies three levels of organizational culture. On the surface are *artifacts* (visible organizational structures and processes), which are held in place by *espoused values* (strategies, goals, and philosophies), which arise from *basic underlying assumptions* (unconscious, taken-for-granted beliefs, perceptions, thoughts, and feelings as the ultimate source of values and action). Schein's work on groups (1988) is also instructive here in looking at culture as it plays out for the individual. When individuals in an organization seek to change their status, role, membership, or level in an organization, they must cope with four factors: *identity, control and influence, needs and goals,* and *acceptance and intimacy.*

- **Be aware of the characteristics of the organization's culture and the client's fit within the context.** Coaching an individual in an organization often begins at the first level (artifacts) and moves down to the third (basic underlying assumptions) as the work progresses, but all three levels are areas for development because each of them reinforces the others.

- **Encourage the client to build support for herself into the coaching process.** This may involve meetings with her supervisor that can include you. For a client working within an organization, any changes she makes through coaching must be sustainable in the culture of that organization.

- **Be alert to basic underlying assumptions that are unexamined in the client and that drive behavior and attitudes in the organization.** Stay informed and connected with the organization. Listen to your client, notice the environment, and be alert to the presence or absence of cues that he is picking up from the culture. Help the client become more aware of the assumptions and biases that operate within the organization's environment.

- **If possible, work with the client's direct reports and peers.** This helps create a more receptive context for change.

- **Be aware of the organization's culture (as defined by Cameron & Quinn, 2005) and its potential effect on your client's behaviors and expectations.** Especially in large or multinational organizations, different cultures can exist in various parts of a company, either organizational or geographic. Do not let the client assume that one division or department within a large company will have the same culture and values as another, especially if they are geographically remote.

- **Encourage your client to raise his awareness and understanding of the organization's culture and how he relates to it.** You might say, *Your behavior, attitude, and way of functioning in this organization may have something to do with who you are as an individual, but it also is heavily influenced by the culture and system within which you work. Part of our coaching will involve understanding both this culture and system and your relationship to it.*

- **Challenge the client to explore the impact of a proposed change from the perspective of the organizational culture.** In the client's excitement around a solution, she may create unintended consequences that cause concern within the organization.

ORGANIZATIONAL SYSTEMS: HANDY, WHEATLEY, MORGAN, AND SENGE

The broad scientific field of systems theory has yielded some important concepts that are applicable to understanding organizations, particularly the nature and processes of change. Jantsch (1980) describes a system as a "set of coherent, evolving, interactive processes which temporarily manifest in globally stable structures that have nothing to do with the equilibrium and the solidity of technological structures." An important and often humbling realization for coaches is to recognize the complex and interdependent forces inherent in the system in which a client operates. Various authors, such as Gareth Morgan (1997) and Charles Handy (1993), describe organizations through a series of metaphors. Morgan characterizes organizations as machines, as organisms, as brains, as political systems, as flux and transformation, as psychic prisons, and as instruments of domination. Peter Senge (1990) describes the complexity of organizations through a systems model. Margaret Wheatley (1994) frames organizational understanding in terms of field theory: "I have come to understand organizational vision as a field—a force of unseen connections that influences employees' behavior—rather than as an evocative message about some desired future state" (p. 13).

Coaching Applications

- **Help your client understand the organization within which he works as a complex system.** A client can then perceive his behavior as part of a complex whole, influenced not only by his personal attitude or abilities but also by the complexity of the system.

- **Encourage your client to consider a systems approach rather than "silo" thinking.** Be alert to a leader who is functioning with silo thinking: people tasked with different jobs and responsibilities can end up working independently on the same problem or project without each other's knowledge or collaboration.

- **One way to help your client understand both herself and the organization is to use a metaphor in coaching.** Having the client select a metaphor for the organization can be emotionally relieving and can free her up to view the situation in a different light.
- **Engage your client to consider his organization as a dynamic system capable of learning and change.** This helps the client expand his perspective about possibilities and learning for him and for the organization.

ORGANIZATIONAL LEARNING AND SYSTEMS THINKING: ARGYRIS, SCHÖN, SENGE, NONAKA, AND TAKEUCHI

Organizational learning, often associated with the field of organization development, provides a perspective and a set of tools with which to reflect not only on the objective world but also on our perceptions, assumptions, and theories of what the world is like. Organizational learning makes the assumption that an organization is able to sense changes in signals from its environment (both internal and external) and adapt accordingly. Argyris and Schön (1974) make the distinction between *espoused theories* and *theories-in-use* in looking at the unconscious gap between what people say and what they do. How we narrate what we are doing is often not reflective of our actual guiding beliefs. Argyris (1999, p. 438) wrote,

> [W]henever undiscussables exist, their existence is also undiscussable. Moreover, both are covered up, because rules that make important issues undiscussables violate espoused norms. . . . It is very difficult to manage [organizational defense routines]. They continue to exist and proliferate because they are relegated to the realm of "underground management" and all sides tacitly agree to this state of affairs. As a result, organizational defense routines often are very powerful.

Argyris and Schön (1978) discuss the concept of single- and double-loop learning. In single-loop learning, individuals, groups, or organizations modify their actions according to the difference between expected and obtained outcomes. In double-loop learning, they question the values, assumptions, and policies that led to the actions in the first place. If they are able to view and modify these, then double-loop learning has taken place. Another way to frame this is to say that double-loop learning is the learning that derives from reflecting on single-loop learning.

Nonaka and Takeuchi (1995) developed a four-stage spiral model of organizational learning. They distinguish two kinds of knowledge in an organization: tacit knowledge and explicit knowledge. Tacit knowledge is personal, context specific, and subjective. Explicit knowledge is codified, systematic, formal, and easy to communicate. Tacit knowledge is transformed into explicit knowledge and back again, as organizational learning spirals through four stages: externalization, when the tacit knowledge of key personnel in the organization is made explicit; internalization, when employees internalize the organization's formal rules; socialization, the tacit sharing of knowledge; and combination, the dissemination of codified knowledge.

Senge (1990) combined the concept of learning with the theory of systems thinking to develop the model of the *learning organization.* According to Senge, "five new 'component technologies' are gradually converging to innovate learning organizations" (p. 6): systems thinking, personal mastery, mental models, building a shared vision, and team learning.

Senge describes each of these technologies in detail and discusses the critical importance of their developing as an "ensemble." His focus on the whole system provides a concrete, easily understood framework for coaching within an organization. It can be a powerful and creative tool for any client.

Coaching Applications

- **Help your client develop his skill in systems thinking and observation from a learning perspective.** Ask him to think about the relationship between organizational systems and his satisfaction or sense of fit within the organization.

- **Support your client as she recognizes "undiscussables" of the organization as well as her own.** Candor and authenticity within a coaching conversation create a safe environment that allows her to discuss what was previously unnoticed or feared.

- **Consider introducing single- and double-loop learning with your client.** Understanding this can greatly help him identify any learning difficulties, both on a personal level and for his team or organization.

- **Discuss with your client how rules, understanding, and organizational behavior are created in an organization.** Reference to Nonaka and Takeuchi's model will help with this.

- **Encourage your client to explore the gap between the espoused theories and the theories-in-use in her organization.** Noticing the difference between what is said and what is done, either by the organization or by her, allows for increased awareness, understanding, and action as she navigates her role within the organization.

Additional Reading

Argyris, C. (1999). *On organizational learning* (2nd ed.). Malden, MA: Blackwell.

A good summary of some of Argyris's seminal insights into the ways in which organizations, and the people in them, defend themselves against challenges to their existing views and how to work with these defenses.

Argyris, C., & Schön, D. (1974). *Theory in practice: Increasing professional effectiveness.* San Francisco: Jossey-Bass.

This book provides the foundation for our understanding of a reflective approach to working with and within organizations.

Argyris, C., & Schön, D. (1978). *Organizational learning: A theory of action perspective.* Reading, MA: Addison-Wesley.

Another good foundation for understanding organizations.

Ashkenas, R., Ulrich, D., Jick, T., & Kerr, S. (2002). *The boundaryless organization: Breaking the chains of organizational structure.* San Francisco: Jossey-Bass.

This book provides insight into how an organization can not only remove the obvious boundaries and obstacles but also transform itself. Based on the work the authors did within GE, it provides insight and practical tools for application within complex organizations.

Galbraith, J. (2001). *Designing organizations: An executive guide to strategy, structure, and process.* San Francisco: Jossey-Bass.

This foundational book introduces Galbraith's STAR model, which is widely used and very helpful in identifying both culture and performance issues in organizations.

Hofstede, G. (2001). *Culture's consequences* (2nd ed.). Thousand Oaks, CA: Sage.

Originally published in 1980, this is a classic text on the study of culture. Hofstede's research provides insight into organizational culture locally and globally.

Morgan, G. (1997). *Images of organizations.* Thousand Oaks, CA: Sage.

A scholarly and provocative look at four types of organizations and how each type inherently gives rise to different system characteristics.

Pascale, R. T. (1990). *Managing on the edge: How successful companies use conflict to stay ahead*. London: Viking Penguin.

A well-researched book filled with case studies that speak to the issues facing those who seek to help organizations change.

Pellerin, C. (2009). *How NASA builds teams*. Hoboken, NJ: Wiley.

A useful model for the coach working with individuals or teams within organizations. The book has a strong focus on accountability for individuals and teams in an organization that has a combination of functional, project, and matrix management.

Schein, E. H. (1999). *The corporate culture survival guide*. San Francisco: Jossey-Bass.

A handy work filled with case studies and practical implications for understanding and working with issues of culture in organizations.

Senge, P. M. (1990). *The fifth discipline: The art and practice of the learning organization*. New York: Doubleday.

The book that enabled systems thinking and organizational learning to become part of the common language in talking about organizational processes and leadership.

Weisbord, M. R. (1987). *Productive workplaces: Organizing and managing for dignity, meaning, and community*. San Francisco: Jossey-Bass.

A wonderful book that traces the history of approaches to understanding culture and improving performance in the workplace.

Wheatley, M. J. (1994). *Leadership and the new science*. San Francisco: Berrett-Koehler.

A popular layperson's guide to the implications of current scientific thinking for organizational life and those who lead.

chapter SEVENTEEN

Team and Group Behavior

Laura Hauser

Coaching in organizations has generally been conducted in a dyadic (one-on-one) format designed to improve individual effectiveness. But increasingly, organizations are using teams to accomplish complicated work. A growing awareness that what matters is the performance of the team, and that individual coaching might overlook the impact of systemic factors, has given rise to the practice of *team coaching*. Research in team coaching has so far been sparse, but there is plenty to be learned from related disciplines. This chapter integrates general small group theory and coaching practice to deepen our understanding of how teams and groups may be coached toward higher performance.

The words *group* and *team* have overlapping meanings, and will be used interchangeably for most of this chapter, but it can be useful to distinguish between them. A group is a collection of individuals who come together for a common purpose. A team is generally understood to be a specific type of group. Katzenbach and Smith (2003) defined a team as "a small number of people with complementary skills, who are committed to a common purpose, performance goals, and approach, for which they hold themselves mutually accountable" (p. 45). A team or small group usually has fewer than twenty members.

A FRAMEWORK FOR UNDERSTANDING THEORIES OF SMALL GROUPS AND TEAMS: *WHAT, HOW,* AND *WHEN*

What we know about groups primarily comes from theories created in the fields of psychology, sociology, and communication. These theories can help us understand how groups function, interact, and develop. Organizing these into three main categories—group task (*what* the group does), group process and dynamics (*how* the group operates), and group development (how the group develops *over time*)—provides a set of lenses through which we can observe and understand the workings of the group. Choosing from among these three would lead to different coaching choices and different results. But although each perspective offers insight, each one alone is incapable of fully explaining what is happening. Understanding all three will lead to more informed and more effective coaching.

GROUP TASK PERSPECTIVE: *WHAT* THE GROUP DOES

The group task perspective assumes that groups exist to accomplish goals. What a group does is defined by its task. Nobel laureate Herbert Simon (1944), an American economist, psychologist, and professor, pioneered studies to explain how people in organizations make decisions. He coined the term *bounded rationality* to suggest that organizations can never be totally rational because their members have limited abilities to process information. He concluded that when making decisions, individuals and organizations engage in *satisficing*—reaching "good enough" (rather than optimal) decisions. It is important for groups to accept this limitation, because circumstances and information constantly change. Otherwise, groups risk falling into a state of permanent indecision, sometimes called *analysis paralysis*.

Central to a group's ability to perform tasks is its structure. Responsibilities and formal authority are allocated, and these affect the members' relationships (Greenberg & Baron, 2008). Structure also affects the amount of interdependence and coordination required between team members and between the team and its environment in order to effectively accomplish its work (Campion, Medsker, & Higgs, 1993). For example, a group that produces a Web site would need close coordination to dovetail the efforts of software developers, copywriters, and graphic designers. In contrast, a group of grocery store checkers can work relatively independently of each other. Group structure has to be appropriate to the task.

Toward a Task Perspective of Team Coaching: J. Richard Hackman and Ruth Wageman

Hackman and Wageman (2005) were the first to propose a theory of team coaching. They suggest that the primary job of the coach is to help the team perform its task successfully, and they define team coaching as "direct interaction with a team intended to help members make coordinated and task-appropriate use of their collective resources in accomplishing the team's work" (p. 269). They propose that team coaching interventions are more effective in increasing a team's performance when certain conditions are present. Ideally the organization will allow the team to manage (1) the level of *effort* the members exert, (2) the adoption of *strategies*, such as distributing roles or deciding when to break into subgroups, and (3) the level of relevant *knowledge and skill* the members bring to the task. It's also helpful if the team is well designed and the organizational context within which it operates supports rather than impedes the team's work. Coaching will be more effective if the team is well structured and supported—for example, by having an appropriate reward system in place that recognizes not only the performance of the individual but also of the team.

Whether or not the organizational circumstances are optimal, Hackman and Wageman (2005) argue that the coach should focus on task performance processes rather than interpersonal relationships or processes that are not under the control of the team. It's also important to take into account the team's life cycle. Motivational coaching is most helpful when provided at the beginning of a performance period to increase the level of commitment; consultative coaching, such as facilitated problem solving, is helpful at the midpoint; educational coaching, such as reflective learning, is appropriate after performance activities have been completed and the team is ready to capture and internalize lessons learned from the experience.

Coaching Applications

- **Help the team clarify what it has been tasked to accomplish and how its members will help accomplish the task.** Vague terms like "raising the bar for the division" often lead to confusion and misunderstanding. As a coach, you can help by asking such questions as *Raised by how much? In what way is the bar raised? Are we to reduce expenses or increase revenue, customer satisfaction, employee satisfaction?*

- **Help the team design and implement an effective decision-making process.** You can help by clarifying the decisions that the team needs to make, identifying realistic alternatives, assessing the benefits and consequences of the alternatives, and determining the resources needed to implement the decision. Identify not only what decisions need to be made but also who would need to approve the decision and who would be affected by it. If a team appears to become stuck in analysis paralysis, inquire if the group has enough information to make a "good enough" rather than optimal decision.

- **Match the coaching intervention to the function, timing, and conditions.** Be conscious of the stage the team has reached in its life cycle; help the team consider whether the members need help with their effort, strategy, or skill; and help the team identify ways of enhancing factors that support their work and removing obstacles.

GROUP PROCESS AND DYNAMICS PERSPECTIVE: *HOW* THE GROUP OPERATES AND INTERACTS

In contrast to the task perspective that focuses primarily on what a team does, the group process and dynamics perspective looks at how the group interacts and how underlying emotional and psychological processes influence the group's ability to perform its tasks effectively. There exists no general agreement on the distinction between *group dynamics* and *group process*, and the terms are often used interchangeably. But *process* tends to refer to underlying emotional and psychological issues, whereas *dynamics* suggests more the pattern of interactions among the team members.

Unconscious Basic Assumptions: Wilfred Bion

While a group works toward its task, it also operates on an emotional level that can help or hinder the group's performance. Wilfred Bion (1961), a British psychoanalyst, examined how members' deep-seated emotions affected group behavior and asserted that groups operate at two levels: the *work group*, which works toward achieving the group's tasks, and the *basic assumptions group*, which focuses on emotion-related behaviors, such as anxiety, that can derail the accomplishment of the group's task. Bion identified three primary emotion-related behaviors, all of which represent the group's way of coping with anxiety:

1. **Dependence.** When the group members perceive the leader as all-powerful while considering themselves inadequate, they depend on the leader unrealistically to meet all their needs, such as providing material and emotional nourishment, solving their problems, and reducing their anxiety. When the leader fails to deliver, group members attack the leader and seek a replacement. Dependency behaviors often show up early in a group's life.

2. **Pairing.** Pairing occurs when two group members pair up and take the lead to establish a new leader. This pair believes that new leadership offers hope of protecting them from conflicts and dependency that they consider to be dangerous. They feel hopeful that the group's anxiety and suffering will end with the establishment of a new leader.

3. **Fight or flight.** When a group experiences what is viewed as a common internal or external enemy, the group goes into fight-or-flight mode. Members attempt to resolve their anxiety or conflict about the enemy by fighting, which may involve splitting into subgroups and fighting each other, or fleeing by withdrawing from the conflict.

The GROUP Coaching Model: Saul Brown and Anthony Grant

Brown and Grant's GROUP model (2010) offers a practical approach for structuring a team coaching session. GROUP is an acronym for *goal, reality, options, understanding of others,* and *performance.* An important facet of the GROUP model is that it combines both the task perspective as well as the group process and dynamics perspective by addressing the team's goal and external environment, as well as the forces of group dynamics and group processes. Brown and Grant offer specific actions you can take as a coach to guide coaching conversations when you want to develop systems thinking and foster real change at the individual, group, and organizational levels.

Goal. Ask the group to clarify what they want to achieve from the coaching session, with such questions as *What do you want to achieve in this session? How would you like to feel afterwards?*

Reality. Raise awareness of the group's present realities. Examine how the current situation is impacting the group's goals. Consider asking *What have you tried so far? What worked? What didn't work?*

Options. Identify and assess available options. Encourage solution-focused thinking and brainstorming. Consider asking *What possible options do you have? What has worked for you in the past? What haven't you tried yet that might work?*

Understand others. Help group members deeply observe and understand the situation within the group as well as their own internal reactions to what is occurring and being said. Consider asking *What is your view? What is her view? What was your internal dialogue when you were listening to that? How can we integrate the broader perspective?*

Perform. Help the group determine next steps by developing individual and group action plans. Build motivation and ensure accountability. Consider asking *What are the next steps? What might get in the way? Who can support you? How will you feel when this is done?*

Coaching Applications

- **Help the group address both the group's goals as well as the dynamics and emotional undercurrents that derail their performance.** State what you observe in the group and engage group members in a conversation about what is happening in the room at this moment. This helps the group understand and examine the emotional and psychosocial processes influencing its behavior.

- **Highlight group dynamics around issues of leadership.** Only rarely will a group member confront the leader inside the group. As a coach, you are in a good position to hear concerns from group participants and the leader and to help the group identify actions that can move the group forward in a positive way. Also stay aware of dynamics that relate to you as the coach: just as a team can become too dependent on a leader, it can become too dependent on the coach. Avoid being viewed as the expert or leader.

- **Examine your own contribution to the dynamics of the team.** Manage your own emotions and do not become entangled in those of the group. Ask yourself how your emotional and psychological states influence the group dynamics. Consider applying the GROUP model to yourself, asking yourself the same questions described earlier as a way to assess your effectiveness as a team coach.

GROUP DEVELOPMENT: HOW THE GROUP DEVELOPS *OVER TIME*

The third lens, group development, assumes that groups are living organisms that grow and develop over time. Each phase of development can be characterized by certain needs and challenges. Typically, models of group development follow a progression of stages, each stage being contingent on successful completion of the prior one. Three well-known and widely used models are offered by Bennis and Shepard (1956), Schutz (1958, 1971, 1994), and Tuckman (1965; Tuckman & Jensen, 1977). These models summarize well-established knowledge about group development.

Dependence, Counterdependence, and Interdependence: Warren Bennis and Herbert Shepard

In the late 1940s, the National Training Laboratories Institute in Bethel, Maine, pioneered the use of the sensitivity training group, or T-group, to raise participants' awareness of how they interact with others. Bennis and Shepard built on their experience with T-groups to identify three phases of group development: *dependence,* focusing on harmony; *counterdependence,* focusing on infighting; and *interdependence,* focusing on performance (Minahan, 2006). During the dependence phase, questions arise about who has power and authority as the group seeks a leader to rely on. This early period is characterized by *flight from conflict,* with members tending to act cohesively. The phase of counterdependence, also called the *fight* stage, triggers personal and intimacy issues as members experience interpersonal conflict and disenchantment. By the final, interdependence phase, interpersonal conflicts have been resolved, and effective task-oriented work becomes possible. Each phase is developmental and features a key issue that must be resolved: harmony in phase 1, power in phase 2, and performance in phase 3. Bennis and Shepard believed that a group had to complete each phase before moving to the next. Thus a group might progress through all three or might become frozen at any stage. Only after members have confronted and resolved issues of authority, for example, can they address the relationships among themselves.

Fundamental Interpersonal Relationship Orientation: Will Schutz

While Bennis and Shepard were researching group development, American psychologist Will Schutz (1958, 1971, 1994) was conducting naval research with crews in nuclear submarines, who were under enormous stress while conducting missions at sea of up to 180 days at a time. Schutz published his findings in 1958, establishing the Fundamental Interpersonal Relationship Orientations (FIRO) model, and followed this up with a well-known and widely used instrument, the FIRO-B. The model explains the interpersonal needs of people in the context of a group. According to the FIRO model, groups develop in predictable stages based on basic human needs, dealing first with the needs for *inclusion,* then needs for *control* or power, and lastly needs for *affection* or openness, repeating the cycle each time the group convenes.

As the group develops through these stages, each member has her own preferences for inclusion, control, and openness. Each need is measured along two dimensions: the extent to which the member expresses or demonstrates that need to others and the extent to which the member wants to receive that behavior from others. The more quickly the group and its members have their needs met, the more quickly they are able to move to the higher level of affection and openness, which allows them to spend more time and energy accomplishing the task rather than dealing with interpersonal issues.

So how might these needs be demonstrated and observed during a group interaction? During the inclusion stage, members may ask, "What's my role?" or say, "I don't understand what we are supposed to do." Both of these suggest that the members' inclusion needs are unmet. Inclusion behaviors may also show up as politeness or the formation of in-groups and out-groups. During the control stage, a member may advocate for his own position and fail to listen to others or ask about their ideas. He may shut down or exhibit passive aggressiveness through behaviors designed to control others, such as sarcasm or eye-rolling. During the affection stage, helping behaviors may be noticeably present or absent, personal stories may be shared or withheld, and there may be more or less smiling and eye contact. These are indicators of the extent to which openness is present among the members. Greater openness makes for higher levels of performance.

Form, Storm, Norm, Perform, and Adjourn: Bruce Tuckman

From his small group research, Bruce Tuckman concluded that groups develop in four stages: forming, storming, norming, and performing (1965). He later added the fifth stage of adjourning (Tuckman & Jensen, 1977). During each stage of the group's life, the members simultaneously deal with the interdependent tasks of building relationships and accomplishing work. Progress in one dimension affects progress in the other. Interpersonal conflict will tend to thwart the accomplishment of tasks, for example, and interpersonal harmony will support the task. Tuckman added that the core issues of each stage must be resolved before the group evolves to the next stage:

Forming. The first stage deals with finding direction and testing the group's interpersonal and tactical boundaries. During forming, members depend on the leader and each other to find their bearings. In this stage, members often are polite as they test suitable attitudes and behaviors.

Storming. Once members find their bearings and start organizing for their task, conflict tends to erupt over issues of power and control. Defensiveness, competitiveness, arguing, and withdrawal are typical at this stage. Members often question who is responsible for what, what the rules are, what the reward system is, and what the criteria are for evaluation.

Norming. When conflict gives way to mutual problem solving and cohesion, the group enters the norming stage. Standards of behavior are established regarding members' working relationships, meeting attendance, information sharing, conflict resolution, leadership, and decision making. Common behaviors at this stage include friendly joking, confiding personal information, and expressing criticism constructively.

Performing. Some groups evolve to a higher level of task performance characterized by interdependence. At this stage, roles and authorities tend to adjust dynamically as needed to channel the group's energy into optimal task performance and to develop group members and the group as a whole.

Adjourning. The final stage involves termination of task behaviors and dissolution of the group. Activities include recognizing each other's accomplishments and expressing personal good-byes. Members often experience a sense of both accomplishment and loss during this stage, especially when the group is dissolved suddenly or with little planning.

Coaching Applications

- **Design interventions appropriate to the developmental phase of the team.** During the forming stage, help the group clarify roles, goals, purpose, norms, procedures, and performance measures. If a group becomes stuck during the storming stage due to control and authority issues, name the observable behavior and inquire how their knowledge of group development could explain their current issue. Support the group in shifting from controlling behaviors (advocating one's position) to problem-solving behaviors (listening and asking questions to understand each other's viewpoints) as a way to become unstuck and move on to next steps. When a team adjourns, support the group to close out their work in an appreciative way that creates a sense of completion and satisfaction.

- **Increase the team's understanding of group development as a means of improving their performance.** Invite the team to refer to one or more models to periodically assess their level of development. Invite discussion about the group's major strengths and weaknesses and help them develop a plan of action to support the team's performance. Start a conversation about how the group could build team development into their work together. For example, the group could begin each team meeting with a check-in to help people be present and feel included. During the meeting, revisit the group's ground rules to deal with control issues, such as ensuring equity of airtime, clarifying the outcomes for the meeting, and observing the group's problem-solving method. At the end of each meeting, the group could conduct a checkout to acknowledge each other, highlight the group's accomplishments and key learnings, and identify next steps.

Additional Reading

Clutterbuck, D. (2007). *Coaching the team at work*. London: Brealey.
    A practical book filled with models, mini case studies, and useful tips and suggestions.
Collins, J. (2000). *Good to great*. New York: HarperCollins.
    A best seller based on a study of eleven companies that recorded extraordinary results over the course of fifteen years.
Forsyth, D. R. (2009). *Group dynamics* (5th ed.). Belmont, CA: Wadsworth.
    Theory and research on group dynamics applied to fourteen extended case studies and illustrated with practical activities.
Hackman, J. R., & Wageman, R. (2005). A theory of team coaching. *Academy of Management Review, 30*, 269–287.
    This journal article presents the first theory about team coaching. Excellent resource for coaches who want to understand the theoretical underpinnings of team coaching,

and who seek guidance about the task-related factors that impact team coaching interventions.

Jones, B., & Brazzel, M. (Ed.) (2006). *The NTL handbook of organization development and change: Principles, practices, and perspectives*. San Francisco: Pfeiffer.

A comprehensive textbook with core theories and practical methods. This is an essential resource for organization development consultants, coaches, and students who want to know how to effectively bring about meaningful and sustainable change in individuals, groups, and organizations.

Katzenbach, J. R., & Smith, D. K. (2003). *The wisdom of teams: Creating the high-performance organization*. New York: Collins Business.

In this groundbreaking classic, the authors offer a comprehensive approach to understanding groups and overcoming the problems that often paralyze group members, the group as a whole, and relations between groups. Also see *The Discipline of Teams Workbook* by the same authors.

LaFasto, F.M.J., & Larson, C. E. (2001). *When teams work best*. Thousand Oaks, CA: Sage. This popular and practical book based on surveys of more than six thousand team members and leaders across industries discusses the five key dynamics that impact team effectiveness.

Poole, M. S., & Hollingshead, A. B. (2005). *Theories of small groups: Interdisciplinary perspectives*. Thousand Oaks, CA: Sage.

A research-based and readable collection of original essays that introduce different perspectives on small groups. It includes findings about group composition, group structure, and decision making.

Ward, G. (2008). Towards executive change: A psychodynamic group coaching model for short executive programs. *International Journal of Evidence Based Coaching and Mentoring*, 6(1), 67–78.

A good article measuring effectiveness of group coaching.

chapter EIGHTEEN

Situational and Contextual Issues in the Workplace

Mary Wayne Bush

Coaching has become an important strategy for corporate leadership development and for dealing with change as well as fundamental aspects of managing a workforce, such as performance development and succession planning. A recent study from the American Management Association/Institute for Corporate Productivity (Thompson et al., 2008) found that companies report using coaching to improve individual performance and productivity (79 percent) and to address leadership development and succession planning (63 percent).

Coaching involves conversation focused on discovery and actions, and helps a person, group, or team achieve their desired outcome or goal. It can be seen in the workplace context as providing relationship-based, on-the-job learning, which is becoming a business imperative in today's fast-paced, global, high-tech organizations. Although coaching has traditionally been offered for leadership development, often using external expert consultants, organizations are increasingly seeing the benefit of coaching to develop a more capable workforce at all levels, increasing knowledge transfer, accelerating change, and driving improved performance. Managers and HR professionals alike are adding coaching to their skill portfolios, and many organizations are developing internal coaching capabilities.

This chapter outlines current theories and considerations for coaching in three common workplace situations:

1. Performance management

2. Organizational change

3. Leadership assimilation

COACHING AND PERFORMANCE MANAGEMENT

Performance management can be defined as a strategic, integrated approach to increasing organizational effectiveness by improving the performance of the people who work in organizations and developing the capabilities of teams and individual contributors. Managing performance is linked to increases in profit and employee satisfaction, as well as decreases in defects, waste, and rework (Armstrong & Baron, 2008).

Many organizations have now recognized the relationship between setting objectives and linking these objectives to organizational strategy. Performance management is the method for achieving this, utilizing multiple strategies that include cascading strategic and operational objectives and linking them to specific objectives for each individual. This ensures that everyone in the organization knows his or her part in achieving the objectives, and gives managers the means to measure how team members are performing (Potgieter, 2005).

Full Time Performance Management

Performance management has evolved from a focus on performance appraisals and reviews, and has become a valuable tool to link business performance to strategy, improving retention by offering employees better recognition of their achievements and better opportunities to advance their careers. Current trends include replacing the annual evaluation process with Full Time Performance Management (FTPM) using a performance diary to capture relevant notes on performance-related issues throughout the year. FTPM also encourages ongoing, regular dialogue between employees and management about performance (Potgieter, 2005).

Performance Pyramid: John Wedman and Steve Graham

The performance pyramid (Wedman, 1998) is a straightforward model that identifies the basic elements needed to analyze and improve performance of individuals, groups, and organizations. At the base of the pyramid lie the larger organizational concerns relating to vision and strategy. Above that are tools and processes, expectations and feedback, and rewards and incentives. Next come performance capability and motivation, with knowledge and skills at the top.

Balanced Scorecard: Robert Kaplan and David Norton

In simple terms, the balanced scorecard (Kaplan & Norton, 1996), is a tool for an organization to measure its own effectiveness, breaking its operation down into different areas. In its classic form, the balanced scorecard consists of a four-section chart representing strategic perspectives. At the center is the vision statement and the strategic goal. Radiating from that are four different perspectives: financial, customer, learning and growth, and internal process, each with a list of criteria for measuring performance. Since Kaplan and Norton first developed the balanced scorecard, new elements have been added.

Coaching Applications

- **When coaching a leader, inquire how she sets expectations, tracks accountability, and ensures alignment of performance to overall organizational goals.** Performance management involves helping leaders and groups establish contingency plans for getting back on track if goals are not met or alignment dissipates. This works well at all levels of organizations, and can be implemented by midlevel managers.

- **As a coach of leaders, help establish a regular rhythm of conversation between levels—leader to direct reports and leader to his or her own boss.** Most performance management goals rely on regular dialogue between manager and employee.

- **Help your client raise his awareness around establishing clear expectations.** Good performance management starts with the leader setting clear expectations. This includes regular feedback about how the expectations are being met—both from the leader, who may comment on the quality, quantity, and timeliness of performance, and from the employee, who may have comments about the project or assignment, or the tools, training, and resources needed to get it done to a satisfactory standard.

- **Encourage your client to be proactive in identifying goals and objectives that align with the overall goals of the organization.** Suggest the use of a performance diary to note questions, accomplishments, and other aspects of her performance to discuss with her leader. This ensures that there is direct "line of sight" between what she does each day and the success of the organization. Holding regular performance discussions and clarifying performance expectations with leaders, as well as asking for the time, training, and other resources needed to do the job satisfactorily will assist your client in achieving her goals.

COACHING AND ORGANIZATIONAL CHANGE

Coaching can be applied to change management in ways that develop resilience and agility at all levels and support both the success and sustainability of the change effort. Theorists have studied various aspects of change in organizations, emphasizing the process of managing change, the systemic nature of change, and the psychological impact on the individual. Three of these theorists will serve to illustrate the range.

Change as a Transition: William Bridges

Bridges (1991) was the first to identify the implications of change as a personal psychological process and explain the individual experience of transition and its implications. He delineated a three-stage process to be managed.

1. Ending, losing, letting go—in which the change is recognized as the loss of something that "has been" or "is." This stage is about helping people deal with their tangible and intangible losses and mentally prepare to move on.

2. The neutral zone—in which critical psychological realignments and repatterning take place. This is all about helping get people through the change and capitalize on the confusion they are experiencing by encouraging them to be innovators.

3. The new beginning—in which the new state, or changed state, is recognized and embraced for the possibilities it holds. This stage involves helping

people develop the new identity, experience the new energy, and discover the new sense of purpose that together make the change begin to work.

Bridges maintains that the situational changes are not as difficult for companies to make as the psychological transitions of the people impacted by the change. The function of the Bridges model is to help employees place themselves emotionally in the process. Understanding change as a psychological transition frames the process in a manner that helps employees move forward.

Change as a Process: John Kotter

Kotter (2007) offers an eight-step process for organizational change, emphasizing the need for leaders to take a strong role in driving change. Leaders must identify the compelling business case for change, increase the sense of urgency around the intended change, form a powerful sponsoring coalition, and articulate and drive a positive vision of the future. Leaders must also communicate to all stakeholders and remove obstacles for those implementing the change. Celebrating short-term wins keeps up the momentum, and it is the responsibility of leaders to ensure that the changes are sustained in the organization through policies, structures, and processes. Kotter shows us that change is a process that can be managed through leadership support and sponsorship.

Resistance to Change: Rick Maurer

Maurer (1996) identifies several elements of successful change, including understanding why people might support or resist proposed changes. He suggests that resistance is often as much about the way a change is being led as it is about the proposed change itself, and distinguishes three levels of resistance: not understanding or agreeing with the rationale; not liking the proposed change for individual reasons of inconvenience or loss of job status or employment; and not liking or trusting the way the change is being led. Maurer encourages coaches and other professionals to investigate what causes resistance, so that it becomes easier to address it and build support for ideas.

Coaching Applications

- **Help your client clarify and communicate the business case and strategy for the change, as well as the actions that will be needed at each level.** Coach the leader to communicate not only what will be different, but why—and why it is personally important to him.

- **When working with a client experiencing change, help her both understand her new role and develop the interpersonal skills needed for making this change.** Individual employees need to be clear on what they must do differently and why. This may also be an opening for coaching at other levels of the organization, especially if the individuals are influential or demonstrate resistance.

- **Encourage your client to pay attention to how his own behaviors support or resist the change.** He may need coaching on becoming a role model and on how to encourage, recognize, and celebrate successes in change implementation.

- **Help leaders think about how to embed the new changes into existing processes, structures, and systems.** This will help institutionalize the changes that have been made.

- **Propose coaching the team leaders as a group on a regular basis.** If teams are deployed for projects or change implementation, coach the team leaders to engage team members, manage resistance, and track accountability and project success.

COACHING FOR LEADERSHIP ASSIMILATION

In the 1990s, as organizations adopted less hierarchical methods and responded to global and economic forces with flatter structures, downsizing, and mergers and acquisitions, assimilation coaching became a distinct specialty. Leadership assimilation, sometimes referred to as *onboarding* or *transition*, is designed to achieve two major objectives: shortening the productivity curve of the new leader and increasing engagement and reducing turnover in the organization (Conger & Fishel, 2007). Coaching aims to minimize risk and expense for organizations by assisting leaders in understanding their new roles and objectives, setting up operations, defining their leadership vision, and developing a new network of colleagues within the first few months of employment. Typically, coaching is used to help the leader orient herself in the new situation, identify key stakeholders, build the new team, clarify and achieve short-term objectives, and successfully manage the personal emotions of transition.

Coaching for leadership assimilation is gaining popularity in business organizations and becoming a standard practice for HR professionals. It is important for organizations to help new hires make a successful transition into the new positions and environments early in their employment. Research has consistently shown that attitudes and beliefs that new hires develop toward their organization generally form very early in employment and remain relatively stable (Bauer & Green, 1994). In fact, some studies report that about 90 percent of new employees make their decision to stay at a company within the first six months on the job (Aberdeen Research, 2006). It takes a mid- to senior-level manager an average of 6.2 months to reach a break-even point, the point at which his contribution to the organization begins to surpass the company's costs of bringing him on board (Wells, 2005). According to Bradt, Check, and Pedraza (2006), 40 percent of leaders entering new organizational roles fail during their first eighteen months. The estimated organizational costs of a failed executive-level hire can be as high as $2.7 million (Bossert, 2004). Consequently, it is important for organizations to support successful transitions early in a leader's employment, and coaching is excellent for this application.

Coaching Applications

- **Ask the leader or manager to identify what is new for him.** Has he moved into a completely new organization or industry, or to a different branch or division of the same organization? Have his functional responsibilities changed—for example, in a move from engineering to operations? Is the change lateral, with the same level of responsibility, or is it a promotion to a new level that may not be familiar? What is the nature of the move? Is the new position a training or development opportunity, or is the leader expected to turn around a faltering business or implement best practices from another location?

- **Talk with the leader about her support system.** Whom does she go to for help and assistance? How will she build a strong network in the organization? In addition to your client, you may have an opportunity to include her new boss, deputy, HR partner, or administrative assistant in the coaching process.

- **Understand the organizational context: mission, vision, values, and culture.** What are some of the stories, legends, and unique traditions? Talking about a company or division in these terms helps build cohesion among the employees and create new pathways for assimilation.

- **Ask the new leader to articulate his responsibilities.** What are his business objectives? What are his priorities for execution? What issues or concerns does he currently have with regard to the way the organization is operating? Has he discussed or confirmed any of this with his boss?

- **Help your client identify how success will be measured.** Who will be assessing her success? Who are the new leader's major stakeholders, besides her boss and team?

- **Help your client identify and communicate his own vision and values for the organization.** Encourage the leader to meet with his direct reports to let them know his leadership style and expectations of them. Alignment within the organization depends on leaders being able to convey the mission and strategy of the organization.

- **Introduce the multirater (360) feedback assessment once your client has been in position long enough for the organization and direct reports to get to know her.** This will help her understand how she is being perceived by the boss, direct reports, customers, and others.

Additional Reading

Bridges, W. (2009). *Managing transitions: Making the most of change.* Reading, PA: Addison-Wesley.

Bridges explains the individual experience of transition and its implications for managing change. Great information here for coaches on how to work with leaders and those who demonstrate resistance.

Cohen, D. S. (2005). *The heart of change field guide: Tools and tactics for leading change in your organization.* Boston: Harvard Business School Press.

This is a good resource for tools and worksheets to use in implementing Kotter's eight-step change model.

Conner, D. R. (1992). *Managing at the speed of change: How resilient managers succeed and prosper where others fail.* New York: Villard Books.

Conner identifies roles within the successful change process and gives suggestions for coaching the change leaders who hold these roles.

Downey, D., March, T., & Berkman, A. (2001). *Assimilating new leaders: The key to executive retention.* New York: AMACOM.

Describes a four-stage process for leadership transition planning and coaching.

Lee, R., & Valerio, A. M. (2005). *Executive coaching: A guide for the HR professional.* San Francisco: Jossey-Bass.

Offers an HR partner perspective for transition coaching.

Niven, P. R. (2006). *Balanced scorecard step-by-step: Maximizing performance and maintaining results*. Hoboken, NJ: Wiley.

Provides tools, methodologies, and steps necessary to understand and execute balanced scorecard performance management.

Rummler, G. A., & Brache, A. P. (1995). *Improving performance: How to manage the white space in the organization chart* (2nd ed.). San Francisco: Jossey-Bass.

An excellent resource for performance management coaching.

Watkins, M. (2003). *The first 90 days: Critical success strategies for new leaders at all levels*. Boston: Harvard Business School Press.

Outlines a strategy for the new leader in a new role to establish goals and reputation for the first ninety days in a new job, secure some early successes, set up expectations for direct reports, and build a peer network.

Watkins, R., & Leigh, D. (2010). *Handbook of improving performance in the workplace* (Vol. 2). San Francisco: Pfeiffer.

A comprehensive resource for selecting and implementing performance interventions of all kinds.

PART FOUR

Traditions from Self-Help, Personal Growth, and Spirituality

The self-help and human potential movements of the 1960s and 1970s, and the accompanying interest in noninstitutionalized forms of spirituality, constitute an important thread in the underground history of coaching.

Coaching is an art—its skills must be mastered and internalized. It also rests on theoretical foundations—the premise of this book is that there is a knowledge base with which the professional coach should be acquainted. The coaching encounter remains peculiarly democratic, however. The coach must be an expert in coaching, but it is the client who is credited with the greater expertise in the nature of the question, the problem, the aspiration. And it is the client who is the source of the solution. The particular quality of the coaching engagement is this balance between the responsibility of the coach and the empowerment of the client.

If humanistic psychology, and the cluster of developments in therapeutic practice associated with it, can be identified as one of the parents of coaching, then the other is surely to be found in the human potential movements and the search for sources of transformation accessible to all.

chapter NINETEEN

Spiritual and Religious Traditions

Jennifer Sellers

Your sacred space is where you can find yourself again and again.

—Joseph Campbell (1998, p. 180)

In some ways, all coaching is spiritual coaching. Coaching addresses what is important in someone's life. Although clients do not generally come looking for spiritual development, they often present their most intimate concerns, their deepest desires, and their greatest fears. Reflecting on these issues has the potential to touch a person's very essence. It can raise awareness in the client of her relationship to a higher consciousness, whether she experiences that consciousness in nature, in a place of worship, in private meditation, or in any activity that provides her with a feeling of personal peace and harmony.

The stated reason a client comes to coaching is likely to be immediate and tangible. And certainly it is rare that a client's presenting goal or issue is overtly spiritual. She may come with a performance or development goal. But even performance goals can engender spiritual growth, as the client finds herself in the waters of transformational change. In many situations, it is the coach who invites the client into these waters. Jenny Rogers encourages us "to consciously work with clients to turn their perfectly reasonable transactional goals into transformational goals" (2008, p. 119). Through what she learns in the process of achieving her goals, the client is transformed. Such transformation is in the domain of the spiritual.

For example, a client recently came to a session with the goal to get better at "managing up," at earning the respect of her superiors and getting them to more readily accept her ideas. She left the session with an entirely different perspective on the issue. She developed a new sense of valuing her own work more deeply. As a result, she discovered ways of communicating more effectively that honored both her and the other, and connected them, rather than simply focusing on her own issue.

We can view this session through many lenses. The psychological lens might show the client claiming self-worth, strengthening her boundaries, and disentangling her own opinion of her work from the opinions and reactions of others. A lens of improved social interaction might reveal how she discovered more effective ways of communicating. Through the spiritual lens, what we see is a human being connecting with her own source of heart or spirit. From this connection, she found a more expansive way to honor her own life while at the same time honoring the qualities of her manager.

DESIRE, FEAR, SELF-BELIEFS, AND THEIR RELATIONSHIP TO SPIRITUALITY

As human beings we tend to share certain needs and desires. At the deepest level these include the desire to be loved, recognized, and seen for our accomplishments (Maslow, 1964); the desire to engage in work that is fulfilling and joyful (Csikszentmihalyi, 1990); and the desire to be free from fear and to find purpose in life (Seligman, 2002). Often our inability to achieve what we desire results from fear, and underlying that fear is a belief about ourselves—that we are not good enough, not up to the task at hand, not deserving, not lovable. Exploring desires, fears, and self-limiting beliefs offers the possibility of helping people become more aware of themselves, which in turn offers the opportunity for spiritual growth.

JAMES FOWLER: STAGES OF FAITH

Fowler's seminal work (1981) on the stages of development of faith offers a model that might be helpful in understanding a client's experience. Fowler's research indicates that an individual's faith might go through as many as six stages. Stage I, Intuitive-Projective Faith, refers to children between the ages of three and seven and is not relevant to a coaching application. What follows is a description of stages II through VI.

Stage II—Mythic-Literal Faith. At this stage—common to younger school-age children, but also found in some adolescents and adults—the person begins to take on the beliefs, stories, moral rules, and attitudes of people around him in a literal and one-dimensional way. The logical mind begins to rein in the imagination. The world gains coherence and meaning through story, but the individual is not yet able to step outside the narrative and reflect on it.

Stage III—Synthetic-Conventional Faith. This generally appears in adolescence, though some adults stabilize at this stage. Typically the individual has begun to inhabit a wider world beyond the family, and faith supplies a way to make sense of it all, to help her understand how she fits in and how she sees herself in this larger context. But she is still not able to step out of her own perspective to question deeply held beliefs and values.

Stage IV—Individuative-Reflective Faith. It is at this stage—typically during adolescence or adulthood—that the individual begins to take ownership of the beliefs and attitudes that inform his life. Now the tensions between self-fulfillment and service to others require reflection and exploration, and can give rise to inner conflict. There is a reliance on logic and a new capacity to conceptualize. The individual develops his own perspective. He is able to reflect on his sense of identity and ideological outlook and observe them as factors in how he relates to the world.

Stage V—Conjunctive Faith. At this stage, which is usually associated with midlife, with fuller recognition of life's complexity comes an integration of the cognitive and the imaginative. There is an ability to see one's place in society in a more conscious way; a recovering and revisioning of one's past; a connection to one's deeper self; an acceptance of and interest in paradox; and an attraction to experiences, situations, or people so different that they threaten one's sense of identity and worldview. A thorough understanding of the limitations of the filters through which one views and experiences life becomes possible.

Stage VI—Universalizing Faith. In Fowler's taxonomy, this stage is extremely uncommon. People in this stage feel a oneness with others and the world and a simultaneous appreciation of the particularity of individuals and things. They act from this deeply held sense and encourage it in others. As a result, they are often at odds with the societal structures, systems, and processes that confine and define most people. They love life without grasping at it. They have been described as rare people with a special grace and serenity.

CONTEMPLATIVE SPIRITUAL PRACTICES OF THE WORLD'S RELIGIONS

Spiritual traditions around the globe and throughout the centuries have encouraged contemplative practice. The mystical branches of many religions focus on contemplation as a way of becoming open to a direct experience of the divine.

Various forms of meditative practice, designed to calm and focus the mind, are found in Judaism, Christianity, Buddhism, Hinduism, Islam, and other religious traditions. These might take the form of prayer, the study of scriptures and divine texts, or the silent repetition of sacred words or mantras. In one form or other, most traditions advocate the practice of reflection, taking time out of the day to sit quietly and reflect on a moment, an event, a life. Self-reflection, observing oneself with some degree of detachment, is often a central part of this.

Physical practices designed to connect the practitioner to the divine can be as varied as handling beads or walking mazes. Dance sometimes plays a part—for example, in Hinduism, Sufism (the mystical branch of Islam), and Hasidic Judaism. Focusing on breathing as a way to slow the mind is practiced in many traditions. The word *inspire,* which means to take in breath, suggests an ancient connection between breathing and enlightenment.

Some of these practices have become a part of the secular landscape. Yoga and meditation, for example, both of which have roots in eastern religious traditions, have entered the mainstream of western life and may already be activities a client draws on for support.

UNIVERSAL SPIRITUAL PRINCIPLES AND PRACTICES

Contrasting religious traditions are often linked by underlying spiritual principles. These principles, which show up in the literature of religions around the world and are supported by secular experience, open the heart, put one in touch with a larger consciousness, and expand one's vision. A few examples:

Acceptance. Central to Buddhism and other spiritual traditions, acceptance is simply the ability to take life as it comes and to be at peace with oneself and one's circumstances. Simple, but not always easy. "The curious paradox is that when I accept myself as I am, then I change," said Carl Rogers (1995, p. 17).

Trust. An individual is more resourceful, less fearful, and knows how to live when she trusts that what is needed in a given situation will become available; when she relies on inner resources; and when she has enough confidence to believe that even if something does not work out as intended, she can handle it. With trust, one often realizes that difficult situations produce desired growth or an even better outcome than the one imagined.

Gratitude. Many spiritual and religious traditions teach—and many individuals have learned through experience—the power of being grateful for what is beautiful and important in this life. Gratitude can have a profound impact on one's attitude and on one's emotional strength and abilities.

Compassion. This compassion is both for self and for others. The Dalai Lama has said, "My religion is very simple. My religion is kindness." Compassion, kindness, love. These words speak to the friendliness of spirit for oneself and for others and remind us of our connection to one another and to our deepest selves.

Connection. That we are connected to one another, not separate entities, is a theme in spiritual life. To awaken to our connection is to value the life around and within us. Connection to our own purpose and meaning powers our actions toward life-giving goals and visions.

Coaching Applications

- **Be sensitive to the client's spiritual and religious orientation.** Remember that this is both a personal and possibly sensitive topic of discussion.

- **Avoid projecting your own spiritual or religious beliefs onto your client.** The possibility of a spiritual discussion should emerge only from the client's thoughts and feelings. Spiritual or religious beliefs and practices are central to one's sense of self, and this area must be approached with sensitivity and discrimination.

- **Stay focused on the client's agenda.** If the coaching discussion moves to spirituality or religion, make your values explicit if this is appropriate, or let go of discussing them if this is what is best for the client.

- **Consider beginning each coaching session with a centering process that you and your client undertake together.** In the initial contracting phase of a coaching engagement, if it feels authentic to you, agree on a practice at the beginning of each session that helps set the tone for the client's safe self-exploration. You might agree to take a breath with the client, to repeat to him some of the values and principles you have harvested in your initial conversations, or to simply remind him that this session is for him alone and to take a moment to tap in to his own resourcefulness. Centering oneself before beginning a coaching conversation is also a good way to be fully present and ready for your client.

- **Be aware of your beliefs and values around spirituality and spiritual practice.** Increase your own self-awareness, relaxation, and alignment with your highest aspirations through a practice that is right for you.

- **Talk with your client about quiet time and reflection as a process for centering and connection.** Ask her to consider a minimum of three minutes each day to be quiet. She might practice driving with no radio on, no music playing, and no cell phone in operation. Or she might find a quiet place in her home or outside to sit in stillness and reflect at the beginning or end of each day.

- **Know that the client is united with his own higher power or source and that the coaching process is larger than both of you.** The client is inspired by what he learns for himself and about himself. It is exhilarating to feel the rush of insight that comes from connecting to one's own wisdom and to one's own energetic source. This is the client living from his innermost spirit. Remember that this is about your client's connection to something larger than himself and not about you.

Additional Reading

Brach, T. (2003) *Radical acceptance: Embracing your life with the heart of a Buddha.* New York: Bantam Books.
  Brach is a therapist, yogi, and Buddhist meditation teacher. She focuses on the two wings of mindfulness, awareness and compassion, as she shows the reader how to let

go of the suffering of self-judgment and other internal conflicts that destroy our happiness and diminish our lives.

Katie, B. (2002). *Loving what is: Four questions that can change your life*. New York: Three Rivers Press.

The Work of Byron Katie, described and demonstrated in this book, gives you as a coach a process for helping clients see inside their own thinking, to get free of their stressful thoughts, and therefore to get in touch with what is ultimately important to them.

Ruiz, M. (2001). *The four agreements: A practical guide to personal freedom, a Toltec wisdom book*. San Rafael, CA: Amber-Allen.

The four agreements are simple yet powerful agreements you make with yourself—and clients can make with themselves—in order to live in integrity and alignment. Ruiz talks about them in a way that inspires, weaving in stories from his Toltec heritage.

chapter TWENTY

The Self-Help and Human Potential Movements

Leni Wildflower

A variety of self-help and self-improvement movements sprang up during the 1960s and 1970s, mainly in the United States, and spread across the western world. These movements embodied ideas, philosophies, and ways of teaching that were to become vital forces in shaping the construction and protocols of coaching as we know it today. Though they took a variety of forms, they shared the premise that transformation is within one's own power; that through the development of one's innate potential, one can experience an improved quality of life, characterized, at best, by happiness, creativity, inner peace, and fulfillment. Some of these movements tended toward the mystical, whereas others were more pragmatic in emphasis; but they generally embraced a form of spirituality that was humanistic and postreligious in the value it placed on the present experience of life.

Many of these movements had roots that dated back well before the 1960s and 1970s, drawing on the work of such figures as psychotherapist and psychological theorist Carl Jung, writer Aldous Huxley, spiritual teacher Krishnamurti, and philosophers William James and Rudolf Steiner. In addition, Alcoholics Anonymous, founded in the 1930s in America, played an important role in influencing the concept of self-help and self-healing.

The self-help movements coincided with the development of humanistic psychology and were influenced by the approaches of Carl Rogers, Abraham Maslow, Rollo May, and other psychologists studying new ways of conducting therapy.

Included in this explosion of ideas were new forms of body awareness and body work, such as Rolfing and Heller Work, Alexander Technique, Reichian therapy and Primal Scream therapy, and such group practices as NTL (National Training Laboratory), the encounter group, Gestalt therapy (Fritz Perls), est (Erhard Seminars Training), and Transactional Analysis (Eric Berne). Early influences and practices that were co-opted or adapted included yoga, tai chi, and meditation.

The Esalen Institute in Big Sur, California, which was founded in 1962, became a meeting point and a center for these movements. At some point during the 1960s and 1970s, all the major figures in these modern movements visited Esalen. Some of the most innovative work was developed, encouraged, or cross-pollinated there:

> Esalen appealed to those who were trying to make sense of what was happening in society and to those who were interested in making more personal and immediate changes in their own lives: rediscovering their bodies, opening up their senses, learning to feel and communicate their desire. (Anderson, 1983, p. 146)

This was a very rich time in the growth of human awareness and development.

The Esalen Institute is still in existence, and many of the humanistic traditions continue to be practiced there. The sense of creative ferment has diminished, but the influence on coaching methodology has been profound.

Probably the greatest impact of the human potential movements was on the development of life coach training, particularly in America. As the field of coaching has expanded to include work on executive coaching for business, nonprofits, medical institutions, schools, and so on, coaching has shifted to accommodate knowledge about organizations, leadership, and business in general. Nonetheless, core psychological and spiritual principles that found fresh expression in these movements—principles fundamental to an understanding of how human beings operate and what is necessary to live a more productive, joyful life—continue to serve as important insights into the human predicament. At the same time, it should be noted that this territory is no less subject to market forces than any other, and arguably more open to exploitation than most.

LANDMARK EDUCATION

Of the many disciplines that have influenced the development of coaching, aside from humanistic psychology, the teachings found in est and later Landmark Education (see www.landmarkeducation.com) may be the most influential. These programs are based on the premise that transforming one's life is possible and that what is crucial to this transformation is to take responsibility for one's life. Landmark Education purchased the est training from Werner Erhard, modified it, and currently conducts trainings throughout the world. In the Landmark Forum, the basic program is arranged as a discussion in which the course leader presents ideas and the participants voluntarily share with the leader and the group how the ideas presented apply to their lives. The following are among Landmark's precepts:

- There is a difference between what happens in my life and the meaning I impose on it. I limit myself and get stuck in old patterns with the stories I construct. An attachment to what I'm good at (a "strong suit") can be as limiting as an attachment to a narrative of failure, weakness, or suffering (a "racket").

- My behavior is often governed by unnecessary fear of others and the need to avoid humiliation.

- It is liberating to communicate with people with whom I have unresolved conflicts in order to express forgiveness and to acknowledge responsibility for my own behavior. (The Landmark process encourages participants to phone significant people immediately, during breaks.)

- My life is richer if I *choose* or embrace joyfully those things I am unable to change.

- I can transform my life by imagining and articulating a new possibility for myself. As a social creature, I construct my reality in my interactions with other people. I draw them into my narratives, "enrolling" them in my new possibilities (just as I have enrolled them in my negative "stories"). Communicating this new possibility to others is essential.

- **Encourage your client to see the difference between an event in her life and the meaning she has attached to it.** Helping her reframe her experience in the light of this distinction can be a powerful tool for helping her let go of negative or self-defeating feelings.

- **Support your client in being less than perfect.** He can sometimes let go of being the best, looking good, or fulfilling other people's unreasonable or inappropriate expectations.

- **Encourage your client to gain the freedom that comes from forgiveness.** Where she is stuck in resentment, support her to make the contact necessary to free her. Where she is stuck in regret, help her recognize how these negative emotions are holding her back.

- **Help your client envision the life he would like to be leading.** Support him in taking steps toward that future, and encourage him to speak to other people about this, so that they are more likely to support and amplify his new sense of who he is.

TIM GALLWEY: THE INNER GAME

Tim Gallwey's book *The Inner Game of Tennis* (1974) described a new approach to mastering tennis. Gallwey's approach soon became a metaphor for approaches to many activities, including other sports, aspects of business, and stress reduction. His premise, which has roots in eastern philosophies and meditation, is based on visualization and nonjudgmental observation of what is happening in the moment. It is the process of trying, competing, self-criticizing, and self-analyzing that holds an individual back in any performance. According to Gallwey, the inner game methodology involves three principles: nonjudgmental awareness, trust in one's own self, and the exercise of free and conscious choice.

A relaxed, aware state of being and a focused, centered mind will produce the following:

- A feeling of confidence and an absence of anxiety and self-doubt

- No obsession with success and no fear of failure

- An absence of competitiveness, the focus being on playing (or working) beautifully and excellently

- A peak performance that comes without effort and when not thinking about it

Gallwey's methodology was revolutionary at the time and was soon being employed extensively in corporations around the world. Csikszentmihalyi's concept of flow, which emerged later, has a different emphasis, but the two overlap in interesting ways. Gallwey remains a prominent figure in the history of coaching.

Coaching Applications

- **Help your client work through self-judgment.** Focusing on past failures will reduce the chances of present and future success.

- **Remind your client that all change is accompanied by fear.** Fear, like any feeling, will diminish if one lets oneself feel it while continuing to move forward in life.

- **Discuss with your client the value of quieting the mind.** Relaxing and taking time away from the struggle to achieve can sometimes be the most effective route to achievement.

JOHN GRINDER AND RICHARD BANDLER: NEURO-LINGUISTIC PROGRAMMING

Neuro-Linguistic Programming (NLP) is a set of tools for communication that was developed during the 1970s by John Grinder and Richard Bandler.

Grinder and Bandler began by analyzing the linguistic strategies of two highly effective therapists, Fritz Perls and Virginia Satir. They observed the way these therapists challenged the utterances of their clients in three specific ways—identifying distortions, generalizations, and deletions—thereby leading the clients to look beneath the surface structure of their utterances and recognize the underlying deep structure. Bandler and Grinder (1975) codified this procedure into what they called a *meta model*. New models followed, together with a series of strategies including *anchoring*—creating a trigger for a desired emotional state—and *reframing*—defusing a problem by viewing it in a different context or perspective.

Bandler and Grinder (1979) claimed that NLP would be instrumental in helping people make deep and lasting changes quickly and easily. They emphasized its practical effects rather than any insight it might offer.

We call ourselves *modelers*. What we essentially do is to pay very little attention to what people say they do and a great deal of attention to what they do. And then we build ourselves a model of what they *do*. We are not psychologists, and we're also not theologians or theoreticians. We have *no* idea about the "real" nature of things, and we're not particularly interested in what's "true." The function of modeling is to arrive at descriptions which are *useful*. . . . We're not offering you something that's *true*, just things that are *useful*. (p. 7)

From its therapeutic origins, NLP has shifted into other fields, including marketing, motivation building, and helping people become more personally effective. Originally a system of alternative therapy, it is now seen primarily as a set of tools to aid communication and behavior modification. There is a considerable amount of controversy surrounding NLP. It has been criticized as being more attuned to manipulation than to self-discovery. It has also suffered from internal rifts, a progressive shift in focus, and a lack of empirical support for its assumptions.

BILL WILSON AND BOB SMITH: ALCOHOLICS ANONYMOUS

Alcoholics Anonymous was founded in the United States in the middle of the Depression by Bill Wilson and Bob Smith, two nonprofessionals who helped each other stay sober. The organization grew rapidly. In 2006, AA reported 106,202 groups worldwide. Although distinctly Christian in its early days, the program has evolved to include people of all faiths and nonbelievers. Participants are encouraged, however, to be open to the possibility of accepting a "higher power" in their lives as a part of the program.

In part, it is the structure of Alcoholics Anonymous that has kept it growing and thriving for so many years. AA groups are self-supporting and are neither businesses nor charities. There are no dues or membership fees. Groups rely on voluntary membership donations to pay for room rental, refreshments, literature, and any other expenses. There is no hierarchical leadership. No member of the organization is allowed to contribute more than $3,000 per year, and AA returns contributions mailed from outside sources. The principles of AA have been adapted for use by other groups, including Narcotics Anonymous (NA) and Al-Anon, a group for family members of alcoholics.

In AA, the effort to stop drinking is accompanied by an effort to change behavior and thinking patterns. This process, which AA calls a "spiritual awakening," is achieved by following a twelve-step program. Steps include admitting that your life is out of control, surrendering to a higher power, examining your life carefully to make changes that are necessary for a better life, making amends to people you have harmed, and helping other alcoholics recover. AA contends that without following this twelve-step program, alcoholics will not stay sober. AA has adopted a version of what has come to be known as the Serenity Prayer, written in the 1930s by the theologian Reinhold Niebuhr: "God, grant me the serenity to accept the things I cannot change, courage to change the things I can, and wisdom to know the difference." Central to AA's approach is the importance of taking "one day at a time."

As an informal element of structure, the tradition of sponsorship is essential. Newcomers, as they are called, are encouraged to get a sponsor—someone who has been in the program for a substantial period of time. Old timers are encouraged to sponsor others. The practice of one person assisting another to be his best self, holding him to account on his own behalf, is not unlike what coaches do. Other concepts central to AA have been incorporated and adapted by many self-help groups.

Coaching Applications

- **Remind your client that what she feels at any given moment is not what should dictate her behavior.** Explain the importance of acting "as if" (a familiar phrase in AA). This is not about faking behavior. Feelings come and go, and often don't have much to do with external reality. If she attends to what needs to be done, her attitude will probably shift in response to the change in behavior.

- **Encourage your client to clean up areas of guilt or regret by seeking forgiveness.** This is an important step toward freedom from negative feelings. Forgiving oneself is as important as being forgiven by others.

- **Help your client determine what he can and can't change in his life.** This might not be as easy as it sounds. He might have limiting beliefs about his own ability or freedom that are keeping him stuck. Or he might be faced with tough circumstances that are genuinely beyond his control. Teasing out the options could be a crucial step.

Additional Reading

Alcoholics Anonymous. (1990). *Daily reflections: A book of reflections by A.A. members for A.A. members.* New York: Alcoholics Anonymous World Service.

Spiritual and self-help advice from recovering alcoholics.

Alcoholics Anonymous. (2002). *Alcoholics Anonymous—Big Book.* New York: Alcoholics Anonymous World Service.

The AA "bible," describing the program and telling the history of the organization and how it was founded.

Bartley, W. W. (1978). *Werner Erhard, The transformation of a man: The founding of est.* New York: Clarkson N. Potter.

The story of Werner Erhard and the insights that led to the creation of est. Informative reading.

Csikszentmihalyi, M. (1997). *Finding flow: The psychology of engagement with everyday life.* New York: Basic Books.

A classic on strengthening one's ability to notice and create peak experience and happiness.

Gallwey, W. T. (2009). *The inner game of stress: Outsmart life's challenges and fulfill your potential.* New York: Random House.

One of Gallwey's follow-up books to his first book, this is full of rich exercises and resources.

Jeffers, S. (1987). *Feel the fear and do it anyway: How to turn your fear and indecision into confidence and action.* London: Arrow Books.

A popular book that deals with managing fear and uncertainty.

O'Connor, J., & Seymour, J. (1993). *Introducing NLP: Psychological skills for understanding and influencing people.* London: Harper Thorsons.

A good primer for understanding the components of NLP.

Ram Dass. (1974). *The only dance there is.* New York: Random House.

A persuasive discussion of spirituality from a Harvard professor who became a Hindu scholar and practitioner. It translates eastern concepts effectively into western language.

Richo, D. (2002). *How to be an adult in relationships: The five keys to mindful loving.* Boston: Shambhala.

An excellent guide to creating healthy intimacy and friendships—and understanding what makes this task so difficult. Contains helpful charts and diagrams.

Robertson, N. (1988) *Getting better: Inside Alcoholics Anonymous.* New York: Morrow.

Provides a clear understanding of the founding of AA, the individuals involved, and how the organization came to be what it is today.

Ruiz, M. A. (1997). *The four agreements.* San Rafael, CA: Amber-Allen.

An inspiring book that encourages exploration and acceptance of personal responsibility and choice.

Mindfulness

Janet Baldwin Anderson, Francine Campone, and Jennifer Sellers

Mindfulness means moment-to-moment awareness. It is learning to wake up to each moment of your life so that you are fully living your life in this moment. . . . Mindfulness is not a mysterious mystical state; rather it is being fully aware of the reality around you. Mindfulness is maintaining awareness of the sensations in your body, the flow of thoughts through your mind, the sounds and sights in your surroundings. Thus, mindfulness is awareness expanded into ourselves and outward into the world.

—McQuaid and Carmona, 2004, p. 12

Mindfulness is a state of being in which one is aware of what is happening moment to moment and maintains the ability to be conscious both of oneself and of others. Mindfulness is not meditation, although meditation is an important pathway to awareness of oneself. Mindfulness has become recognized as a crucial component of effectively working with others.

Mindfulness has ancient traditions with deep roots in many areas of knowledge and fields of practice, such as psychology and psychotherapy, spiritual and wisdom traditions, and health and wellness. Wisdom traditions have long associated the practices of self-reflection and mindful awareness with the development of human consciousness and well-being. However, it is only within recent decades that scientific advances have permitted us to observe what is going on within the living brain in the act of experiencing. These advances help deepen our understanding of the mind, reveal how the mind and the brain create each other, and suggest how our everyday reflective practices of mindfulness may be understood through a lens of neurobiology—the biological study of the brain and nervous system and its ability to adapt and transform itself (Doidge, 2007).

In recent years, findings about the brain—from such disciplines as cognitive science, human development, biology, psychology, and medicine—have led to the emergence of a multidisciplinary science that studies the brain from the perspectives of the physiological, developmental, and psychological processes involved in the formation of the mind. This new science—a joining of cognitive neuroscience and psychotherapy—has been referred to as *interpersonal neurobiology* (Siegel, 2007), reflecting a focus on brain function and structure that develops not only within the body but also in relation with others. The new knowledge about the brain has implications for any endeavor designed to increase well-being, foster capabilities, and improve performance. Coaches stand to benefit from the integration of this new knowledge, as we seek to apply it in our coaching practices and in our own lives. Whether from the eastern or western roots, mindfulness is being researched in the social and biological sciences and has made its way into popular culture.

ATTENTION, PURPOSE, AND NONJUDGMENT: JON KABAT-ZINN

In the late 1970s, Jon Kabat-Zinn, a molecular biologist working at the stress reduction clinic at the University of Massachusetts Medical Center, developed a program called mindfulness-based stress reduction (MBSR). Kabat-Zinn's *Full Catastrophe Living* (1990) described the program in detail and gave countless readers access to the concept of mindfulness, and clear instruction in how to employ it in their everyday lives.

Three elements of Kabat-Zinn's concept of mindfulness are especially relevant to reflective coaching practice: attention, purpose, and nonjudgment. The reflective practitioner is one who engages mindfully in the moment of practice, gathering a full spectrum of data on intentions, actions, and the outcome of actions.

MBSR spawned much research on mindfulness in a wide range of circumstances and fields. Programs that teach or encourage mindfulness are now found in the institutions, organizations, and agencies of domains as diverse as health, education, recreation, psychotherapy, and business.

Kabat-Zinn's study of mindfulness was informed by his exposure to the ancient Buddhist practice of meditation. The humanistic movement in psychology, philosophy, and psychotherapy has given rise to other lines of exploration. The "mindfulness" encouraged in Gestalt therapy, cognitive behavioral therapy, and rational emotive behavior therapy is focused on calm acceptance of what is, on self-acceptance, and on nonjudgmental attention and observation (Dryden & Still, 2006).

The Harvard social psychologist Ellen Langer contrasts mindfulness with the mindless state, when one is trapped in thinking that adheres to rigid categories and perspectives. In a mindful state, one constantly creates new categories, welcomes new information, and is open to different points of view or perspectives (Carson & Langer, 2006).

MINDFULNESS AND ATTUNEMENT WITH OTHERS: DANIEL SIEGEL

According to Siegel, who has developed the concept of interpersonal neurobiology, mindfulness may be seen as an attuned relationship with oneself (focusing on one's own internal world) as well as an attuned relationship with others (focusing on the internal world of another). The focus on the mind of another person harnesses neural circuitry that enables two people to "feel felt" by each other. Siegel sees a commonality of mechanisms between the two forms of internal and interpersonal attunement, and both are cultivated by a direct focus of mindful awareness. In *The Mindful Brain*, Siegel writes that in this way we "come to not only know the mind, but to embrace our own inner world and the mind of others with kindness and compassion" (2007, p. 2).

REFLECTIVE PRACTICE: DONALD SCHÖN

Donald Schön proposes that practitioners in such fields as psychotherapy, education, and medicine are in effect experimenting with each intervention they offer and thus need to direct attention to the nature of the experiment and the outcomes in order to correct course. Schön suggests that practitioners consciously or unconsciously choose a response or intervention in order to elicit more information (exploratory experiments), to see what kind of response is generated (move-testing experiments), or to test an assumption about the essential nature of a problem (hypothesis-testing experiments). Through mindful reflection, the practitioner is able to nonjudgmentally gather data and better understand the interdependence of coaching strategies and their impact.

Schön suggests that practitioners can easily fall into a "parochial narrowness of vision" (1983, p. 60). By purposefully directing attention to what we do as coaches, nonjudgmentally noticing the impact and outcomes of our actions and reflecting on our initial intentions, we can learn to avoid the traps of habituated professional behaviors and selective attention. This application of mindfulness is especially relevant to evidence-based coaching, as it invites practitioners to be mindful of their own mental models as well as the multiple dimensions of the client and the coaching context.

MINDFUL REFLECTION AND CHANGING HABITS OF PRACTICE

Psychotherapist Bonnie Badenoch (2008) offers a brain-based perspective on the effects of mindful reflection. There is a shift, she argues, from "top-down" to "bottom-up" processing. Top-down processing engages the layers of the brain, which contain ideas about what will happen next based on past experience. Bottom-up processing engages us in the sensory experiences of the moment, enabling us to insert additional information that may disrupt or challenge those ideas. A mindful and reflective stance in practice helps liberate us from learned patterns. As coaching practitioners, when we experience dissonance in the moment and reflect on that experience, we create the opportunity to develop more complex and nuanced behaviors.

For Doug Silsbee (2008), the practice of "self-observing over time" changes our relationship with a habit, inevitably leading to greater self-awareness and choice. Self-observation of our own habits cultivates the internal observer and begins to foster "present moment awareness" that leads us to notice the impulse *before* the behavior (pp. 145–146).

Shauna Shapiro and Linda Carlson (2009) write about the creation of a "witness self," which helps practitioners move away from a habitual problem-solving orientation. They call the ability to separate oneself from the contents of one's own consciousness "reperceiving." For coaches who have previously worked as consultants, therapists, or educators or in any other expert role, this shift might be particularly necessary. Shapiro and Carlson argue that for the practitioner, mindful reflection encourages self-compassion. Acknowledging the universality of being human, flaws and all, strengthens the bond of true empathy, not as a cognitive experience but as an experienced connection. Through mindful reflection, practitioners create a holding space for their own feelings as well as those of the client.

For Mark Hubble, Barry Duncan, and Scott Miller (1999), founders of the Institute for the Study of Therapeutic Change, mindful reflection allows practitioners to direct attention to the changes that are taking place in the client, affirming what the client has done and directing attention toward pathways that support continuation of change. Gathering data supports the coach in accurately estimating the client's readiness for change, enabling the coach to design appropriate interventions to encourage forward momentum.

Coaching Applications

- **Maintain an authentic and nonjudgmental presence.** By accepting both your client's emotions and your own, without becoming overpowered by them, you become better able to shift perspectives and help the client do so. The greater your mastery of mindfulness, the more likely you are to embody this nonjudgmental and flexible presence.

- **Maintain your focus on the client and the client's agenda during the session.** It is natural for the mind to wander. Mindfulness encourages us to notice our inner dialogue and the extent to which this distracts us from or influences our perceptions of our client. If your mind does wander, bring attention back to the client without self-judgment.

- **Help the client practice mindfulness in the session.** Encourage her to bring her focus into the present, to slow down her reaction to her situation, to feel it in her body, and to notice and accept her internal responses. Allow her to acknowledge self-judgment and steer her toward compassion for herself.

- **Experiment with mindfulness practices for yourself.** Try on various practices to find what fits best for you. These might include some form of meditation, meditative reading, yoga, tai chi, connecting with nature, or listening to music. Strengthening yourself allows you to be at your best as you relate and work with others.

Additional Reading

Kabat-Zinn, J. (1994). *Wherever you go there you are: Mindfulness meditation in everyday life*. New York: Hyperion.

This book describes, explains, and encourages the experience of mindfulness. It is intended both for beginners and for those who have extensive practice. It offers pragmatic techniques, helpful practices, and a rich exploration of mindfulness.

Schön, D. A. (1983). *The reflective practitioner: How professionals think in action*. New York: Basic Books.

In this classic work, Schön demonstrates that it is through reflection that the practitioner utilizes a repertoire of understandings, images, and actions to reframe a troubling situation and thereby generate problem-solving actions.

Siegel, D. J. (2007). *The mindful brain: Reflection and attunement in the cultivation of well-being*. New York: Norton.

Siegel uses theory, science, and anecdote to show that mindfulness meditation, secure attachment, and effective psychotherapy each has a similar neural mechanism. By integrating the science of mind, mindfulness, and neurobiology, this book reveals how to transform the brain and promote well-being.

Silsbee, D. K. (2008). *Presence-based coaching: Cultivating self-generative leaders through mind, body, and heart*. San Francisco: Jossey-Bass.

Silsbee writes from a stance of reflective mindfulness while giving clear instruction, practical suggestions, and thought-provoking insights into serving the client through presence.

PART FIVE

Coaching Specific Populations

One of the exciting things about coaching is its adaptability. It can transform itself while remaining true to its core principles. It crosses the globe and faces a spectrum of needs and circumstances.

Education and coaching would seem like a natural fit, but whereas the business environment has been enthusiastic in embracing the promise of coaching, the world of elementary and secondary education has been more resistant. Perhaps the simple imperatives of the market make outcomes in business less contested and more directly measurable. Perhaps chronic underfunding of education and the pressure of externally created initiatives set up resistance to yet another time-consuming idea. Nevertheless, coaching is making inroads into schools and achieving dynamic results.

Sustainability is of ever-increasing concern, but the problems can seem so vast that the individual, overwhelmed and despondent, slips into a state of denial. Here too coaching has a role to play. And the challenges and possibilities of various dimensions of diversity—gender, culture, and age—make demands that coaching must continue to meet.

Education

Kathy Norwood and Mary Ann Burke

I believe coaching is the missing ingredient from our school improvement efforts, and when a well designed coaching program is successfully implemented, school systems, staff and students will soar.

—Reiss, 2007, p. 4

Coaching is a growing phenomenon in school systems throughout the world and has become a form of embedded professional learning for staff members (Darling-Hammond, Chung Wei, Andree, Richardson, & Orphanos, 2009). But the value of coaching in its full sense is still in contention. Coaching has been seen as an adjunct to more familiar roles or has been grafted onto emerging administrative positions, including teacher leader, literacy coordinator, consultant, staff developer, mentor, school improvement specialist, data specialist, and content area coach.

Educational coaching roles extend beyond conventional coaching (Norwood & Burke, 2008). Trained coaches are leaders who help build leadership capacity, support teachers in analyzing student data and refining instructional practices, and facilitate teams in collaborative exchanges through professional learning communities. The overarching purpose is to enhance student learning by increasing leadership and teaching competence. Coaching in education has now expanded to include coaching for students, and executive coaching for school leaders and administrators.

Increasingly, as coaching becomes recognized, schools are hiring specialist or independent coaches to teach coaching skills to educators and for coaching with teachers and principals. In addition, programs focused on coaching high school or college students are beginning to emerge.

The effectiveness of coaching in education cannot be overstated. Research has shown that traditional staff development and training programs produce limited results in changing classroom practices or implementing and sustaining school initiatives (Showers & Joyce, 1996). When a theory is presented and even modeled by a trainer, 85 percent of teachers will understand the concept, 15 to 18 percent will attain the new skill, but only 5 to 10 percent will apply it in the classroom, resulting in little influence on students' learning. When coaching is added to the mix, 90 percent learn the concept, 90 percent attain the skill, and 80 to 90 percent apply it in the classroom.

COMBINING COACHING AND STAFF TRAINING

School administrators in the United States have been slower than business organizations to embrace coaching. Coaching has been introduced as a way of supporting the implementation and sustainability of best practices, so coaches are often in a hybrid role. For example, after teachers have attended a workshop on current practice, coaches will typically work with teams and individuals, modeling lessons, observing classroom instruction, and helping teachers incorporate district standards and assessments into their teaching.

The coaching conversations themselves tend to be more structured than those in conventional coaching, with most educational coaches using conversation maps with lists of prescribed questions. As educational coaches become more skilled, they internalize the conversation maps and learn to intuitively allow the client to guide the conversation. But the open-ended coaching conversation that flows along the client's line of thought is not yet the accepted model.

Even in this limited role, however, coaching is proving effective, as published research and anecdotal information are beginning to demonstrate. Biancarosa, Bryk, and Dexter (2008) studied the effects of professional development in literacy collaboration, combined with coaching, on students and teachers from eighteen schools in eight states. Their midstudy data showed significant improvement in student literacy rates—16 percent in the first year and 29 percent in the second.

One of the authors provided literacy professional development and coaching in Walnut Creek School District in California from 1997 to 2000. Student performance data from one school illustrated the positive impact that training combined with coaching had on teachers and students. In the final year, 77 to 91 percent of K–5 students were achieving at or above grade level in reading compared to 64 to 79 percent recorded in the first year. During this time, the number of English language learners increased from 6 percent to 10 percent, and special education referrals dropped from 6 percent to 3 percent.

State standards math scores in a high school in Centennial School District in Oregon increased from 49 percent in 2007–08 to 69 percent in 2008–09. Administrators attributed this, in part, to the work of their coach. The high school had established professional learning communities (PLCs) (DuFour & Eaker, 1998), and the coach had been trained in a variety of coaching methodologies. The coach incorporated the International Coach Federation's coaching core competencies, standards, and ethical guidelines in her work. Student data were analyzed to customize an action plan for each teacher, which was implemented during a six-session coaching cycle (first introduced by Norwood & Burke, 2008).

COACHING APPROACHES IN EDUCATION

The Self-Regulation Empowerment Program (Cleary & Zimmerman, 2004) is an application of social-cognitive theory and research. In this program, the self-regulated learning coach teaches students to use Zimmerman's cyclical feedback loop of self-regulation (2000). Students discover how to apply learning strategies and positive self-motivation techniques.

Another promising approach for coaching students toward self-directed learning is positive education (Seligman, 2008), which involves teachers coaching students to apply principles of positive psychology—cultivating positive emotion, character traits, and resilience—to strengthen their learning experiences. In 2008, Seligman and colleagues from Penn State University trained one hundred teachers from Geelong Grammar School (Australia) in how to teach positive psychology to their students, who range from age three through grade 12. The school Web site (see www.ggs.vic.edu.au/Positive-Education/Teaching-Programme.aspx) reports that by 2011, more than nine hundred students will have been trained in positive psychology skills with the intention of increasing levels of creativity, critical thinking, positive emotion, and ability to cope with negative feelings.

Another study conducted in Australia with high school students, this one focusing on year 11 females, has provided encouraging results in building personal resilience. In an exercise in evidence-based life coaching (Green, Grant, & Rynsaardt, 2007), teachers were trained as coaches to provide life coaching, in a ten-session cycle, using a cognitive behavioral, solution-focused coaching framework. Participants set goals and were coached to "identify personal resources . . . [and] develop self-generated solutions and specific action steps, systematically working through the self-regulation cycle of setting goals, developing action plans, monitoring and evaluating progress" (p. 27). The results of personal coaching were linked to increased levels of hope and cognitive hardiness (a dimension of resilience that protects mental health) and decreased levels of depression.

COGNITIVE AND INSTRUCTIONAL COACHING

Two methodologies important to educational coaching of teachers and administrators are Cognitive Coaching and instructional coaching. Each is grounded in research and is applicable to most teaching situations.

Cognitive Coaching (Costa & Garmston, 2002) was developed from Cogan and Goldhammer's clinical supervision model (1969). It was designed to help administrators support teachers' growth toward self-directed learning by applying humanistic principles in teacher evaluations. This methodology works on changing "mental models" (Auerbach, 2006)—beliefs about ourselves, other people, and life in general—to arrive at less restrictive ways of thinking. Working from the assumption that "behaviors change after our beliefs change" (Knight, 2007, p. 10), cognitive coaches use maps (planning, reflecting, problem solving) to navigate the conversation.

Instructional coaching (Knight, 2007) combines the knowledge and expertise of coaching competencies with the experience of effective best practices across a broad spectrum of instruction, including content areas, student assessment, and classroom management. Instructional coaches are full-time coaches employed by the school system, who work with teachers to help them incorporate research-based instructional practices (2007). Instructional coaches must have strong skills in communicating and building relationships with others, the ability to empathize, and a broad and deep understanding of and experience with instructional practices and assessments.

- **Clarify your role as a coach.** Be clear about your client's expectations and the expectations for coaching within the school system. When your coaching is supported by an organization, you are accountable both to your client, the individual participating in the coaching, and to the sponsor, the organization paying for the coaching. Depending on the school system, policies and processes around coaching and reporting requirements may challenge the confidentiality of the relationship. Establishing clear expectations at the start for open, honest communication supports the client and sponsor in achieving successful outcomes.

- **Learn about the organizational structure and hierarchy of the school system you are working in.** Whether you are an internal coach or contracted externally, it helps to understand the context within which your client works.

- **Support your client to strengthen her skill and knowledge in navigating change.** The educational environment can be subject to frequent reorganization, new demands, and shifting priorities. Understanding the process of change and her own response to it allows the client to gain perspective and learning as she moves forward toward her personal goals.

- **Explore resistance with your client using a cognitive coaching approach.** An experience of cognitive coaching allows him to integrate learning as an educator. Be alert to any resistance you experience and self-manage or seek support with your own coach.

STRATEGIES FOR SUSTAINABILITY

Coaches can learn to apply various strategies that support sustainability. These strategies are also effective for classroom teachers coaching students toward self-directed learning.

The Coaching Continuum is a flexible model of coaching that requires that one learn to flow between the roles of consultant, collaborator-mentor, and coach (Lipton, Wellman, & Humbard, 2003) to stimulate and fuel an accelerated model of learning. Each role has a different purpose. At times, coaching situations call for the use of multiple approaches that are more direct, action-oriented, and skills-based.

This approach is most effective when one combines it with the gradual release of responsibility model (Pearson, Roehler, Dole, & Duffy, 1992). Originally developed for children's learning, this model is easily transferred to adult learning. The premise is that teachers are not expected to fully implement new concepts before they have seen the concepts modeled and have practiced with one who is more expert. Four phases progressively build the client's capacity to reflect on his or her practice, increase professional self-awareness, and facilitate self-directed learning.

Phase one. The coach initially serves as consultant and instructs the client in best practices by teaching or directly modeling a concept or strategy for the client.

Phase two. The coach serves as a mentor to the teacher. The mentor and mentee participate as equals in collaborative activities, such as teaching, planning lessons, analyzing student data, reflecting and problem solving, or developing curriculum. The mentor might coteach with the mentee, and together they debrief the lesson and look at student learning.

Phase three. The coach *coaches*. This stance is a "non-judgmental mediation of thinking and decision-making" (Lipton, Wellman, & Humbard, 2003, p. 21). A coach will provide opportunities for a planning conference, observation of the lesson, and a reflection conference with the client as she practices new teaching behaviors.

Phase four. The coach and client celebrate and share concise feedback for a job well done. The client is now practicing the new best-practice behavior independently and successfully.

This type of performance coaching becomes a fluid dance between consulting, mentoring, and coaching. As teachers become more proficient, a coach has an increased opportunity to stay in the coaching role.

The cycle of inquiry (Militello, Rallis, & Goldring, 2009) is an approach that entails continuous, ongoing action research based on teaching practices. It requires that teachers define questions about their practice, analyze data, identify gaps in student achievement, design instruction to address teaching gaps, and then determine whether those changes improved student learning. Green, Grant, & Rynsaardt's solution-focused life coaching framework (2007) and Zimmerman's cyclical model of self-regulation (2000) describe how this model could be applied to working with students.

- **Develop a broad scope of coaching skills and knowledge to support the varied roles that may be required of you within education.** Recognize which role you are called on to provide at any given time, whether coach, mentor, consultant, or teacher.

- **Help your client raise his awareness around how he can effect change within his environment.** A school principal or headmaster is faced with daily challenges, often juggling administrative and budgetary concerns with the needs of students. A teacher's challenges may include managing diverse student needs, limited resources, and dense curriculum requirements. Coaching allows your client a time to reflect and find perspective and focus, so that he is better able to take action on what lies within his control.

- **Establish a support system for yourself.** Whether you are internal to the school system or contracted as an external coach, develop a peer network, participate in coaching for yourself, work with a mentor coach, and reflect on your learning as part of your ongoing professional development. And most important, allow yourself time to reenergize so that you embody sustainability as a person and a professional.

POTENTIAL IMPACT OF SCHOOL CULTURE ON COACHING

Teachers, administrators, and coaches may be unaware of the most pervasive cultural patterns in their schools. School culture operates on conscious and subconscious levels (Lindahl, 2006, p. 3):

- Highly observable manifestations (behavior, language, rituals)
- Somewhat less observable aspects (unwritten rules that "everyone" knows)
- Deeply embedded subconscious core operations (common, unquestioned, fundamental assumptions and values)

The most embedded patterns of school culture are the most persistent and are consequently the most difficult to identify and change, for coaches and teachers alike.

Coaches must practice and teach their staff the art of critical reflection—especially critical self-reflection—in order to examine aspects of school culture that undermine the change process:

- What do teachers expect of their students and themselves? What are their feelings about their students and themselves? How do these expectations and feelings affect their teaching?

- What do coaches expect of their clients and themselves? What are their feelings about their clients and themselves? How do these expectations and feelings affect their coaching?

Coaches must consider the culture of the schools in which they work in order to match coaching to the teachers' needs. Although each individual school has its own character, one may discover general cultural trends that distinguish elementary schools from secondary schools.

IMMUNITY TO CHANGE: ROBERT KEGAN AND LISA LAHEY

The Immunity to Change process was developed by Robert Kegan and Lisa Lahey to help people recognize and overcome their own hidden obstacles to change (2009). Kegan and Lahey have been working extensively with groups of school administrators and teachers on an adaptive change model that challenges them to identify the *competing commitments* that prevent them from bringing about the changes in education to which they are committed (2001). Competing commitments include (1) the desire to support learner-centered education versus the sense that good leadership in education requires command and control; (2) the commitment to pushing children to excel educationally versus the compassionate tendency to avoid demanding high academic performance from underprivileged children who are already burdened with life conditions; (3) the commitment among teachers to embrace new ways of teaching versus the belief that their role of teacher as authority figure must be maintained (2009).

By revealing competing commitments and the assumptions that underlie these commitments, the Immunity to Change process, which has been used and researched extensively in public education, can aid all school personnel in expanding their awareness of what prevents them from making the change they desire.

Coaching Applications

- **Learn to administer the Immunity to Change process.** This can provide you with a powerful tool in helping clients change both their thinking and behaving. The process can be conducted with individuals or groups.

- **In the early stages, be willing to support your client in simply observing his competing commitments and living with them.** The Immunity to Change process encourages a compassionate view of internal conflict and contradiction. The process is powerful, however, and simply discovering where one is stuck may be enough to initiate change.

- **Challenge your client to test the validity of her competing commitments or underlying assumptions.** Once she has become aware of what is standing in the way of change, coaching might involve devising activities to test the validity of the commitment or the underlying assumption that fuels it.

- **Help your client be a curious observer of himself rather than a critic.** Although the Immunity to Change process might begin with practical concerns and external goals, it can bring up deeply personal beliefs and long-held assumptions. Encourage your client to view the competing commitments that are holding him back not as signs of weakness or personal failure but as part of his human complexity, and to trust that observing them without judgment will allow him the freedom to change.

Additional Reading

Costa, A., & Garmston, R. (2002). *Cognitive coaching: A foundation for Renaissance schools* (2nd ed.). Norwood, MA: Christopher-Gordon.
A comprehensive book on cognitive coaching that includes theory, application, coaching maps, a toolkit, and research.

Kegan, R., & Lahey, L. L. (2009). *Immunity to change: How to overcome it and unlock the potential in yourself and your organization.* Boston: Harvard Business School Press.
The most recent book on the subject. This simplifies the developmental model and offers concrete ways to use the Immunity to Change process in organizations.

Killion, J., & Harrison, C. (2006). *Taking the lead: New roles for teachers and school-based coaches.* Oxford, OH: National Staff Development Council.
This book identifies ten roles for school-based coaches and discusses strategies for school coaching programs; the accompanying CD-ROM offers an extensive toolkit for coaches.

Knight, J. (2007). *Instructional coaching: A partnership approach to improving instruction.* Thousand Oaks, CA: Corwin Press.
A well-researched guide to understanding and implementing instructional coaching programs in schools. Includes a toolkit for coaches in the appendix.

Norwood, K., & Burke, M. A. (2008). *Coaching for transformational change.* Henderson, NV: Lulu.

A coaching manual for coach trainings that combines theory and practical applications. Includes a coaching conversation model, suggestions for working closely with principals, an extensive toolkit, and a resource guide.

Wagner, T., & Kegan, R. (2006). *Change leadership: A practical guide to transforming our schools*. San Francisco: Jossey-Bass.

An excellent reference providing insight into actual work and results with leadership and change within schools.

Issues of Aging

chapter TWENTY-THREE

Connie S. Corley

*[M]ore than half of all the human beings who have ever
lived beyond age 65 are alive today.*

—Moody, 2010, p. xxix

*I'm convinced that the challenge of aging isn't to stay young;
it's not only to grow old but to grow whole—to come into your own.
The aging process is woven into human destiny.
It's your time to embrace that challenge and figure out who you are,
now that you're not who you were.*

—Goldman, 2009, p. 12

Growing old is inevitable, but what that means is far from constant. In the United States and many countries globally, living to sixty-five and beyond is increasingly common. Although the age of sixty-five is typically used to define the older adult population in the United States, in fact, the body's organs and sensory systems start aging much earlier. Yet what historically has been seen as the mark of aging, a number that varies by country and is typically based on the age of pension eligibility, is constantly being redefined. Planning for longevity is a complex and comprehensive process, yet many people react only after an issue arises or a crisis is faced. Recent economic factors have affected the retirement plans of many, and people are staying in the workforce longer or "retooling" in order to find new sources of income (Walker & Lewis, 2009). Entrepreneurship is also growing in the mid- to later-life population because of economic factors and the desire among many individuals to engage in work about which they feel a sense of passion (Freedman, 2008). Essential to optimal aging is to understand and prepare for the many changes that occur as people grow older, and to foster their engagement in ways to manage challenges while thriving along the way.

NEW MODELS OF AGING

As the population of older adults burgeons worldwide, especially with the aging of the baby boomers (Moody, 2010), the field of gerontology is likewise burgeoning. Different challenges and opportunities arise depending on whether you look at aging from a population perspective or an individual perspective. Advances in cognitive science are interfacing with the biological, social, and behavioral sciences, leading to "the changing tenor in the field of aging—from inevitable decline to new opportunities" (Kryla-Lighthall & Mather, 2009, p. 38).

Whether a person is living in optimal circumstances or in the context of challenging life situations, the quality of life in the later years can be enhanced through a variety of measures. Coaches are in a prime position to work with individuals and groups in midlife and well into older adulthood to optimize the aging experience.

In the twenty-first century, interest in creative aging and discoveries about brain changes have led to new pathways for engagement in life (Cohen, 2006). Such terms as "positive aging" and "conscious aging" (Moody, 2010) have also come into the landscape and represent an interest in how people can access inner resources, while highlighting the contributions that older adults can make to society. Cohen (2000) suggests that in the later years of life, there is an "Encore" phase characterized by restating and reaffirming life themes and finding novel ways to explore them. This phase to some extent parallels Erikson's psychosocial stage of "generativity versus stagnation" (Erikson, Erikson, & Kivnick, 1986), when attention is focused on care and concern for future generations, although Cohen's Encore phase comes much later (age seventy and beyond). Vaillant's longitudinal research on factors contributing to vital aging (2002), with its emphasis on generativity, reinforces the importance of meaningful activity in later life.

One theory, among many, for understanding and optimizing the later years of life identifies four major domains: awareness, activity, affiliation, and attitude. The "four A" approach offers a simple framework that can guide coaches to specific areas of attention when working with midlife and older clients. (For additional information about the four A approach, see www.conniecorleyphd.com.) The remainder of the chapter discusses each of these four domains.

AWARENESS OF THE AGING PROCESS

In 1997, two MacArthur Fellows, John Rowe and Robert Kahn, released a widely cited book titled *Successful Aging.* One of the three principles Rowe and Kahn identified is "avoidance of disease and disability." It's important to be aware of predisposition to illness. Various estimates suggest that up to one third of aging can be attributed to genetic factors. Awareness of family history of major causes of death, such as heart disease and cancer, can lead to lifestyle changes that reduce the likelihood of disability associated with certain diseases.

Coaching Applications

- **Help your client identify what support or information she needs in caring for her health and well-being.** Exploring self-care, health, and wellness in a coaching conversation allows her to consider what else she needs to know and what actions she should take as she ages.

- **Learn more about resources available for information on aging.** One resource that may be helpful is the National Institute on Aging: www.nia.nih.gov/AboutNIA/.

- **Recognize that implementing lifestyle changes can be challenging.** There is often a time lag between knowing that you need to make changes and actually being able to make the change. Help your client look, without guilt or self-blame, at what he needs to do but hasn't yet done. At the same time, gently probe with such questions as *What do you need that would help you change your eating habits?*

- **Encourage your client to explore resources available online or via mobile phone, iPod, or other technology to support her healthier lifestyle choices.** Examples of available resources include the Living to 100 Life Expectancy Calculator (www.livingto100.com/) and Vitality Compass (www.bluezones.com). These relatively simple programs are useful in helping people identify risk factors, many of which are modifiable, that can affect their longevity.

ACTIVITY

Early theories of aging focused on what was seen as a withdrawal from social engagement. Cumming and Henry (1961) considered this process of "disengagement" inevitable. Some contemporary thinking, such as an approach called "activity theory" (Adams & Sanders, 2010), challenges this view. There is a contrasting concern about the "busy ethic" (Ekerdt, 2010), which can lead some people to become more active to compensate for losses, such as retirement or layoff from a job. In some instances, becoming "busy" leads to other challenges that come from avoiding the feelings that may be part of a natural grieving process—after loss of a spouse or partner, for example. But for some older adults, curtailing activities and social contacts is seen as a natural process that can "maximize positive affect and promote identity maintenance" (Adams & Sanders, 2010, p. 2), according to socioemotional selectivity theory (Frederickson & Carstensen, 1990).

In the area of social activity, the groundbreaking work of Gene Cohen (2000, 2006) and colleagues has highlighted the role of the arts in promoting well-being. The National Center for Creative Arts (www.creativeaging.org) identifies arts programs that may be beneficial. For Rowe and Kahn, high functioning both cognitively and physically is one of three components of successful aging (1997). Activity that engages mind and body is crucial to midlife and later life wellness. Lifelong learning is another venue for midlife and older adults to become intellectually stimulated, socially engaged, and often physically active (Hooyman & Kiyak, 2008). Numerous programs in the United States, such as those associated with OASIS (www.oasisnet.org) and Osher Lifelong Learning Institutes (http://usm.maine.edu/olli/national/), offer classes, events, and volunteer opportunities. Road Scholar (www.roadscholar.org; formerly known as Elderhostel), for example, runs educational tours to more than ninety countries.

Creating a "social portfolio" helps one tap into creative potential in later life. Cohen (2000) suggests that this portfolio is just as important as a financial portfolio in lifelong planning. The social portfolio is conceptualized along two dimensions: individual or group efforts in relation to mobility and energy levels.

Where a person is situated along these dimensions determines what types of activity would be appropriate. An individual activity for someone with low mobility and low energy, for example, might be the creation of a "secret recipes" family cookbook (Cohen, 2000).

Coaching Applications

- **Build your familiarity and credibility to work with older or aging individuals.** The primary requirement in working with an older or aging population is credibility. This doesn't mean you need to be the same age as your client, but your credibility depends on your familiarity with issues of aging and, to some extent, how much experience you have in this area.

- **Focus on the issue of activity, which is central when working with a client on issues around aging.** The importance of physical activity is almost always an issue with clients of any age when they are working on improving their quality of life. But it becomes critical in aging.

- **Work with your client to identify what kind of physical activity she enjoys.** Help her explore what will support her in achieving and maintaining her health goals.

- **Encourage your client to build a plan that balances activity with periods of rest and contemplation.** Finding the right balance can be challenging in the aging population.

- **Work on creative ways to gently help your client move toward trying new things.** Cognitive behavioral coaching experiments (see Chapter Two) are often an effective way to move forward. Chances are your client has already been told by his doctor, children, and friends what he should do. Sometimes unconditional support will allow him to actually begin making changes.

AFFILIATION

As people age, there are many opportunities for connection and fulfillment, and coaches can help people identify activities that are engaging and enlivening. There is a vast body of research affirming the benefits of social engagement in enhancing well-being, even in the face of illness, such as mind-body skills groups for cancer (Gordon & Harazduk, 1999). As people age, they may experience cumulative losses, such as the deaths of parents, siblings, friends, spouses, or partners. Some people are at a loss as to how to cope with feelings of anger and sadness. Especially for people who are at a distance from family members, finding support beyond the initial stage of mourning the loss of a partner may be difficult. Churches or synagogues and hospice organizations offer bereavement and social support, which are great resources for the coach to recommend to grieving clients and their families and to widowed older adults (Silverman, 2004).

A resilient community is more likely to provide care; resilient communities "grow out of positive personal relationships and sufficient nurturing resources" (Greene, Cohen, Gonzalez, Lee, & Evans, 2007, p. 229). For midlife and older adults who are caregivers (and most are or will be caregivers for one or more older adults), an assessment of the challenges and risks is important, balanced by an awareness of the "gifts of caregiving" (Goldman, 2002). Being in a community, such as a support group for caregivers of persons with dementia or other debilitating conditions, provides reinforcement for this crucial role and often respite to help energize the caregiver and prepare him or her for the known and unknown challenges ahead.

Communities support social engagement; in fact, "Social connectivity is critical to longevity and aging in place" (Abbott, Carman, Carman, & Scarfo, 2009, p. 4). Preparing for one's own possible social, physical, psychological, spiritual, and health needs requires awareness of the resources in one's current living environment.

Coaching Applications

- **Brainstorm with your client to identify opportunities for connection and community.** Once he is aware of groups, programs, or organizations, consider cognitive behavioral experiments to help him explore further through action. For a reluctant client, trying something out—one time—can be an excellent first step to opening him up to connecting more with others.

- **Help your client move to action.** For instance, if your client is tired and reluctant to act (and many older people are), selecting what she wants to connect to may seem like an overwhelming and unwelcome task. Coaching takes patience. Your client's initial connection may be her sessions with you.

- **Focus on caregiving if it impacts your client's life.** Whether your client is a caregiver or receiving care, self-care is critical and can be enhanced through support groups. Encourage your client to find a support group for caregivers.

This type of group would allow him to share experiences and gain resources with others in similar situations.

- **Encourage your client to explore social networking as an option to connect with others.** "Meetup" groups (www.meetup.com) can easily be found or initiated based on interest and geographical location. Meetup.com's motto is "do something, learn something, share something, change something."

ATTITUDE: POSITIVE AGING

Since the late 1990s, a new movement known as positive psychology has emerged and taken hold in the popular press as well as in academic circles. Although only limited attention has been paid specifically to older adults in this movement, there is a parallel interest in resilience associated with growing older (Hooyman & Kiyak, 2008), for example among survivors of earlier life trauma (Greene, 2010; Corley, 2010). While reflection and solitude have positive benefits in later life, it is important to balance these with activity. "Continuity theory" (Neugarten, Havighurst, & Tobin, 1968) suggests that people's lifelong propensities help them adapt to aging. The burgeoning area broadly defined as "positive aging" has spawned an annual conference and related activities. As Moody states, "It's been said that the best way to predict the future is to create it . . . and positive aging is the future we want to create" (personal communication, February 2010).

In gerontology specifically, there are theories related to spirituality, such as gerotranscendence (Tornstam, 2005), which shed light on the importance of reflection and represent a shift in perspective "from a materialistic, rational view of the world to a more cosmic and transcendent one, normally accompanied by an increase in life satisfaction" (Hooyman & Kiyak, 2008, p. 311). Erikson (cited in Hooyman & Kiyak, 2008) similarly posits that the final psychosocial stage of "ego integrity versus despair" concerns self-acceptance and finding meaning in the whole of one's life (Hooyman & Kiyak, 2008).

There is increasing attention to such activities as reminiscence, life review, and autobiography in the aging field to help older adults integrate their life experiences and leave a legacy when possible (Hooyman & Kiyak, 2008; Cohen, 2000). Structured approaches, such as Guided Autobiography (Birren & Svensson, 2006; Birren & Cochran, 2001; Birren & Deutchman, 1991) and the Illuminated Life (www.illuminatedlife.hawaii.edu), provide a group experience for reflection and sharing of life experiences and worldview, as well as engaging in a creative process around life themes. Creating a "Third Age Life Portfolio" will help mindfully integrate and diversify personal investments in "creativity, work, play, love, service, learning, community, selfcare, and spirituality" (Sadler, 2006, p. 17).

Coaching Applications

- **Work with your client to strengthen her awareness around attitude.** Although all of the components of aging (awareness, activity, affiliation, and attitude) influence each other, attitude may be the most critical component as people grow older.

- **Focus on ways to improve attitude.** Be open to exploring with your client the variety of ways she can change her attitude, including everything from spiritual practices to card playing to adopting a pet to taking up yoga.

Additional Reading

Cohen, G. (2000). *The creative age: Awakening human potential in the second half of life.* New York: Avon.

The late Gene Cohen weaves research, stories, and suggestions for how creativity enhances well-being and the management of adversity in the later years, and also outlines four stages of development in later life.

Goldman, C. (2002). *The gifts of caregiving: Stories of hardship, hope and healing.* Minneapolis, MN: Fairview Press.

Many a caregiver has been inspired by this book of uplifting stories crafted by journalist Connie Goldman; there is an accompanying CD of selected contents from the radio broadcast.

Goldman, C. (2004). *Ageless spirit: Reflections on living life to the fullest in midlife and the years beyond.* Minneapolis, MN: Fairview Press.

Inspiration and reflection are triggered by reading fifty poignant stories in the words of writers, artists, actors, and other well-known personalities, including cartoonist Charles Schulz and poet May Sarton.

Goldman, C., & Mahler, R. (2007). *Secrets of becoming a late bloomer: The art of staying creative, involved, and aware in mid-life and beyond.* Minneapolis, MN: Fairview Press.

This book is full of inspirational tales from extraordinary ordinary older individuals about overcoming limitations, accepting new challenges, examining values, and contemplating the meaning of life, along with strategies to bring out the late bloomer in each of us.

Moody, H. R., & Carroll, D. (1998). *Five stages of the soul: Charting the spiritual passages that shape our lives.* New York: Random House.

Spiritual growth is a key element of positive aging, and this classic book highlights distinct stages (the call, the search, the struggle, the breakthrough, and the return) in the process.

Richardson, C. (2002). *Life makeovers: 52 practical and inspiring ways to improve your life one week at a time.* New York: Random House.

Although this book from a prominent coach is not targeted to the aging population, many of the chapters (one for each week of the year) address fitness and wellness with direct guidelines and resources for taking action.

Rowe, J., & Kahn, R. (1997). *Successful aging.* New York: Random House.

This classic book based on research funded by the MacArthur Foundation identifies three key components of successful aging, along with practical suggestions and advice for optimizing well-being in later life.

Sinetar, M. (2002). *Don't call me old, I'm just awakening! Spiritual encouragement for later life.* Mahwah, NJ: Paulist Press.

This book, which applies equally well to the Attitude section that follows, is based on a series of letters between two women friends as they share their wisdom on growing older, highlighting the role of connection in well-being.

Vaillant, G. (2002). *Aging well: Surprising guideposts to a happier life from the landmark Harvard study of adult development.* New York: Little, Brown.

Using data from multiple longitudinal surveys along with anecdotal stories of elders, Vaillant discusses important factors associated with wellness, including exercise and maintaining a healthy weight as well as social and intellectual stimulation.

chapter TWENTY-FOUR

Culture and Cultural Intelligence

Katrina Burrus

What *is* culture exactly? A few definitions: "Culture is the way in which a group of people solves problems and reconciles dilemmas. . . . A problem that is regularly solved disappears from consciousness and becomes a basic assumption, an underlying premise" (Trompenaars & Hampden-Turner, 1998, pp. 3, 7). "Culture consists of shared mental programs that condition individuals' responses to their environment" (Hofstede, quoted in Thomas & Inkson, 2003, p. 22). "[Culture is] the sum total of all the shared, taken-for-granted assumptions that a group has learned throughout its history. It is the residue of success" (Schein, 1992, p. 29).

Culture has been compared to an iceberg. Its visible tip represents behaviors, words, customs, and traditions; the larger part of culture remains hidden, representing beliefs, values, assumptions, and thought processes.

In today's interconnected, global world, failing to integrate culturally within an organization is the most important cause of derailment (Watkins, 2003). A coaching process that heightens the leader's cultural intelligence (Plum, 2007) can accelerate the integration process, bringing with it faster bottom-line value. The coach plays an important role in a client's transition to a new position or country and can benefit from knowing some key cultural concepts. A coach should facilitate understanding of different types of culture: national (United States versus France versus Korea), regional (New York versus California), organizational (for profit versus nonprofit), and functional (marketing versus accounting). A coach may also encounter two different types of clients: those who have lived overseas as adults and those who while growing up had significant experiences abroad that affected their cultural identities.

DIMENSIONS OF CULTURAL DIFFERENCES: HOFSTEDE

A pioneer in the study of defining cultures by certain variables, Geert Hofstede (1980) analyzed a large database of employee value scores within IBM from seventy countries around the world. He later extended his studies to other population categories, demonstrating that national and regional cultural groupings affect the behavior of societies and organizations persistently across time. He developed a cultural dimension model that reflects major cultural differences in how people from certain cultures think, feel, and behave over time.

CULTURAL INTELLIGENCE: GOLEMAN

The concept of cultural intelligence was based on Goleman's theory of emotional intelligence or EQ (1998) and Gardner's work on multiple intelligences (1983). Plum (2007) defines cultural intelligence as "the ability to make oneself understood and the ability to create a fruitful collaboration in situations where cultural differences play a role" (p. 1). Emotional intelligence as conceived by Goleman does not explain the worldview developed by a person with a multicultural identity. Someone can be emotionally intelligent and yet clueless as to how to adapt to a new cultural environment. Nor does high EQ insight necessarily lead to success in a cross-cultural environment. Individuals need to be willing and able not only to adapt their behavior to the cultural context (Plum, 2007) but also to shift assumptions that are usually held at a preconscious level.

CULTURAL DIFFERENCES: TROMPENAARS AND HAMPDEN-TURNER

According to Trompenaars and Hampden-Turner (1998), culture operates at essentially three different levels:

1. National or ethnic

2. Organizational or corporate

3. Functions within an organization

At each of these levels, one can look at the following three aspects of culture: relationships, time, and environment. Particular characteristics can be assessed on a continuum, with each variable at opposite ends of the scale. These dimensions of cultural differences are not intended to label or discriminate but rather to allow for learning and understanding of the similarities and differences across cultures. The first five of these aspects of culture concern relationships; the next two are about attitudes to time; the last one deals with the way an individual relates to the cultural environment.

Universalism Versus Particularism

Universalist cultures respect the rules first, whereas particularist cultures place friendship before abstract societal rules. Trompenaars and Hampden-Turner demonstrated this cultural opposition using the example of a car accident (1998). In universalist cultures, the majority of the population is not ready to "lie" to help out a friend who is responsible for a car accident, whereas in particularist cultures, most people would "lie" and testify in a friend's favor.

Members of universalist cultures believe that what is right and good can be defined and applied to all situations. They place legal contracts and rules above relationships. A trustworthy person is one who honors his word or contract. There is only one truth or reality: that which has been agreed on. For particularists, legal contracts are merely a starting point and can be readily modified. What is right depends on relationships and circumstances. A trustworthy person is the one who honors changing mutualities.

Individualism Versus Collectivism

Members of individualist cultures take care of themselves and close family; ideally they achieve alone and assume personal responsibility. Work-related decisions are made on the spot by representatives. Groups are more widely defined in collectivist cultures and include close and more distant relatives and friends. Achievements are attributed to groups, and decisions are referred back to the organization. Collectivists are likely to enjoy going on vacations in organized groups or with extended friends and family, whereas individualists often travel alone or in pairs.

Neutral Versus Emotional

Members of neutral cultures do not express feelings and emotions in public, remaining cool and self-controlled. Emotions occasionally explode. Physical contact, gesturing, and strong facial expressions are often taboo, unlike in emotional cultures, where thoughts are revealed verbally and nonverbally. Sharing one's emotions is viewed as a way of releasing tension.

Specific Versus Diffuse

Whereas specific cultures separate public and private lives and define business by contract, diffuse cultures involve the whole person in the business relationship. Morality in a diffuse culture is highly situational, depending on the person and the context. Tact is valued. People from specific cultures, who want to get straight to the point and close the deal, may find it hard to understand people from diffuse cultures, viewing their behavior as evasive and ambiguous. Turnover rates are far higher in specific cultures, where results are expected to come quickly, than in diffuse cultures, where managers try to motivate failing employees.

Achievement Versus Ascription

Achievement-oriented cultures judge people by their accomplishments, whereas in ascription-oriented cultures, status results from birth, kinship, gender, age, and connections. In an achievement-oriented culture, titles are relevant only when linked to one's competencies. Respect toward superiors is based on their effectiveness, and competent people in authority vary in age and gender. It is not unusual to see young people in positions of authority. In ascription-oriented cultures, titles are used extensively, and people respect hierarchy. Most high-level positions are held by middle-aged men qualified by their background.

Past Versus Future Orientation

Whereas some cultures tend to look toward the future, others are fatalistic and look toward the past to predict the future. In past-oriented cultures, the respect shown for ancestors, predecessors, and elders is paramount. It is unlikely for the boss to be younger than an employee. Future-oriented cultures focus on youth and potential. People aim for future successes and enthusiastically engage in planning and strategizing.

Sequential Versus Synchronic

In cultures with a sequential or monochronic orientation, time is precisely divided, and more importance is given to schedules than to relationships. People generally prefer doing one activity at a time according to a well-established plan. In synchronic or polychronic cultures, in contrast, people tend to do several things at once and are less likely to respect schedules. Importance is given to the completion of the task and to communication rather than to preestablished planning.

Internal Versus External

In cultures with an inner-directed orientation, convictions are readily expressed through conflict and resistance; focus is on oneself, one's group, and one's organization; and people feel discomfort when their environment—business, social, or political—seems out of control. Cultures with an outer-directed orientation adopt a more flexible attitude and are more likely to seek compromise and maintain harmony. Focus is on others—customers, partners, colleagues—and change is viewed as natural.

Coaching Applications

- **Be willing to adapt your coaching style to the culture of your client.** Coaching in a universalist culture may entail laying out an organized, formal plan. In contrast, coaching in a particularist culture may involve a considerable amount of time invested in developing the relationship before the coaching begins.

- **At the same time, in accommodating to the foreign environment, don't abandon the skills and patterns you have developed in your own culture.** A client from a diffuse culture, for example, might be comfortable letting things gradually unfold, whereas a client from a specific culture might expect efficiency, structure, and having the process made explicit in advance. Be conscious of separating your incidental cultural preferences from your professional understanding of what is required for a successful coaching engagement.

- **Support your client in adapting his work style to the culture of his new work environment.** You might, for example, assist a general manager from an individualist culture who is working in a communitarian work environment in adjusting the organization's reward systems and ways of managing direct reports so that rewards go to the team.

CROSS-CULTURAL MANAGEMENT: SCHWABENLAND, SACKMANN, AND PHILLIPS

The dominant theories in the field of cross-cultural management are based on the idea that "national cultures can be defined, measured and located on dimensions representing various sets of values" (Schwabenland, 2006, p. 102). This type of generalization may be perceived as simplistic and no longer applicable to today's reality. "In a multi-cultural and diverse society, culture can no longer be implicitly defined as a substitute for nation, and members of such societies can no longer be assumed to identify solely or most strongly with their country of national origin or citizenship" (Sackmann & Phillips, 2004, p. 384).

The classical concepts do not portray the complexity and ambiguity of today's multicultural environment. After World War II, there was a mass migration of human populations worldwide. As a consequence, many expatriates spent extensive periods of time in foreign countries. Their children developed a sense of belonging to both home and host cultures, with the result that they blend elements from different cultures, producing a "third" culture (Van Reken & Pollock, 2009). These children have been termed *third culture kids* (TCKs).

Many TCKs developed a multicultural intelligence that corresponds to Bennett's "most extreme case of ethnorelativism: Integration" (Bennett & Bennett, 2004, p. 163). "In this case identity is meant as maintaining a meta-level to one's experience" (p. 157). With a bicultural or multicultural perspective, the individual is able to see multiple worldviews and maintain a meta- or higher-level look without being attached to any one culture or perspective. This attitude stands in contrast to ethnocentrism, which places experiences of one's own culture as "central to reality" (Bennett, 2004, p. 1), where beliefs and behaviors of early socialization remain unquestioned. Ethnorelativism means to "experience one's own beliefs and behaviors as just one organization of reality among many viable possibilities" (p. 62).

GLOBAL NOMADIC LEADERS: BURRUS

Amid accelerating change and globalization, companies are increasingly faced with the difficult challenge of developing global and highly mobile leaders. Global nomadic leaders (GNLs) were raised in multiple countries, speak multiple languages, and have moved multiple times. They are *global* and very comfortable working everywhere and living anywhere. If you ask them where they come from, they hesitate to answer with any specific country. A leader may have been born in India, grown up in Saudi Arabia, and attended university in the United States, and now works in Europe. An example of a GNL is President Obama. He is multiracial; his parents come from different continents. He has had significant experiences in Indonesia and moved many times while growing up. GNLs are *nomadic* in the sense that from their early years they have experienced multiple moves and have integrated a migratory instinct that they perpetuate as adult leaders. Some decide consciously and deliberately to remain grounded for periods of their life. Here we shall focus on those who continue their mobile lifestyles.

Research shows that GNLs possess multicultural intelligence and are sought after by multinationals for their worldview. It seems that being relatively detached from specific cultures, they are able to develop a greater cross-cultural sensitivity.

Companies are in dire need of leaders who possess an exceptional ability to accelerate business development in complex cultural environments. The chairman and past CEO of Nestlé, Peter Brabeck-Letmathe, also emphasizes the need for multicultural intelligence combined with firsthand international experience in multinational companies: "You cannot limit yourself to knowing just one culture, for you need to have an understanding of and respect for different national cultures. . . . When you are selling food . . . you are participating in the consumers' cultural relationship with food, and this requires a much stronger understanding of the country's culture. The consumers' relationship to food is highly emotional and culturally specific" (quoted in Burrus-Barbey, 2000, p. 498).

GNLs demonstrate multicultural intelligence in a number of ways. They

- Thrive on complex situations and need new challenges

- Distinguish more readily what is common to all humans from what is culturally specific

- Compare and contrast different cultural emotions, perceptions, and behaviors, always negotiating within themselves their multiple cultural identities

- Question the local status quo to push forward objectives by using a different set of assumptions and developing competencies to respond appropriately and blend in

- Use the capacity for empathy that derives from their multicultural status—the ability to put themselves in the other person's shoes (Thomas & Inkson,

2003)—in order to negotiate multiple cultural identities in the search for a broader perspective (Burrus, 2009)

- Adapt rapidly, enjoying the challenge and variety, and being open and curious while viewing their experience at a metalevel (Bennett, 2004; Burrus, 2009), which allows them to more readily suspend judgment, observe, learn, and negotiate

A possible downside might be a lack of long-term commitment. GNLs can feel rootless during periods of their lives; become exasperated when they lose one of their anchors, such as an important relationship or job; or become disenchanted with their mission. In reaction to feeling rootless, certain leaders will purchase homes where they have created an emotional tie, where they want to create a home base for their children, or where they want to connect to the roots of their partner.

Coaching Applications

- **Assess whether a client identifies with a specific culture, or several.** A background history helps determine what significant cultural experience she has had and what her rhythm of change has been. If you ask her which country she comes from, any hesitation or a long explanation of all the places she has lived might indicate that her identity is multicultural.

- **Identify any sense of rootlessness the client is experiencing by verifying whether there is a sudden desire to change jobs, apartments, or homes.** While some GNLs will respond to discomfort by purchasing homes or reconnecting with lost friends or family so as to feel more grounded, many will instigate change. Explore with your client what drives his need for change. Is it restlessness, boredom, or the desire to avoid a painful situation?

- **When working with a GNL, explore with her what serves as a stabilizing factor in her mobile lifestyle.** Possible stabilizing factors might be the company, the family, a corporate mission, a house, a significant relationship, or a virtual network of people. Ask her what she must have to feel good anywhere.

- **Identify the local cultural and leadership needs and expectations.** This is essential in adapting the GNL's abilities to the leadership needs of the multinational organization. It might be appropriate to interview the client's boss, peers, and employees to highlight different values, priorities, and assumptions. It might also be important to ask what is rewarded and what is taboo within the organization.

- **Be alert to the GNL's characteristic talents: flexibility, tolerance, curiosity, adaptability, and a capacity to contain complexity and nuance.** Explore with your client when and how he enacts these qualities. Coaching GNLs requires you to be able to grasp the complexity of multiple perspectives (Sackmann, 1997).

Additional Reading

Burrus, K. (2009). Coaching managers in multinational companies: Myths and realities of the itinerant executive. In G. Abbott (Ed.), *The Routledge companion to international business coaching* (pp. 230–238). London: Routledge.

This handbook offers the first comprehensive and detailed introduction to the theory and practice of international business coaching.

Hofstede, G. (2009). Geert Hofstede Cultural Dimensions. www.geert-hofstede.com/.

Hofstede's Web site provides an interactive resource to compare the cultural dimensions for various cultures. The site also includes information on business etiquette around the world.

Thomas, D. C., & Inkson, K. (2003). *Cultural intelligence: People skills for global business.* San Francisco: Berrett-Koehler.

This reviews what type of cultural intelligence is necessary in a global environment.

Trompenaars, F., & Hampden-Turner, C. (1998). *Riding the waves of culture: Understanding cultural diversity in global business.* New York: McGraw-Hill.

This book is a classic and reviews cultural differences mainly across nations, but it also explicates corporate culture.

Rosinski, P. (2003). *Coaching across cultures: New tools for leveraging national, corporate, and professional differences.* London: Brealey.

Rosinski clarifies the connection between personal, organizational, and community goals. He takes a multiple-perspective approach to linking local and global cultures.

Issues of Gender

chapter TWENTY-FIVE

Karen Tweedie and Leni Wildflower

Sally Helgesen (1995), Deborah Tannen (1990, 1994), and Carol Gilligan (1982), among other feminist researchers, argue that there is a culture specific to the female gender. Helgesen states that there are qualities women leaders bring to organizations. Tannen postulates that men and women have different ways of speaking, both in their personal and professional lives. And according to Gilligan, women's moral development is culturally distinct from moral development in men. Both styles—male and female—are equally valid. The tension comes in the effort of each to understand and appreciate the other style. Arlie Hochschild (1989, 1997) argues that gender continues to place women at the center of housework and family life, even when both partners are working full-time. Gersick and Kram (2002) looked at high-achieving women at midlife to research the issues and needs of this particular cohort. Consistent with the findings of Tannen and others, Gersick and Kram confirmed that the women in their study derived great benefit from having access to, and conversations with, women at similar stages of life who are facing similar challenges.

GENDER AND DEVELOPMENT OF MORALITY: CAROL GILLIGAN

The conflict between self and other constitutes the central moral problem for women, posing a dilemma whose resolution requires a reconciliation between femininity and adulthood. . . . It is precisely this dilemma—the conflict between compassion and autonomy, between virtue and power—which the feminine voice struggles to resolve in its effort to reclaim the self and to solve the moral problem in such a way that no one is hurt. (Gilligan, 1998, p. 356)

Gilligan's groundbreaking book, *In a Different Voice: Psychological Theory and Women's Development* (1982), theorizes that women's moral development is different from men's, organized around notions of responsibility and care. Gilligan challenged Lawrence Kohlberg's theory of moral development (1976), objecting that his findings were based only on studies of men and boys, and arguing that, for women, transitions between the stages of moral development are fueled by changes in a sense of self rather than changes in cognitive capability. According to Gilligan, women make moral choices based less on rules (the traditionally masculine method) and more on an understanding of the context for moral choice. Women focus on the needs of individuals and on relationships, and this guides their moral choices and decisions. In addition to moral development, female identity and conceptions of self are rooted in a sense of connection and relatedness to others.

Coaching Applications

- **Remember that the best theories and findings on gender difference can only reveal tendencies.** They cannot predict how any particular person will think or act or feel. The extent to which individuals emphasize rules or context in making moral choices, for example, may or may not be shaped by their gender. In your role as a coach, always listen for your client's unique perspective.

- **Be alert to signs of tension in your client between the need for autonomy and the need for connection.** A capacity for caring and relationship can be a great asset in the workplace. It can also be a liability. Women in particular may need coaching to become more assertive and independent in professional situations.

- **Be aware that your client may need support in promoting a culture at work that is more collaborative and sympathetic.** Most business organizations are dominated by men, and are often "masculine" in culture—hierarchical, competitive, individualistic. With reference to Gilligan, you can help your female client understand this culture better, while supporting her in asserting the benefits of feminine ways of functioning.

GENDER AND WORK-LIFE BALANCE:
ARLIE RUSSELL HOCHSCHILD

[G]ender shapes time usage and quality. Not only is employed women's total time commitment to paid and unpaid work equal to or greater than that of employed men, but women's work in the home is different—more arduous, less flexible, and more likely to be interrupted. These factors . . . suggest that women will feel that it is more difficult to balance work and family than men will. (Milkie & Peltola, 1999, p. 480)

In two of her important researched works, *The Second Shift* (1989) and *The Time Bind* (1997), Hochschild describes a variety of complications faced by working couples with families. *The Second Shift* concentrates on the various strategies couples have used to pursue full-time careers while simultaneously raising a family. The second shift refers to the jobs that need to be done to keep the family going—cooking, cleaning, spending time with children, and so on. Hochschild refers to the current position of women as the "stalled revolution." The women's movement got women out of the home and into the first shift of paid employment, but, in her opinion, resulted in little change in the second (domestic) shift. In 80 percent of the working couples Hochschild interviewed, women still assume the major burden of house and family care. Moreover, Hochschild, among other researchers, reports that the type of housework working men most commonly perform allows them more flexibility and is usually deemed more challenging—such as lawn maintenance and house or car repair work. In contrast, the work of cooking, cleaning, washing dishes, and caring for sick children—the territory most women inhabit—is repetitive, performed on a daily basis, and often not particularly challenging.

Coaching Applications

- **Help your client visualize how her time is spent.** This is probably one of the most common issues when coaching working women. There are no easy answers, but the balance wheel is an excellent tool to begin exploring allocation of time. Published in various versions, the balance wheel is essentially a pie chart with six or eight segments that represent aspects of a well-rounded life, such as work, relationships, financial stability, spiritual well-being, physical health, fun, personal growth, and contribution to others' lives (Richardson, 1999; Whitworth, Kimsey-House, & Sandahl, 1998). Ask your client to describe what an ideal balance wheel would look like for her. What is she neglecting? Where does she need to cut back?

- **Ask the client how she takes care of herself.** The segment of the balance wheel that women most often neglect is attending to their own physical, mental, and spiritual well-being. When appropriate, help your client devise activities for self-care and self-renewal, such as relaxation techniques, exercise, reading, meditation, and so on.

- **Encourage your client to develop a plan for her personal life.** She may have to negotiate with her partner about second-shift responsibilities. Help her outline a reasonable division of labor in the family and devise strategies for negotiating toward a productive outcome.

- **Help your client acknowledge loss and to work through grief.** Women are sometimes encouraged to believe that they can have it all, even to feel that they've failed if they haven't achieved this. But the fact is that if a working mother wants to be with her infant during the first months of life or longer, she has to interrupt her career. More children mean more interruptions, which may threaten her advancement over the long run. Whatever the details of her situation, helping her grieve what she doesn't have will enable her to cope with life's limitations and move on.

- **Be aware that a male client may also be juggling the demands of a job with domestic responsibilities.** Second-shift issues, though characteristic of the female experience, are not unique to women.

GENDER AND CONVERSATIONAL STYLES: DEBORAH TANNEN

Deborah Tannen has written extensively on the different ways in which gender affects conversational style (1990, 1994). According to Tannen, men and women have different ways of communicating and derive different meanings from language.

> There are gender differences in ways of speaking, and we need to identify and understand them. Without such understanding, we are doomed to blame others or ourselves—or the relationship—for the

otherwise mystifying and damaging effects of our contrasting conversational styles. . . . Recognizing gender differences frees individuals from the burden of individual pathology. . . . Taking a sociolinguistic approach to relationships makes it possible to explain these dissatisfactions without accusing anyone of being crazy or wrong, and without blaming—or discarding—the relationship. (Tannen, 1990, p. 17)

Where women characteristically use language to seek confirmation, make connections, and reinforce intimacies, men are more likely to use it to protect their independence and negotiate status. These patterns are not immutable, however. Both men and women can learn to understand, appreciate, and even adopt some of each other's language styles in an effort to improve both communication and relationships. The following are examples of stereotypical gender contrasts taken from Tannen's work. They can best be understood not as descriptions of how individual men and women behave but as characteristic male-female dichotomies.

Status versus support. Conversation for men is often a contest, either to achieve the upper hand or to prevent other people from pushing them around. For women, talk is more likely to be a way of expressing mutual support.

Independence versus intimacy. Women often use conversation to preserve intimacy, whereas men use it to assert their independence.

Advice versus understanding. Often, women want someone to listen to their problems with understanding, whereas men are inclined to give advice and look for solutions.

Orders versus proposals. When a woman says "Let's park over there," a man can hear it as an order. "Do you want to clean up now, before lunch?" can come across as an attempt to manipulate.

Conflict versus compromise. Generally, men are more comfortable with verbal conflict. Women tend not to ask directly for what they want. She sees him as being confrontational. He sees her as being manipulative.

Coaching Applications

- **Consider explaining Tannen's male-female dichotomies to your client if she or he has trouble communicating with a boss, direct report, or partner of** the opposite sex. Both men and women can benefit from learning to understand and interpret each other's language styles. (You might recommend Tannen's *You Don't Understand*, 1990, or, for a more popular treatment of the same concept, John Gray's *Men Are from Mars, Women Are from Venus*, 1992.)

- **With a client encountering difficulties in this area, suggest Tannen's dichotomies as a framework for discussing the problem with the other person.** Tannen's work takes the "blame game" out of gender-based misunderstandings and is alert to the humor of male-female misunderstandings. Brainstorm with your client ways to present this material in a way that would ease the tension.

- **Be conscious of the subtle ways in which your own style as a coach might be influenced by your gender.** Be alert for signs of misunderstanding between you and a client of the opposite sex, which might be rooted in different ways of thinking or talking.

GENDER AND FEMALE LEADERSHIP: SALLY HELGESEN

Sally Helgesen asserts that because of a variety of factors, women in leadership positions display certain distinct leadership qualities that have become both needed and valued in today's world. Her research (1995) found the following behaviors particular to female managers:

- Women worked at a steady pace, but with small breaks scheduled throughout the day.

- Women did not view unscheduled tasks and encounters as interruptions. They tended to view them as part of caring, being involved, helping, and being responsible.

- Women made time for activities not directly related to their work.

- Women maintained a complex network of relationships with people outside their organization.

- Women saw their identities as complex and multifaceted.

From this research, Helgesen (1995) concludes that women leaders have developed skills that are multifaceted, collaborative, networked, creative, and democratic. These qualities present the possibility of a qualitatively different kind of leadership style—one that is more democratic and inclusive.

Coaching Applications

- **If it seems appropriate, introduce your client to Helgesen's work.** It can be inspiring reading for young female managers, providing perspective on successful role models who have developed networked, collaborative ways of leading, and making them more conscious of their own styles of leadership. Male leaders also might benefit from a knowledge of different leadership styles. A client, whether male or female, who is facing an unexpected or intractable challenge can sometimes achieve a breakthrough by trying out a style more characteristic of the other gender.

- **As with any gender-based distinctions, be aware that these generalizations might not apply to an individual client.** Such findings can alert us to trends, but are not one-size-fits-all descriptions of human behavior.

- **When coaching clients of the opposite sex, be aware that their aims, ways of working, and ways of interacting might be different from yours.** Good coaching always involves tuning in to the particular concerns and priorities of the client. Awareness of gender difference just adds another dimension.

GENDER AND HIGH-ACHIEVING WOMEN AT MIDLIFE: CONNIE GERSICK AND KATHY KRAM

Using Levinson's model of adult development, Gersick and Kram (2002) conducted an exploratory study that involved interviewing a small cohort of high-achieving executive women ages forty-five to fifty-five from the financial services industry. The authors were interested in the patterns of individuals' lives over the whole life course. They outlined participants' developmental work in terms of finding a life role (in their twenties), managing career-family trade-offs (in their thirties), and coming into their own (at fifty and beyond). Among the women they interviewed, Gersick and Kram found that by the fifties transition, some women had begun some fundamental changes in the character of their lives. They had newfound confidence in their abilities and a zest for new learning that they had not expected during these years.

Specific findings from Gersick and Kram's in-depth interviews with this group of high-achieving women at midlife include the following:

- Whereas for men, separateness seems to be an indicator of maturity, for women, relationships are of fundamental importance to the construction of their lives. (This supports Gilligan's findings on female emotional and moral development.)

- There is often internal conflict between the "traditional" woman, who must have the security of marriage and family, and the "antitraditional" woman, who eschews dependency and seeks control over her own life—even though she may not have role models or be sure what this could look like.

- There is an absence of mentoring available to women after their thirties. As women become more senior at work, face new challenges, have increasing visibility and responsibility in their jobs, and approach the glass ceiling, there is an increase in complexity in their life structure that can be mastered only with great flexibility and creativity.

- Most women interviewed wanted promotions and other rewards for their contributions at work, but were not prepared to devote themselves to "strategizing" solely for the purpose of getting ahead in the business world.

- Women saw a difference between leadership and being at the top. In a male hierarchy, being at the top means being dominant. For these women, the role of the leader was to be a catalyst. In their view, an adaptive organization was one with multiple leaders serving as catalysts.

- These women assumed there were limitations to their opportunities for career advancement. And they were acutely aware of the need for personal and family trade-offs when faced with the challenge of the two-career household.

- The timing of childbearing did not appear to be a significant factor in a woman's career and family satisfaction. Most important were the strategies she used to balance the different aspects of her life.

Coaching Applications

- **Let your high-achieving female client know that she's not alone.** She may not be connected to a peer group of women of the same status. It might help her to know that other women of a similar age, having achieved a similar level of success, are dealing with equivalent issues.

- **Be ready to help your midlife female client develop in new directions, away from her current career ladder.** This may not be the stated issue at the beginning of the coaching engagement. It may be something she hasn't thought much about yet, or acknowledged as an ambition. But be prepared for it to come up.

- **Discuss with your client what she might like to spend more time on, and how to make more room in her life for activities not related to her own work.** This might involve taking up new interests or cultivating interests and talents she has neglected.

- **Help a client who has achieved success in a predominantly male environment to remember the value of connecting with other women.** This might range from mentoring younger women in her workplace to attending to friendships outside work.

Additional Reading

Bateson, M. C. (1989). *Composing a life*. New York: Grove Press.
  Daughter of the famous anthropologist Margaret Mead, Mary Catherine Bateson looks at the lives of a range of different women in terms of choices they made and their notions of what creates a sense of accomplishment in life.

Elgin, S. H. (1993). *Genderspeak: Men, women, and the gentle art of verbal self-defense*. Hoboken, NJ: Wiley.
  A popular, practical book giving specific examples of how women can use language skillfully to manage a range of personal and professional situations.

Gilligan, C. (1982). *In a different voice: Psychological theory and women's development*. Cambridge, MA: Harvard University Press.
  Academic in tone, but very accessible, Gilligan's classic work outlines her theory about women and learning styles.

Helgesen, S. (1995). *The female advantage: Women's ways of leadership*. New York: Doubleday Currency.
  An excellent book for new managers. It's instructional and also supportive of female managers and leaders.

Helgesen, S., & Johnson, J. (2010). *The female vision: Women's real power at work*. San Francisco: Berrett-Koehler.
  A look at the ways in which what Helgesen terms female ways of working can be a powerful force.

Hochschild, A. R. (1989). *The second shift*. New York: Penguin Books.
  The study that reignited interest in the pressures on working families. Full of engaging case studies.

Hochschild, A. R. (1997). *The time bind: When work becomes home and home becomes work*. New York: Henry Holt.
  Very accessible reading about the pressures of career and home.

Tannen, D. (1990). *You just don't understand: Women and men in conversation.* New York: Ballantine Books.

This book focuses on differences in conversation style often occurring in male-female relationships.

Tannen, D. (1994). *Talking from 9 to 5: How women's and men's conversational styles affect who gets heard, who gets credit, and what gets done at work.* New York: Morrow.

This book applies the concepts of *You Just Don't Understand* to the workplace.

chapter TWENTY-SIX

Environmental Sustainability

Katrina S. Rogers

Sustainability has become a new and exciting topic for coaches working both with individuals and within organizations. Sustainability can best be understood as a system of changing the way people and organizations function. It involves basically three areas of work: social, economic, and environmental.

According to one influential model (Adams, 2006) any two of these factors might be in alignment without the conditions of full sustainability being achieved. When social and environmental needs for sustainability are met, conditions are described as *bearable*. Meeting environmental and economic needs makes things *viable*. When economic and social conditions align, conditions are *equitable*. Sustainable development occurs only when all three are in concert, when the needs of all three are met and nothing is sacrificed. Although this model directs attention to the conditions of sustainability, it does not accurately reflect that the natural resources from the environment are what lie at the basis of economies and societies.

Scholars arguing for sustainable development have suggested that showing that economy and society have natural constraints is a first step in creating more sustainable systems (Adams, 2006). There is now abundant evidence that humankind is living unsustainably on the planet (for example, see the Earth Policy Institute Web site, www.earth-policy.org/). These data further support the idea that organizations and their leaders are, or soon will be, under pressure to design systems to support healthier organizations within natural constraints. In this

251

conceptualization, economy and society are seen as nested within the larger circle of the natural environment.

To operationalize a deeper understanding of sustainability in her professional life, the sustainable coach requires a toolkit for sustainability. This toolkit comprises three elements: a change in thinking toward a more sustainable worldview; a willingness to build a skill set in sustainability, and knowledge of the latest sustainable frameworks used in the field.

Consistent with theories of adult development, people's thinking about sustainability evolves as they mature over their life course (Boiral, Cayer, & Baron, 2009). As a coach, you need to be aware of the different phases of sustainability understanding as a client matures. As we move away from simple concepts about the external world, we also develop the capacity to think in ways that lend themselves to sustainability.

Sustainable thinking has three basic characteristics: (1) moving from short-term thinking to taking a long view of things; (2) moving from thinking of the economy as something outside of nature to something that is integrated with and supported by nature; and (3) moving from thinking about a linear flow of resources to thinking about the ways resources flow through a system.

There are several frameworks that are useful for understanding the ways in which the concept of sustainability is being applied across organizational settings. These frameworks are the ecological footprint, the natural step, natural capitalism, industrial ecology, cradle-to-cradle, and biomimicry. They exemplify the latest research and practice in the field of sustainability, and will be of most use to coaches working with sustainability in organizational settings.

THE ECOLOGICAL FOOTPRINT

The *ecological footprint* is a measure of human demand on the Earth's ecosystem (Rees, Wackernagel, & Testemale, 1996). The term is now in use by many organizations and on Web sites dedicated to discussions about calculating the carrying capacity of the Earth. This carrying capacity is a measure of how much land and water area a human population requires to produce the resources it consumes and to absorb its wastes. The ecological footprint for all of humankind is currently calculated at 1.4, meaning that humankind consumes 1.4 planet Earths per year. (For more information, see the Global Footprint Network Web site, www.footprintnetwork.org/en/index.php/GFN/). Another way to think about this number is that it takes the Earth 1.4 years to regenerate what we use in a year. This is the very definition of unsustainable.

THE NATURAL STEP

The concept of the natural step emerged as a response to the way a cell works as a system. Robèrt, a Swedish scientist, examined how a cell works to maintain health and prevent sickness. He went on to ask whether it would be possible to create a framework that mimicked the efficiency and sustainability of a cell. The framework became known as the *natural step framework* (Robèrt, 1991). Also known as the *framework for strategic sustainable development,* this builds on science and draws from many disciplines to create a plan that allows researchers to measure change toward sustainability.

Becoming sustainable through the natural step framework means eliminating the following from current developmental processes:

1. The impact on the global environment of substances extracted from the earth
2. The buildup of chemicals produced by society
3. The destruction of nature and natural processes
4. Conditions that undermine people's capacity to meet their basic needs

The planning method used by the natural step framework facilitates organizations in considering their nonsustainable activities and plotting a pathway to becoming more sustainable.

NATURAL CAPITALISM

Natural capitalism is a framework used mostly by for-profit companies to reconceptualize their organizations so that they achieve economic goals without degrading the environment. On the basis of work by Paul Hawken, Amory Lovins, and Hunter Lovins (2008), natural capitalists argue that business and environmental interests increasingly overlap, and that a company's next transformation will be to redesign its work so that customer demands are satisfied, profits increase, and environmental needs are met. Natural capital is defined as the total of the natural resources and ecosystem services that make possible all economic activity. This capital is now recognized as having immense economic value, yet we currently work within a set of practices that do not take natural capital into account. This failure to value our natural assets as they connect to economic activity is one of the reasons for the wasteful use of our resources.

The first significant principle of natural capitalism is to radically increase an organization's resource productivity. This entails a complex process of accounting for every element in a production process or organizational flow that is consumed, created, or wasted. Implementing this first principle can reduce waste and create the financing for the other three elements of natural capitalism: redesigning industry on biological models with closed feedback loops, shifting from the sale of goods to the provision of services, and reinvesting in natural capital.

INDUSTRIAL ECOLOGY

Industrial ecology is a field of study that uses a framework for sustainability based on viewing the environment, economics, and technology from a broad sociological perspective. Based on systems theory, industrial ecology focuses on understanding emergent behavior at the point of intersection between human and natural systems (Allenby, 2006).

Organizations that utilize an industrial ecological framework aim to create an industrial system that behaves like an ecosystem, in which the wastes of one species may be resources for another. The goal is to make the outputs of one industry the inputs of another, thus reducing use of raw materials, reducing pollution, and saving on waste treatment. A famous example used by industrial ecologists is a Danish industrial park in the city of Kalundborg. The linkages between the various elements make this an excellent example of industrial ecology in practice. In what is considered to be the world's most elaborate industrial ecosystem, steam and various raw materials, such as sulfur, fly ash, and sludge, are exchanged by users (Peck, 2010). This exchange reduces costs for disposal, improves resource use, and improves sustainable performance. For example, the electrical power station in Kalundborg has been able to use the gas from the oil refinery that used to go to waste. By sending the gas to the power station, the refinery has saved thirty thousand tons of coal a year.

CRADLE-TO-CRADLE

Sustainable frameworks for organizations have at their theoretical core that all organizational processes must be seen through a systems perspective. The *cradle-*

to-cradle framework is premised on the same assumption, but focuses on promoting ecologically intelligent design. In their book *Cradle to Cradle*, McDonough and Braungart (2002) argue that industrial processes themselves are not antithetical to nature, but rather are the outcomes of a time when natural resources seemed infinite.

Given that the Industrial Revolution has had devastating consequences for the environment, the next revolution will be to re-create design to mirror our new thinking about natural resources. In this new spirit of an economic existence constrained by the limited availability of natural resources, designers can employ the intelligence of natural systems. Proponents of cradle-to-cradle thinking use innovative design principles as a way to invent new ways of conducting themselves. The book *Cradle to Cradle* is itself a treeless product made of synthetic paper and resin that can be easily recycled, although it is also durable and waterproof. In every organization, there are countless opportunities to practice ecologically intelligent design.

BIOMIMICRY

Similar to the cradle-to-cradle focus on design, *biomimicry* is an emerging field that imitates elements of nature in design and processes. Originally named by the scientist Janine Benyus (1998), this work focuses on the practical application of ideas gleaned from natural processes. Some examples include the web silk that some spiders create, which is as strong as the Kevlar used in bulletproof vests. Engineers could use this material in such items as parachute lines or suspension bridge cables. Other research has proposed harvesting water from the fog the way a beetle does and creating adhesive glue from mussels, solar cells whose structure is similar to that of leaves, bionic cars inspired by the boxfish, fabric that emulates shark skin, and more. The Biomimicry Institute has compiled a list of "Nature's 100 Best Innovations" inspired by animals, plants, and other organisms. (This list is available at www.n100best.org/innovation/case01.html.)

All these frameworks share the idea that sustainability is both a process that begins with changed thinking and a skill-building task that must be accomplished for organizational health. The following list lays out the various aspects of the coaching sustainability toolkit.

Coaching for Sustainability Toolkit

Change Thinking	Build a Sustainable Skill Set	Know Sustainable Frameworks
Developing a long-term view	Understanding science	Ecological footprint
Understanding environmental constraints	Creating a set of ethical guidelines	The natural step
	Working intentionally toward sustainability	Natural capitalism
Seeing resource flows through systems		Industrial ecology
	Developing systems thinking competency	Cradle-to-cradle
		Biomimicry

Coaching Applications

- **Learn more about the science of sustainability.** There are several excellent books in the field, including *Environmental Science: A Global Concern* (Cunningham & Cunningham, 2009). This work serves as an excellent primer on environmental science for nonscientists, and includes thoughtful analysis of the role of science in decision making. Having a rudimentary knowledge of the science will allow you to begin defining the parameters of the organizational system in which you are working, identifying the nonsustainable elements, and appropriately valuing the resources within the organization.

- **Build a competency in systems thinking, which involves an understanding that elements of the system, product, and process are parts of an integrated whole.** All the parts are related to each other and interdependent, both within the system and between the system and the outside world. When systems thinking is used in sustainability reasoning, then unsustainable activities become exposed, and it is easier to address issues from a longer-term perspective. For example, Nokia wanted to reduce its carbon emissions by reducing its product packaging. Its initial premise was simple: the company asked customers if they would buy phones that didn't come in elaborate packaging. Customers reported that they were happy to purchase phones without packaging, and a sustainable idea was born. According to the Nokia Web site (www.nokia.com/corporate-responsibility/environment/sustainable-behavior/clarity), this change removed twelve thousand trucks from the road and reduced paper use by one hundred tons. Additional examples of systems thinking and organizational sustainability can be found in Paul Hawken's book *The Ecology of Commerce* (1993).

- **Learn to recognize system boundaries within organizations.** It is helpful to conceptualize systems within systems, much like Russian nesting dolls. Helping your client envision where she is located within a system and how her area relates to others will establish this concept of seeing the whole and its parts.

- **Stretch your client's thinking to consider what may sound like abstract notions.** Ask such questions as *How can this coaching engagement meet our moral obligations to both current and future generations? Are there ways to build more community inclusiveness in this work? Are there questions I can ask you that may stimulate conversation about diversity, social equity, and the value of nature to these organizational processes?* As a coach, you might have the opportunity to raise these questions in organizational settings. The report *Our Common Future* (World Commission on Environment and Development, 1987) contains the original definition of sustainable development and can be used to create a set of ethical guidelines for sustainability.

- **To achieve deep engagement with your client, work from a position of intentionality.** In terms of sustainability, this intentionality takes the form of seeking to

  - Use a systems approach to describe and develop sustainability competencies
  - Enhance meaningful work by seeing work as part of a whole
  - Incorporate environmental factors as a foundation for economic and social values
  - Avoid problem solving, focusing instead on managing environmental problems for the long term
  - Look for breakthrough technologies that are sustainable in nature
  - Support decision-making processes that are systemic and based on long-term thinking

- **Help both individuals and organizations open up to the possibility of change.** Learning about the environmental state of the planet often leaves individuals with a sense of paralysis and helplessness about their potential role. As a result, there is a tendency to deny the problem or to ignore it, thinking of environmental problems as something external to their working lives. Encourage your client to consider manageable steps that are within his range.

- **Discuss with your client how she feels about the current environmental situation.** Explore her fears and concerns. Support her in strengthening her skills to manage change. There is a relationship between the ability to overcome fear, denial, or inertia and the ability to begin working for sustainable change. Talking about sustainability at a personal level can help open your client to making changes in her life and in the world.

- **Learn new ways of making sustainable changes, both personally and at the organizational level.** Brainstorm ideas with your client. Having knowledge about innovative ideas in the field of sustainability is a way to give back to leaders and organizations.

- **Communicate to your client the latest ideas in sustainability.** This will have the advantage of fostering projects that bring diverse people together. Doing sustainable work helps organizational leaders broaden their horizons and extend their knowledge of different people and cultures (Senge, 2008).

- **As a coach, and also as a caring individual, take personal action to reduce your ecological footprint in whatever system you are engaged in.** An available resource is the ecological footprint calculator, available at www .ecologicalfootprint.com/ (British version) or www.myfootprint.org/en/visitor _information/ (international version), with which to evaluate your client's (and your own) ecological footprint. Some variables include place of habitation, income, transportation, climate zone (to analyze energy use), size of dwelling, energy habits, and location of dwelling.

Additional Reading

Banerjee, S. B. (2003). Who sustains whose development? Sustainable development and the reinvention of nature. *Organizational Studies, 24*, 143–180.
This article focuses on different conceptualizations of sustainable development and implications for organizations. It is useful to see how the field of organizational studies has begun to be influenced by sustainable development ideas.

Capra, F. (1982). *The turning point.* New York: Simon & Schuster.

This is one of the first works to emphasize the importance of systems thinking in relation to sustainability. Capra argues that solutions to environmental degradation can be found only if the structure of the system itself can be changed.

Daly, H., & Cobb, J. B. (1989). *For the common good.* Boston: Beacon Press.

Written by economists, this book argues that modern economics presents a mechanistic worldview that has created the conditions for environmental degradation. In order to create more sustainable economies, we need to focus on rooting interests at the local level and reestablishing human-based and human-sized communities.

Hawken, P. (1993). *The ecology of commerce.* New York: HarperBusiness.

Hawken lays out the case that the environment is being destroyed by current industrial demands. We can have both a thriving economy and a thriving environment if we change the way we think about doing business. He argues for a restorative economy, which is based on mirroring natural systems that minimize waste and maximize efficiency.

Meadows, D. H., Meadows, D. L., Randers, J., & Behrens, W. W. (2004). *The limits to growth* (2nd ed.). London: Earthscan.

This book is useful for understanding how the environmental movement began to take shape in the 1970s. The authors investigated five major trends—accelerating industrialization, population growth, widespread malnutrition, depletion of nonrenewable resources, and a deteriorating environment—and revealed the downward trajectory of the environment as a result of industrialization.

Schmidheiny, S., & Business Council on Sustainable Development. (1992). *Changing course.* Boston: MIT Press.

This important book examines the role that business needs to play in creating a more sustainable world. Arguing that the for-profit sector must support civil society and governments, the author uses many examples of sustainable companies that lead the way and can inspire other organizations.

Wright, R. T., & Nebel, J. (2002). *Environmental science: Toward a sustainable future* (8th ed.). Upper Saddle River, NJ: Prentice Hall.

Written as a primer for understanding environmental science, this is an excellent text for learning about the fundamental ecological principles underlying nature. It is helpful to understand these principles in thinking about how to create social, economic, and organizational systems that mirror natural processes.

PART SIX

Creative Applications

Coaching has always benefited, and will continue to benefit, from a creative interaction with other disciplines. Specific approaches developed in other fields have been fruitfully applied to coaching.

From therapy, for example, comes the solution-focused approach, with its emphasis on future possibilities rather than past problems and its concern with the efficient use of limited contact time. Other coaches have borrowed the principles of Appreciative Inquiry from the field of organization development, and effectively applied to the coaching engagement a process that preempts an analysis of the perceived problem with a focus on what is already working.

Two approaches with more ancient roots involve attending to the body, with its capacity to contain and express experience; and listening to the stories we tell about ourselves, their structures and turning points and the openings they offer for the creation of new stories.

chapter TWENTY-SEVEN

Coaching and the Body

Terrie Lupberger

Mr. Duffy . . . lived at a little distance from his body.

James Joyce, "A Painful Case," 1914/1993, p. 104

The way we shape ourselves will have people move towards us, away from us, against us, or be indifferent to us.

—Richard Strozzi-Heckler, 2007, p. 91

When it comes to the body, we adorn it, feed it, exercise it, rest it, nip and tuck it—but don't always acknowledge the impact it has on who we are in the world. Science is now proving what we've intuitively known for centuries—that our physiology influences our learning, thinking, and actions. As far back as the time of the Greek philosopher Socrates, but especially in recent centuries, the western world has privileged a particular interpretation of what it means to be human. That interpretation is summed up by René Descartes, French philosopher and physicist, who asserted in the mid-1600s that mind and body are separate and that our actions are controlled by the mind.

In the early to mid-1900s, the groundbreaking work of psychoanalysts Wilhelm Reich and his student Alexander Lowen, among others, sought to understand and prove a deep relationship between the mind, psychological issues, and the body.

263

Despite this, the western world has continued its privileging of rationalism and objectivism over other ways of knowing and has encouraged an understanding of the body as simply the mechanism that allows us to put our thoughts into action. This view has promoted a separation between thinking and the body that has had enormous consequences for our species.

LEGITIMACY OF THE FELT EXPERIENCE

The body's *felt* experience has not been trusted as a legitimate means of navigating the world. Humberto Maturana, a Chilean biologist and philosopher, and his student, biologist and neuroscientist Francisco Varela, wrote a pioneering book titled *The Tree of Knowledge* (1987), which makes a powerful, scientific case for the way biology shapes our understanding of reality.

Among the claims they make, two are particularly critical for coaching. First, as human beings, we are *structurally determined*. What this means is that our "knowing" is rooted in our biology and that "reality" isn't something "out there" that everyone can agree on, but rather occurs to us in ways that depend on our own filters—biology, physiology, experiences, history. The authors' second claim is that through *structural coupling,* our own physiology reacts to the physiologies of those around us. The consequence of this is that we human beings are not as independent in our thinking or actions as we tend to assume. According to Maturana and Varela,

> In the interactions between the living being and the environment, the perturbations of the environment do not determine what happens to the living being . . . ; rather it is the structure of the living being that determines what change occurs in it. (1987, pp. 95–96)

Coaching Applications

- **Challenge the "reality" your client describes in his stories.** His stories are influenced by his biology, physiology, and experience.

- **Encourage your client to become more aware of what she is feeling, experiencing, and noticing about herself and her environment.** Raising her awareness allows her to expand her perspective and her learning about herself and others.

SOMATIC COACHING AND THE PIONEERS

Somatics is from the Greek word *soma*, which literally translates as "the living body in its wholeness" (Strozzi-Heckler, 2007, p. 93). A somatic approach to coaching requires the coach to understand the body as fundamental to learning and to change. Strozzi-Heckler, a pioneer and expert in the fields of coaching and leadership, trains coaches in how to coach from this vantage point. The coach learns how to observe the movement of the individual and the shape of his or her physicality, and to recognize how these impact his or her thinking and responses to life. The coach transcends the traditional understanding that mind is separate from body, and works on the assumption that working with the "whole" can produce a structural, biological transformation.

Another way to think about a somatic approach to coaching is that the coach is aiming to support clients to cultivate versatility in their thinking and free themselves from automatic responses and habits. In *Retooling on the Run*, Stuart Heller and David Surrenda (1994), two other leaders in the field of observing bodies, leadership, and coaching, write,

> Versatility is most effectively learned with a whole body approach. Your words are not the only source of your meaning. You telegraph your attitudes and beliefs with every inflection, gesture, and movement. You think, feel, move, communicate, interact, and imagine with your body. (p. xvi)

Including a somatic orientation in your coaching means listening to more than the words. It means listening to how your clients' physiologies affect their thinking and their ability to take actions consistent with what they say matters to them. As a coach, you support your clients in becoming aware of their conditioned tendencies and habits of reacting. Awareness provides them with the power to choose, to act rather than react, to replace habits with choices.

Coaching Applications

- **Develop your somatic self-awareness by spending time paying attention to what is happening in your own body in different situations.** Is your habit to contract in a particular situation, or to relax and expand? What are your moods, emotions, and automatic assessments in response to this situation? Are you centered or thrown off center? Open or closed? Extended or withdrawn?

Connected or disconnected? Engaging or resisting? After you become good at noticing these things when you're alone, pay attention to what happens when you're in conversations. Don't judge; just observe. Keep a journal of your observations. At intervals, make assessments of your developing capacity for somatic awareness, self-awareness, and awareness of others.

- **Listen beyond the words of your client.** In the somatic approach to coaching, you are encouraged to listen differently. Start paying attention to your client's voice, tone, pace, breathing, rhythm, emotions, shape. What questions can you ask to generate new awareness? What practices can you develop so that they bring a different shape or body to the situation?

- **Help your client become comfortable with uncertainty and "not knowing."** As a coach, you have the opportunity to support your clients in developing a physiology that can hold uncertainty in a mood of peace. Coaching is fundamentally about learning, and in learning we face the unknown. How can you help your clients develop the capability to be physically at ease with "not knowing"?

- **Develop simple somatic exercises for your client.** Have him walk in a pleasant place at least three times a week, noticing his surroundings. This will help develop his capacity to pay attention to others.

- **Experiment with exercises that allow your client to be grounded and present.** As you begin the coaching session, ask your client to take a few deep, slow breaths. Then ask her if she is willing to go through the Centered Presence Exercise (see the next Coaching Applications list in this chapter). Finally, ask your client to sit quietly for sixty seconds and relax every muscle—from the jaw and shoulders down to the feet—before beginning the coaching engagement.

ONTOLOGICAL COACHING: JULIO OLALLA

Ontological coaching is a practice that facilitates the emergence of new possibilities in the personal and/or professional life of an individual (or group) by making him aware of his participation in the construction and co-creation of the reality he perceives. (Olalla, 2004, p. 48)

Although theorist Fernando Flores and biologist Humberto Maturana are key contributors to the understanding that body and physiology are integral to coaching, it is Julio Olalla who is credited with embedding this concept in the coaching approach known as Ontological Coaching. Ontological Coaching requires that the coach observe how the client uses language, emotions, and the body to generate—or fail to generate—results. The ontologically trained coach uses these three doorways—language, body, and emotions—to respectfully explore with the client how she has constructed her worldview, how this worldview impacts her thinking and actions, and how, through new learning, she can shift in order to generate new possibilities for action. In his book *From Knowledge to Wisdom*, Olalla (2004, p. 48) states,

> As humans, we are not just embodied minds. We have physical bodies and experience emotions, sensations, and spiritual impulses. Once again, however, our reliance on reason as the only reliable source of knowledge and power leads us to devalue these experiences.

Coaching Applications

- **Get your client moving.** Whether it's listening to music, dancing, walking, fencing, practicing yoga or aikido, the point here is to encourage her to try out new shapes by moving through different experiences. The conversations will be different according to which shape she adopts.

- **Expand your own range of movements and emotions in your coaching.** Explore ways to expand your thinking, feeling, movement. The coach's own physiology and shape impact how he works with a client. If he is tense or contracted, his coaching approach and questions will be influenced by his tension. Cultivate a versatile coaching posture and be constantly aware of the need to pay attention and speak from your center.

- **Invite your client to try this simple experiment.** Say *For the next fifteen seconds, think of an experience that generates a positive, happy feeling for you (your children's hugs, a recent promotion, an acknowledgment from someone that matters, and so on). Now, while still thinking of this experience, physically collapse your spine, hunch your shoulders, and cast your eyes down to the ground. Notice the quality of your feeling.* Something has likely changed. Most people report that it is hard to hold on to happy feelings in that contracted body shape.

- **Try the Centered Presence Exercise from Heller and Surrenda's book *Retooling on the Run* (1994).** It is a simple yet effective way for you and your clients to begin cultivating your attention and awareness so as to bring you to more choice when reacting to circumstances around you.

- **Find your feet.**

  Feel your feet touching the floor.

  Notice the pressure and the contact between your feet and the floor.

  Feel the insides of your feet. Feel the muscles and bones.

  Let the sensations grow in strength and spread throughout your body.

  While maintaining this quality of sensation, let a new breath emerge.

- **Find your hands.**

  Feel what you are presently holding or touching.

  Notice the pressure and the contact between it and your hands.

  Feel the insides of your hands. Feel the muscles and bones.

  Let the sensations grow in strength and spread throughout your body.

  While maintaining this quality of sensation, let a new breath emerge.

- **Find your head.**

  Look and listen to what is going on around you and within you.

  Tune in to your senses of smell and taste.

  Notice how your head balances on the top of the spine.

  Let the sensations grow in strength and spread throughout your body.

  While maintaining this quality of sensation, let a new breath emerge.

- **Find your breath.**

  Inhale and exhale on purpose.

  Focus your attention on the middle of your torso.

  Relax and let your breath move to its own rhythm.

  Let the sensations grow in strength and spread throughout the body.

Additional Reading

Dunham, R. (2010). *The innovator's way.* Cambridge, MA: MIT Press.
    Speaks to the interweaving of language and emotions and body to generate and *apply* innovation.

McDermott, I., & Jago, W. (2001). *The NLP coach*. London: Piatkus.

Looks with a different lens at somatics and the body's impact on action and thinking.

Olalla, J. A. (2004). *From knowledge to wisdom*. Boulder, CO: Newfield Press.

Introduction to Ontological Coaching and the concerns of being human.

Strozzi-Heckler, R. (2007). *The leadership dojo: Build your foundation as an exemplary leader*. Berkeley, CA: Frog Books.

Interesting stories on how somatics impact presence and leadership.

Zeman, S. (2009). *Listening to bodies: A somatic primer for coaches, managers and executives*. Richmond, CA: Shasta Gardens.

A good resource with practices to help increase your own awareness and development; it is also beneficial as you work with others.

chapter TWENTY-EIGHT

A Narrative Approach to Coaching

David B. Drake

O ur lives are in many ways defined by the stories we tell about them. The stories themselves are drawn from a rich tapestry of historical, contextual, cultural, and mythical narratives. However, in this time of what often feels like an ever-accelerating *now*, many people experience a strong need to continuously recalibrate their personal stories and social narratives in order to grow, relate well to others, and express themselves.

In part as a response to these demands, narrative coaching has emerged over the past ten years as a holistic approach to help people shift their stories about themselves, about others, and about life itself. Working this way helps people to (1) become more aware of their own implicit and explicit stories, told and untold, (2) recognize how these stories shape their identity and their behavior at both conscious and unconscious levels, (3) understand that these stories are personally and socially constructed, and (4) create new stories about how they want to be, relate, and act in the world.

FOUNDATIONS OF NARRATIVE COACHING

The primary focus in narrative coaching is to work with the stories, as they emerge from clients in conversations, as vehicles for greater awareness, authorship, agility, and accountability. This approach draws primarily on three bodies of work:

1. *Narrative psychology* (and related work in other social sciences) as a way to understand and connect with the client as a narrator—exemplified by William James's distinction (1927) between the "I" (as subject) and the "Me" (as object) and Kenneth Gergen's work on the social construction of identity (1994).

2. *Narrative structure* as a way to elicit and understand the material in the stories—exemplified by Kenneth Burke's work on story grammars (1969) and Joseph Campbell's work on the heroic journey (1973).

3. *Narrative skills* as a way to work with the dynamics in the conversational "field"—exemplified by Carl Jung's work on collective and unconscious processes (1970), Michael White and David Epston's work on narrative therapy (1990), and Clandinin and Connelly's use of three-dimensional narrative inquiry space (2000).

Coaching Applications

- **Focus on real-time attention to the client's narrative process and content.** Commit to your own ongoing development to help you do so, by increasing your ability to be present, your ability to self-regulate when triggered, your emotional range, and your responsive repertoire.

- **Take a kaleidoscopic view of the client's situation and her story.** Be willing to draw on a variety of frames in order to be able see her in new and more complete ways. Know where your strengths and your blind spots are as you work with her. Think about how you might develop and incorporate other modalities to help her tell her whole story—for example, by using somatic practices, such as attending to breathing and using the body expressively, to surface the preverbal influences that have shaped her identity and issues.

- **Recognize the power of a person's context and the influence of language.** Begin by continuously surfacing and maturing your own unconscious biases around gender, nationality, epistemology (our understanding of what constitutes knowledge), and so on. In particular, be conscious of any unexamined privilege you bring to coaching conversations, especially if it is not a part of your client's experience. Be open to challenging the collective stories in which he lives, and work as well at helping him liberate his personal stories in whatever way he chooses.

- **Pay attention to the process of narration (including your own role) as well as the structure of the material that emerges.** The path to resolution is often found in exploring what happens "one day . . . ," the turning point in most stories. The *story spine* is a good frame to use as you invite people to tell their stories: (1) Once upon a time . . . (2) Every day . . . (3) But one day . . . (4) Because of that . . . Until finally . . . (5) And ever since then . . . (6) The moral of the story is . . . At the same time, don't get so caught up in the drama of the story that you overlook its larger purpose as a vehicle for change.

NARRATIVE IDENTITY IN COACHING

A distinguishing feature of a narrative approach to coaching is its emphasis on the crucial role of identity in understanding and supporting people's development and performance. It suggests that coaches should think of identity as relational action (Gergen & Gergen, 2006) and an adaptive performance (Mishler, 1999) more than as a unitary and static object, and as authored in the present and shaped by the perceived potential of the future (Markus & Nurius, 1986) more than just as a product of a fixed past. In other words, identity is fluid. It's an ongoing process in which people navigate between fitting in and functioning well in their environment, and authentically expressing themselves and getting their needs met. A narrative approach works well with identity issues because it mirrors the innate storytelling nature of our minds to see and navigate the world in spatial, temporal, and volitional terms.

Coaching Applications

- **Help clients come to their stories with less judgment.** We develop defenses to protect aspects of our identity where we feel vulnerable. The goal in coaching is to increase clients' sense of secure attachment and their "window of tolerance" (Drake, 2009) by softening their need for these defenses—and the stories that reinforce them—so they can develop greater awareness, gain more trust in themselves, make more conscious choices, and attain better results.

- **Build rapport by providing both an interpersonal structure and a narrative structure in which your client can safely and fully engage with her**

story. Drawing on Winnicott (1971), think of yourself as a "good enough" professional who can both match your client where she is now and invite her to experience new ways of being, relating, and narrating. Work with her in the moment as much as possible, regardless of whether she is talking about the past, present, or future.

- **Realize that people tell stories to make, confirm, or experiment with ways of being in the world and being seen by the world.** In your role as coach, ask yourself, *What is this person trying to achieve through telling this story, particularly at an emotional level, and how are his current narration strategies working for him?* If his strategies are not working well, ask him what results he is hoping for and how he might draw on his relational and behavioral strengths in new ways.

- **Support change by helping the client imagine and create new possibilities.** Help her identify narrative data from her life that support an alternate view of who she is and how she wants to be in the world, what the narrative therapists call "unique outcomes" or "exceptions." At the same time, realize that in order for new stories or new relations between stories to take hold in her life, she must build on elements of familiar stories.

- **Realize that people can see only as far as their stories will take them; they can act only as far as their stories will back them.** Help your client see both the old patterns and the new possibilities in how he currently connects his identities, stories, and behaviors. If he wants to adopt new behaviors or attain new results, help him build an identity and a new narrative from which, in time, he can naturally do so. To sustain that new identity, he will need to learn and repeatedly enact new behaviors—and the story that goes with them.

NARRATIVE SKILLS IN COACHING: LISTENING FOR THE WHOLE STORY

Given the emphasis in narrative coaching on context, culture, and the conversational "container," it is no surprise that listening plays a particularly key role in this approach. Coaches can best discern the path forward in the conversation moment to moment and act as a guide along the way through simultaneously paying attention to themselves, the other person, the field between them, and the stories as they emerge. In doing so, they stay present to the lived experience of the conversation as much as possible and work with what is there. The research on attachment (Wallin, 2007) and on mindfulness, presence, and rapport (Siegel, 2007) provide a strong evidence base for this approach. Kramer's work (2007) on relational meditation is particularly helpful here in reminding the coach to pause, relax, and remain open in order to trust in the process, listen without assumption, and speak only when it seems important.

This commitment to deep yet fluid listening is reflected in the narrative coach's decentered position in the conversation. This can be seen, for example, in Drake's Narrative Diamond model (2007, 2008) in which the aim is to listen carefully for

What is said—as a witness for the storyteller and to foster greater trust

What is not said—as an advocate for the whole story and to identify the agenda for change

What wants to be said—as a steward for the emerging story and to support a vision for new options

What is being said differently—as an ally for changes that are already happening and to use them as a structure for new behavior

The goals of this work are to

- Help people become more aware of the contours of their available narratives and reframe them or their relationship to them

- Guide them in discovering and developing new options (often hidden as gems in their own stories) and a more evolved repertoire

- Help them successfully launch their new story (Hewson, 1991) as the basis for fulfilling their aspirations

The last of these is important because any story told in a coaching session, even if it has been transformational in that setting, must survive the "retellings" if clients are to sustain the changes they have begun.

Coaching Applications

- **Start with the client's preferred ways of processing and narrating her experience, and use this as a foundation for engaging other aspects of her story and self.** Once you have built up sufficient trust and attunement with your client, you can more easily engage her in telling more of the story. For example, draw out more of the untold factual, sequential, and verbal elements to enrich the personal, contextual, nonverbal parts that were originally shared. Change often comes from the integration of this new material into the story.

- **Create a rich narrative field for the conversation.** Be actively engaged yet nonattached, notice what appears, and remain connected even in silence. Use your inner experience in the session as one gauge for what is going on for the client and in the field. Invite yourself and your client to stay "in" his story as it unfolds across a series of present moments so that the material and the dynamics become more apparent and available for renegotiation.

- **Put more emphasis on generating experiences and less on rushing to interpretation, meaning, or action.** In doing so, you will more fully engage the whole person and create conditions more similar to what your client will encounter after the session. This is important because stories are a great lens into people's mental models, beliefs, and assumptions about how things are "supposed to be." Remember that everything you need is right in front of you.

- **Trust that the client will begin where he is ready and that the critical themes will emerge in time, regardless of which stories he shares first.** Any story or set of stories can be a portal into the larger issues at play for the client and the path to reaching his resolution or aspiration. So track how he organizes his story—which events are included, which themes are central, which characters are portrayed as significant, and which voices are privileged in the telling. Use the ordinary as a gateway to the extraordinary.

- **Listen for the gaps, the thresholds, where the client's habitual emplotment strategies (patterns in forming stories) have broken down or are no longer working.** These gaps in how she makes sense and meaning of events can be seen as "breaches" (Bruner, 2002) and the story she tells as an attempt to resolve the discrepancy between what she expected and what has transpired. These gaps are an opportunity to help her formulate a different story and create a different outcome because it is in these spaces in between—where the old story is challenged but the new one is not yet formed—that growth most often occurs.

- **Pay close attention to the ethics of working with clients' stories.**

  Clients expect their coach to create a safe environment for their storytelling.

  Clients expect their stories to be heard in a nonjudgmental, nonassumptive manner.

Clients expect to have their community and cultural stories taken seriously.

Clients have the right to tell their own story in their own way.

Clients tell and understand their story as best they can at the time.

Clients have the right to change their stories, lives, and selves as they choose.

Clients are accountable for the impact of their stories on themselves and others.

Clients expect their coach to manage his or her own stories, agendas, and participation.

Clients expect their coach to be an exemplary steward of the stories that are told.

Additional Reading

Bruner, J. (2002). *Making stories: Law, literature, life*. Cambridge, MA: Harvard University Press.
  A later work from a key figure who as an educational psychologist brings a literary frame to narrative and writes beautifully about its place in contemporary life.
Cozolino, L. (2002). *The neuroscience of psychotherapy: Building and rebuilding the human brain*. New York: Norton.
  One of several books from a psychotherapist and professor who writes accessibly and well about the human experience and the art of helping others thrive.
Drake, D. B. (2008). Thrice upon a time: Narrative structure and psychology as a platform for coaching. In D. B. Drake, D. Brennan, & K. Gørtz (Eds.), *The philosophy and practice of coaching: Insights and issues for a new era* (pp. 51–71). San Francisco: Jossey-Bass.
  This chapter focuses on the understanding and use of narrative structure and analysis as a foundation for a narrative approach to coaching.
Freedman, J., & Combs, G. (1996). *Narrative therapy: The social construction of preferred realities*. New York: Norton.
  A clear and approachable introduction to how narrative therapy is done, written by two of its leading practitioners.
McAdams, D. P. (1993). *The stories we live by: Personal myths and the making of the self*. New York: Guilford Press.
  A useful introduction to narrative psychology, particularly in terms of the reciprocal links between identity and stories.
McKee, R. (1997). *Story: Substance, structure, style and the principles of screenwriting*. New York: HarperCollins.

A guidebook from a well-known Hollywood screenwriting teacher that provides a great introduction to narrative structure and flow.

Schank, R. A. (1990). *Tell me a story: A new look at real and artificial memory*. New York: Scribner.

A provocative and fascinating book that jump-started my professional interest in narrative as it applies to learning and development from a cognitive perspective.

Siegel, D. J. (2007). *The mindful brain: Reflection and attunement in the cultivation of well-being*. New York: Norton.

A wonderful book by a psychiatrist and professor who brings together mindfulness, what he calls "interpersonal neurobiology," and human development.

Wallin, D. J. (2007). *Attachment in psychotherapy*. New York: Guilford Press.

An excellent overview of the development of attachment theory, related neuroscience and mindfulness research, and their respective applications in professional practice.

White, M., & Epston, D. (1990). *Narrative means to therapeutic ends*. New York: Norton.

The classic that launched the field of narrative therapy; see also White's later work (2007) for a clear outline of the core practices.

chapter TWENTY-NINE

Solution-Focused Coaching and the GROW Model

Carol Wilson

During the 1950s, there was a major shift in thinking, represented by the work of psychologists including Carl Rogers, Abraham Maslow, and Fritz Perls. The view held by psychologists in the first half of the century—namely, that clients were patients who needed to be fixed—was turned on its head; the new therapists viewed people as whole and resourceful rather than as dysfunctional and needy. In the 1980s, Steve de Shazer, Insoo Kim Berg, and colleagues at the Brief Family Therapy Center in Milwaukee, Wisconsin, built on earlier work by Milton Erickson and others to arrive at the solution-focused model used most commonly today.

Solution-focused therapy, also known as brief therapy, focuses on the present and future. It differs from previous therapeutic approaches in that sessions are usually conducted over a short period of time (one to five sessions), focus on the client's strengths, and dwell on future possibilities rather than past problems. Since the late 1990s there has been a steady increase in the research specific to coaching that is beginning to establish solution-focused coaching as an evidence-based practice (Green, Oades, & Grant, 2006).

"The solution-focused approach . . . may seem simplistic to some, but . . . takes pride in keeping it simple. Staying focused on the solution is the essence of great coaching" (Grant, 2006, p. 89).

279

SOLUTION-FOCUSED BRIEF COACHING

Solution-focused coaching is a constructivist practice that places primary emphasis on assisting the client to define a desired future state and to construct a pathway in both thinking and action to move toward that future state (Cavanagh & Grant, 2010). A solution-focused approach assumes that clients have the capability to be active participants in solving their own problems and that they have an opportunity for building skill in self-directed learning. What is distinct about solution-focused coaching, according to O'Hanlon & Beadle (1996), is that the two main tasks of solution-focused coaching are to *change the viewing* (help the client see the situation in a different light) and *change the doing* (help them develop new behaviors). The work centers on two critical practices: supporting clients to explore their preferred futures; and exploring when, where, with whom, and how parts of this preferred future are already happening.

Coaching Applications

- **Help your client envisage a solution to his problem.** The "miracle question," an essential tool of solution-focused coaching, involves asking the client how the future would be different if the problem were no longer present. Explore this question with the client to help him create a first step toward a solution.

- **Follow up the miracle question with questions that focus on the possibility of change.** For example, ask *What are you already doing in your life, or what is currently happening in your life, that might be leading toward this desired future?*

- **Ask your client "scaling questions."** Collaborate with your client in constructing a scale—say, from 1 to 10, with 1 signifying the worst the problem has ever been and 10 signifying the best things could ever be. Ask such questions as *What is stopping you from slipping one point down the scale?* or *Where would you like to be on the scale?*

- **Work toward moving your client away from absolutes.** Encourage her to recognize exceptions, times when the problem has been absent or less severe. For example, ask if there has been a time when she did something that improved the situation.

- **Reinforce the client's resilience in coping with the situation, however difficult.** For example, ask questions that focus on his ability to get up in the morning, to make it through the day, to show up at work. If he's feeling a loss of confidence in certain areas, ask about circumstances or times when he *was* successful in accomplishing these tasks.

THE GROW MODEL

In the 1970s, Tim Gallwey, a Harvard graduate on sabbatical as a tennis coach, noticed that his students seemed to be more successful at teaching themselves than by learning from an instructor. Gallwey's work (see, for example, Gallwey, 1997) was discovered by an English baronet and ex-racing driver, Sir John Whitmore, who opened a tennis and ski school to develop the techniques. Eventually Whitmore's team was invited by corporations to inject a day of tennis coaching into their management training courses to help managers embrace the principle of self-directed learning. The GROW model, which sets the pattern for the coach's questions, emerged from a group that included Sir John Whitmore, who later popularized it in his book *Coaching for Performance.* GROW is an acronym for which various definitions have emerged over the years. The following describes the acronym as defined in the 2009 edition of Whitmore's book:

G   **Goal** setting for the session as well as for the short and long term

R   **Reality** checking to explore the current situation

O   **Options** and alternative strategies or courses of action

W   **What** is to be done, **When,** by **Whom,** and the **Will** to do it

Other versions in existence include TGROW, with Topic at the start and the W standing for Wrap up.

The GROW model is a useful framework for any activity, not only in coaching conversations but also in project management, disciplinary exchanges, and life in general. It enables people to think clearly and keep moving forward toward positive solutions and achievements.

Goal

In effective GROW coaching, establishing the goal means far more than simply asking the client what he or she wants to achieve. The whole of the first session might usefully be spent exploring the client's goals, which may at the end of that time be quite different from the ones with which the client came into the session. We often run our lives according to agendas set by others—parents, teachers, or bosses. We aim for what we think we *should* achieve rather than what we want to achieve. However, if we can identify what we really want, in line with our own values, interests, and talents, not only are we more likely to achieve the goal, but the experience along the way will be a lot more fun.

Goal questions throw the focus of attention forward, past barriers and self-limiting beliefs. A technique widely used by professional golfers is to imagine hitting the winning shot. This is based on the dual theories that the brain is unable to tell fact from fiction (which is why we cry at sad films) and that every time we repeat an action we ingrain a new habit. Therefore, by picturing the winning shot, we are tricking our brains not only into believing we have done it, so that it will be easier a second time, but also creating the neural pathways of a new habit.

The original SMART goal setting model was created for managers to set targets for their teams. SMART stands for *specific, measurable, achievable/agreed, realistic/relevant*, and *time bound*. When one sets goals for others, one tends to aim too high, hence the "achievable" and "relevant" elements of SMART. When one sets one's own goals, however, one tends to aim too low, being limited by lack of confidence or baggage from the past. When coaching, we are enabling clients to set goals for themselves, so a slightly different model is required. One adaptation developed for coaching is the EXACT model (Wilson, 2007). The following is a comparison between SMART and EXACT.

S	Specific	E	Explicit
M	Measurable	X	Xciting
A	Achievable/Agreed	A	Accessible
R	Realistic/Relevant	C	Challenging
T	Time bound	T	Time framed

The limiting elements of SMART are replaced by "challenging" to stretch clients past their own limiting beliefs. Also, whereas a SMART goal can be negative ("Get out of the bottom division"), an EXACT goal has to be positively framed ("Get into the top division"), which encompasses the solution focus of coaching, directing our minds to where we want to be instead of what we want to get away from.

Reality

Reality is the part that is missing in everyday conversation. People tend to leap straight from the past ("He said I was always late, so I said I wasn't") to the future ("I'm going to resign"), taking all of their emotional baggage into tomorrow's decision. Reality questions enable clients to step off the emotional track, gain some new perspectives, and make decisions from a calmer state of mind.

Options

The purpose of this stage is to brainstorm all possible ideas, not just the ones that are immediately obvious. Having recognized what stands in their way, clients are capable of being very creative in finding ways to move forward.

Will

This is the part of the GROW model where awareness and new insights are pinned down to practical action. Will is about discovering what a client will commit to doing, not just compiling a list of possible actions. An effective action is one that excites and motivates the client, is simple and clear with a single focus, and is the very first step in a possible chain of actions. If it is not the first step, confusion is liable to set in, and the client will procrastinate.

The following are sample GROW questions:

Goal: What do you want? Over what time frame? How will you know when you have achieved it? Imagine you have achieved it: What do you see, hear, and feel?

Reality: What is happening at the moment? How important is this to you? If an ideal situation is 10, what number are you at now? What impact is this having on you? on others? What are you doing that is working toward your goal? What are you doing that is getting in the way of your goal?

Options: What are your options? What could you do? What else? What might someone else do in your position?

Will: What will you do? How, when, and where will you do that? What is your first step? How committed are you? What might get in your way? What will it take for you to commit to that action?

Coaching Applications

- **Start with a Goal question.** The GROW framework is flexible and does not have to be adhered to chronologically, but Goal questions raise the client's energy and expand her vision. Goal questions are useful throughout the coaching conversation to motivate and provide a sense of purpose.

- **Ask Reality questions when the client seems stuck.** The Reality part of GROW is useful for gaining perspective and awareness.

- **Ask plenty of Goal and Reality questions.** Options and actions will then tend to spring into the client's mind without effort, along with the energy required to carry them out. If a client ever says, *I don't know what to do,* Goal and Reality questions are likely to clear confusion and give rise to new insights.

- **Encourage the client to reframe from a negative perspective to a positive one.** For example, if he says, *I want to feel less stressed,* ask him, *How would you like to feel?*

- **Use scaling questions to allow the client to assess progress.** For example: *Where are you now on a scale of 1 to 10? Where would you like to be six months from now?*

- **Ask the client what she is learning.** For example: *What do you know now that you didn't know before? What is your insight about that? How could you use that elsewhere in your life and work? Now that you know you are capable of that, what else could you do?*

Additional Reading

Berg, I., & Szabo, P. (2005). *Brief coaching for lasting solutions*. London: Norton.
This book describes how to conduct conversations that are most useful to clients in achieving their goals within a brief period of time.

Greene, J., & Grant, A. M. (2003). *Solution-focused coaching: Managing people in a complex world*. London: Momentum Press.
Backed by psychological theory, this book features practical tools and techniques for enhancing life experience and work performance.

Whitmore, J. (2009). *Coaching for performance* (4th ed.). London: Brealey.

This book lays out the foundation principles of coaching as devised by the team who developed performance coaching from Gallwey's Inner Game in the early 1980s.

Wilson, C. (2007). *Best practice in performance coaching: A handbook for leaders, coaches, HR professionals and organizations.* London: Kogan Page.

Complete with worksheets and exercises, evaluations and international case studies, this is a guide to performance coaching for managers and coaches.

chapter THIRTY

Appreciative Inquiry

Jacqueline Binkert and Ann L. Clancy

The theoretical foundation of Appreciative Inquiry (AI) is based on powerful assumptions about human change that are positive and life generating by nature. AI introduced a major shift in the practice of organization development by offering a mode of inquiry that was both generative and philosophical and that would not constrain imagination (Cooperrider & Srivastva, 1987). Developed by David Cooperrider and his adviser Suresh Srivastva, along with other graduate students at Case Western Reserve University in the 1980s, AI offered a generative model of organizational action research and change that challenged the traditional problem-based action research model. It is considered to be *life affirming* by practitioners due to its core propositions around the power of inquiry; that is, inquiry begins with appreciation, generates useful information, can stir people to action, and should be collaborative (Cooperrider, Whitney, & Stavros, 2003).

AI has become a force to be reckoned with in the arena of positive group and organizational change. It has been called a philosophy, a revolutionary force, a transformational change process, a life-giving theory and practice, and even a new worldview (Watkins & Mohr, 2001; Whitney & Trosten-Bloom, 2003). The success of AI is marked by the application of its principles and process beyond the organizational context, into such areas as team building (Whitney, Trosten-Bloom, Cherney, & Fry, 2004); self-help (Kelm, 2005); strategic planning (Stavros & Hinrichs, 2009); and coaching (Orem, Binkert, & Clancy, 2007).

UNDERLYING CONCEPTS

The spark that launched Cooperrider was the observation that organizations move toward what they study, a profound realization at the time. The essential concepts that underlie AI can be summarized as follows:

- In every society, organization, or group, something works.
- What we focus on becomes our reality.
- Reality is created in the moment, and there are multiple realities.
- The act of asking questions of an organization or group influences the group in some way.
- People have more confidence and comfort to journey to the future (the unknown) when they carry forward parts of the past (the known).
- If we carry parts of the past forward, they should be what is best about the past.
- It is important to value differences.
- The language we use creates our reality.

The theories and practices of AI are firmly rooted in the new scientific paradigm. Instead of conceiving of an objective, predictable, and controllable universe, scientists in the twenty-first century describe a vastly different world based on quantum physics and the new sciences of chaos theory, self-organizing systems, and complexity theory (Wheatley, 1992). In the past, change was mostly defined as incremental, linear, and predictable in terms of simple cause and effect. Now scientists see change in the context of complexity, subjectivity, interconnectedness, collaboration, self-organization, multiple sources of cause and effect, and the collective use of language to create social reality.

AI recognizes that inquiry and change occur simultaneously. The very first questions laser attention in a certain direction and sow the seeds of change. The kinds of questions asked help set the stage for what clients discover about themselves and their situations. The right questions can lead clients to conceive, talk about, and construct a positive future as well as to experience a sudden shift in perspective that liberates them from limiting patterns of thought.

Coaching Applications

- **Ask AI-type questions to help your client reflect on himself in a more positive light and begin thinking outside the box.** Asking positive, life-enhancing questions underscores the power of the present in effecting personal change for your client. Some examples of positive inquiry include *Tell me about a quality moment in your life; Tell me about a time you experienced positive energy in your life; Recall a time you worked with someone you considered an inspirational leader; Tell me about a time when you received recognition, appreciation, or acknowledgment for your work;* and *Tell how you learn best.*

- **Use positive inquiry to help the client reflect on when she is at her best.** Begin coaching sessions with positive AI questions; they will make a difference in the outcome of the session. Research shows that there is constant interaction between the individual and her environment, with no temporal sequencing; that is, the environment influences the person, and the person influences the environment in the same moment. Neither one precedes the other in time; therefore, one can have an immediate impact on the other. This is the positive dynamic between coach and client.

- **Watch for pivotal moments in coaching conversations.** These are moments when the client sees himself or his situation with new eyes. Pay attention to the client's internal questions about himself; they are as important as your questions. Shifting his internal dialogue from one of blame (*What's wrong with me? Why can't I get this right?*) to one of discovery (*When have I been successful? What actions can I experiment with?*) is a powerful tool to pivot him toward acknowledging his choices in creating a more positive future.

- **Help the client move forward, carrying parts of her past that are positive and comforting.** As people mature, their understanding of themselves and the world around them grows and deepens. A new situation or experience (whether positive or negative) provides an opportunity for the client to reinterpret and free herself from limited ways of seeing herself, her situation, and her range of possibilities.

FIVE AI PRINCIPLES

As a philosophy, AI involves five core principles that are woven together and support one another in guiding change away from problem solving and toward an appreciative outlook.

1. *The constructionist principle* states that how humans communicate, interact, create symbols, and construct metaphors with one another creates social

reality. Thus social knowledge and destiny are intertwined. What people know about themselves and how they know it are fateful or full of destiny because these are the only ways individuals know how to understand and relate to themselves, their past, and their potential for the future (Chaffee, 2004).

2. *The positive principle* states that building and sustaining momentum for change requires large amounts of positive affect and social bonding. Emotions such as hope, excitement, inspiration, caring, camaraderie, a sense of purpose, and even sheer joy help people create something meaningful together.

3. *The simultaneity principle* recognizes that inquiry and change happen at the same time; that is, how organizations and individuals think, talk about, discover, and imagine the future—the seeds of change—are sown in the first questions they are asked.

4. *The poetic principle* invites organizations and individuals to view themselves not as problems to be solved but, like poetry, as an open book of possibilities, as a story that they continually rewrite, incorporating learnings from the past, present, and future.

5. *The anticipatory principle* states that humans have infinite resources for generating constructive change through their collective imagination and their discourse about the future. In other words, creating a clear positive image of the future, filled with desires and possibilities, guides current actions and behaviors.

Coaching Applications

- **Develop a productive relationship with your client.** Creating change involves social collaboration. The relationship between you and your client must be one of partnership and mutual respect.

- **View your client as a *mystery to be appreciated* rather than a problem to be solved.** Generally the client does not want to be "fixed" but is looking to you for support in constructing a better future for herself. Help her feel permitted to view herself in a new, more holistic way.

- **In preparation for each coaching session, become mindful of your own feelings and thoughts and seek to become centered and focused on the upcoming**

time to be spent with your client. Emotions are contagious. By preparing yourself for the coaching conversation, you take the lead to become *positively* contagious with your client. When a client has negative emotions or dark days, empathetically connect with him to help him step back and see a bigger picture. Support him by holding faith in his dreams through times of difficulty.

- **Support your client by helping her create a picture of a desired future that directs her toward what she *wants*.** Humans are aspirational beings, hard-wired to anticipate the future. Unfortunately, clients are often more likely to articulate what they *don't* want, rather than what they would like to move toward. Remember, the seeds of the future exist in the present.

- **Integrate the five principles of AI into your approach to coaching.** The appreciative approach is more than technique. It is an expression of a positive and generative view of life and change. Decide for yourself whether these principles are in alignment with your own beliefs and experiences around individual change.

SOCIAL CONSTRUCTIONISM: BERGER AND LUCKMANN

A key perspective of AI and the new emerging paradigm is social constructionism. Postmodern thought, from which social constructionism springs, rejects the notion of static underlying structures and a search for truth in favor of a belief in multiple, contextual realities (Watkins & Mohr, 2001). The construction of social meaning is made through language (Berger & Luckmann, 1966), a uniquely human ability that differentiates us from the physical world. Integral to social constructionism and thus to the appreciative approach is the notion of individuals as active, independent, and spontaneous beings who, consciously or not, form images of the future toward which they then grow.

Coaching Applications

- **Become aware of your language as a coach, as well as your own beliefs and philosophy around change.** Because you (just like your client) create your social reality through conversation, the language you use and how you express your beliefs about change have great impact on your client.

- **Listen to the language of your client; it provides clues to her thinking patterns and beliefs about herself.** Reflect her choice of language back to her to help her shift to a more empowering and productive view of herself and her circumstances. Where possible, gently move your client from problem language to discovery and appreciative language.

HOLISTIC VIEW OF TIME

AI incorporates an expanded view of time beyond the legacy of Newtonian Absolute Time, which was considered an unchanging physical reality, independent of human consciousness (Newton, 1687/1990). Instead of accepting an individual as the sum total of his past with the locus of control outside of him, a holistic view of time embraces the simultaneous interplay of past, present, and future as an integrated whole, each part influenced by the other parts (Clancy, 1996). A holistic perspective of time incorporates the following assumptions:

- Both the present and future influence change.
- Individuals are agents of their own change.
- People can change in ways inconsistent with their past and are best understood in relation to their present context.
- People access multiple experiences of time.

Coaching Applications

- **Consider your client's beliefs about his present and future to be as significant as the events of the past.** Both the present and future influence change as much as events of the past, so it is important to realize how the past, present, and future influence one another in your client's ability to change.

- **Move your client forward in the coaching process by focusing more attention on the strengths of the present and possibilities of the future.** Individuals are agents of their own change. From the beginning, engage your client in an interchange that supports building or sustaining a positive self-reinforcing cycle of growth.

- **Help the client become aware that recurring negative thoughts are rooted in the past and are habits that are no longer useful in the present.** People can change in ways inconsistent with their past and are best understood in relation to their present context. Becoming aware of this potential can help break negative patterns by opening the possibility for new action. You can help the client reconstruct the meanings of her past and support her in creating new practices.

- **Assist the client to trust his own sense of timing, intuition, and insight into his process of internal change.** People have access to multiple experiences of time beyond the pervasiveness of linear clock time. Such experiences include biological rhythms (best times of energy during the day), sudden shifts in understanding ("aha" moments), a sense of flow (when time seems to disappear), subjective feelings of how quickly or slowly time passes, and the unfolding of possibilities. Helping the client become more aware of his own sense of time enables him to experience his days more richly and productively.

FOUR AI STAGES

The practice of AI occurs in four main stages that are dynamic, interrelated, and iterative. The *discovery stage* is about reflecting and celebrating strengths and successes to help organizations and individuals truly appreciate what gives life to them. The *dream stage* is about articulating potential, and uses an appreciative process to create a dream or a future picture. The *design stage* is about directing attention and action to become designers of the future. The period of time between the articulation of a dream and its manifestation is the focus of this stage. The *destiny stage* is about recognizing the state of being in which organizations and individuals have embraced the reality of their dream in the present. They are moving forward (becoming) yet living life fully and well in the present (being).

Coaching Applications

- **Guide your client in discovering and remembering her best self.** Begin the coaching engagement by guiding her conversation to successes of her past as well as to her current and past strengths and abilities. This will help move the coaching conversation forward in a positive, life-enhancing direction.

- **Help your client find clarity and hope in defining a desired future for himself.** A person's self-awareness and destiny are interwoven (Mohr, 2004). Encouraging your client to talk about himself and his desires in the present and for the future is an important part of supporting him to reveal what he most wants for himself—his dreams.

- **Lead your client in creating a foundation and structure to proactively attain her dream.** People are both the designers of their world and the product of their own designs. It is important for the client to influence her destiny by making choices and acting in ways that reflect her most positive core and her desired future. Your job is not only to affirm the reality of the client's dreams but also to support her in making mindful choices and actions in moving forward.

- **Enable the client to expand his own capacity to appreciate himself, stretch beyond what's familiar, recognize his own progress, and reach out to others for support.** People's lives and destinies are always in the process of creation. Destiny is not about endings or beginnings but about living life fully and well. The client may feel that his capacity to create the future he wants is lacking, or it may seem overwhelming to sustain the energy and focus needed to attain his dream. Help him recognize aspects of his dream that are already in the present. What people focus on becomes their reality.

- **Use Appreciative Coaching as a dynamic, iterative process.** People don't live their lives linearly, but in a continual cycle of discovery, learning, and action. Effective coaching reflects this natural rhythm; therefore, the Appreciative Coaching process is meant to guide clients, not direct them.

Additional Reading

Adams, M. G. (2004). *Change your questions, change your life: 7 powerful tools for life and work*. San Francisco: Berrett-Koehler.

Adams introduces QuestionThinking, a simple system of tools for using positive inquiry to transform one's thinking, actions, and therefore results. She contrasts the power of discovering and using "learner" questions with the limiting and negative effect of "judger" questions.

Berg, I. K., & Szabo, P. (2005). *Brief coaching for lasting results*. New York: Norton.

This book blends solution-focused theory with brief, short-term coaching sessions. It teaches coaches how to conduct useful conversations to help clients achieve their goals within a brief period of time. Solution-focused approaches put energy into discovering and highlighting what works instead of being problem oriented with clients.

Berger, P. L., & Luckmann, T. (1966). *The social construction of reality*. New York: Doubleday.

This treatise introduces the term *social construction*, meaning that persons and groups interacting together in a social system form, over time, concepts or mental representations of each other's actions, which eventually become habituated into reciprocal roles. In the process of this institutionalization, knowledge and people's conception (and belief) of what reality is become embedded in the institutional fabric of society. Social reality is therefore said to be socially constructed.

Cooperrider, D. L., & Srivastva, S. (1987). Appreciative Inquiry in organizational life. In R. W. Woodman & E. Pasmore (Eds.), *Research in organizational change and development: An annual series featuring advances in theory* (Vol. 1, pp. 129–169). Greenwich, CT: JAI Press.

This is the seminal article that launched the concept and eventual practice of the Appreciative Inquiry approach to organizational change.

Cooperrider, D. L., & Whitney, D. (2005). *Appreciative Inquiry: A positive revolution in change.* San Francisco: Berrett-Koehler.

This book provides an overview of the newest findings related to the definitions, principles, and practices of AI as a model for change leadership. It draws on more than twenty years of practice and includes positive and inspiring experiments in businesses and communities around the world.

Gergen, K. J., & Gergen, M. (2004). *Social construction: Entering the dialogue.* Chagrin, OH: Taos Institute.

This book is geared toward students, colleagues, and practitioners who desire to gain a basic understanding and appreciation of the power and drama of social construction. Important theoretical developments are outlined as well as constructionist ideas in action—organizations, psychotherapy, education, conflict resolution, social research, and everyday life.

Hammond, S. A. (1998). *The thin book of Appreciative Inquiry* (2nd ed.). Plano, TX: Thin Book.

This book offers a rich summary of the major concepts, assumptions, and tools in the theory and practice of AI.

Orem, S. L., Binkert, J., & Clancy, A. L. (2007). *Appreciative Coaching: A positive process for change.* San Francisco: Jossey-Bass.

This book describes a positive, life-enhancing approach to coaching rooted in AI. Based on research, the Appreciative Coaching model weaves theory with practical, hands-on knowledge, including tools and concrete steps for incorporating this evidence-based method into any existing coaching practice.

Slife, B. (1993). *Time and psychological explanation.* New York: State University of New York.

Slife reveals how the concept of time in the field of psychology has been neither studied nor debated. The unquestioned acceptance of Newtonian, linear time has had dramatic and limiting implications for psychological theory and therapy. He traces the historical legacy of Newtonian time and then presents two opposing assumptions of time, also with deep historical roots, that challenge the Newtonian framework and provide a holistic temporal alternative.

Slife, B. (1995). Newtonian time and psychological explanation. *Journal of Mind and Behavior, 16*(1), 45–62.

This article examines the five characteristics of Newton's conception of Absolute Time—objectivity, continuity, linearity, universality, and reductivity—which have had a profound influence on psychology. It presents criticisms of Newton's framework by contemporary philosophers and physicists who have abandoned these temporal characteristics as well as the concept of Absolute Time.

Wheatley, M. J. (1992). *Leadership and the new science: Learning about organization from an orderly universe.* San Francisco: Berrett-Koehler.

This groundbreaking classic helps readers understand what it means to work within Newtonian organizations in a quantum age. Wheatley offers an alternative view of organizational structure and management based on revolutionary discoveries in quantum physics, chaos theory, and evolutionary biology. These new scientific concepts provide a participative, open, and adaptive understanding of how work and people are organized.

PART SEVEN

Components of Effective Coaching

Assessments are ubiquitous. Although no substitute for the real work of engaging with the client, an assessment can sometimes provide a useful beginning to a coaching conversation. Many clients will have previously been assessed by various instruments—perhaps many times—and a knowledge of what form different assessments take, and what might be learned from them, is invaluable. Included here is a comprehensive survey of commonly used assessments.

More surprising, perhaps, is the range of research that has already been conducted in the field of coaching, including inquiries into what coaches do, and the impact and outcome of their work. There is a need for continuing outcome research and for more extensive reviewing and sharing of findings.

First, though, comes a dynamic and challenging contribution to a discussion of standards in coaching and what constitutes "coach maturity." This chapter sets about confronting some common myths and assumptions, and proposes an approach to a definition of quality, touching on elements that include the quality of the process, the quality of the relationship, the efficacy of the engagement, the adherence to ethical standards, and the return on investment. In doing so, it offers a particular angle on the central concern of this book: what it is we do when we coach, and on what foundations our practices are based.

chapter THIRTY-ONE

Coach Maturity: An Emerging Concept

David Clutterbuck and David Megginson

oaching sometimes seems like Keats's rainbow—the more we try to define it, dissect it, classify it, and demystify it, the more we diminish it and lose its essence. One of the concerns both of us have about so much of the coaching literature is that it represents attempts to confine coaching within the partisan wrappings of a particular school, philosophy, or approach. Often the motivation seems to be less about holistic understanding than about staking out territory, laying claim to the high ground in order to compete with or dislodge competing ideas. Such narrow and sometimes self-serving perspectives seem to us to be completely at odds with the essential ethos of coaching—to be enquiring, open, inclusive, subtle, and multiperspective. This approach has been called "relational coaching" by Erik de Haan and colleagues (de Haan, 2008).

At the same time, we accept and encourage the notion of quality in coaching, even though we may struggle in defining what that means. Ingredients in a definition of quality of coaching might be posited to include

- The delivery of intended and positive unintended outcomes. Simply delivering against the initial, presented goal is not necessarily an indicator of quality, for a number of reasons:

- The goal may be the wrong one for the client or the organization (or both).

- Achieving goal clarity may be the end point, not the beginning of the coaching assignment; many clients need coaching to establish what they want and why, but are self-sufficient in thinking through how they are going to achieve it.

- Even coaching at a relatively low level of competence can achieve change in the client. Simply being there and allowing the client to talk things through can be remarkably effective, where the client needs only to structure his or her own thinking. The primary skills required in such cases are attentive listening and knowing when to shut up!

- Depth of rapport, which may in turn relate to attentiveness, awareness of one's own values, and authenticity.

- Energy. Observation of coaches in assessment center "real plays" suggests that the most effective coaches simultaneously create an intense stillness and an intense energy field. Increasingly used by organizations in Europe, assessment centers are typically customized programs that put coaches through a variety of exercises to assess their skills and suitability. The space between them and the client almost crackles! By contrast, the least effective coaches seem to suck energy from the room, dissipating energy as they flail about seeking to "plug in" to the client and his or her issues.

- A systemic approach to the coaching dynamic. The coaching context extends beyond the individual client to the human and organizational systems in which he or she operates.

OBSERVATIONS ABOUT COACHES AND COACHING

Our observations of many coaches in and out of action in the context of coach assessment centers suggests that it may be easier to define what does *not* define quality. For example:

Having a certificate or diploma. At best this is a hygiene factor, indicating that the coach has undergone some form of training in the role. But rigorous assessment shows that many "certified" coaches are severely lacking in competence, whereas many of the most effective coaches are "naturals" who bring to the role a mixture of innate intuitiveness and reflection on experience.

Having individual accreditation. The International Coach Federation, the Association for Coaching, the European Mentoring and Coaching Council, and others (Brennan & Whybrow, 2010) have set up systems for individual accreditation. This seeks—more directly than certification—to measure something akin to maturity. However, it largely shows that the coach is good enough, rather than how far on a personal journey he or she has traveled.

Client satisfaction. Some clients may overrate the efficacy of their coaches, confusing empathetic conversation (simply having someone listen to them) with transformational dialogue.

Fee rates. We have found a variation of fifteen to one in fees charged per hour, but no significant correlation with quality of coaching delivered.

You may note that we have used the terms *quality* and *efficacy* (or *effectiveness*) interchangeably here. In practice, efficacy—the delivery of positive results—is one aspect of quality. Other aspects potentially include process quality, relationship quality, ethicality, and return on investment.

Efficacy itself is difficult to pin down. Given that the presented goal is often only a starting point or an easy win, is efficacy, in the sense of achieving outcomes, the delivery of the initial objective or of the emerging objective? Moreover, if efficacy is related to outcomes, is it adequate to assess those outcomes solely in terms of changes for or within the client? Taking a systemic perspective, efficacy also concerns the impact on the client's team and a variety of other stakeholders. And, given that coaching is expected to be a two-way learning relationship, to what extent can we include learning and personal change for the coach as elements of coaching efficacy?

Our reflections to reconcile the spontaneity, dynamism, and variety of coaching with the need to maintain standards lead to the conclusion that simplistic classifications are likely to be divisive and of dubious validity. What's needed is a conceptual framework that reflects the evolution of complexity in coaches' way of thinking about themselves, their clients, and the context in which they operate.

A possible solution may lie in the context of maturity. A number of authors have proposed models of the evolution of maturity, in the sense of the development of human beings. These models broadly assume that changes in the structure of thinking about oneself and the world with which we interact evolve slowly and in recognizable, sequential patterns; that higher levels involve a greater degree of awareness about the individual's environment, and greater complexity in how she interprets her environment; that evolving through one level is an essential precursor to the next; that cognitive and socioemotional responses at earlier levels may remain open and available, even though the individual's "center of gravity" is at a higher level; that people evolve at different rates; and that only a small proportion of the population become centered in the highest levels of maturity. These models tend to emphasize either cognitive-reflective processes or ego development (Bachkirova & Cox, 2007), by which they mean the development of self-identity and maturing of interpersonal relationships. Key authors here include Torbert (1991), Wilber (2000), Cook-Greuter (2004), Beck and Cowan (1996), and Kegan (1992).

As Bachkirova and Cox (2007, p. 330) express it,

> What is particularly important in relation to development of coaches is that each stage enriches individual capacity for reflection and effective interaction with others. Their ability to notice nuances and details of situations is increasing. The resultant self-awareness gives them a better opportunity to articulate, influence and potentially change these situations.

Otto Laske (2006, 2009), who has built in particular upon Kegan's approaches, maintains additionally that in a coaching context, the relative maturity of the coach and client is significant in the relationship dynamic. Most important, if the coach is less cognitively or socioemotionally mature than the client, this is likely to have a significant and negative impact on the quality of the coaching process. Chandler and Kram (2005) make a similar point with regard to the related activity of mentoring.

MIND-SETS AND MODELS

Our own interpretations of coach maturity are not based on empirical research, but we hope they will stimulate such research and serve as a starting point for debate. Our model derives from observation in a variety of contexts, but particularly within coach assessment centers, where it is possible to benchmark coaches against consistent criteria and hence to reflect on characteristics and thinking patterns exhibited by coaches of different levels of demonstrated competence. It is important to emphasize here that we are not equating maturity and competence as the same construct. However, it is reasonable to conclude that they are closely related.

From these observations and reflections, four coaching mind-sets emerged, which do appear to represent a progression for many, if not all, coaches. (Having presented these to hundreds of coaches now, we are reasonably confident that coaches who possess a sense of having evolved with their practice appreciate the implied journey and accept the highest level of maturity as an aspiration for committed coaches.) The four levels are *models based, process based, philosophy or discipline based,* and *systemic eclectic.*

Models-based coaches are often very new to the field and seek the reassurance of a closely defined approach that they can take into any situation they might meet. Most often, the model they choose is GROW, or one of its derivatives. This type of coaching is characterized by mechanistic conversations in which following the model is more important than exploring the client's world. It is about doing rather than being; it tends to be about coaching *to* the client rather than coaching *with* the client and about the coaching intervention rather than the coaching relationship. The driving need to find a solution often rests with the coach rather than the client. The dangerous myth that a good coach can coach anyone in any situation appears to stem from this very narrow perception of coaching.

Process-based approaches allow for more flexibility. They can be considered as a structured linking of related techniques and models. The coach has a number of specific tools to use in helping the client's thinking, but the toolkit is still relatively limited. A solutions-focused approach, for example, assumes that the client's immediate need is to find a solution, but in practice, many clients simply want to build a greater understanding of their situation or come to terms with a problem that is inherently insoluble. CLEAN language offers a number of powerful questions, which prevent the imposition of the coach's agenda. Yet there are many coaching situations where the emotional engagement between coach and client provides the most powerful resource for change.

Philosophy- or discipline-based mind-sets tend to offer a still wider portfolio of responses to client needs, because they operate within a broad set of assumptions about helping and human development. They can still be applied mechanistically, however. What prevents them being so is the coach's ability to reflect on his or her practice, both while coaching and after each coaching session. This level of reflexivity is inherent in, say, Gestalt, where self-awareness in the coach is core to helping clients understand themselves and their situation.

The fourth, most liberating mind-set is the systemic eclectic. Coaches with this mind-set have a very wide array of ways of working and a toolkit amassed from many sources, both within coaching and from very different worlds. They have integrated this into a self-aware, personalized way of being with the client. They exhibit an intelligent, sensitive ability to select a broad approach, and within that approach, appropriate tools and techniques that meet the particular needs of a particular client at a particular time. This relates to what Webb (2008) calls coaching for wisdom.

Observation of and discussion with a sample of systemic eclectic coaches suggests that

- They have immense calm, because they have confidence in their ability to find the right tool if they need it.
- They hardly ever use tools. When they do, the tools are subtly and almost seamlessly integrated into the conversation. Indeed, these coaches allow the conversation to happen, holding the client in the development of insight and steering with only the lightest, almost imperceptible touches.
- They place great importance on understanding a technique, model, or process in terms of its origins within a philosophy.
- They use experimentation and reflexive learning to identify where and how a new technique, model, or process fits into their philosophy and framework of helping.
- They judge new techniques, models, and processes on the criterion of *Will this enrich and improve the effectiveness of my potential responses to client needs?*
- They use peers and supervisors to challenge their coaching philosophy and as partners in experimenting with new approaches.
- They take a systemic and holistic view of the client, the client's environment, and the coaching relationship; this makes them more sensitive to nuances of the situation and hence to what approaches they can employ.

Table 31.1 shows a comparison of the four levels of coaching maturity in coaching conversations.

CHARACTERISTICS OF A SYSTEMIC ECLECTIC COACH

Observation in coach assessment centers gave us the basis for proposing an approach that closely parallels other models of maturation. Areas where mature coaches demonstrate that they have reflected deeply include

Table 31.1
Four Mind-Sets for Coaching

Coaching Approach	Style	Critical Questions
Models based	Control	How do I take the client where I think he needs to go? How do I adapt my technique or model to this circumstance?
Process based	Contain	How do I give enough control to the client and still retain a purposeful conversation? What's the best way to apply my process in this instance?
Philosophy based	Facilitate	What can I do to help the client do this for herself? How do I contextualize the client's issue within the perspective of my philosophy or discipline?
Systemic eclectic	Enable	Are we both relaxed enough to allow the issue and the solution to emerge in whatever way they will? Do I need to apply any techniques or processes at all? If I do, what does the client context tell me about how to select from the wide choice available to me?

- Their personal philosophy of coaching
- Understanding of the business context
- Freedom from the tyranny of the question
- Use of coach supervision and mentoring
- Maintaining professional development and integrating learning
- Identifying and managing boundaries
- Their personal journey as a coach
- Knowing the kind of clients and situations with which they work best

- Understanding what makes a fully functioning individual
- Understanding what makes an effective organization

Personal Philosophy of Coaching

"Ontological coaching" has developed specific meaning as a genre of coaching practice. However, in the more generic sense of ontology as "being about being," coaches tend to reflect more deeply, as they mature, on the nature of the interaction between themselves and their clients. Their reflections lead them to an understanding of this interaction that goes far beyond textbook explanations of the coaching process, whether these derive from models-based, process-based, or discipline-based approaches.

They integrate their formal learning with reflection on their experiences with clients, so as to develop *and articulate* a unique and personal perspective of the coaching dynamic. Some parallels can be drawn here with Kegan's stages of adult maturity (1992). Absorbing values and beliefs of others—accepted wisdom—whether consciously or unconsciously, is perhaps typical of Kegan's level three. As they mature, coaches question these "given" beliefs and begin to develop their own, self-authored perspectives, based on their own experience and reasoning. This suggests Kegan's level four. Some go a step further, challenging their own self-focused assumptions, embracing uncertainties, and letting go of any sense of needing to exert control over the conversation. For example, they may see coaching as a process of shared meaning-making in which the client's values and perspectives have equal validity to their own.

Understanding the Business Context

One of the most pernicious myths about coaching is that coaches need no contextual knowledge of the client's world. Whether born of self-aggrandizement or a mechanistic view of coaching, this is manifestly untrue, on two counts: client safety (and hence ethicality) and efficacy. In sports coaching, it is important to know enough to ensure that the client is not led to adopt behaviors that might be detrimental to himself. Similarly in the business world, a coach who works with top managers but who has poor knowledge of corporate governance rules poses a risk both to the clients and to himself or herself. Indeed, legislation in many countries incorporates the concept of a "shadow director," which places partial responsibility for managerial neglect or malpractice on individuals who have influenced the company's decision making. And in a banking environment, for example, it is probably important to have at least a basic understanding of compliance rules.

From an efficacy perspective, the coach has to have enough contextual knowledge, first, to demonstrate empathy and build rapport and credibility with the client and, second, to construct questions that stimulate significant insight.

Coach assessment observations show clearly that the most effective coaches ask questions and make supportive comments that demonstrate

- A broad understanding of the client's world (not necessarily of the client's specific job role or function)
- Knowledge of the "big themes" affecting the organization and the industry
- An ability to link the client's day-to-day issues with these big themes

Of course, having too close an understanding of the client's world also has its downside. In particular, it leads the coach instinctively to come up with his or her own answers, and suppressing these may divert attention from listening to the client. Coaches who have themselves been senior executives in a previous career often visibly struggle to manage this dilemma. Mature coaches work to avoid a directive, "I've been there" approach. Our observation has been that the most effective coaches are often those who have enough knowledge to contextualize questions, yet are able to maintain a deep, curious, and constructive naiveté.

It has been interesting to observe in this regard the reactions of observers and panelists from the companies using assessment centers. Those with HR and line manager backgrounds express frustration that many executive coaches have not made even simple attempts to peer through the windows of the clients' worlds. Failure to take such basic steps as conducting a simple Web search to better understand the client's world is interpreted as arrogance and a sign that the coach has little genuine sense of caring for the client.

Freedom from the Tyranny of the Question

Systemic eclectic coaches give themselves permission to do less, with resultant great efficacy. In classroom experiments, we have artificially limited the number of times coaches can speak to only once in every ten minutes, on average. In almost all cases, the coaches' and coachees' perceived quality of the dialogue and, in particular, of the questions asked is higher than under normal conditions. Our observation of systemic eclectics is that they are almost miserly with their questions, giving their clients maximum time for reflection before they will nudge them gently along in their thinking.

Use of Coach Supervision and Mentoring

Although all the major coaching professional bodies require member coaches to have some form of coach supervision or mentoring, remarkably few coaches seem to have developed a mental model that embraces supervision as a core activity in their practice. For many, it appears to be a tick-the-box requirement, with little proactivity and little practical relevance to their development as coaches. Peer coaching, in particular, can become a collusive, self-congratulatory activity.

We have very little evidence with regard to how coaches at different levels of maturity approach supervision, but we can posit that there might be differences in

- How they choose their coach supervisor or mentor
- The psychological contract they have with their supervisor
- How they decide what to take to supervision
- How they prepare for supervision
- How they reflect upon supervision
- How they ensure the quality of the supervision they receive
- Their awareness of specific changes that have happened in them and in their practice as a result of coach supervision

We suspect—but do not yet have evidence to support—that mature coaches would tend to have more developed, more proactive approaches to coach supervision and mentoring. Certainly, in assessment centers, more mature coaches tend to give clearer, more specific responses to all of the seven issues mentioned above. From comments by systemic eclectics, we glean a number of possible differentiators, which include

- A sense of needing to be challenged fundamentally by supervision—and hence to choose supervisors whose background and perspective are dissimilar to their own

- The use of more than one supervisor, so as to provide different perspectives and challenges—for example, one with a strong formal psychological background and one with a deeper business background

- Integration of supervision and self-supervision

Personal Development

What might a mature approach toward self-development as a coach look like? On the basis of our observation of a small sample of systemic eclectics, we suggest that they might exhibit

- Openness to a wide spectrum of learning opportunities—reading, exploration with peers, supervision, conferences, workshops, and so on

- Self-coaching—proposing insightful questions to themselves

- Networked learning—building around them a network of peers who bring different perspectives but a similar dedication to learning

- Engagement with research and development of the profession—for example, using writing as a vehicle for self-discovery

Boundaries

You don't have to be a psychologist to recognize such phenomena as projection, dependency, or sociopathy. But you do need at least some understanding of psychological and behavioral processes. Assessment centers have, however, revealed some very dangerous coaches who have little appreciation of boundaries—for example, the coach who claimed to have done four thousand hours of coaching, but could not think of a single occasion when he had met a boundary issue!

Maturity in terms of boundary management might conceivably involve

- Both theoretical knowledge and practical experience of a range of psychologically based boundary issues.

- A highly developed sense of the ethics of being a coach. A code of practice can be very helpful as a guide, particularly for inexperienced coaches, but it is only an external instrument. Mature coaches might be expected to have internalized the values within a code of practice and aligned these with their own values, to the extent that they become instinctive, moral responses based on reflection on "choices in action" from the coaches' own experience with clients.

- Having a network of advisers to consult with on new situations, who will offer different perspectives.

- Being able to step outside the coaching relationship from time to time to examine motivations and gain as objective as possible a perspective on the dynamics of the relationship. To some extent, supervision can assist in this (see Hawkins and Smith's seven-eyed process model of supervision, 2006). However, it can be argued that even more value can be gained from supervision in this context if the coach is able to "self-detach" from time to time.

Both boundary management and self-management in coaching are potentially fruitful areas for research.

Personal Journey as a Coach

Common to all theories of maturity is a sense of progression. Inherent in the concept of wisdom is the use of reflection to raise awareness of both current and precursor states. Integral to the assessment center design is a description of the coach's learning journey—how she makes current sense of her evolution toward her current level of practice. For many, the learning journey appears to have begun and ended with a certificate or other formal recognition as a coach. These coaches' practical experience with clients has largely reinforced the "given" knowledge, rather than inspired them to question it.

We extrapolate that further along the maturity spectrum, coaches are able to articulate critical shifts in their awareness of themselves as coaches, of the coach-client relationship, and of the coaching process. A little further along again, they are able to describe—albeit often with hesitancy—where the journey appears to be taking them. It seems that, as with other maturity models, they are aware that the center of gravity of their maturity level is shifting, and they are searching for client opportunities, insights, and pivotal conversations that will assist that movement, even if their vision of where it will take them is still somewhat hazy.

In addition, many of the responses that we would classify as more mature tend to show the following movements:

- From a narrow perspective of coaching toward a broader perspective

- From a need for certainties and solutions to comfort with uncertainties and evolutions

- From a focus on solving just the client's current problem toward a focus on helping him achieve self-understanding that will enable him to avoid future problems

- From a focus on doing to a focus on being

- From preoccupation with the client (client focus) to a balance between the client and the systems of which the client is a part

- From the coaching conversation to the coaching relationship (for example, placing increased emphasis on the client's internal conversations between meetings)

Knowing With Whom They Work Best

It is arguable that every coach is better suited to some clients and situations than others. Key factors here may be

- Whether transfer (of knowledge and expertise) is an important dynamic in the role

- The client's perceptions (right or wrong) about the importance of the coach's background and experience either inside or outside the context of coaching

- The depth of psychological and behavioral competence required to help the client understand her issues and maintain client safety

- The perceived relative status of coach and client

Coaches bring different kinds of life experience, and corporate buyers tend to place a higher value on coaches who have credibility with clients by virtue of their own experience at the senior executive level. (However, assessment center data suggest that a high level of experience in management, when not accompanied by a high level of coaching maturity, represents poor value for the money and may sometimes do more harm than good.)

So what would maturity look like in this case? Some possible components might be

- A clear articulation of their strengths and weaknesses as a coach

- A realistic analysis (in other words, not the public relations story) of situations where they have made the greatest and least impact on a client's awareness, situation, and behavior

- A sense of which clients most pique their professional curiosity and personal engagement

- A realistic sense of their own impact—where they come across as most credible

- Use of reliable, systemic methods of gathering client feedback, along with evidence of analysis of this data and how, through reflection, the data have been used to improve and focus their practice

Conception of a Fully Functioning Person

For many coaches, Rogers's conception (1961) of a fully functioning person may describe the coach's perception of what it means to be human. Many former executives have a much more businesslike model. Whatever model a coach has, it is useful to articulate it so that clients know where the coach is coming from, and the coach realizes that views or hints about what the client might do or aspire to come from a position rather than appearing out of thin air.

Conception of an Effective Organization

What we've said about the coach's views on individual functioning also applies to his view of organizations. Some may feel that Argyris has captured the intractability and difficulty of organizing (see, for example, Senge, Ross, Smith, Roberts, & Kleiner, 1994); others may value the simple nostrums of Peters and Waterman (1982). Again, whatever the source of the coach's views, those views need to be acknowledged.

BECOMING A SYSTEMIC ECLECTIC COACH

So how can and do coaches mature into systemic eclectics? One ingredient is likely to be *time*. Malcolm Gladwell (2008) summarizes research into exceptional performance in a range of activities from business to sport and suggests that it takes ten thousand hours to achieve mastery in any field. Certainly, all the systemic eclectics we have observed have been involved with coaching—or with related disciplines—for a good many years. But putting in the hours does not automatically create mastery—there must also be an immense amount of reflection, experimentation, and adaptation of practice.

We observe that for systemic eclectics, the learning they acquire shows them how much more they could learn. Their experience is like that of climbing a mountain: the higher they ascend, the bigger and more distant the horizon. We suspect that feeling comfortable with this diminishing perspective of one's own importance and competence relative to what might conceivably be possible requires a great deal of personal maturity.

Presented with this metaphor, relatively inexperienced coaches often express concern to us about the scale of the learning journey ahead of them. Our response is to expand the metaphor. What is the point of a long journey with no clear end point if you don't stop periodically and enjoy the view? If there is one characteristic of systemic eclectics that can potentially be learned and used by coaches at any level of maturity—and can possibly speed the transition between levels—it is this ability to savor where you are, to contextualize it and to be able to look both forward and backward along the path. Accepting and valuing your current state may be the critical component in achieving the next level of maturity!

chapter THIRTY-TWO

Use of Assessments in Coaching

Mary M. Nash, Dian Christian, and Janet Baldwin Anderson

O ur belief is that an assessment is *only* as effective as the coaching discussion that follows it. This chapter provides an introduction to the wide variety of assessments utilized in coaching. It offers guidelines for determining whether, when, what, and how assessments may be used, as well as brief annotations of many assessments that are widely used in coaching today.

In the hands of a knowledgeable and experienced coach, assessments can serve as effective and efficient means to inform both the client and the coach about client preferences, styles, skills, and abilities, in order to advance the coaching process. Although much of this information could be collected through conversations with the client, assessments may provide a shortcut (Rogers, 2004), establish a common language for the coach and client, and build a foundation for developing the coaching plan. Assessment data, whether self-reported or received through multirater feedback (such as a 360-degree feedback instrument) or other means, can provide the client with new self-awareness and insights, as well as the ability and language to articulate these new understandings.

Sometimes a client comes to a coaching engagement with a rich portfolio of assessment results, current or historical. These assessments can be a starting place for understanding and appreciating more about the client. If the coach is not certified and experienced with a given assessment, partnering with a coach who *is* can help make the data more useful. A coach who abides by the ethical standards set by the professional coaching and testing bodies recognizes her limits and does not attempt to interpret or use data from assessments unless trained, knowledgeable, and experienced in their use. As in medicine: *above all, do no harm.*

Included here are the assessments currently most commonly utilized in coaching. Each has been reviewed for the availability of psychometric evidence (such as validity, and reliability when relevant), research studies documenting its use, and anecdotal reports of its usefulness by certified practitioners and clients. This is not a comprehensive compilation, but a selection intended to represent some of the best examples among the range of assessments available. Our purpose here is to provide a concise overview as a resource.

At the end of this chapter is Table 32.1, which provides information to help the reader identify appropriate assessments for a given engagement or situation. The table also includes information on Web-based and other resources for learning more about an assessment. But before we go into the review, let us first look at the *why, which, when, who,* and *how* of using assessments in coaching.

WHY CONDUCT ASSESSMENTS?

The coach needs to be acutely aware of *why* she wishes to conduct an assessment in the first place. What will she do with the new information? How can this information enable the client to gain insights that were not recognized prior to the assessment? (Rogers, 2004). Appropriate purposes include enhancing self-discovery and awareness on the part of the individual client, and improving performance, group process, or team functioning. In addition, assessments can provide a common language for the coach and client(s) to discuss current status and monitor change and progress (Harper, 2008). The client will not be best served if the coach relies on the assessment as a substitute for a coaching discussion, refers to the assessment when she feels "stuck" as to where to go next in the coaching engagement, uses the assessment as a way to forward her own agenda instead of the client's, or discusses the assessment without clear intention merely because this is required by the client's organizational coaching protocol. Other important preliminary considerations include the readiness and maturity of the client and, where appropriate, the coach's familiarity with professional standards for measurement and assessment (American Educational Research Association, American Psychological Association, & National Council on Measurement in Education, 1999).

WHICH ASSESSMENTS, AND WHEN?

Once a coach and client have identified a coaching issue for which an assessment may be appropriate, the next questions are *which* assessment to use, and *when*? In some engagements, and particularly in organizations with an established coaching culture and protocol, specific assessments may be conducted just prior to beginning a coaching engagement, but whenever possible it is beneficial for the coach and client to establish rapport and trust before embarking on an assessment process. The client might have historical data (such as previous 360-degree feedback results); re-administration could be enlightening. Benchmark data could be helpful in monitoring progress or growth.

WHO SHOULD BE ASSESSED, AND HOW?

Closely following these considerations, or aligned with them, is the question of *who* should participate in the assessment. Is self-report data likely to provide the necessary awareness, for example, or would multirater assessment better facilitate breakthrough insights? These issues are best addressed through the coach's mindful reflection on the particular engagement and through collaboration with the client and, where appropriate, the client's organization. In making these decisions, it is important to be aware of the danger of "survey fatigue," both for other raters and the client.

Whatever assessment is chosen, the coach will need to know *how* to conduct it. One critical consideration is to ensure that the coach has the necessary qualifications and experience. This is in the best interest of both the coach and the client. Some instruments require specific training or certification. It is strongly recommended that coaches not administer assessments that they have not taken themselves. Participating in an assessment, however, does *not* constitute adequate training for administering it with a client.

The use of assessments can facilitate the coach's own self-knowledge. That, along with open-minded curiosity and unconditional positive regard, can help the coach create the nonjudgmental presence needed to remain open to the client and all that he brings to the engagement.

Once the assessments have been conducted and scored, and the results interpreted, the real coaching begins. The results are a beginning point for a conversation with the client. They help the coach decide what approach or style might work best in this coaching relationship (Auerbach, 2001). Some assessment results may be completely new to the client; others may be familiar and have positive or negative connotations. The client may have taken an assessment in the past and either forgotten about it or had a less than favorable experience. He may have never thought about what he prefers, how he tends to behave in certain situations, or what processes for thinking or learning he most often uses. He may be startled by the accuracy of the assessment findings or may be skeptical and deny that the data are relevant to him in any way. Regardless of the initial response, an experienced and fully present coach can help facilitate rich, reflective dialogue and useful insight.

Assessments are valuable in the workplace because often people avoid being frank with each other, and many leaders get little honest, transparent, or constructive feedback (Peltier, 2001). In the coaching relationship, assessments are beneficial because they can create a fast track toward a deep conversation. Often clients who desire to make productive changes appreciate the ability of assessments to accelerate the progress of establishing trust and rapport with the coach, developing self-awareness, and establishing the coaching goals. Although a client is more than the snapshot captured by one or even a combination of assessments, and may at times act in ways that are not consistent with the results, the data, discussed in the context of an effective coach-client relationship, can lead clients to new ways of feeling and thinking about themselves, and of being.

An assessment is merely a tool, one method for the coach and client to gain information and insight. While it is important to select appropriate assessments purposefully, it is also important to acknowledge that the way in which the coach uses the assessment, the process and use of self, is key. Even the best assessment can't take the place of deep listening, nonjudgmental curiosity, following the client's agenda, and cocreating an action plan that moves the client forward.

REVIEW OF ASSESSMENTS

Following are brief descriptions of many assessments commonly utilized in coaching engagements. Included are the Web sites from which the reader can gain further information.

16 Personality Factors (16PF)

The 16PF, developed by Raymond Cattell, includes measurements of the following: warmth, reasoning, emotional stability, dominance, liveliness, rule-consciousness, social boldness, sensitivity, vigilance, abstractedness, privateness, apprehension, openness to change, self-reliance, perfectionism, and tension. It has been studied extensively, and the sixteen factors have been shown to overlap with the five higher-order factors known as the Big Five (see NEO PI-R). (www.pearsonassessments.com)

Belbin Team Role Questionnaire

Developed by Dr. R. Meredith Belbin, this assessment categorizes team roles as action-oriented, people-oriented, or cerebral, and defines nine specific roles: shaper, implementer, completer finisher, co-ordinator, teamworker, resource investigator, plant, monitor evaluator, and specialist. Awareness of the roles we play can help us be more intentional about which role is most helpful to the overall performance of the team. (www.belbin.com)

Birkman Method

The Birkman Method, developed by Roger Birkman, aims to identify a person's everyday interpersonal style, underlying motivation, expectations, and signs of stress behavior. This tool helps individuals gain understanding about how and why they lead, learn, think, decide, and relate to others. (www.birkman.com)

California Psychological Inventory (CPI 260 and CPI 434)

Utilized and researched for over fifty years, these assessments provide insight to support individual and leadership development, and performance improvement. The CPI 260 provides results on more than two dozen scales in five areas: dealing with others, self-management, motivations and thinking style, personal characteristics, and work-related measures. The CPI 434 includes two scale profiles, one with gender-specific norms, the other with total norms, and includes results on scales including creative temperament, managerial potential, and tough-mindedness. (www.cpp.com)

Campbell Leadership Index (CLI)

Developed by David P. Campbell of the Center for Creative Leadership, the CLI is a 360-degree multirater assessment that measures personal characteristics related to the demands of leadership and to an individual's leadership success. Comparing self-ratings with the average ratings of observers, the measured characteristics are organized into the following five broad orientations: leadership, energy, affability, dependability, and resilience. The survey also provides twenty-one measures of more specific leadership characteristics. The scored results yield a profile of strengths and areas for improvement. (www.vangent-hcm.com)

Career Anchors

Career Anchors Self-Assessment, developed by Edgar Schein, facilitates discovery of one's career motivators. Schein believed there is one driving motivator for most people and that their preferences for a career generally match this motivator. The career anchors are technical/functional competence, general managerial competence, autonomy/independence, security/stability, entrepreneurial creativity, service/dedication to a cause, pure challenge, and lifestyle. The questionnaire helps the client understand what the primary motivator is for her. (www.careeranchorsonline.com)

Clifton StrengthsFinder

This assessment was developed by Marcus Buckingham and Donald Clifton of Gallup Organization, the authors of *Now, Discover Your Strengths* (2001). It identifies the client's top five signature themes out of thirty-four potential themes, and is based on the assumption that one can become more productive by focusing and developing strengths than by working on weaknesses. Themes include achiever, activator, and developer, among others. (www.gallup.com)

Cultural Orientations Framework (COF) Assessment Questionnaire

This was developed from a framework of the same name by Philippe Rosinski. The COF was designed to assess and compare cultures, and includes a range of cultural dimensions or orientations grouped in seven categories: sense of power and responsibility, time management approaches, definitions of identity and purpose, organizational arrangements, notions of territory and boundaries, communication patterns, and modes of thinking. (www.philrosinski.com)

Cultural Orientations Indicator (COI)

COI measures a person's work style preferences against ten dimensions of culture. Results can be compared against colleagues' profiles as well as team and country profiles. (www.tmcorp.com)

DiSC/DISC

The DiSC (with a lowercase *i*) assessment uses nonjudgmental language to explore behavior styles across four primary dimensions: dominance, influence, steadiness, and conscientiousness. DISC (with an uppercase *I*) measures dominance, influence, steadiness, and compliance. These assessments are used with an individual or a team to foster awareness, enhance individual or team performance, develop better communication, and reduce conflict. Both are based on the work of Dr. William Moulton Marston. (DiSC: www.inscapepublishing.com) (DISC: www.extendeddisc-na.com)

Emotional Competence Inventory (ECI), also Emotional and Social Competency Inventory (ESCI)

This instrument provides self-, manager, direct report, and peer ratings on a series of behavioral indicators of emotional intelligence, based on emotional competencies defined by Daniel Goleman. The ECI comprises twenty competencies in four clusters: self-awareness, self-management, social awareness, and relationship management. The ESCI is the latest 360-feedback tool based on the ECI. The ESCI measures twelve competencies organized into four clusters: self-awareness, self-management, social awareness, and relationship management. (www.haygroup.com)

Emotional Quotient Inventory (EQ-i) and the EQ-360

Developed by Reuven Bar-On, the EQ-i is a self-report measure of emotionally and socially intelligent behavior that provides an estimate of emotional-social intelligence. Ten of the fifteen scales have been confirmed in factor analysis: self-regard, interpersonal relationships, impulse control, problem solving, emotional self-awareness, flexibility, reality testing, stress tolerance, assertiveness, and empathy. The other five scales (optimism, self-actualization, happiness, independence, and social responsibility) are retained as "facilitators" of social and emotional intelligence. Reports are available in several formats for individuals and teams, including leadership, development, group, individual to group, group to group, and group across administration. The EQ-360 is a multirater version of the EQ-i. It comprises eighty-eight items in the form of short sentences and employs a five-point response format. (www.mhs.com)

Fundamental Interpersonal Relationships Orientation–Behavior (FIRO-B)

Developed by Will Schutz for the U.S. Navy during the Korean War, the FIRO-B predicts how individuals will work together in groups. The model identifies three interpersonal needs: inclusion, control, and affection. The six-cell model shows expressed behavior and desired behavior for the three interpersonal needs, helping clients gain insight into their own behavior and that of others while working or interacting in groups. (www.cpp.com)

Herrmann Brain Dominance Instrument (HBDI)

This assessment identifies one's preferred approach to thinking. Based on whole-brain thinking, the categories are emotional, analytical, structural, and strategic. William Herrmann, developer of the assessment, suggests that it may be used for better understanding of self and others, as well as enhanced communication and productivity. (www.hbdi.com)

Hogan Personality Inventory (HPI)

Based on the Five Factor Model (see NEO PI-R) and adapted by Dr. Robert Hogan for the business community, this measurement includes seven primary scales and six occupational scales. The primary scales are adjustment, ambition, sociability, interpersonal sensitivity, prudence, inquisitive, and learning approach. The occupational scales are service orientation, stress tolerance, reliability, clerical potential, sales potential, and managerial potential. (www.hoganassessments.com)

International Personality Item Pool (IPIP)

Lewis Golberg developed this questionnaire, based on the Five Factor Model, to measure extraversion, agreeableness, conscientiousness, emotional stability, and intellect. (http://ipip.ori.org)

Leadership Effectiveness Analysis (LEA) 360

Based on decades of research on leadership competencies, this multirater assessment provides feedback on twenty-two leadership practices, as well as normative data from international peer groups. The resultant report focuses on opportunities for development through provision of profiles, narratives, and strategic implications. This assessment is available in fourteen languages and with nineteen country- or region-specific norms. (www.mrg.com)

Learning Styles Inventory (LSI)

Based on David Kolb's experiential learning theory, this self-scoring assessment determines an individual's learning style—accommodating, assimilating, diverging, or converging. The insights gained from this assessment help the client understand how she actually learns and how she might create situations for learning that are consistent with her preferred style. Understanding learning situations that are not as useful to the client would also be beneficial and can enhance the potential to avoid less effective strategies in the future. (www.haygroup.com)

LH-System for Testing and Evaluation of Potential (LH-STEP)

The LH-STEP is a comprehensive assessment battery designed to compare a person's scores against a normative sample of higher-level professionals and executives, as well as to a company-specific position or job family. It is used to help an organization match an applicant's individual capabilities to specific job requirements by measuring skills, abilities, and potential for success. Developed by psychologists at the University of Chicago's Human Resource Center, the assessment provides information for objective decisions related to hiring, training, and promoting. It helps uncover hidden assets in the workforce and identifies strengths and areas for development for an individual or an entire department. (www.vangent-hcm.com)

Leadership Practices Inventory (LPI 360)

LPI 360 is a comprehensive leadership development tool created by James M. Kouzes and Barry Z. Posner as part of the Leadership Challenge program. LPI 360 provides a way for individual leaders to measure and receive feedback on the frequency of their own specific leadership behaviors on a 10-point scale. (www.lpionline.com)

Mayer-Salovey-Caruso Emotional Intelligence Test (MSCEIT)

Developed by John Mayer, Peter Salovey, and David Caruso, the MSCEIT is a refinement of their Multifactor Emotional Intelligence Scale (MEIS) following further empirical research in this domain. This is also a shorter assessment than its predecessor, without sacrificing its psychometric properties. The MSCEIT is an ability-based model that assesses the respondent's ability to perceive, use, understand, and regulate emotions. (www.mhs.com)

Myers-Briggs Type Indicator (MBTI)

The MBTI, one of the most widely used assessments globally, indicates a person's preferences for where he gets his energy, how he gathers data, how he makes decisions, and how he orders his life. Based on the work of Carl Jung and developed by the mother-and-daughter team of Katherine Briggs and Isabel Briggs Myers, the MBTI measures preferences on four personality dichotomies: introversion (I)/extroversion (E), sensing (S)/intuiting (N), thinking (T)/feeling (F), and perceiving (P)/judging (J), resulting in a four-letter type (for example, INTP). The MBTI Step II, which helps clients understand how they differ from others with the same type, provides feedback on twenty additional subscales or facets. (www.cpp.com)

NEO Personality Inventory-Revised (NEO PI-R) and NEO Five-Factor Inventory (NEO-FFI)

Based on research on human personality, the NEO PI-R assessment was developed by Paul Costa and Robert McCrae to identify the overarching factors of human personality known as the Five Factor Model. These factors are openness to experience, conscientiousness, extraversion, agreeableness, and neuroticism (OCEAN). The NEO PI-R has 240 items and two versions: one for self-assessment and one for observers. The NEO-FFI is shorter, with only 60 items, but is still a valid and reliable assessment. (www4.parinc.com)

Parker Team Player Survey (TPS) and Parker Team Development Survey (TDS)

The TPS, which was developed by Glenn Parker, identifies the team member styles of contributor, collaborator, communicator, and challenger. This style preference helps individuals see how they respond in team situations as well as see what style their team members use in the team setting. Parker's TDS offers a way to measure how well a team is performing and can also be used as a team-building activity or a basis for a workshop on team effectiveness. (www.cpp.com)

Riso-Hudson Enneagram Type Indicator (RHETI)

The Enneagram, an ancient geometric figure, delineates nine basic personality types and the ways in which the nine types are related to each other. The RHETI is an independently scientifically validated assessment of Enneagram preferences. The assessment helps foster awareness and personal growth by helping clients notice patterns that exist in their daily life. (www.enneagraminstitute.com)

Social Style Model

This assessment looks at the dimensions of assertiveness and responsiveness in natural behavioral patterns. The intersection of these two dimensions creates four social styles: analytical, driving, expressive, and amiable. The practical application of understanding one's social style preference and that of others can lead to insights about how to improve interpersonal skills. (www.tracomcorp.com)

Strong Interest Inventory (SII)

Based on the six RIASEC categories developed by John Holland (realist, investigative, artistic, social, enterprising, and conventional), the SII measures a client's interests in a range of occupations, work and leisure activities, and school subjects for the purpose of finding a match in her work or school life. By comparing her interests with those of people who have found satisfaction in a particular career, the report helps the client see where new career options might exist. (www.cpp.com)

Subject-Object Interview (SOI)

Based on the work of Robert Kegan, the SOI enables coaches to know their own developmental level, as well as those of their clients, through the lens of Kegan's model of adult development. This understanding helps facilitate communication and development of appropriate coaching goals. The SOI is conducted through a focused semistructured interview that requires transcription and qualitative data analysis. (www.mindsatwork.com)

Team Development Assessment (TDA) 4-D Systems

Developed by Charles Pellerin, PhD, former director of NASA's astrophysics division, the four-dimensional, eight-item assessment is designed to measure the social context of the team, which Pellerin defines as a group of people with sufficient social interaction to develop common behavioral norms. The assessment supports individual leader and team development. (www.4dsystems.com)

Thomas-Kilmann Conflict Model Instrument (TKI)

Kenneth Thomas and Ralph Kilmann developed this assessment to look at individual behavior in conflict situations. Using the two basic dimensions of assertiveness and cooperativeness, they found five specific methods people use in dealing with conflict: competing, collaborating, compromising, avoiding, and accommodating. The TKI is valuable in both individual and team coaching settings. (www.cpp.com)

Values in Action (VIA) Survey of Character Strengths

Martin Seligman and Christopher Peterson developed this survey to measure twenty-four character strengths—creativity, curiosity, and open-mindedness, among others. (www.viasurvey.org)

Table 32.1.
Selected Assessments by Construct Assessed

Assessment	Adult Development	Behavior Style	Career	Cognitive Abilities	Conflict	Culture	Emotional Intelligence	Leadership	Personality	Strengths	Team Development	Values
16 Personality Factors (16PF)									X			
Belbin Team Role Questionnaire											X	
Birkman Method		X										
California Psychological Inventory (CPI)		X							X			
Campbell Leadership Index (CLI)								X				
Career Anchors			X									
Clifton StrengthsFinder										X		
Cultural Orientations Framework (COF)						X						
Cultural Orientations Indicator (COI)						X						
DiSC/DISC		X										
Emotional Competence Inventory (ECI)							X					
Emotional Quotient Inventory (EQ-i) (self-assessment)							X					
EQ-360 (multirater assessment)							X					
Fundamental Interpersonal Relationships Orientation-Behavior (FIRO-B)		X										
Hermann Brain Dominance Inventory (HBDI)		X										
Hogan Personality Inventory (HPI)									X			
International Personality Item Pool (IPIP)									X			
Leadership Effectiveness Analysis (LEA) 360								X				
Leadership Practices Inventory (LPI 360)								X				
Learning Styles Inventory (LSI)		X										

(Continued)

Table 32.1.
Selected Assessments by Construct Assessed (*Continued*)

Assessment	Adult Development	Behavior Style	Career	Cognitive Abilities	Conflict	Culture	Emotional Intelligence	Leadership	Personality	Strengths	Team Development	Values
LH-System for Testing and Evaluation of Potential (LH-STEP)				X								
Mayer-Salovey-Caruso Emotional Intelligence Test (MSCEIT)							X					
Myers-Briggs Type Indicator (MBTI)									X			
NEO Personality Inventory-Revised (NEO PI-R) and NEO Five-Factor Inventory (NEO-FFI)									X			
Parker Team Development Survey (TDS)											X	
Parker Team Player Survey (TPS)											X	
Riso-Hudson Enneagram Type Indicator (RHETI)									X			
Social Style Model		X										
Strong Interest Inventory (SII)			X									
Subject-Object Interview (SOI)	X											
Team Development Assessment (TDA) 4-D Systems											X	
Thomas-Kilmann Conflict Model Instrument (TKI)					X							
Values in Action (VIA) Survey of Character Strengths												X

Current Research on Coaching

Francine Campone

What are other coaches doing? How have they been trained? Are they applying particular theories or models? What kinds of results are they getting? What do clients think about the experience? Coaches are curious about such questions—and appropriately so.

Scholarly coaching-specific studies have proliferated in the past ten years. They provide numerous sources of information on these and other topics. This chapter presents an overview of coaching-specific research, with an eye toward gaining a better understanding of what coaching scholars and practitioners are studying and where to locate findings that might be of use to readers of this book. The studies included here have all appeared in peer-reviewed journals within the past ten years, and all are empirical, resting on evidence gathered in the course of a formal research process. A key source in the preparation of this chapter is Grant's annotated bibliography (2009) and the search engines ProQuest and Wilson Select, which can be accessed through a library with subscription privileges.

Given the relatively young state of coaching-specific research, it may be too soon to draw conclusions about coaching impact, processes, or the field in general. Results are sometimes contradictory and suggest many avenues for further study. Nonetheless, coach practitioners can identify what is being studied, learn how coaching research is conducted, and use the results to inform their own practice. Becoming familiar with coaching research is not as daunting as it might initially appear, and can be useful in various ways. It allows practitioners to benchmark their own experiences and answer the question, *Is this how others do it?* It helps them make better-informed decisions about how to respond to particular clients or situations; for example, client perception studies, studies in the impact of cognitive behavioral and other models, and studies on coaching special populations can give them insight into how to apply best practices. Reading studies can help practitioners stretch their understanding of earlier learning on competencies, boundaries, and models. Finally, it opens doors for skilled practitioners to gain a deeper understanding of the science behind the art.

The studies are presented in four sections: (1) studies of the coaching field—what coaches do, who they are, and the nature of the industry; (2) coaching impacts and outcomes; (3) research on coaching special populations; and (4) deep investigations of coaching literature to generate evidence-based theories and models of coaching.

PRACTICE, PRACTITIONERS, AND THE INDUSTRY

Research topics in this area include the different dimensions of the coaching process (what coaches do); client perceptions of what aspects of coaching are most helpful; coach characteristics; the coaching industry, including coach training; and coaching provided by leaders or managers as a strategy for carrying out their leadership roles. These studies were all conducted with internal or external coaches for whom coaching is a primary role.

What Coaches Do

Coaches often wonder what other coaches do and what specific coaching strategies and interventions seem to be most useful in helping clients effect change. By analyzing the narratives of coaching conversations, Stein (2008) identifies and defines the multiple roles taken by coaches in the course of dialogue. Dawdy (2004) provides a comparative analysis of coaching methods based on client feedback. Seamons (2006) explores clients' and their supervisors' perspectives on the most effective aspects of coaching. Creane's exploratory study (2003) of client perceptions of personal coaching identifies thirteen dimensions of what personal coaching is and how it impacts clients.

Ballinger (2000) and Luebbe (2005) identified those factors in coaching that clients perceived as most important in contributing to behavior change. Longhurst (2006) explored the dimensions and impact of the "aha" moment in coaching.

Blow's qualitative study (2005) identified aspects of the coaching process that supported experts in more effectively sharing their expertise. The impact of the coaching relationship was explored in studies by Baron and Morin (2009), Huggler (2007), and Orenstein (2002).

Authors studying client perceptions of what coaches do include Peterson and Millier (2005), Olsen (2006), and Gyllensten and Palmer (2007). The executive experience and perceptions of coaching are explored in several studies, including Sztucinski (2002), Fanasheh (2003), Bush (2005), Terrell (2004), and Stevens (2005). Blattner's case study of coaching a downwardly mobile executive (2005) provides insight into coaching processes. Boespflug (2005) compares the attitudes of male future business managers toward coaching and psychotherapy.

The method of coaching delivery, whether face-to-face, distance, phone, or videoconferencing also appears to have an impact. Charbonneau (2003) and Bell (2006) both offer insight into the medium selection process and discuss the implications of media choices. Hancyk (2000) and Yedreshteyn (2009) explore best practices for introducing and implementing coaching programs in a corporate environment.

Who Coaches Are and How They're Trained

What coaches know, how they were trained, their original field of education and practice, and several other dimensions of the coach have an impact on coaching outcomes. Grant and Zackon (2004) conducted a large-scale survey of coaches' knowledge bases, theories, techniques, and outcomes, with responses from 2,529 members of the International Coach Federation. Similarly, Spence, Cavanagh, and Grant (2006) surveyed the skills, experience, and training of Australian coaches; Brooks and Wright (2007) studied the characteristics of coaches in New Zealand. Liljenstrand (2004) and Liljenstrand and Nebecker (2008) compared the practices of coaches with backgrounds in business, clinical psychology, or related fields, or industrial-organizational psychology or related fields. Newsom (2009) analyzed the work behaviors of coaches, with an interest in comparing these with the work practices used in counseling.

The training and practices of coaching psychologists is explored in Whybrow and Palmer's study (2006). Braham (2006) explores the impact of Vipassana meditation practice on coaches' practice. Coaches' theories of emotions figure as the focus of Bachkirova and Cox's study (2007); coaching practices that enact theories of emotion are explored in Cox and Bachkirova (2007). Traynor (2000) demonstrates the coaching-related skills of clinical psychologists and offers a framework for their involvement through coaching, training, mentoring, and therapy.

Studies examining the impact of different approaches to coach training and education include long-term supervision (Butwell, 2006), short- and long-term skills development programs (Grant, 2007), and personal life coaching for coaches in training (Grant, 2008). Grant and Cavanagh (2007) report on preliminary results of a study seeking to validate a coaching skills self-report instrument. Erik de Haan's studies of critical incidents in coaching (2008a, 2008b) present the experiences of novice and experienced coaches and discuss implications for coach development.

The Coaching Industry

Ozkan's dissertation (2008) offers a context for the emergence and evolution of coaching as a field and a culture. Several studies of the coaching industry are centered in Australia, including Clegg, Rhodes, Kornberger, and Stilin's survey (2005) of potential challenges and Grant and O'Hara's exploration (2006) of the self-presentation and business characteristics of Australian coaching schools. The characteristics of coach training and education in Australia are documented by Binstead and Grant (2008) and Grant and O'Hara (2008). Ahern's survey (2005) of provider type and characteristics compares the quality of coaching offered by three different sizes of provider groups. Rogers (2005) conducted an action research survey of business plans for life coaches.

Leaders and Managers as Coaches

The studies in this section examine the impact coaching has on staff performance when leaders or managers provide the coaching, and the impact of coaching received by leaders or managers.

Konczak, Stelly, and Trusty (2000) developed and tested the Leader Empowering Behavior Questionnaire as a means of identifying the dimensions of leadership behavior related to improved job satisfaction and organizational commitment. Wenzel (2001) proposed and tested a model for managers as coaches, identifying manager characteristics that are predictive of successful coaching performance. Longenecker and Neubert's study (2005) presents junior managers' perceptions of manager coaching behaviors considered to be most critical. Wacholz (2000) examined multiple dimensions of coaching sessions between supervisors and sales agents. In a comparative study, Noer, Leupold, and Valle (2007) examined coaching behaviors of Saudi Arabian and U.S. managers and the role of underlying cultural values.

Miller's case study (2003) presents the impact of a manager training seminar that included performance coaching skills in the context of an action learning process. Using a quasi-experimental design, Wangsgard (2007) introduces a model for training managers in coaching skills, and documents the impact of the training model.

The study by Ellinger, Ellinger, and Keller (2005) examined the impact of manager coaching on the performance of warehouse workers in the logistics industry. Morgeson (2005) examined the impact of external leader coaching on team performance. Hamlin, Ellinger, and Beattie (2006) presented a cross-cultural comparison of empirical findings from prior studies of manager coaching effectiveness. Using a case study framework, Law, Ireland, and Hussain (2006) sought to develop a universal integrated framework of coaching and evaluate its impact on participants and organizations.

COACHING IMPACTS AND OUTCOMES

The impact of coaching has been measured in a wide variety of ways, both quantitative and qualitative. This section looks at studies of coaching impacts and outcomes (1) in organizational contexts, (2) related to specific theories or models of coaching, and (3) as an element of a multidimensional development program.

Organizations

There is a growing body of data that document coaching impact on the individual client, on teams, and on the organization. Two studies present alternatives for the measurement of coaching outcomes: Leedham (2005) offers a holistic scorecard method, and Parker-Wilkins (2006) proposes elements for assessing the value proposition in coaching. Some insight into the value proposition may also be gained from reading Dagley's interviews (2006) of HR professionals, which document perceptions of efficacy, effectiveness, and return on investment.

Several studies have measured the impact on specific dimensions, including manager effectiveness (Jones, Rafferty, & Griffin, 2006; Styhre & Josephson, 2007), learning agility (Trathen, 2008), feedback ratings (Smither, London, Flautt, Vargas, & Kucine, 2003), and self-efficacy (Evers, Brouwers, & Tomic, 2006; Sparrow,

2007). Both studies by Ascentia (2005a, 2005b) as well as a study by Bowles, Cunningham, Rosa, and Picano (2007) document the impact of coaching on managers and their teams. Kombarakaran, Baker, Yang, and Fernandes (2008) present the results of a survey of coaches and clients to demonstrate the impact of executive coaching and characteristics of effective program design. One study explicitly sought to identify those executives who might most benefit from coaching (Kampa-Kokesch, 2002), while another looked at the impact, benefits, and limitations of coaching within large organizations (McDermott, Levenson, & Newton, 2007).

The impact of coaching on individual development, workplace health, and absenteeism formed the focus of several studies. Hurd (2003) took a phenomenological approach to better understand how coaching impacted individual clients in personal, career, and organizational dimensions, as well as to identify a link between coaching, adult development, and organization development. Wales (2003) described the impact of an externally provided coaching program and the impact of internal changes, such as increased self-awareness and confidence, on external behaviors. Gyllensten and Palmer (2005, 2006) applied both quasi-experimental and qualitative methods to explore the impact of a workplace coaching program on levels of stress. Dujits, Kant, van den Brandt, and Swaen (2007, 2008) demonstrated the impact of coaching on absence rates of high-risk employee populations. Wasylyshyn, Gronsky, and Haas (2006) documented the impact of coaching on the emotional competence of high-potential employees; Feggetter (2007) studied coaching perceptions and coaching outcomes with this group. Goal quality and self-concordance were shown to be enhanced by coaching in Burke and Linley's study (2007).

Studies have been conducted on coaching impact outside the corporate sector as well. Populations include military leaders (Bowles & Picano, 2006), teachers in the United Kingdom (Allan, 2007), school principals (Gravel, 2007), and nursing leaders (Mackenzie, 2007). Winum's case study (2005) documents both the format and impact of coaching on an African American executive.

Particular Theoretical Models

The impact of cognitive behavioral coaching is examined and documented in several studies. Grant (2002, 2003) tested an integrative framework of solution-focused, cognitive behavioral coaching in a series of studies, measuring the impact on metacognition, mental health, and goal attainment. The impact of peer and professional life coaching on goal striving and well-being is also documented in Spence and Grant (2007). Green, Oades, and Grant (2006) similarly examined the impact of a cognitive behavioral coaching approach in life coaching; Libri and Kemp (2006) studied the impact of a cognitive behavioral coaching model on executives. A cognitive behavioral approach to coaching was shown to have a positive impact on hopefulness and cognitive hardiness when employed by teacher coaches with a high school population (Green, Grant, & Rynsaardt, 2007). Palmer and Gyllensten (2008) present a case study that documents the impact of cognitive behavioral coaching with a client suffering from depression. Case study is also the platform for Karas and Spada's study (2009) of the impact of brief cognitive behavioral coaching on procrastination.

In the health arena, three studies examine the impact of coaching by health care providers on patient choices and behaviors: Bennett and Perrin (2005); Allen, Lezzoni, Huang, Huang, and Leveille (2008); and Gattellari et al. (2005). Mindfulness training and health coaching were combined in an approach documented by Spence, Cavanagh, and Grant (2008); and Butterworth, Linden, McClay, and Leo (2006) studied the impact of motivational interview–based coaching on employees' physical and mental health.

Clark (2003) and Bell (2006) both studied the use of the Meyers-Briggs Type Indicator as a key element of coaching programs. Czigan (2008) looked at the use of personality indicators in the design of coaching. Other integrative models include a principle-based intervention that integrates an understanding of mind, thought, and consciousness (Roy, 2007); a spirituality and transformational learning approach in coaching (Brantley, 2007); and a whole-system approach to coaching (Fahy, 2007).

With Other Development Activities

Conway (2000) utilized both a multirater feedback instrument and the Developmental Challenge Profile as integral elements of a feedback-with-coaching intervention, and measured the differences of impact for several delivery methods. Coaching was combined with other delivery methods as a tool for enhancing the learning of motivational interviewing in Miller, Yahne, Moyers, Martinez, and Pirritano's study (2004). Mulec and Roth's study (2005) examined the impact of team coaching in combination with action learning and reflection. Schnell's case study (2005) followed the evolution of a multidimensional program over the course of a five-year period of organizational growth and development. Emotional intelligence served as the focus for Blattner and Bacigalupo's study (2007) of executive, team, and organization development using a program cofacilitated by a consultant and coach. A study by Grant, Curtayne, and Burton (2009) examined the impact of an executive coaching program that combined 360-degree feedback, a half-day workshop, and four individual coaching sessions. Sue-Chan and Latham's two-continent study (2004) compared the effects of peer, external, and self-coaching on team behaviors of MBA program participants.

Beyond the corporate sector, Griffin (2005) reported on the impact of a multidimensional intervention program on behaviors of young African American men. In this case study, Navalta, Goldstein, Ruegg, Perna, and Frazier (2006) examined the impact of a multidimensional program on an adolescent with mood disorder. Coaching was one element of Kanne's study (2006) of emotional intelligence and the transformational learning journey of thirty pastors.

SPECIAL POPULATION NEEDS AND IMPLICATIONS FOR COACHING

Studies in this section place a spotlight on coaching populations that are more narrowly defined than such broad categories as "executive." In these studies, the coaching needs of clients are identified on the basis of a number of differentiating traits, including personality, gender, ethnicity, and position status.

Within the broader category of executive or leadership coaching, several studies examined the needs and relevant strategies for working with clients at different ends of the performance spectrum. Levy, Cober, and Miller (2002) offered suggestions for coaching transformational leaders. Vloeberghs, Pepermans, & Thielmans (2005) examined coaching and other elements of a multidimensional leadership development program for high-potentials in Belgian companies. Hymes (2008) provided a case study illuminating the coaching needs of emerging leaders; Jones and Spooner (2006) used interviews to determine the coaching needs of high achievers. Hughes (2003) interviewed psychologists providing executive coaching to investigate strategies used in coaching narcissistic executives. Characteristics and needs of abrasive executives, and a model for coaching them, are offered in Crawshaw's dissertation study (2006).

Coaching in specific organizational contexts serves as a focus for three studies. Rundle-Gardiner and Carr (2005) examine the tolerance threshold in a workplace that discourages achievement motivation, and the implications this has for coaching. Volz-Peacock's study (2006) of team values and cohesiveness discusses results with implications for coaching teams. Vance and Paik (2005) examine the learning needs of host country nationals working for multinational organizations.

Women executives received attention in three studies. Dupuis (2004) and Martell (2005) studied the characteristics and needs of women executives, with implications for coaching to facilitate development. The impact of executive coaching, as perceived by executive women, was examined in Starman's dissertation (2007). The needs of midlife males were examined in Ellinger, Ellinger, and Keller (2005). Winum (2005) presented the elements of coaching a male African American executive. The coaching needs of leaders outside the corporate sector were explored in three studies. Duran-Whitney (2005) drew upon the literature to explore the needs of aspiring small business owners and generated a model for coaching this population. Using an action-research approach, Williamson (2005) sought to capture the impact of a shared governance model on the leadership and coaching skills of nurse managers.

Four studies considered coaching adolescents and other nonadult populations. Cleary and Zimmerman (2004) studied the effect of a learning coaching program on adolescents' ability to self-regulate. Physically inactive twelve- to fourteen-year-olds were the focus of a study by Gorczynski, Morrow, and Irwin (2008), which examined the impact of a co-active approach on behavioral control. Van Zandvoort, Irwin, and Morrow (2009) studied the impact of co-active coaching on obese female university students. Nonadult students were the focus of Passmore and Brown's study (2009) of the impact of coaching on examination performance.

THEORETICAL COACHING MODELS

The studies in this section bring theories from the literature of coaching and foundational fields into the practice field to generate coaching-specific theories or models for practice. The integrative section presents models of coaching that combine two or more theoretical approaches to create a multifaceted framework for coaching. The second section is an overview of studies using the single-frame model; the authors have translated principles and practices from a single theoretical framework into coaching models.

Integrative Models

The integrative models present what Orenstein (2000) refers to as a "coaching technology." Several studies investigate the dimensions of the coach experience and methods employed by coaches to effect change, resulting in a multifaceted model of coaching that integrates those principles and practices that appear to contribute most to successful coaching outcomes. Both Kleinberg (2001) and Kappenberg (2008) incorporated client perceptions to support their findings. Turner's dissertation (2003) examined the perceptions and experiences of executives who had received coaching, as a means of developing a grounded theory of executive coaching; Wilkins (2000) employed a grounded theory method to develop a model for personal coaching. Through analysis of critical incidents offered by executive and life coaches, Marshall (2007) proposed six critical factors implicated in successful coaching outcomes. Jackson's study (2005) was directed at developing a typology of coaching approaches and offered a five-dimensional construct that could be used to support the development of a multidimensional coaching strategy. Recognizing the role of organizational culture, Peel (2006, 2008) studied and documented the impact of context on coaching outcomes.

Single-Theory Models

Within the group of single-theory models, adult development theory and its applications in coaching emerge as a focus of theoretical interest. Astorino (2004) integrates the literature of adult development, with particular focus on Robert Kegan's constructive developmental theory, with conceptual models of executive coaching. Building on postconstructivist theories of adult development, Akrivou (2008) explores self-integration and discusses the implications for coaching. Exploring subject-object interviewing in coaching, Berger and Atkins (2009) discuss uses and challenges of the subject-object interview in a coaching context.

Positive psychology is also examined in a coaching context. In their investigation of optimistic managers and their influence, Arakawa and Greenberg (2007) provide guidance for coaches working with executives in the development of a positive leadership style. Strengths theory and positive psychology are also factors in Govindji and Linley's study (2007) of coaching, self-concordance, and well-being. Grezemkovsky (2006) uses a qualitative approach to examine and define the construct of happiness and the role of coaching in the evolution of the construct.

The role of verbal and nonverbal communication is examined in several studies. Two models of communication competence are presented in Carpenter's study (2006), and their relevance to executive coaching is discussed. The use of nonviolent communication principles was studied by Cox (2005) as a means of enhancing online coaching and mentoring. In Topp's dissertation (2007), a presence-based coaching model was applied with entrepreneurs and the outcomes documented. Drum (2007) proposed a grounded theory of elements used by theatre directors to create a learning environment, and suggested potential applications in coaching. Creativity is a focus in McVea's study (2007) of the impact of spontaneity theory and role theory in freeing client creativity.

Two studies explore theories of intelligence applied in coaching. Harding's action research project (2006) employed the theory of multiple intelligences in a coach-mentor learning program, resulting in the development of a multiple intelligences model and a coaching and mentoring toolkit. Bricklin (2002) synthesized the literature on executive coaching and emotional intelligence to provide a proposed model for improving emotional intelligence in executive coaching clients. Cultural intelligence was examined in St. Claire-Ostwald's review (2007) of the literature on cultural dimensions and cultural awareness as they apply in cross-cultural coaching.

Coaching models may also incorporate psychodynamic and personality theories. Mansi (2007) discusses the integration of psychometric tools in a psychodynamic approach to coaching. Choong and Britton's (2007) exploration of covariance between character strengths and MBTI types offers implications for coaching psychology. Terrell (2004) seeks to define a psychology of leadership with implications for executive coaching. Stewart, Palmer, Wilkin, and Kerrin (2008) examine the influence of personality on coaching success. Ernst (2008) develops and explores the impact of a coaching model that integrates motivational interviewing and health coaching on the patient's behavioral change.

Afterword
Challenges Ahead

Jenny Rogers

Coaching has come a long way since my own early dabblings some twenty years ago, when I and my colleagues, already intrigued and enthralled by the activity we naively believed that we, uniquely, had discovered, were perplexed by what to call it. We described it as "one to one work"—a bland label that now quite pleases me because we did not use the feeble word "help." And thank god we had no idea that other people, also early adopters, were using the word "mentoring" with all its long-lasting potential for confusion. Since that time, coaching has grown immeasurably, but what are the challenges ahead?

There is no getting away from the probable damage that global recession will inflict. As I write, I see long-standing organizational clients drawing back from commissioning coaching—sometimes, it seems, out of fear that when money is tight, coaching will be seen as an indulgence. Even where coaching has supporters, development budgets may disappear—a luxury that the organization believes it cannot afford. In my own early years as a coach, there was far less competition and, in the early 1990s, nothing like the savagery of today's problems. I was able to build my hours, quietly making innumerable mistakes with clients who were, in retrospect, amazingly forgiving. That is going to be far more difficult for today's newcomers whose careers as coaches may stall before they can accelerate.

All of this coincides with some shrewd attacks on coaching, for instance by the U.S. writer Barbara Ehrenreich in *Bait and Switch* or the British journalist

Lucy Kellaway in *Who Moved My BlackBerry?* —both of whom have drawn attention to the absurdly grandiose claims we coaches can make for ourselves. In Lucy Kellaway's book, a "diary" of e-mails between a wonderfully incompetent fictional coach and her credulous client, the coach gives her client platitudinous advice that keeps on coming as long as the client keeps on paying the fees. The empty nonsense of the coach's "techniques" faithfully reflects many well-known coaching books. As satire it precisely hits the spot because it is only a little more exaggerated than the reality. These are attacks we have brought upon ourselves. My conclusion is that we have to be much more honest and realistic about what we can do. It is not true that "anyone" can be coached. The client needs to be a willing volunteer, open to change, and brave. We should be more prepared to say no when these preconditions are not met.

Establishing how coaching is a return on investment and not just a cost is a vital task for all coaches. We need good, hard evidence that goes beyond us chanting, "Coaching is a good thing because we say it is." It helps here that buyers of coaching are now much more knowledgeable and discriminating. They understand what coaching is and what it can do. Increasingly I also meet potential clients whom I privately call coaching divorcees. They are on their second or even third attempt to find a decent coach. They typically describe two problems that for me sum up the subtleties and challenges of doing a first-class job as a coach. First there is the coach who merely reflects back and seems incapable of challenging. As one divorcee said,

> I would say, "I'm stressed about this," and he would go, "So you're feeling stressed . . ." I never felt we got anywhere. I completed the program my organization paid for, but all we did was tackle trivial problems like how to make sure the photocopier got serviced on time.

The second common problem is the coach who gets too fixed on finding answers and is terrified of stillness and reflection, afraid that if the client leaves without a pat solution or an action plan, the coaching is a failure. Such coaches can mistake the initial issue for the underlying need, vigorously harassing the client with "techniques" and "tools" that lead nowhere.

How has this happened? One cause is the myth that coaching is easy and that anyone can do it. Once you swallow this, then you may also believe that a few days of training are all you need before you are fully qualified, a belief sustained by companies offering cheap, low-quality training—the same companies who encourage the false idea that there is a vast market for "life coaching" when the truth is that there is not.

Coaching is far from easy. It is a high-level skill, one that looks easy when you see a superb practitioner at work because it seems effortless. I tell my own trainees that it takes one thousand hours of practice and feedback to learn the basics, three thousand hours to deal with the mainstream of what clients will bring, and ten thousand hours to feel that little a client can say or do will unsettle you. This is no different from any other profession, but we old hands must be prepared to be frank with newcomers about the determination one needs to reach anything like mastery.

In this tough climate, we need tough ways of ensuring that what we do is the best it can be. Coach supervision only goes so far because essentially it is two people talking about the work one has done when the other was not present. It depends critically on extraordinary levels of self-awareness and candor on both sides. If we really care about quality, we should do what other businesses do: mystery shopping, feedback questionnaires administered by a third party, subjecting our actual coaching to observation and critical comment.

Disputes over how to define coaching are a distraction. Our obsession with definition betrays our immaturity as a profession. We should get on with the coaching and worry less about the exact words we use to describe it. I believe we are overly concerned with boundaries, especially between coaching and therapy. The difference between some kinds of therapy and some kinds of coaching can be so thin as to be invisible. I welcome this. Rather than trying to erect stout walls between ourselves and therapists, we need to learn from therapy and to be bolder. Inexperienced coaches often seem to live in terror of *getting in too deep*, or *doing harm*, and may make a point of avoiding working with feelings. To me it is obvious that no issue worthy of attention by client and coach is without an emotional element. All coaches should feel confident of working respectfully with clients in the "being" as well as the "doing" domain.

Some people claim that as an executive coach you do not really need knowledge of the business environment. I disagree. Of course it is true that our objectivity as outsiders is invaluable. But we do also need to become thoroughly versed in the knotty issues of our clients' organizations. Only then are we likely to understand the irrationality of so much executive behavior—for instance, their refusing to delegate and working very long hours, despite these executives' knowing perfectly well that they are endangering their health and family life by doing so.

Neither behavioral approaches nor insight alone will produce transformation. Skilled self-sabotage lies behind the difficulty of making the changes we humans say we want and yet resist so expertly. Working at this level requires psychological sophistication, courage, confidence, an ability to ask wise rather than clever questions, and a willingness to suspend judgment and create impeccable rapport. Easy to say, so much harder to do; but when we can, the rewards—for us and for our clients—are immense.

REFERENCES

Chapter 1: Humanistic and Transpersonal Psychology

Assagioli, R. (2007). *Transpersonal development: The dimension beyond psychosynthesis.* Findhorn, Scotland: Smiling Wisdom.

Grof, S. (2000). *Psychology of the future: Lessons from modern consciousness research.* Albany, New York: State University of New York Press.

Maslow, A. (1968). *Toward a psychology of being.* Hoboken, NJ: Wiley.

Perls, F. S., Hefferline, R., & Goodman, P. (1994). *Gestalt therapy: Excitement and growth in the human personality.* Gouldsboro, ME: Gestalt Journal Press.

Rogers, C. (1961). *On becoming a person.* London: Constable.

Chapter 2: Cognitive Behavioral Therapy and Related Theories

Bandura, A. (1977). *Social learning theory.* New York: General Learning Press.

Beck, A. T. (1976). *Cognitive therapy and the emotional disorders.* New York: International Universities Press.

Burns, D. (1980). *Feeling good: The new mood therapy.* New York: Avon Books.

Ellis, A., & Dryden, W. (1997). *The practice of rational emotive behavior therapy.* New York: Springer.

Padesky, C. A., & Greenberger, D. (1995). *Clinician's guide to mind over mood.* New York: Guilford Press.

Palmer, S., & Szymanska, K. (2007). Cognitive behavioural coaching: An integrative approach. In S. Palmer & A. Whybrow (Eds.), *Handbook of coaching psychology: A guide for practitioners.* Hove, England: Routledge.

Pellerin, C. (2009). *How NASA builds teams: Mission critical soft skills for scientists, engineers, and project teams.* Hoboken, NJ: Wiley.

Peltier, B. (2001). *The psychology of executive coaching: Theory and application.* Ann Arbor, MI: Sheridan Books.

Reinecke, M. A., & Clark, D. A. (Eds.) (2004). *Cognitive therapy across the lifespan: Evidence and practice.* Cambridge, England: Cambridge University Press.

Williams, H., Edgerton, N., & Palmer, S. (2010). Cognitive behavioural coaching. In E. Cox, T. Bachkirova, & D. Clutterbuck (Eds.), *The complete handbook of coaching* (pp. 37–51). London: Sage.

Chapter 3: Positive Psychology

Biswas-Diener, R., & Dean, B. (2007). *Positive psychology coaching: Putting the science of happiness to work for your clients.* Hoboken, NJ: Wiley.

Boniwell, I. (2006). *Positive psychology in a nutshell.* London: Personal Well-Being Centre.

Csikszentmihalyi, M. (1990). *Flow: The psychology of optimal experience.* New York: HarperCollins.

Csikszentmihalyi, M. (1990). Flow. In S. Lopez (Ed.), *The encyclopedia of positive psychology* (pp. 394–400). Chichester: Blackwell.

Fredrickson, B. (2004). The broaden-and-build theory of positive emotions. *Philosophical Transactions of the Royal Society of London, Series B: Biological Sciences, 359,* 1367–1377.

Fredrickson, B. (2009). *Positivity: Groundbreaking research reveals how to embrace the hidden strength of positive emotions, overcome negativity, and thrive.* New York: Crown.

Fredrickson, B., & Losada, M. F. (2005). Positive affect and the complex dynamics of human flourishing. *American Psychologist, 60,* 678–686.

Fredrickson, B., Tugade, M., Waugh, C., & Larkin, G. (2003). What good are positive emotions in crises? A prospective study of resilience and emotions following the terrorist attacks on the United States on September 11th, 2001. *Journal of Personality and Social Psychology, 84,* 365–376.

Grant, A. M. (in press). Coaching and positive psychology. In K. M. Sheldon, T. B. Kashdan, & M. Steger (Eds.), *Designing the future of positive psychology.* Oxford: Oxford University Press.

Grant, A., M., & Spence, G. B. (in press). Using coaching and positive psychology to promote a flourishing workforce: A model of goal-striving and mental health. In A. Linley, S. Harrington, & N. Page (Eds.), *Oxford handbook of positive psychology and work.* Oxford: Oxford University Press.

Hodges, T. G., & Clifton, D. O. (2004). Strengths-based development in practice. In A. Linley & S. Joseph (Eds.), *Positive psychology in practice* (pp. 256–268). Hoboken, NJ: Wiley.

Kauffman, C., & Scouler, A. (2004). Toward a positive psychology of executive coaching. In A. Linley & S. Joseph (Eds.), *Positive psychology in practice* (pp. 287–302). Hoboken, NJ: Wiley.

Linley, P. A., & Harrington, S. (2006). Playing to your strengths. *Psychologist, 19*(2), 86–89.

Lyubomirsky, S. (2006). Happiness: Lessons from a new science. *British Journal of Sociology, 57,* 535–536.

Lyubomirsky, S. (2008). *The how of happiness: A practical guide to getting the life you want.* London: Sphere.

Papageorgiou, C., & Wells, A. (2003). Nature, functions, and beliefs about depressive rumination. In C. Papageorgiou & A. Wells (Eds.), *Depressive rumination: Nature, theory, and treatment* (pp. 3–20). Chichester, England: Wiley.

Park, N., Peterson, C., & Seligman, M. (2004). Strengths of character and well-being: A closer look at hope and modesty. *Journal of Social and Clinical Psychology, 23,* 628–634.

Peterson, C., & Seligman, M. (2004). *Character strengths and virtues: A handbook and classification.* New York: Oxford University Press.

Reivich, K., & Shatte, A. (2002). *The resilience factor: 7 keys to finding your inner strength and overcoming life's hurdles.* New York: Broadway Books.

Seligman, M. (2002). *Authentic happiness: Using the new positive psychology to realize your potential for lasting fulfilment.* New York: Free Press.

Seligman, M., & Csikszentmihalyi, M. (2000). Positive psychology: An introduction. *American Psychologist, 55*(1), 5–14.

Seligman, M., Steen, T. A., Park, N., & Peterson, C. (2005). Positive psychology progress: Empirical validation of interventions. *American Psychologist, 60,* 410–421.

Sheldon, K. M., & Elliot, A. J. (1999). Goal striving, need satisfaction, and longitudinal well-being: The self-concordance model. *Journal of Personality and Social Psychology, 76,* 482–497.

Sin, N. L., & Lyubomirsky, S. (2009). Enhancing well-being and alleviating depressive symptoms with positive psychology interventions: A practice-friendly meta-analysis. *Journal of Clinical Psychology, 65,* 467–487.

Chapter 4: Transactional Analysis

Berne, E. (1964). *Games people play.* New York: Grove Press.

Harris, T. (1967). *I'm OK, You're OK.* New York: Grove Press.

Karpman, S. (1968). Fairy tales and script drama analysis. *Transactional Analysis Bulletin, 7,* 26.

Chapter 5: Adult Development

Axelrod, S. D. (2005, Spring). Executive growth along the adult development curve. *Consulting Psychology Journal: Practice and Research,* pp. 118–125.

Belenky, M. F., Clinchy, B. M., Goldberger, N. R., & Tarule, J. M. (1986). *Women's ways of knowing: The development of self, voice, and mind.* New York: Basic Books.

Erikson, E. (1980). *Identity and the life cycle.* New York: Norton.

Erikson. E. (1982). *The life cycle completed.* New York: Norton.

Fisher, D., & Torbert, W. (2000). *Personal and organizational transformations: The true challenge of continual quality improvement.* New York: McGraw-Hill.

Jung, C. G. (1961). *Memories, dreams, and reflections.* New York: Random House:.

Kegan, R. (1982). *The evolving self: Problem and process in human development.* Cambridge, MA: Harvard University Press.

Kegan, R. (1994). *In over our heads: The mental demands of modern life.* Cambridge, MA: Harvard University Press.

Kegan, R., & Lahey, L. (2001). *How we talk can change the way we work.* San Francisco: Jossey-Bass.

Kegan, R., & Lahey, L. (2009). *Immunity to change: How to overcome it and unlock potential in yourself and your organization.* Boston: Harvard Business School Press.

Koestler, A. (1967). *The ghost in the machine.* London: Hutchinson.

Levinson, D. J. (1978). *The seasons of a man's life.* New York: Random House.

Levinson, D. J. (1997). *The seasons of a woman's life.* New York: Random House.

Loevinger, J., & Blasi, A. (1976). *Ego development: Conceptions and theories.* San Francisco: Jossey-Bass.

Stein, M. (1983). *In midlife: A Jungian perspective.* Dallas, TX: Spring.

Vaillant, G. E. (1993). *The wisdom of the ego.* Cambridge, MA: Harvard University Press.

Wilber, K. (1993). *The spectrum of consciousness, 20th anniversary edition: Integral psychology and the perennial philosophy.* Boston: Shambhala. (First edition published 1973)

Chapter 6: Theories of Intelligence

Albrecht, K. (2006). *Social intelligence: The new science of success.* San Francisco: Jossey-Bass.

Bar-On, R. (1997). *Bar-On Emotional Quotient Inventory (EQ-i): Technical manual.* Toronto: Multi-Health Systems.

Boring, E. G. (1923). Intelligence as the tests test it. *New Republic, 35,* 35–37.

Carroll, J. B. (1993). *Human cognitive abilities: A survey of factor analytic studies.* New York: Cambridge University Press.

Cattell, R. B. (1963). Theory of fluid and crystallized intelligence: A critical experiment. *Journal of Educational Psychology, 54,* 1–22.

Gardner, H. (1983). *Frames of mind.* New York: Basic Books.

Gibbs, N. (1995, October). The EQ factor. *Time, 146*(14), 60–68.

Goleman, D. (1995). *Emotional intelligence: Why it can matter more than IQ.* London: Bloomsbury.

Goleman, D. (2004, January). What makes a leader? *Harvard Business Review, 82*(1), 82–91. (Original work published 1998)

Gould, J. G. (1981). *The mismeasure of man.* New York: W. W. Norton.

Herrnstein, R. J., & Murray, C. (1994). *The bell curve: Intelligence and class structure.* New York: Free Press.

Mayer, J. D., Caruso, D. R., & Salovey, P. (2000). Selecting a measure of emotional intelligence: The case for ability scales. In R. Bar-On & J. D. Parker (Eds.), *The handbook of emotional intelligence* (pp. 320–342). San Francisco: Jossey-Bass.

Mayer, J. D., & Salovey, P. (1997). What is emotional intelligence? In P. Salovey & D. Sluyter (Eds.), *Emotional development and emotional intelligence: Implications for educators* (pp. 3–31). New York: Basic Books.

Salovey, P., & Mayer, J. D. (1990). Emotional intelligence. *Imagination, Cognition, and Personality, 9,* 185–211.

Sternberg, R. J. (1985). *Beyond IQ: A triarchic theory of human intelligence.* New York: Cambridge University Press.

Thurstone, L. L. (1931). Multiple factor analysis. *Psychological Review, 38,* 406–427.

Chapter 7: Neuroscience

Adams, M. (2004). *Change your questions, change your life: 7 powerful tools for life and work.* San Francisco: Berrett-Koehler.

Begley, S. (2007). *Train your mind, change your brain: How a new science reveals our extraordinary potential to transform ourselves.* New York: Ballantine Books.

Bowlby, J. (1951). *Maternal care and mental health.* Monograph series no. 14. Geneva: World Health Organization.

Bowlby, J. (1969). *Attachment and loss: Vol. 1. Attachment.* London: Hogarth.

Brothers, L. (1997). *Friday's footprint: How society shapes the human mind.* New York: Oxford University Press.

Brothers, L. (2001). *Mistaken identity: The mind-brain problem reconsidered.* Albany: State University of New York Press.

Dennett, D. (1991). *Consciousness explained.* New York: Penguin.

Fredrickson, B. L. (2009). *Positivity: Top-notch research reveals the 3-to-1 ratio that will change your life.* New York: Three Rivers Press.

Goleman, D. (1995). *Emotional intelligence: Why it can matter more than IQ.* New York: Bantam Books.

Kopp, R. R. (1995). *Metaphor therapy: Using client-generated metaphors in psychotherapy.* New York: Bruner/Mazel.

Libet, B. (1985). Unconscious cerebral initiative and the role of conscious will in voluntary action. *Behavioral and Brain Sciences, 8,* 529–566.

Lieberman, M. D. (2007) Social cognitive neuroscience: A review of core processes. *Annual Review of Psychology, 58,* 259–289.

Michael M. Merzenich Award for distinguished scientific contributions. (2001). *American Psychologist, 56,* 878–881.

Ochsner, K. N., & Lieberman, M. D. (2001). The emergence of social cognitive neuroscience. *American Psychologist, 56,* 717–734.

Ollwerther, W. R. (2010, January 13). Fast track for neuroscience? *Princeton Alumni Weekly,* p. 16.

Rizzolatti, G., & Sinigaglia, C. (2008). *Mirrors in the brain: How our minds share actions, emotions, and experience* (F. Anderson, Trans.). New York: Oxford University Press.

Rock, D. (2008). SCARF: A brain-based model for collaborating with and influencing others. *NeuroLeadership Journal, 1,* 44–52.

Rock, D., & Page, L. J. (2009). *Coaching with the brain in mind: Foundations for practice.* Hoboken, NJ: Wiley.

Schwartz, J. M., & Begley, S. (2002). *The mind and the brain: Neuroplasticity and the power of mental force.* New York: Regan Books.

Schwartz, J. M., Stapp, H. P., & Beauregard, M. (2004). Quantum physics in neuroscience and psychology: A neurophysical model of mind–brain interaction. *Philosophical Transactions of the Royal Society of London, Series B: Biological Sciences.* Published online www.jstor.org/journals/00804622.html.

Senge, P., Scharmer, C. O., Jaworski, J., & Flowers, B. S. (2005). *Presence: An exploration of profound change in people, organizations, and society.* New York: Doubleday/Society for Organizational Learning.

Siegel, D. J. (1999). *The developing mind: Toward a neurobiology of interpersonal experience.* New York: Guilford Press.

Siegel, D. J. (2007). *The mindful brain: Reflection and attunement in the cultivation of well-being.* New York: Norton.

Siegel, D. J. (2010). *Mindsight: The new science of personal transformation.* New York: Bantam.

Stapp, H. P. (2007). *Mindful universe: Quantum mechanics and the participating observer.* Berlin: Springer-Verlag.

Zander, R. S., & Zander, B. (2000). *The art of possibility: Transforming professional and personal life.* Boston: Harvard Business School Press.

Chapter 8: Theories of Adult Learning

Bolton, G. (2004). *Reflective practice: Writing and professional development.* Thousand Oaks, CA: Sage.

Cox, E. (2006). An adult learning approach to coaching. In T. Grant & D. Stober (Eds.), *Evidence-based coaching handbook: Theory and practice* (pp. 193–219). Hoboken, NJ: Wiley.

Dewey, J. (1916). *Democracy and education: An introduction to the philosophy of education.* New York: Macmillan.

Dewey, J. (1938). *Experience and education.* New York: Touchstone.

Freire, P. (1969). *Pedagogy of the oppressed.* New York: Continuum International Publishing Group.

Honey, P., & Mumford, A. (1992). *The manual of learning styles* (3rd ed.). Maidenhead, England: Peter Honey.

Knowles, M., Holton, E. F., & Swanson, R. (2005). *The adult learner: The definitive classic in adult education and human resource development* (6th ed.). Boston: Elsevier. (First edition published 1973)

Kolb, D. (1984). *Experiential learning: Experience as the source of learning and development.* Englewood Cliffs, NJ: Prentice Hall.

Lewin, K. (1997). *Resolving social conflicts and field theory in social science.* Washington, DC: American Psychological Association.

Merriam, S. (2001). *The new update on adult learning theory*. San Francisco: Jossey-Bass.

Mezirow, J. (1991). *Transformative dimensions of adult learning*. San Francisco: Jossey-Bass.

Mezirow, J. (Ed.). (2000). *Learning as transformation: Critical perspectives on a theory in progress*. San Francisco: Jossey-Bass.

Schön, D. A. (1983). *The reflective practitioner: How professionals think in action*. New York: Basic Books.

Whitmore, J. (2009). *Coaching for performance, 4th edition: GROWing human potential and purpose*. London: Brealey.

Chapter 9: Social Constructionism

Anderson, H. (1997). *Conversation, language, and possibilities: A postmodern approach to therapy*. New York: Basic Books.

Buber, M. (1970). *I and thou* (W. Kaufmann, Trans.). New York: Touchstone.

Burr, V. (2003). *Social constructionism*. New York: Routledge.

Cooperrider, D. L., Whitney, D., & Stavros, J. M. (2005). *Appreciative inquiry handbook: The first in a series of AI workbooks for leaders of change*. Brunswick, OH: Crown Custom.

Gergen, K. J. (1973). Social psychology as history. *Journal of Personality and Social Psychology, 26*, 309–320.

Gergen, K. J. (1999). *An invitation to social construction*. London: Sage.

Gergen, M., & Gergen, K. J. (Eds.). (2003). *Social construction: A reader*. London: Sage.

Hosking, D., & McNamee, K. (Eds.). (2006). *The social construction of organization*. Herndon: Copenhagen Business School Press.

Langer, E. J. (1997). *The power of mindful learning*. Cambridge, MA: Da Capo Press.

McNamee, S., & Gergen, K. J. (Eds.). (1999). *Relational responsibility: Resources for sustainable dialogue*. London: Sage.

Pearce, W. B. (2007). *Making social worlds*. Malden, MA: Blackwell.

Chapter 10: Theories of Change

Bridges, W. (2003). *Managing transitions: Making the most of change (2nd ed)*. Cambridge, MA: Da Capo Press.

Burke, B. L., Arkowitz, H., & Menchola, M. (2003). The efficacy of motional interviewing: A meta-analysis of controlled clinical trials. *Journal of Consulting and Clinical Psychology, 71*, 843–861.

Kegan, R., & Lahey, L. (2009). *Immunity to change: How to overcome it and unlock potential in yourself and your organization*. Boston: Harvard Business School Press.

Kübler-Ross, E. (1973). *On death and dying*. New York: Routledge.

Prochaska, J. O., DiClemente, C. C., & Norcross, J. C. (1992). In search of how people change: Applications to addictive behaviors. *American Psychologist, 47,* 1102–1114.

Rollnick, S., & Miller, W. R. (1995). What is motivational interviewing? *Behavioral and Cognitive Psychotherapy, 23,* 325–334.

Chapter 11: Communication Theory

Anderson, H. (1993). On a roller coaster: A collaborative language systems approach to therapy. In S. Friedman (Ed.), *The new language of change: Constructive collaboration in therapy* (pp. 323–344). New York: Guilford Press.

Anderson, H. (1995). Collaborative language systems: Toward a postmodern therapy. In R. Mikesell, D. D. Lusterman, & S. McDaniel (Eds.), *Integrating family therapy: Family psychology and systems theory* (pp. 27–44). Washington, DC: American Psychological Association.

Anderson, H. (1997). *Conversation, language, and possibilities: A postmodern approach to therapy.* New York: Basic Books.

Anderson, H. (2007). The heart and spirit of collaborative therapy: The philosophical stance: "A way of being" in relationship and conversation. In H. Anderson & D. Gehart (Eds.), *Collaborative therapy* (pp. 43–62). New York: Routledge.

Anderson, R., Cissna, K. N., & Arnett, R. (Eds.). (1994). *The reach of dialogue: Confirmation, voice, and community.* Cresskill, NJ: Hampton Press.

Bruner, J. (1990). *Acts of meaning.* Cambridge, MA: Harvard University Press.

Buber, M. (1965). *Between man and man* (R. G. Smith, Trans.). New York: Macmillan.

Buber, M. (1970). *I and thou* (W. Kaufmann, Trans.). New York: Scribner.

Holmgren, A. (2004). Saying, doing and making: Teaching CMM theory. *Human Systems, 15*(2), 89–100.

Littlejohn, S. W. (1999). *Theories of human communication* (6th ed.). Belmont, CA: Wadsworth.

Pearce, W. B. (2005). The coordinated management of meaning (CMM). In W. B. Gudykunst (Ed.), *Theorizing about intercultural communication* (pp. 35–54). Thousand Oaks, CA: Sage.

Pearce, W. B., & Cronen, V. (1980). *Communication, action, and meaning.* New York: Praeger.

Pearce, W. B., & Pearce, K. A. (2000). Combining passions and abilities: Toward dialogic virtuosity. *Southern Communication Journal, 65,* 161–171.

Stelter, R. (2007). Coaching: A process of personal and social meaning making. *International Coaching Psychology Review, 2,* 191–201.

Tannen, D. (1984). *Conversational style: Analyzing talk among friends.* Norwood, NJ: Ablex.

Tannen, D. (1986). *That's not what I meant! How conversational style makes or breaks relationships.* New York: Ballantine Books.

Tannen, D. (1990). *You just don't understand: Women and men in conversation.* New York: Ballantine Books.

Tannen, D. (1994a). *Gender and discourse*. New York: Oxford University Press.

Tannen, D. (1994b). *Talking from 9 to 5: How women's and men's conversational styles affect who gets heard, who gets credit, and what gets done at work*. New York: Morrow.

Chapter 12: Conflict Management

Brinkert, R. (1999, July). *Challenges and opportunities for a campus conflict education program*. Paper presented at the Conflict Resolution in Education Network (CREnet) conference, Boston.

Cloke, K., & Goldsmith, J. (2000). *Resolving conflicts at work*. San Francisco: Jossey-Bass.

Fisher, R., & Ury, W. (1991). *Getting to yes: Negotiating agreement without giving in*. New York: Penguin Books.

Jones, T. S., & Brinkert, R. (2008). *Conflict coaching: Conflict management strategies and skills for the individual*. Thousand Oaks, CA: Sage.

Patterson, K., Grenny, J., McMillan, R., & Switzler, A. (2002). *Crucial conversations: Tools for talking when stakes are high*. New York: McGraw-Hill.

Tidwell, A. (1997). Problem solving for one. *Mediation Quarterly, 14*, 309–317.

Chapter 13: Systems Theory and Family Systems Therapy

Bateson, G. (1972). *Steps to an ecology of mind: Collected essays in anthropology, psychiatry, evolution, and epistemology*. Chicago: University of Chicago Press.

Bateson, G., Jackson, D. D., Haley, J., & Weakland, J. (1956). "Towards a Theory of Schizophrenia." *Behavioral Science, 1*, 251–264.

Becvar, D. S., & Becvar, R. J. (1999). *Systems theory and family therapy: A primer*. Lanham, MD: University Press of America.

Bowen, M. (1975). Family therapy after twenty years. In S. Arieti (Ed.), *American handbook of psychiatry* (Vol. 5). New York: Basic Books.

Bowen, M. (1978). *Family therapy in clinical practice*. Northvale, NJ: Aronson.

Gergen, K. (1985). The social constructionist movement in modern psychology. *American Psychologist, 40*, 266–275.

Gerson, R., McGoldrick, M., & Petry, S. (2008). *Genograms: Assessment and intervention*. New York: Norton.

Minuchin, S. (1974). *Families and family therapy*. Cambridge, MA: Harvard University Press.

Minuchin, S. (1993). *Family healing: Strategies for hope and understanding*. New York: Free Press.

Nichols, M. P., & Schwartz, R. C. (1995). *Family therapy: Concepts and methods*. New York: Simon & Schuster.

Schultz, S. J. (1984). *Family systems thinking*. Northvale, NJ: Aronson.

Schwartz, R. C. (1997). *Internal family systems therapy*. New York: Guilford Press.

Schwartz, R. C. (2001). *Introduction to the internal family systems model*. Oak Park, IL: Trailheads.

von Bertalanffy, L. (1968). *General system theory*. New York: Braziller.

Chapter 14: Transition and Career Management

Arruda, W., & Dixson, K. (2007). *Career distinction: Stand out by building your brand*. Hoboken, NJ: Wiley.

Bolles, R. (2010). *What color is your parachute?* Berkeley, CA: Ten Speed Press.

Bridges, W. (1991). *Managing transitions: Making the most of change*. Reading, MA: Addison-Wesley.

Csikszentmihalyi, M. (2003). *Good business: Flow, leadership and the making of meaning*. New York: Viking.

Frankl, V. (1959). *Man's search for meaning*. New York: Pocket Books.

Kübler-Ross, E. (1997). *On death and dying*. New York: Touchstone. (Original work published 1960)

Watkins, M. (2003). *The first 90 days: Critical strategies for new leaders at all levels*. Boston: Harvard Business School Press.

Williams, L. (2008). *Ultimate interview*. London: Kogan Page.

Chapter 15: Leadership

Bennis, W. G. (1994). *On becoming a leader*. New York: Perseus Books.

Bennis, W. G., & Thomas, R. J. (2008). Resilience and the crucibles of leadership. In J. V. Gallos (Ed.), *Business leadership: A Jossey-Bass reader* (2nd ed., pp. 504–515). San Francisco: Jossey-Bass.

Collins, J. (2001). *Good to great*. New York: HarperCollins.

Goleman, D. (1995). *Emotional intelligence: Why it can matter more than IQ*. New York: Bantam Books.

Goleman, D. (2000, March-April). Leadership that gets results. *Harvard Business Review*, pp. 78–90.

Goleman, D. (2004, January).What makes a leader? *Harvard Business Review*, pp. 82–91.

Heifetz, R. A., & Linsky, M. (2002). *Leadership on the line: Staying alive through the dangers of leading*. Boston: Harvard Business School Press.

Kantrow, A. M. (2009, November). Why read Peter Drucker? *Harvard Business Review*, pp. 65–70.

Kegan, R. (1994). *In over our heads: The mental demands of modern life*. Cambridge, MA: Harvard University Press.

Kouzes, J. M., & Posner, B. Z. (2008). The five practices of exemplary leadership. In J. V. Gallos (Ed.), *Business leadership: A Jossey-Bass reader* (2nd ed., pp. 26–34). San Francisco: Jossey-Bass.

Wheatley, M. J. (2007). *Finding our way: Leadership for an uncertain time*. San Francisco: Berrett-Koehler.

Chapter 16: Organizations and Organizational Culture

Argyris, C. (1999). *On organizational learning* (2nd ed.). Malden, MA: Blackwell.

Argyris, C., & Schön, D. (1974). *Theory in practice: Increasing professional effectiveness*. San Francisco: Jossey-Bass.

Argyris, C., & Schön, D. (1978). *Organizational learning: A theory of action perspective*. Reading, MA: Addison-Wesley.

Burns, J. M. (1978). *Leadership*. New York: Harper & Row.

Cameron, K. S., & Quinn, R. E. (2005). *Diagnosing and changing organizational culture: Based on the competing values framework*. San Francisco: Jossey-Bass.

Deal, T. E., & Kennedy, A. A. (2005). *Corporate cultures: The rites and rituals of corporate life*. New York: Basic Books.

Handy, C. (1993). *Understanding organizations: How understanding the ways organizations actually work can be used to manage them better*. New York: Oxford University Press.

Jantsch, E. (1980). *The self-organizing universe: Scientific and human implications of the emerging paradigm of evolution*. New York: Pergamon Press.

Likert, R. (1967). *The human organization: Its management and value*. New York: McGraw-Hill.

McGregor, D. (1967). *The professional manager*. New York: McGraw-Hill.

Morgan, G. (1997). *Images of organizations*. Thousand Oaks, CA: Sage.

Nonaka, I., & Takuchi, H. (1995). *The knowledge-creating company: How Japanese companies create the dynamics of innovation*. New York: Oxford University Press.

Schein, E. H. (1988). *Process consultation: Its role in organization development*. Reading, MA: Addison-Wesley.

Schein, E. H. (2004). *Organizational culture and leadership* (3rd ed.). San Francisco: Jossey-Bass.

Senge, P. M. (1990). *The fifth discipline: The art and practice of the learning organization*. New York: Doubleday.

Taylor, F. (1911). *The principles of scientific management*. New York: HarperCollins.

Weber, M. (1968). *Economy and society: An outline of interpretive sociology*. Los Angeles: University of California Press. (Original work published 1922)

Wheatley, M. J. (1994). *Leadership and the new science*. San Francisco: Berrett-Koehler.

Chapter 17: Team and Group Behavior

Bennis, W. G., & Shepard, H. A. (1956). A theory of group development. *Human Relations*, 9, 415–437.

Bion, W. R. (1961). *Experiences in groups, and other papers*. New York: Basic Books.

Brown, S. W., & Grant, A. M. (2010). From GROW to GROUP: Theoretical issues and a practical model for group coaching in organisations. *Coaching: An International Journal of Theory, Research and Practice, 3*(1), 30–45.

Campion, M. A., Medsker, G. J., & Higgs, C. A. (1993). Relations between work group characteristics and effectiveness: Implications for designing effective work groups. *Personnel Psychology, 46*, 823–847.

Greenberg, J., & Baron, R. A. (2008). *Behavior in organizations* (9th ed.). Upper Saddle River, NJ: Pearson Prentice Hall.

Hackman, J. R., & Wageman, R. (2005). A theory of team coaching. *Academy of Management Review, 30*, 269–287.

Jones, B. B., Brazzel, M. (Eds.) (2006). *The NTL handbook of organization development and change: Principles, practices, and perspectives.* San Francisco: Pfeiffer.

Minahan, M. (2006). Working with groups in organizations. In B. B. Jones & M. Brazzel (Eds.), *The NTL handbook of organization development and change: Principles, practices, and perspectives* (pp. 264–285). San Francisco: Pfeiffer.

Schutz, W. (1958). *FIRO: A three-dimensional theory of interpersonal behavior.* New York: Rinehart.

Schutz, W. (1971). *Here comes everybody.* New York: Harper & Row.

Schutz, W. (1994). *The human element: Productivity, self-esteem, and the bottom line.* San Francisco: Jossey-Bass.

Simon, H. A. (1944). Decision-making and administrative organization. *Public Administration Review, 4*(1), 16–40.

Tuckman, B. W. (1965). Developmental sequence in small groups. *Psychological Bulletin, 63*(6), 384–399.

Tuckman, B. W., & Jensen, M. A. (1977). Stages of small group development revisited. *Group & Organization Studies, 2*, 419–427.

Chapter 18: Situational and Contextual Issues in the Workplace

Aberdeen Research. (2006, August). *Onboarding benchmark report: Technology drivers help improve the new hire experience.* www.silkroad.com/SiteGen/Uploads/Public/SRT/Whitepaper/OnboardingBenchmarchReport.pdf.

Armstrong, M., & Baron, A. (2008). *Human capital management: Achieving added value through people.* London: Kogan Page.

Bauer, T. N., & Green, S. G. (1994). Effect of newcomer involvement in work-related activities: A longitudinal study of socialization. *Journal of Applied Psychology, 79*, 211–223.

Bossert, R. (2004, September). Transition coaching accelerates leadership success. *Chief Learning Officer.* http://clomedia.com/articles/view/607/1.

Bradt, G., Check, J. A., & Pedraza, J. (2006). *The new leader's 100-day action plan.* Hoboken, NJ: Wiley.

Bridges, W. (1991). *Managing transitions: Making the most of change.* Reading, MA: Addison-Wesley.

Conger, J. A., & Fishel, B. (2007). Accelerating leadership performance at the top: Lessons from the Bank of America's executive on-boarding process. *Human Resource Management Review, 17*(4), 442–454.

Kaplan, R. S., & Norton, D. P. (1996). *The balanced scorecard: Translating strategy into action.* Boston: Harvard Business School Press.

Kotter, J. P. (2007, January). Leading change: Why transformation efforts fail. *Harvard Business Review*, pp. 96–103.

Maurer, R. (1996). *Beyond the wall of resistance: Unconventional strategies that build support for change.* Austin, TX: Bard Press.

Potgieter, L. (2005). *Trends in performance management.* White paper. Performance Management Institute of Australia. www.pmia.org.au/white/trends.pdf.

Thompson, H. B., Bear, D. J., Dennis, D. J., Vickers, M., London, J., & Morrison, C. L. (2008). *Coaching: A global study of successful practices: Trends and future possibilities 2008–2018.* New York: American Management Association.

Wedman, J. (1998). Exploring the performance pyramid. Needs Assessment Basics. University of Missouri, School of Information Science and Learning Technologies. http://needsassessment.missouri.edu/.

Wells, S. J. (2005, March). Diving in. *HR Magazine*, pp. 54–59.

Chapter 19: Spiritual and Religious Traditions

Campbell, J., & Osbon, D. K. (1998). *A Joseph Campbell companion: Reflections on the art of living.* New York: HarperPerennial.

Csikszentmihalyi, M. (1990). *The psychology of optimal experience.* New York: HarperCollins.

Fowler, J. (1981). *Stages of faith: The psychology of human development and the quest for meaning.* San Francisco: Harper & Row.

Maslow, A. (1964). *Religions, values, and peak experiences.* New York: Penguin Books.

Rogers, C. R. (1995). *On becoming a person: A therapist's view of psychotherapy.* Boston: Houghton Mifflin.

Rogers, J. (2008). *Coaching skills: A handbook* (2nd ed.). Berkshire, England: McGraw-Hill Open University Press.

Seligman, M. (2002). *Authentic happiness: Using the new positive psychology to realize your potential for lasting fulfilment.* New York: Free Press.

Chapter 20: The Self-Help and Human Potential Movements

Anderson, W. T. (1983). *The upstart spring: Esalen and the human potential movement: The first twenty years.* Lincoln, NE: iUniverse.

Bandler, R., & Grinder, J. (1975). *The structure of magic: A book about language and therapy.* Palo Alto, CA: Science and Behavior Books.

Bandler, R., & Grinder, J. (1979). *Frogs into princes: Neuro linguistic programming.* Boulder, CO: Real People Press.

Gallwey, W. T. (1974). *The inner game of tennis: The classic guide to the mental side of peak performance.* New York: Random House.

Chapter 21: Mindfulness

Badenoch, B. (2008). *Being a brain-wise therapist: A practical guide to interpersonal neurobiology.* New York: Norton.

Carson, S. H., & Langer, E. J. (2006). Mindfulness and self-acceptance. *Journal of Rational-Emotive & Cognitive-Behavior Therapy, 24*(1), 29–43.

Doidge, N. (2007). *The brain that changes itself: Stories of personal triumph from the frontiers of brain science.* New York: Viking.

Dryden, W., & Still, A. (2006). Historical aspects of mindfulness and self-acceptance in psychotherapy. *Journal of Rational-Emotive & Cognitive-Behavior Therapy, 24*(1), 3–28

Hubble, M. A., Duncan, B. L., & Miller, S. D. (Eds.). (1999). *The heart and soul of change: What works in therapy.* Washington, DC: American Psychological Association.

Kabat-Zinn, J. (1990). *Full catastrophe living: Using the wisdom of your body and mind to face stress, pain, and illness.* New York: Random House.

Kabat-Zinn, J. (2005). *Coming to our senses: Healing ourselves and the world through mindfulness.* New York: Hyperion.

McQuaid, J. R., & Carmona, P. E. (2004). *Peaceful mind: Using mindfulness and cognitive behavioral psychology to overcome depression.* Oakland, CA: New Harbinger.

Schön, D. A. (1983). *The reflective practitioner: How professionals think in action.* New York: Basic Books.

Shapiro, S. L., & Carlson, L. E. (2009). *The art and science of mindfulness: Integrating mindfulness into psychology and the helping professions.* Washington, DC: American Psychological Society.

Siegel, D. J. (2007). *The mindful brain: Reflection and attunement in the cultivation of well-being.* New York: Norton.

Silsbee, D. K. (2008). *Presence-based coaching: Cultivating self-generative leaders through mind, body, and heart.* San Francisco: Jossey-Bass.

Chapter 22: Education

Auerbach, J. (2006). Cognitive coaching. In D. Stober & A. Grant (Eds.), *Evidence-based coaching handbook* (pp. 103–127). Hoboken, NJ: Wiley.

Biancarosa, G., Bryk, A., & Dexter, E. (2008). *Assessing the value-added effects of Literacy Collaborative professional development on student learning.* Paper presented at the Conference of the American Educational Research Association. www.iisrd.org/program_inquiry/publications.shtml.

Cleary, T., & Zimmerman, B. (2004). Self-regulation empowerment program: A school-based program to enhance self-regulated and self-motivated cycles of student learning. *Psychology in the Schools, 41*, 537–550.

Cogan, M., & Goldhammer, R. (1969). *Clinical supervision: Special method for the supervision of teachers.* New York: Holt, Rinehart, and Winston.

Costa, A., & Garmston, R. (2002). *Cognitive coaching: A foundation for Renaissance schools* (2nd ed.). Norwood, MA: Christopher-Gordon.

Darling-Hammond, L., Chung Wei, R., Andree, A., Richardson, N., & Orphanos, S. (2009). *Professional learning in the learning profession: A status report on teacher development in the United States and abroad.* Oxford, OH: National Staff Development Council.

DuFour, R., & Eaker, R. (1998). *Professional learning communities at work.* Bloomington, IN: National Education Service.

Green, S., Grant, A., & Rynsaardt, J. (2007). Evidence-based life coaching for senior high school students: Building hardiness and hope. *International Coaching Psychology Review, 2*(1), 24–32.

Kegan, R., & Lahey, L. L. (2001). *How the way we talk can change the way we work.* San Francisco: Jossey-Bass.

Kegan, R., & Lahey, L. L. (2009). *Immunity to change: How to overcome it and unlock the potential in yourself and your organization.* Boston: Harvard Business School Press.

Knight, J. (2007). *Instructional coaching: A partnership approach to improving instruction.* Thousand Oaks, CA: Corwin Press.

Lindahl, R. (2006). *The role of organizational climate and culture in the school improvement process: A review of the knowledge base.* The Connexions Project (Module m13465). http://cnx.org/content/m13465/1.1/.

Lipton, L., Wellman, B., & Humbard, C. (2003). *Mentoring matters: A practical guide to learning-focused relationships* (2nd ed.). Sherman, CT: MiraVia.

Militello, M. C., Rallis, S. F., & Goldring, E. B. (2009). *Leading with inquiry and action: How principals improve teaching and learning.* Thousand Oaks, CA: Sage.

Norwood, K., & Burke, M. A. (2008). *Coaching for transformational change.* Henderson, NV: Lulu.

Pearson, P., Roehler, L., Dole, J., & Duffy, G. (1992). Developing expertise in reading comprehension. In J. Samuels & A. Farstrup (Eds.), *What research has to say about reading instruction* (pp. 145–199). Newark, DE: International Reading Association.

Reiss, K. (2007). *Leadership coaching for educators.* Thousand Oaks, CA: Corwin Press.

Seligman, M. (2008, August). Positive education and the new prosperity: Australia's edge. *Education Today*, pp. 20–21.

Showers, B., & Joyce, B. (1996). The evolution of peer coaching. *Educational Leadership, 53*(6), 12–17.

Zimmerman, B. (2000). Attaining self-regulation: A social-cognitive perspective. In M. Boekaerts, P. Pintrich, & M. Seidner (Eds.), *Self-regulation: Theory, research, and applications* (pp. 13–39). Orlando, FL: Academic Press.

Chapter 23: Issues of Aging

Abbott, P., Carman, N., Carman, J., & Scarfo, B. (2009). *Re-creating neighborhoods for successful aging.* Baltimore, MD: Health Professions Press.

Adams, K., & Sanders, S. (2010). Measurement of developmental change in late life: A validation study of the Change in Activities and Interests Index. *Clinical Gerontologist, 33*(2), 1–17.

Birren, J., & Cochran, K. (2001). *Telling the stories of life through Guided Autobiography groups.* Baltimore, MD: Johns Hopkins University Press.

Birren, J., & Deutchman, D. (1991). *Guiding autobiography groups for older adults: Exploring the fabric of life.* Baltimore, MD: Johns Hopkins University Press.

Birren, J., & Svensson, C. (2006). Guided Autobiography: Writing and telling the stories of lives. *LLI Review, 1,* 113–119.

Cohen, G. (2000). *The creative age: Awakening human potential in the second half of life.* New York: Avon.

Cohen, G. (2006). Research on creativity and aging: The positive impact of the arts on health and illness. *Generations, 30*(1), 7–15.

Corley, C. (2010). Creative expression and resilience among Holocaust survivors. *Human Behavior in the Social Environment, 20,* 542–552.

Cumming, E., & Henry, W. (Eds.). (1961). *Growing old: The process of disengagement.* New York: Basic Books.

Ekerdt, D. (2010). The busy ethic: Moral continuity between work and retirement. In H. R. Moody (Ed.), *Aging: Concepts and controversies* (6th ed., pp. 416–424). Thousand Oaks, CA: Pine Forge Press.

Erikson, E. H., Erikson, J. M., & Kivnick, H. Q. (1986). *Vital involvement in old age.* New York: Norton.

Frederickson, B., & Carstensen, L. (1990). Choosing social partners: How old age and anticipated endings make people more selective. *Psychology and Aging, 5,* 335–347.

Freedman, M. (2008). *Encore: Finding work that matters in the second half of life.* Cambridge, MA: Perseus Books.

Goldman, C. (2002). *The gifts of caregiving: Stories of hardship, hope, and healing.* Minneapolis, MN: Fairview Press.

Goldman, C. (2009). *Who am I . . . now that I'm not who I was? Conversations with women in mid-life and the years beyond.* Minneapolis, MN: Nodin Press.

Gordon, J., & Harazduk, N. (1999, June 12). *Mind-body skills for cancer.* Center for Mind-Body Medicine. www.cmbm.org/mind_body_medicine_RESEARCH/1999 -Transcripts/sa15.html.

Greene, R. (2010). Holocaust survivors: Resilience revisited. *Journal of Human Behavior in the Social Environment, 20*, 411–422.

Greene, R., Cohen, H., Gonzalez, J., Lee, Y., & Evans, M. (2007). Cultural narratives, older adults, and resilient communities. In R. Greene (Ed.), *Social work practice: A risk and resilience perspective* (pp. 217–238). Belmont, CA: Thomson Brooks/Cole.

Hooyman, N., & Kiyak, A. (Eds.). (2008). *Social gerontology: A multidisciplinary perspective*. Boston: Allyn & Bacon.

Kryla-Lighthall, N., & Mather, M. (2009). The role of cognitive control in older adults' emotional well-being. In V. Bengtson, D. Gans, N. Putney, & M. Silverstein (Eds.), *Handbook of theories of aging* (2nd ed., pp. 323–344). New York: Springer.

Moody, H. R. (2010). *Aging: Concepts and controversies* (6th ed.). Thousand Oaks, CA: Pine Forge Press.

Neugarten, B., Havighurst, R., & Tobin, S. (1968). Personality and patterns of aging. In B. Neugarten (Ed.), *Middle age and aging: A reader in social psychology* (pp. 173–177). Chicago: University of Chicago Press.

Rowe, J., & Kahn, R. (1997). *Successful aging*. New York: Random House.

Sadler, W. (2006). Changing life options: Uncovering the riches of the Third Age. *LLI Review, 1*(1), 11–20.

Silverman, P. (2004). *Widow to widow: How the bereaved help one another* (2nd ed.). New York: Routledge.

Tornstam, L. (2005). *Gerotranscendence: A developmental theory of positive aging*. New York: Springer.

Vaillant, G. E. (2002). *Aging well: Surprising guideposts to a happier life from the landmark Harvard study of adult development*. New York: Little, Brown.

Walker, J., & Lewis, L. (2009). *Work wanted: Protect your retirement plans in uncertain times*. Upper Saddle River, NJ: Pearson Education.

Chapter 24: Culture and Cultural Intelligence

Bennett, J. M., & Bennett, M. J. (2004). Developing intercultural sensitivity. In D. Landis, J. M. Bennett, & M. J. Bennett (Eds.), *Handbook of intercultural training* (3rd ed., pp. 147–164). Thousand Oaks, CA: Sage.

Bennett, M. J. (2004). Becoming interculturally competent. In J. Wurzel (Ed.), *Toward multiculturalism: A reader in multicultural education* (2nd ed., pp. 62–77). Newton, MA: Intercultural Resource Corporation.Burrus, K. (2009). Coaching managers in multinational companies: Myths and realities of the itinerant executive. In G. Abbott (Ed.), *The Routledge companion to international business coaching* (pp. 230–238). London: Routledge.

Burrus-Barbey, K. (2000, September-October). Leadership, global management, and future challenges: An interview with Peter Brabeck-Letmathe, chief executive officer of Nestlé SA. *Thunderbird International Business Review, 42*, 495–506.

Gardner, H. (1983). *Frames of mind: Theory of multiple intelligences.* New York: Basic Books.

Goleman, D. (1998). *Emotional intelligence.* New York: Bantam Books.

Hofstede, G. (1980). *Culture's consequences: International differences in work-related values.* Thousand Oaks, CA: Sage.

Plum, E. (2007). *Cultural intelligence: A concept for bridging and benefiting from cultural differences.* http://iloapp.culturalintelligence.org/blog/www?ShowFile&doc =1237224822.pdf.

Sackmann, S. A. (Ed.). (1997). *Cultural complexity in organizations: Inherent contrasts and contradictions.* Thousand Oaks, CA: Sage.

Sackmann, S. A., & Phillips, M. E. (2004, December). Contextual influences on culture research: Shifting assumptions for new workplace realities. *International Journal of Cross Cultural Management, 4,* 370–390.

Schein, E. (1992). *Organizational culture and leadership.* San Francisco: Jossey-Bass.

Schwabenland, C. (2006, Summer). The influence of cultural heritage on students' willingness to engage in peer assessment. *Investigations in University Teaching and Learning, 3,* 100–108.

Thomas, D. C., & Inkson, K. (2003). *Cultural intelligence: People skills for global business.* San Francisco: Berrett-Koehler.

Trompenaars, F., & Hampden-Turner, C. (1998). *Riding the waves of culture: Understanding cultural diversity in global business.* New York: McGraw-Hill.

Van Reken, R. E., & Pollock, D. C. (2009). *Third culture kids: The experience of growing up among worlds.* London: Brealey.

Watkins, M. (2003). *The first 90 days.* Boston: Harvard Business School Publishing.

Chapter 25: Issues of Gender

Gersick, C., & Kram, K. (2002, June). High-achieving women at midlife: An exploratory study. *Journal of Management Inquiry, 11,* 104–127.

Gilligan, C. (1982). *In a different voice: Psychological theory and women's development.* Cambridge, MA: Harvard University Press.

Gilligan, C. (1998). In a different voice: Women's conceptions of self and of morality. In B. M. Clinchy & J. Norem (Eds.), *The gender and psychology reader* (pp. 347–382). New York: New York University Press.

Gray, J. (1992). *Men are from Mars: Women are from Venus: The classic guide to understanding the opposite sex.* New York: HarperCollins.

Helgesen, S. (1995). *The female advantage: Women's ways of leadership.* New York: Doubleday Currency.

Hochschild, A. R. (1989). *The second shift.* New York: Penguin Books.

Hochschild, A. R. (1997). *The time bind: When work becomes home and home becomes work.* New York: Henry Holt.

Kohlberg, L. (1976). Moral stages and moralization: The cognitive-developmental approach. In T. Lickona (Ed.), *Moral development and behavior: Theory, research and social issues* (pp. 31–53). New York: Holt, Rinehart, & Winston.

Milkie, M. A., & Peltola, P. (1999, May). Playing all the roles: Gender and the work-family balancing act. *Journal of Marriage and the Family, 61,* 476.

Richardson, C. (1999). *Take time for your life.* New York: Random House.

Tannen, D. (1990). *You just don't understand: Women and men in conversation.* New York: Ballantine Books.

Tannen, D. (1994). *Talking from 9 to 5: Women and men in the workplace: Language, sex and power.* New York: Avon Books.

Whitworth, L., Kimsey-House, H., & Sandahl, P. (1998). *Co-active coaching: New skills for coaching people toward success in work and life.* Mountain View, CA: Davies-Black.

Chapter 26: Environmental Sustainability

Adams, W. M. (2006, January 29–31). *The future of sustainability: Re-thinking environment and development in the twenty-first century* (Report of the IUCN Renowned Thinkers Meeting). Geneva, Switzerland: International Union for the Conservation of Nature.

Allenby, B. (2006). The ontologies of industrial ecology? *Progress in Industrial Ecology, 3*(1/2), 29–40. http://cspo.org/documents/IE%20-%20PIE%20-%20IE%20ontologies.pdf.

Benyus, J. M. (1998). *Biomimicry.* New York: HarperCollins.

Boiral, O., Cayer, M., & Baron, C. M. (2009). The action logics of environmental leadership: A developmental perspective. *Journal of Business Ethics, 85,* 479–499.

Cunningham, W., & Cunningham, M. (2009). *Environmental science: A global concern.* New York: McGraw-Hill.

Hawken, P. (1993). *The ecology of commerce.* New York: HarperBusiness.

Hawken, P., Lovins, A., & Lovins, L. H. (2008). *Natural capitalism.* New York: Little, Brown.

McDonough, W., & Braungart, M. (2002). *Cradle to cradle.* New York: North Point Press.

Peck, S. W. (2010). *Industrial ecology: From theory to practice.* http://newcity.ca/Pages/industrial_ecology.html.

Rees, W. E., Wackernagel, M., Testemale, P. (1996). *Our ecological footprint.* Victoria, British Columbia: New Society.

Robèrt, K.-H. (1991, Spring). Educating a nation: The natural step. *Making It Happen,* pp. 10–20.

Senge, P. (2008). *The necessary revolution.* New York: Doubleday.

World Commission on Environment and Development. (1987). *Our common future.* Oxford, England: Oxford University Press.

Chapter 27: Coaching and the Body

Heller, S., & Surrenda, D. (1994). *Retooling on the run*. Berkeley, CA: Frog Books.

Joyce, J. (1993). A painful case. In J. Joyce, *Dubliners*. New York: Penguin Group. (Original work published 1914)

Maturana, H. R., & Varela, F. J. (1987). *The tree of knowledge*. Boston: Shambhala.

Olalla, J. A. (2004). *From knowledge to wisdom*. Boulder, CO: Newfield Press.

Strozzi-Heckler, R. (2007). *The leadership dojo: Build your foundation as an exemplary leader*. Berkeley, CA: Frog Books.

Chapter 28: A Narrative Approach to Coaching

Bruner, J. (2002). *Making stories: Law, literature, life*. Cambridge, MA: Harvard University Press.

Burke, K. (1969). *A grammar of motives*. Berkeley: University of California Press.

Campbell, J. (1973). *The hero with a thousand faces*. Princeton, NJ: Princeton University Press.

Clandinin, D. J., & Connelly, F. M. (2000). *Narrative inquiry: Experience and story in qualitative research*. San Francisco: Jossey-Bass.

Drake, D. B. (2007). The art of thinking narratively: Implications for coaching psychology and practice. *Australian Psychologist, 42*, 283–294.

Drake, D. B. (2008). Thrice upon a time: Narrative structure and psychology as a platform for coaching. In D. B. Drake, D. Brennan, & K. Gørtz (Eds.), *The philosophy and practice of coaching: Insights and issues for a new era* (pp. 51–71). San Francisco: Jossey-Bass.

Drake, D. B. (2009). Using attachment theory in coaching leaders: The search for a coherent narrative. *International Coaching Psychology Review, 4*(1), 49–58.

Gergen, K. J. (1994). *Realities and relationships*. Cambridge, MA: Harvard University Press.

Gergen, M. M., & Gergen, K. J. (2006). Narratives in action. *Narrative Inquiry, 16*(1), 112–121.

Hewson, D. (1991). From laboratory to therapy room: Prediction questions for reconstructing the "new-old" story. *Dulwich Centre Newsletter, 3*, 5–12.

James, W. (1927). *Psychology: Briefer course*. New York: Henry Holt.

Jung, C. G. (1970). *Psychological reflections*. Princeton, NJ: Princeton University Press.

Kramer, G. (2007). *Insight dialogue: The interpersonal path to freedom*. Boston: Shambhala.

Markus, H., & Nurius, P. (1986). Possible selves. *American Psychologist, 41*, 954–969.

Mishler, E. G. (1999). *Storylines: Craftartists' narratives of identity*. Cambridge, MA: Harvard University Press.

Siegel, D. J. (2007). *The mindful brain: Reflection and attunement in the cultivation of well-being*. New York: Norton.

Wallin, D. J. (2007). *Attachment in psychotherapy*. New York: Guilford Press.

White, M. (2007). *Maps of narrative practice*. New York: Norton.

White, M., & Epston, D. (1990). *Narrative means to therapeutic ends*. New York: Norton.

Winnicott, D. W. (1971). *Playing and reality*. New York: Basic Books.

Chapter 29: Solution-Focused Coaching and the GROW Model

Cavanagh, M. J., & Grant, A. M. (2010). The solution-focused approach to coaching. In E. Cox, T. Bachkirova, & D. Clutterbuck (Eds.), *The complete handbook of coaching* (pp. 54–67). Thousand Oaks, CA: Sage.

Gallwey, T. W. (1997). *The inner game of tennis.* London: Random House.

Grant, A. M. (2006). Solution-focused coaching. In J. Passmore (Ed.), *Excellence in coaching: The industry guide* (pp. 73–90). London: Kogan Page.

Green, S., Oades, L. G., & Grant, A. M. (2006). Cognitive-behavioral, solution-focused life coaching: Enhancing goal striving, well being, and hope. *Journal of Positive Psychology, 1*(3), 142–149.

O'Hanlon, B., & Beadle, S. (1996). *A field guide to possibility land: Possibility therapy methods.* London: BT Press.

Whitmore, J. (2009). *Coaching for performance* (4th ed.). London: Brealey.

Wilson, C. (2007). *Best practice in performance coaching: A handbook for leaders, coaches, HR professionals and organizations.* London: Kogan Page.

Chapter 30: Appreciative Inquiry

Berger, P. L., & Luckmann, T. (1966). *The social construction of reality.* New York: Doubleday.

Chaffee, P. (2004). *Claiming the light: Appreciative Inquiry and congregational transformation.* www.congregationalresources.org/Appreciative/Introduction.asp.

Clancy, A. L. (1996). *Toward a holistic concept of time: Exploring the link between internal and external temporal experiences.* Unpublished doctoral dissertation, Fielding Graduate University, Santa Barbara, CA.

Cooperrider, D. L., & Srivastva, S. (1987). Appreciative Inquiry in organizational life. In R. W. Woodman & E. Pasmore (Eds.), *Research in organizational change and development: An annual series featuring advances in theory* (Vol. 1, pp. 129–169). Greenwich, CT: JAI Press.

Cooperrider, D. L., Whitney, D., & Stavros, J. M. (2003). *Appreciative Inquiry handbook.* San Francisco: Berrett-Koehler.

Kelm, J. B. (2005). *Appreciative living: The principle of Appreciative Inquiry in personal life.* Wake Forest, NC: Venet.

Mohr, B. (2004). *Effecting positive change through Appreciative Inquiry.* www.executiveforum.com/PDFs/MohrSynopsis.pdf.

Newton, I. (1990). *Mathematical principles of natural philosophy* (A. Motte, Trans.) (Revised by Florian Cajori). Chicago: University of Chicago Press. (Original work published 1687)

Orem, S. L., Binkert, J., & Clancy, A. L. (2007). *Appreciative Coaching: A positive process for change.* San Francisco: Jossey-Bass.

Stavros, J. M., & Hinrichs, G. (2009). *The thin book of SOAR: Building strengths-based strategy.* Bend, OR: Thin Book.

Watkins, J. M., & Mohr, B. J. (2001). *Appreciative Inquiry: Change at the speed of imagination*. San Francisco: Jossey-Bass.

Wheatley, M. J. (1992). *Leadership and the new science: Learning about organization from an orderly universe*. San Francisco: Berrett-Koehler.

Whitney, D., & Trosten-Bloom, A. (2003). *The power of Appreciative Inquiry: A practical guide to positive change*. San Francisco: Berrett-Koehler.

Whitney, D., Trosten-Bloom, A., Cherney, J., & Fry, R. (2004). *Appreciative team building: Positive questions to bring out the best of your team*. Lincoln, NE: iUniverse.

Chapter 31: Coach Maturity: An Emerging Concept

Bachkirova, T., & Cox, E. (2007). A cognitive developmental approach for coach development. In S. Palmer & A. Whybrow (Eds.), *Handbook of coaching psychology: A guide for practitioners* (pp. 325–350). London: Routledge.

Beck, D., & Cowan, C. (1996). *Spiral dynamics*. Oxford, England: Blackwell.

Brennan, D., & Whybrow, A. (2010). Coach accreditation. In J. Passmore (Ed.), *Excellence in coaching: The industry guide* (pp. 240–259). London: Kogan Page.

Chandler, D. E., & Kram, K. E. (2005). Applying an adult development perspective to development networks. *Career Development International, 10*, 548–566.

Cook-Greuter, S. (2004). Making the case for a developmental perspective. *Industrial and Commercial Training, 36*, 275–281.

de Haan, E. (2008). *Relational coaching: Journeys towards mastering one-to-one learning*. Chichester, England: Wiley.

Gladwell, M. (2008). *Outliers*. London: Allen Lane.

Hawkins, P., & Smith, N. (2006). *Coaching, mentoring and organizational consultancy*. Maidenhead, England: McGraw-Hill.

Kegan, R. (1992). *The evolving self*. Cambridge, MA: Harvard University Press.

Laske, O. (2006). *Measuring hidden dimensions: The art and science of fully engaging adults*. Medford, MA: IDM Press.

Laske, O. (2009). *Measuring hidden dimensions of human systems*. Medford, MA: IDM Press.

Peters, T., & Waterman, R. (1982). *In search of excellence*. New York: Harper & Row.

Rogers, C. R. (1961). *On becoming a person: A psychotherapist's view of psychotherapy*. London: Constable.

Senge, P., Ross, R., Smith, B., Roberts, C., & Kleiner, A. (1994). *The fifth discipline fieldbook*. London: Brealey.

Torbert, W. R. (1991). *The power of balance: Transforming self, society, and scientific inquiry*. Thousand Oaks, CA: Sage.

Webb, P. (2008). Coaching for wisdom: Enabling wise decisions. In D. B. Drake, D. Brennan, & K. Gørtz (Eds.), *The philosophy and practice of coaching: Insights and issues for a new era* (pp. 161–175). Chichester, England: Wiley.

Wilber, K. (2000). *Integral psychology*. London: Shambhala.

Chapter 32: Use of Assessments in Coaching

American Educational Research Association, American Psychological Association, & National Council on Measurement in Education. (1999). *Standards for educational and psychological testing*. Washington, DC: American Psychological Association.

Auerbach, J. (2001). *Personal and executive coaching: The complete guide for mental health professionals*. Ventura, CA: Executive College Press.

Buckingham, M., & Clifton, D. O. (2001). *Now, discover your strengths: How to develop your talents and those of the people you manage*. New York: Simon & Schuster.

Harper, A. (2008, November). Psychometric tests are now a multi-million-pound business: What lies behind a coach's decision to use them? *International Journal of Evidence Based Coaching and Mentoring*, Special Issue No. 2, 40–51.

Peltier, B. (2001). *The psychology of executive coaching: Theory and application*. Ann Arbor, MI: Sheridan Books.

Rogers, J. (2004). *Coaching skills: A handbook*. New York: Open University Press.

Chapter 33: Current Research on Coaching

Ahern, G. (2005). Coaching professionalism and provider size. *Journal of Management Development*, 24(1), 94–99.

Akrivou, K. (2008). *Differentiation and integration in adult development: The influence of self complexity and integrative learning on self integration*. Doctoral dissertation, Case Western Reserve University, Cleveland, OH.

Allan, P. (2007). The benefits and impacts of a coaching and mentoring programme for teaching staff in secondary school. *International Journal of Evidence Based Coaching and Mentoring*, 5(2), 12–21.

Allen, M., Lezzoni, L., Lezzioni, I., Huang, A., Huang, L., & Leveille, S. (2008). Improving patient-clinician communication about chronic conditions: Description of an Internet-based nurse e-coach intervention. *Nursing Research*, 57(2), 107–112.

Arakawa, S., & Greenberg, M. (2007). Optimistic managers and their influence on productivity and employee engagement in a technology organization: Implications for coaching psychologists. *International Coaching Psychology Review*, 2(1), 77–89.

Ascentia. (2005a). Home office—case study team manager coaching. *International Journal of Evidence Based Coaching and Mentoring*, 3(1). www.business.brookes.ac.uk/research/areas/coachingandmentoring/volume/case_studies2.html.

Ascentia. (2005b). Leicester case study feedback group coaching—can it make a difference? *International Journal of Evidence Based Coaching and Mentoring*, 3(1). www.business.brookes.ac.uk/research/areas/coachingandmentoring/volume/case_studies2.html.

Astorino, D. M. (2004). Executive coaching and adult development: An integration of perspectives. *Dissertation Abstracts International*, 65(5), 2611B.

Bachkirova, T., & Cox, E. (2007). Coaching with emotion in organisations: Investigation of personal theories. *Leadership & Organization Development Journal*, 28, 600–612.

Ballinger, M. S. (2000). Participant self-perceptions about the causes of behavior change from a program of executive coaching. *Dissertation Abstracts International, 61,* 4451.

Baron, L., & Morin, L. (2009). The coach-coachee relationship in executive coaching: A field study. *Human Resource Development Quarterly, 20*(1), 85–106.

Bell, S. E. (2006). Myers-Briggs Type Indicator and executive coaching: Participants' self-perceptions about the effectiveness of the two when used together. *Dissertation Abstracts International, 66*(7), 3980B.

Bennett, J. A., & Perrin, N. A. (2005, June). Healthy aging demonstration project: Nurse coaching for behavior change in older adults. *Research in Nursing & Health, 28*(3), 187–197.

Berger, J. G., & Atkins, P.W.B. (2009). Mapping complexity of mind: Using the subject-object interview in coaching. *Coaching: An International Journal of Theory, Research and Practice, 2*(1), 23–36.

Binstead, T., & Grant, A. M. (2008). An exploratory study of Australian executive coaches. *International Coaching Psychology Review, 3*(1), 43–55.

Blattner, J. (2005). Coaching: The successful adventure of a downwardly mobile executive. *Consulting Psychology Journal: Practice and Research, 57*(1), 3–13.

Blattner, J., & Bacigalupo, A. (2007). Using emotional intelligence to develop executive leadership and team and organizational development. *Consulting Psychology Journal: Practice and Research, 59*(3), 209–219.

Blow, S. (2005). Can coaching strategies help experts share expertise? *International Journal of Evidence Based Coaching and Mentoring, 3*(2). www.business.brookes.ac.uk/research/areas/coachingandmentoring/volume/blow.html.

Boespflug, S. A. (2005). Attitudes of future male business managers towards seeking psychotherapy. *Dissertation Abstracts International, 65*(12), 6642B.

Bowles, S. V., Cunningham, C. J., Rosa, G. M., & Picano, J. J. (2007). Coaching leaders in middle and executive management: Goals, performance, buy-in. *Leadership & Organization Development Journal, 28,* 388–408.

Bowles, S. V., & Picano, J. J. (2006). Dimensions of coaching related to productivity and quality of life. *Consulting Psychology Journal: Practice & Research, 58*(4), 232–239.

Braham, B. J. (2006). Executive coaching and the worldview of Vipassana meditators: A heuristic inquiry. *Dissertation Abstracts International, 67*(5), 2864B.

Brantley, M. E. (2007). Executive coaching and deep learning. *Dissertation Abstracts International, 68*(3), 848A.

Bricklin, S. M. (2002). The rapport program: A model for improving the emotional intelligence of executive coaching clients. *Dissertation Abstracts International, 62*(11), 5363B. University Microfilms International.

Brooks, I., & Wright, S. (2007). A survey of executive coaching practices in New Zealand. *International Journal of Evidence Based Coaching and Mentoring, 5*(1), 30–41.

Burke, D., & Linley, P. (2007). Enhancing goal self-concordance through coaching. *International Coaching Psychology Review, 2*(1), 62–69.

Bush, M. W. (2005). Client perceptions of effectiveness in executive coaching. *Dissertation Abstracts International, 66*(4), 1417A.

Butterworth, S., Linden, A., McClay, W., & Leo, M. C. (2006). Effect of motivational interviewing-based health coaching on employees' physical and mental health status. *Journal of Occupational Health Psychology, 11*, 358–365.

Butwell, J. (2006). Group supervision for coaches: Is it worthwhile? A study of the process in a major professional organisation. *International Journal of Evidence Based Coaching and Mentoring, 4*(2). www.business.brookes.ac.uk/research/areas/coachingandmentoring/volume/burtwell.

Carpenter, H. V. (2006). *Reconceptualizing communication competence: High performing coordinated communication competence, HPC 3. A three-dimensional view.* Doctoral dissertation, Fielding Graduate University, Santa Barbara, CA.

Charbonneau, M. A. (2003). Media selection in executive coaching: A qualitative study. *Dissertation Abstracts International, 64*(1), 450.

Choong, S., & Britton, K. (2007). Character strengths and type: Exploration of covariation. *International Coaching Psychology Review, 2*(1), 9–23.

Clark, R. S. (2003). *Leadership development: Continuous improvement through character assessment.* Doctoral dissertation, University of San Diego, CA.

Cleary, T. J., & Zimmerman, B. J. (2004). Self-regulation empowerment program: A school-based program to enhance self-regulated and self-motivated cycles of student learning. *Psychology in the Schools, 41*, 537–550.

Clegg, S. R., Rhodes, C., Kornberger, M., & Stilin, R. (2005). Business coaching: Challenges for an emerging industry. *Industrial & Commercial Training, 37*(5), 218–223.

Conway, R. L. (2000). The impact of coaching mid-level managers utilizing multi-rater feedback. *Dissertation Abstracts International, 60*(7), 2672A. University Microfilms International.

Cox, E., & Bachkirova, T. (2007). Coaching with emotion: How coaches deal with difficult emotional situations. *International Coaching Psychology Review, 2*(2), 178–190.

Cox, E., & Dannahy, P. (2005). The value of openness in e-relationships: Using nonviolent communication to guide online coaching and mentoring. *International Journal of Evidence Based Coaching and Mentoring, 3*(1). www.business.brookes.ac.uk/research/areas/coachingandmentoring/volume/cox&dannahy.html.

Crawshaw, L. A. (2006). *Coaching abrasive executives: Exploring the use of empathy in constructing less destructive interpersonal management strategies.* Unpublished doctoral dissertation, Fielding Graduate University, Santa Barbara, CA.

Creane, V.E.J.R. (2003). *An exploratory study of personal coaching from the client's perspective.* Doctoral dissertation, California Institute of Integral Studies, San Francisco.

Czigan, T. K. (2008). *Combining coaching and temperament: Implications for middle management leadership development.* Doctoral dissertation, Capella University, Minneapolis, MN, www.capella.edu.

Dagley, G. (2006). Human resources professionals' perceptions of executive coaching: Efficacy, benefits and return on investment. *International Coaching Psychology Review*, *1*(2), 34–44.

Dawdy, G. N. (2004). Executive coaching: A comparative design exploring the perceived effectiveness of coaching and methods. *Dissertation Abstracts International*, *65*(5), 2674B.

de Haan, E. (2008a). Becoming simultaneously thicker and thinner skinned: The inherent conflicts arising in the professional development of coaches. *Personnel Review*, *37*, 526–542.

de Haan, E. (2008b). I struggle and emerge: Critical moments of experienced coaches. *Consulting Psychology Journal: Practice and Research*, *60*(1), 106–131.

Drum, J. (2007). A fruitful soil: What coaches can learn from how theatre directors in rehearsal create a learning environment. *International Journal of Evidence Based Coaching and Mentoring*, *5*(2). www.business.brookes.ac.uk/research/areas/coaching andmentoring/volume/drum.html.

Duijts, S., Kant, I., van den Brandt, P., & Swaen, G. (2007). The compatibility between characteristics of employees at risk for sickness absence and components of a preventive coaching intervention. *International Journal of Evidence Based Coaching and Mentoring*, *5*(1). www.business.brookes.ac.uk/research/areas/coachingandmentoring/ volume/duijts.html.

Duijts, S., Kant, I., van den Brandt, P., & Swaen, G. (2008). Effectiveness of a preventive coaching intervention for employees at risk for sickness absence due to psychosocial health complaints: Results of a randomized controlled trial. *Journal of Occupational & Environmental Medicine*, *50*, 765–776.

Dupuis, M. A. (2004). *Spiritual influences on individual optimal performance at work*. Doctoral dissertation, Union Institute and University, Cincinnati, OH, www.myunion.edu.

Duran-Whitney, M. (2005). Understanding occupational stress and mental health in aspiring small business owners. *Dissertation Abstracts International*, *65*(5), 2675B.

Ellinger, A. E., Ellinger, A. D., Keller, S. B. (2005). Supervisory coaching in a logistics context. *International Journal of Physical Distribution & Logistics Management*, *35*, 620–636.

Ernst, D. B. (2008). Motivational interviewing and health coaching: A quantitative and qualitative exploration of integration. *Dissertation Abstracts International*, *69*(1), 674B.

Evers, W.J.G., Brouwers, A., & Tomic, W. (2006). A quasi-experimental study on management coaching effectiveness. *Consulting Psychology Journal: Practice and Research*, *58*(3), 174–182.

Fahy, T. P. (2007). Executive coaching as an accelerator for whole system organizational change. *Dissertation Abstracts International*, *68*(3), 1066A.

Fanasheh, H. A. (2003). The perception of executive coaching among CEOs of America's top 500 companies. *Dissertation Abstracts International*, *64*(3), 736.

Feggetter, A. J. (2007). A preliminary evaluation of executive coaching: Does executive coaching work for candidates on a high potential development scheme? *International Coaching Psychology Review*, *2*(2), 129–142.

Gattellari, M., Donnelly, N., Taylor, N., Meerkin, M., Hirst, G., & Ward, J. (2005, June). Does "peer coaching" increase GP capacity to promote informed decision making about PSA screening? A cluster randomised trial. *Family Practice*, *22*, 253–265.

Gorczynski, P. M., Morrow, D., & Irwin, J. (2008). The impact of co-active coaching on physically inactive 12 to 14 year olds in Ontario. *International Journal of Evidence Based Coaching and Mentoring*, *6*(2). www.business.brookes.ac.uk/research/areas/coachingandmentoring/volume/6-2-2%20%20Gorczynski%20Morrow%20Irwin.pdf.

Govindji, R., & Linley, A. P. (2007). Strengths use, self-concordance and well-being: Implications for strengths coaching and coaching psychologists. *International Coaching Psychology Review*, *2*(2), 143–154.

Grant, A. M. (2002). Towards a psychology of coaching: The impact of coaching on metacognition, mental health and goal attainment. *Dissertation Abstracts International*, *63*(12), 6094.

Grant, A. M. (2003). The impact of life coaching on goal attainment, metacognition and mental health. *Social Behavior & Personality*, *31*, 253–264.

Grant, A. M. (2007). Enhancing coaching skills and emotional intelligence through training. *Industrial & Commercial Training*, *39*, 257–266.

Grant, A. M. (2008). Personal life coaching for coaches-in-training enhances goal attainment, insight and learning. *Coaching: An International Journal of Theory, Research and Practice*, *1*(1), 54–70.

Grant, A. M. (2009, May). *Workplace, executive and life coaching: An annotated bibliography from the behavioral science and business literature.* Coaching Psychology Unit, University of Sydney, Australia.

Grant, A. M., & Cavanagh, M. J. (2007). The goal-focused coaching skill questionnaire: Preliminarily findings. *Social Behavior and Personality*, *35*, 751–760.

Grant, A. M., Curtayne, L., & Burton, G. (2009). Executive coaching enhances goal attainment, resilience and workplace well-being: A randomised controlled study. *Journal of Positive Psychology*, *4*(5), 396–407.

Grant, A. M., & O'Hara, B. (2006). The self-presentation of commercial Australian life coaching schools: Cause for concern? *International Coaching Psychology Review*, *1*(2), 21–33.

Grant, A. M., & O'Hara, B. (2008). Key characteristics of the commercial Australian executive coach training. *International Coaching Psychology Review*, *3*(2), 57–73.

Grant, A. M., & Zackon, R. (2004). Executive, workplace and life coaching: Findings from a large-scale survey of international coach federation members. *International Journal of Evidence Based Coaching and Mentoring*, *2*(2). www.business.brookes.ac.uk/research/areas/coachingandmentoring/volume/grant&zackon.html.

Gravel, T. M. (2007). Principal time commitment and job satisfaction before and after an executive coaching workshop. *Dissertation Abstracts International Section, 68*(4), 1247A.

Green, L., Oades, L. G., & Grant, A. M. (2006). Cognitive-behavioral, solution-focused life coaching: Enhancing goal striving, well-being, and hope. *Journal of Positive Psychology, 1*(3), 142–149.

Green, S., Grant, A. M., & Rynsaardt, J. (2007). Evidence-based life coaching for senior high school students: Building hardiness and hope. *International Coaching Psychology Review, 2*(1), 24–32.

Grezemkovsky, U. (2006). Happiness is the cure: Self-improvement and authenticity in contemporary American life. *Dissertation Abstracts International, 67*(4), 1411A.

Griffin, J. P., Jr. (2005, November). The building resiliency and vocational excellence (BRAVE) program: A violence-prevention and role model program for young, African American males. *Journal of Health Care for the Poor and Underserved, 16*(4, Pt. B), 78–88.

Gyllensten, K., & Palmer, S. (2005). Can coaching reduce workplace stress? A quasi-experimental study. *International Journal of Evidence Based Coaching and Mentoring 3*(2), 75–85.

Gyllensten, K., & Palmer, S. (2006). Experiences of coaching and stress in the workplace: An interpretative phenomenological analysis. *International Coaching Psychology Review, 1*(1), 86–98.

Gyllensten, K., & Palmer, S. (2007). The coaching relationship: An interpretative phenomenological analysis. *International Coaching Psychology Review, 2*(2), 168–177.

Hamlin, R. G., Ellinger, A. D., & Beattie, R. S. (2006). Coaching at the heart of managerial effectiveness: A cross-cultural study of managerial behaviours. *Human Resource Development International, 9*(3), 305–331.

Hancyk, P. (2000). Coaching in the corporate environment. *Dissertation Abstracts International MAI 38/06, p. 1418.*

Harding, C. (2006). Using the multiple intelligences as a learning intervention: A model for coaching and mentoring? *International Journal of Evidence Based Coaching and Mentoring, 4*(2), 19–42.

Huggler, L.A.A. (2007). CEOs on the couch: Building the therapeutic coaching alliance in psychoanalytically informed executive coaching. *Dissertation Abstracts International, 68*(3), 1971B.

Hughes, J. L. (2003). *Adjusting the mirror: Strategies for coaching executives with narcissistic personality features.* Doctoral dissertation, Rutgers, the State University of New Jersey, Graduate School of Applied and Professional Psychology.

Hurd, J. L. (2003). *Learning for life: A phenomenological investigation into the effect of organizational coaching on individual lives.* Doctoral dissertation, Union Institute and University, Cincinnati, OH, www.myunion.edu.

Hymes, A. J. (2008). Leadership development: A case study exploring the coaching needs of emerging leaders. *Dissertation Abstracts International, 69*(6), 3888B.

Jackson, P. (2005). How do we describe coaching? An exploratory development of a typology of coaching based on the accounts of UK-based practitioners. *International Journal of Evidence Based Coaching and Mentoring, 3*(2), 45–60.

Jones, G., & Spooner, K. (2006). Coaching high achievers. *Consulting Psychology Journal: Practice & Research, 58*(1), 40–50.

Jones, R. A., Rafferty, A. E., & Griffin, M. (2006). The executive coaching trend: Towards more flexible executives. *Leadership & Organization Development Journal, 27*, 584–596.

Kampa-Kokesch, S. (2002). Executive coaching as an individually tailored consultation intervention: Does it increase leadership? *Dissertation Abstracts International, 62*(7), 3408B. University Microfilms International.

Kanne, D. W. (2006). Emotional intelligence and the transformational learning journey of 30 senior pastors who participated in LEAD (Leadership Evaluation and Development). *Dissertation Abstracts International, 66*(8), 2962A.

Kappenberg, E. S. (2008). *A model of executive coaching: Key factors in coaching success.* Unpublished doctoral dissertation, Claremont Graduate University, Claremont, CA. ProQuest Dissertations & Theses.

Karas, D., & Spada, M. M. (2009). Brief cognitive-behavioural coaching for procrastination: A case study. *Coaching: An International Journal of Theory, Research and Practice, 2*(1), 44–53.

Kleinberg, J. A. (2001). A scholar-practitioner model for executive coaching: Applying theory and application within the emergent field of executive coaching. *Dissertation Abstracts International, 61*(12), 4853A. University Microfilms International.

Kombarakaran, F., Baker, M. N., Yang, J. A., & Fernandes, P. B. (2008). Executive coaching: It works! *Consulting Psychology Journal: Practice and Research, 60*(1), 78–90.

Konczak, L. J., Stelly, D. J., & Trusty, M. L. (2000). Defining and measuring empowering leader behaviors: Development of an upward feedback instrument. *Educational & Psychological Measurement, 60*, 301–313.

Law, H., Ireland, S., & Hussain, Z. (2006). Evaluation of the coaching competence self-review online tool within an NHS leadership development programme. *International Coaching Psychology Review, 1*(2), 56–67.

Leedham, M. (2005). The coaching scorecard: A holistic approach to evaluating the benefits of business coaching. *International Journal of Evidence Based Coaching and Mentoring, 3*(2). www.business.brookes.ac.uk/research/areas/coachingandmentoring/volume/leedham.html.

Levy, P. E., Cober, R. T., & Miller, T. (2002). The effect of transformational and transactional leadership perceptions on feedback-seeking intentions. *Journal of Applied Social Psychology, 32*, 1703–1720.

Libri, V., & Kemp, T. (2006). Assessing the efficacy of a cognitive behavioural executive coaching programme. *International Coaching Psychology Review, 1*(2), 9–18.

Liljenstrand, A. M. (2004). *A comparison of practices and approaches to coaching based on academic background.* Doctoral dissertation, Alliant International University, San Diego, CA.

Liljenstrand, A. M., &, Nebeker, D. M. (2008). Coaching services: A look at coaches, clients, and practices. *Consulting Psychology Journal: Practice and Research, 60*(1), 57–77.

Longenecker, C. O., & Neubert, M. J. (2005). The practices of effective managerial coaches. *Business Horizons, 48*, 493–500.

Longhurst, L. (2006). The "aha" moment in co-active coaching and its effects on belief and behavioural changes. *International Journal of Evidence Based Coaching and Mentoring, 4*(2), 61–73.

Luebbe, D. M. (2005). The three-way mirror of executive coaching. *Dissertation Abstracts International, 66*(3), 1771B.

Mackenzie, H. (2007). Stepping off the treadmill: A study of coaching on the RCN Clinical Leadership Programme. *International Journal of Evidence Based Coaching and Mentoring, 5*(2). www.business.brookes.ac.uk/research/areas/coachingandmentoring/volume/mackenzie.html.

Mansi, A. (2007). Executive coaching and psychometrics: A case study evaluating the use of the Hogan Personality Inventory (HPI) and the Hogan Development Survey (HDS) in senior management coaching. *Coaching Psychologist, 3*(2), 53–58.

Marshall, M. K. (2007). The critical factors of coaching practice leading to successful coaching outcomes. *Dissertation Abstracts International, 67*(7), 4092B.

Martell, N. G. (2005). *The voice of leadership: Critical success factors of executive women.* Unpublished doctoral dissertation, Widener University, Institute for Graduate Clinical Psychology, Chester, PA.

McDermott, M., Levenson, A., & Newton, S. (2007). What coaching can and cannot do for your organization. *Human Resource Planning, 30*(2), 30–37.

McVea, C. (2007). Freedom to act in new ways: The application of Moreno's spontaneity theory and role theory to psychological coaching. *Australian Psychologist, 42*, 295–299.

Miller, P. (2003). Workplace learning by action learning: A practical example. *Journal of Workplace Learning: Employee Counselling Today, 15*(1), 14–23.

Miller, W. R., Yahne, C. E., Moyers, T. B., Martinez, J., & Pirritano, M. (2004). A randomized trial of methods to help clinicians learn motivational interviewing. *Journal of Consulting & Clinical Psychology, 72*, 1050–1062.

Morgeson, F. P. (2005, May). The external leadership of self-managing teams: Intervening in the context of novel and disruptive events. *Journal of Applied Psychology, 90*, 497–508.

Mulec, K., & Roth, J. (2005). Action, reflection, and learning and coaching in order to enhance the performance of drug development project management teams. *R&D Management, 35*, 483–491.

Navalta, C. P., Goldstein, J., Ruegg, L., Perna, D. A., & Frazier, J. A. (2006). Integrating treatment and education for mood disorders: An adolescent case report. *Clinical Child Psychology and Psychiatry, 11*, 555–568.

Newsom, G. (2009). A work behavior analysis of executive coaches. *Dissertation Abstracts International, 69*(7), 2617A.

Noer, D. M., Leupold, C. R., & Valle, M. (2007). An analysis of Saudi Arabian and US managerial coaching behaviors. *Journal of Managerial Issues, 19*, 271–287.

Olsen, C. M. (2006). Potential coaching clients and their perceptions of helpful coaching behaviors: A Q-methodological study. *Dissertation Abstracts International, 66*(7), 3985B.

Orenstein, R. L. (2000). Executive coaching: An integrative model. *Dissertation Abstracts International, 61*(04), 2257B.

Orenstein, R. L. (2002). Executive coaching: It's not just about the executive. *Journal of Applied Behavioral Science, 38*, 355–374.

Ozkan, E. (2008). Executive coaching: Crafting a versatile self in corporate America. *Dissertation Abstracts International, 69*(2), 651A.

Palmer, S., & Gyllensten, K. (2008). How cognitive behavioural, rational emotive behavioural or multimodal coaching could prevent mental health problems, enhance performance and reduce work related stress. *Journal of Rational-Emotive & Cognitive Behavior Therapy, 26*(1), 38–52.

Parker-Wilkins, V. (2006). Business impact of executive coaching: Demonstrating monetary value. *Industrial & Commercial Training, 38*, 122–127.

Passmore, J., & Brown, A. (2009). Coaching non-adult students for enhanced examination performance: A longitudinal study. *Coaching: An International Journal of Theory, Research and Practice, 2*(1), 54–64.

Peel, D. (2006). An analysis of the impact of SME organisational culture on coaching and mentoring. *International Journal of Evidence Based Coaching and Mentoring, 4*(1). www.business.brookes.ac.uk/research/areas/coachingandmentoring/volume/peel3.html.

Peel, D. (2008). What factors affect coaching and mentoring in small and medium sized enterprises. *International Journal of Evidence Based Coaching and Mentoring, 6*(2). www.business.brookes.ac.uk/research/areas/coachingandmentoring/volume/6-2-3%20%20Peel.pdf.

Peterson, D. B., & Millier, J. (2005). The alchemy of coaching: "You're good, Jennifer, but you could be really good." *Consulting Psychology Journal: Practice & Research, 57*(1), 14–40.

Rogers, K. L. (2005). An action research study of life coaches: The benefits of a specialized life coaching business plan template designed specifically for the life coaching industry. *Dissertation Abstracts International, 65*(10), 3665A.

Roy, A. F. (2007). An examination of the principle-based leadership trainings and business consultations of a group private practice. *Dissertation Abstracts International, 68*(5), 3437B.

Rundle-Gardiner, A. C., & Carr, S. C. (2005, November). Quitting a workplace that discourages achievement motivation: Do individual differences matter? *New Zealand Journal of Psychology*, *34*(3), 149–156.

Schnell, E. R. (2005). A case study of executive coaching as a support mechanism during organizational growth and evolution. *Consulting Psychology Journal: Practice and Research*, *57*(1), 41–56.

Seamons, B. L. (2006). The most effective factors in executive coaching engagements according to the coach, the client, and the client's boss. *Dissertation Abstracts International*, *67*(1), 588B.

Smither, J. W., London, M., Flautt, R., Vargas, Y., & Kucine, I. (2003). Can working with an executive coach improve multisource feedback ratings over time? A quasi-experimental field study. *Personnel Psychology*, *56*(1), 23–44.

Sparrow, J. (2007). Life coaching in the workplace. *International Coaching Psychology Review*, *2*, 277–297.

Spence, G. B., Cavanagh, M. J., & Grant, A. M. (2006). Duty of care in an unregulated industry: Initial findings on the diversity and practices of Australian coaches. *International Coaching Psychology Review*, *1*(1), 71–85.

Spence, G. B., Cavanagh, M. J., & Grant, A. M. (2008). The integration of mindfulness training and health coaching: An exploratory study. *Coaching: An International Journal of Theory, Research and Practice*, *1*(2), 145–163.

Spence, G. B., & Grant, A. M. (2007). Professional and peer life coaching and the enhancement of goal striving and wellbeing: An exploratory study. *Journal of Positive Psychology*, *2*(3), 185–194.

St. Claire-Ostwald, B. (2007). Carrying cultural baggage: The contribution of socio-cultural anthropology to cross-cultural coaching. *International Journal of Evidence Based Coaching and Mentoring*, *5*(2). www.business.brookes.ac.uk/research/areas/coachingandmentoring/volume/stclaireostwald.html.

Starman, J. (2007). The impact of executive coaching on job performance from the perspective of executive women. *Dissertation Abstracts International*, *68*(5), 1783A.

Stein, I. F. (2008). Enacting the role of coach: Discursive identities in professional coaching discourse (doctoral dissertation, Fielding Graduate University, 2008). *Dissertation Abstracts International*, *69*(3).

Stevens, J. H., Jr. (2005). Executive coaching from the executive's perspective. *Consulting Psychology Journal: Practice and Research*, *57*(4), 274–285.

Stewart, L. J., Palmer, S., Wilkin, H., & Kerrin, M. (2008). The influence of character: Does personality impact coaching success? *International Journal of Evidence Based Coaching and Mentoring*, *6*(1), 32–42.

Styhre, A., & Josephson, P. E. (2007). Coaching the site manager: Effects on learning and managerial practice. *Construction Management & Economics*, *25*, 1295–1304.

Sue-Chan, C., & Latham, G. P. (2004). The relative effectiveness of external, peer, and self-coaches. *Applied Psychology*, *53*, 260–278.

Sztucinski, K. (2002). The nature of executive coaching: An exploration of the executive's experience. *Dissertation Abstracts International, 62*(10), 4826B.

Terrell, J. D. (2004). Leaders and the psychology of leadership. *Dissertation Abstracts International, 65*(5), 2654B.

Topp, E. M. (2007). Presence-based coaching: The practice of presence in relation to goal-directed activity (mindfulness, coaching). *Dissertation Abstracts International, 67*(7), 4144B.

Trathen, S. A. (2008). Executive coaching, changes in leadership competencies and learning agility amongst Microsoft senior executives. *Dissertation Abstracts International, 69*(1), 727B.

Traynor, S. J. (2000). The role of psychologist in leadership development: Training, coaching, mentoring, and therapy. *Dissertation Abstracts International, 61*(4), 2225B.

Turner, C. E. (2003). Executive coaching as a leadership development strategy. *Dissertation Abstracts International, 64*(4), 1332.

van Zandvoort, M. I., Irwin, J., & Morrow, D. (2009). The impact of co-active life coaching on female university students with obesity. *International Journal of Evidence Based Coaching and Mentoring, 7*(1). www.business.brookes.ac.uk/research/areas/coachingandmentoring/volume/7-1-4%20van%20Zandvoort%20Irwin%20Morrow%20-%20Impact%20of%20Co-active%20life%20coaching.pdf.

Vance, C. M., & Paik, Y. P. (2005). Forms of host-country national learning for enhanced MNC absorptive capacity. *Journal of Managerial Psychology, 20*, 590–606.

Vloeberghs, D., Pepermans, R., Thielmans, K. (2005). High-potential development policies: An empirical study among Belgian companies. *Journal of Management Development, 24*, 546–558.

Volz-Peacock, M. (2006). Values and cohesiveness: A case study of a federal team (doctoral dissertation, The George Washington University). *Dissertation Abstracts International, 67*(5), 2868B.

Wachholz, P. O. (2000). Investigating a corporate coaching event: Focusing on collaborative reflective practice and the use of displayed emotions to enhance the supervisory coaching process. *Dissertation Abstracts International, 61*(2), 587A.

Wales, S. (2003). Why coaching? *Journal of Change Management, 3*, 275–282.

Wangsgard, T. G. (2007). A construct of coaching skills and the effect of an original treatment on management behavior. *Dissertation Abstracts International, 67*(8), 3071A.

Wasylyshyn, K. M., Gronsky, B., & Haas, J. (2006). Tigers, stripes, and behavior change: Survey results of a commissioned coaching program. *Consulting Psychology Journal: Practice and Research, 58*(2), 65–81.

Wenzel, L. H. (2001). Understanding managerial coaching: The role of manager attributes and skills in effective coaching. *Dissertation Abstracts International, 61*(8), 4462B. University Microfilms International.

Whybrow, A., & Palmer, S. (2006). Taking stock: A survey of coaching psychologists' practices and perspectives. *International Coaching Psychology Review, 1*(1), 56–70.

Wilkins, B. M. (2000). A grounded theory study of personal coaching. *Dissertation Abstracts International, 61*(5), 1713A.

Williamson, T. (2005, November). Work-based learning: A leadership development example from an action research study of shared governance implementation. *Journal of Nursing Management, 13,* 490–499.

Winum, P. C. (2005). Effectiveness of a high-potential African American executive: The anatomy of a coaching engagement. *Consulting Psychology Journal: Practice and Research, 57*(1), 71–89.

Yedreshteyn, S. (2009). A qualitative investigation of the implementation of an internal executive coaching program in a global corporation, grounded in organizational psychology theory. *Dissertation Abstracts International, 69*(7), 4471B.

THE EDITORS

Diane Brennan is passionate about coaching. She works with leaders and teams in organizations to expand thinking, navigate change, and create a learning culture. She took on leadership roles in the International Coach Federation (ICF) in order to promote global conversations and professionalization across the community, and served as the ICF global president in 2008. Diane is an executive coach, consultant, and author, and coedited *The Philosophy and Practice of Coaching* (Jossey-Bass, 2008). She was the first director of training for Fielding Graduate University's Evidence Based Coaching Program. She holds an MBA and an ICF Master Certified Coach designation, and is a board-certified medical practice executive and fellow of the American College of Medical Practice Executives. She can be reached at diane@coachdiane.com.

Leni Wildflower is a leading teacher and practitioner of knowledge-based coaching. With a master's degree in health education from the University of Hawaii and a doctorate from Fielding Graduate University in human and organizational development, she has taught at Fielding for over ten years, authoring courses in change management, conflict resolution, quality of work, leadership, and executive coaching. She envisioned, designed, and launched Fielding's Evidence Based Coaching Program, a pioneering blend of theory and skills training. Leni has a private practice in coaching and designs coaching programs and trainings for organizations, corporations, and nonprofits. She can be reached at leniwildflower@gmail.com.

THE CONTRIBUTORS

Janet Baldwin Anderson, PhD, is a coach, writer, and educator, and is on the faculty of Fielding Graduate University's Evidence Based Coaching Program. As president of JBA Coaching Services, LLC, she helps clients cultivate presence and authenticity in work and in life. (janet@jbacoaching.com)

Jacqueline Binkert, PhD, is a principal of Appreciative Coaching Collaborative, LLC, and coauthor of *Appreciative Coaching: A Positive Process for Change* (Jossey-Bass, 2007). She specializes in executive coaching, working with clients ranging from nonprofit organizations to international corporations. (jbinkert@ AppreciativeCoaching.com)

Diane Brennan, MBA, MCC, FACMPE, works with leaders and teams in health care, aerospace, engineering, science, and technology, and is president of Brennan Associates, a global leader in coaching. (diane@coachdiane.com)

Mary Ann Burke, PhD, is an author and consultant specializing in organizational hegemony, the politics of reform, and deep change in educational organizations. (drmab@cox.net)

Katrina Burrus, PhD, MCC, is the founder of MKB Conseil, Global Nomadic Leadership Development Institute. An executive coach of global nomadic leaders, abrasive leaders, and talents, Katrina's clients include the United Nations, the United Nations High Commissioner for Refugees, Nestlé, and Novartis. (drburrus@mkbconseil.ch)

Mary Wayne Bush, EdD, is an executive coach, consultant, and speaker. She is senior manager of organization effectiveness for a Fortune 100 company in the United States. (Marywayne@earthlink.net)

Francine Campone, EdD, MAC, MCC, helps mature professionals reinvent life by reinventing work (www.francinecampone.com) and is director of the Evidence Based Coaching Program at Fielding Graduate University. (Francine@reinventinglife.net)

Dian Christian, MBA, MSOD, PCC, is a business coach and consultant with a focus on using assessment in coaching. Some of her certifications include MBTI and Gallup Strengths Performance Coach. Dian is a doctoral student at Fielding Graduate University. (Dian@DianChristianConsulting.com)

Ann L. Clancy, PhD, is a principal of Appreciative Coaching Collaborative, LLC, and coauthor of *Appreciative Coaching: A Positive Process for Change* (Jossey-Bass, 2007). A business and executive coach, she specializes in coaching high-performing, high-potential individuals. (aclancy@AppreciativeCoaching.com)

David Clutterbuck is visiting professor of coaching and mentoring at Oxford Brookes and Sheffield Hallam Universities, practice leader at Clutterbuck Associates, and author of fifty books, fifteen in this area. (dclutterbuck@gpworldwide.com)

Connie S. Corley, MSW, PhD, is a professor at Fielding Graduate University School of Human and Organizational Development and at California State University, Los Angeles, Applied Gerontology and School of Social Work. (ccorley@fielding.edu)

David B. Drake, PhD, is executive director of the Center for Narrative Coaching, teaches internationally on the evolution of coaching, and helps organizations use coaching and narrative to guide culture change. (ddrake@narrativecoaching.com)

Sherry Harsch-Porter, BSBA, MA, PhD (expected June 2011), is president of the Porter Bay Group, Inc. Sherry is an executive coach and business consultant serving primarily Global 1000 companies, teaches graduate courses at Washington University, and is chapter chair for the Women Presidents' Organization. (sherry@porterbay.com)

Laura Hauser, MA, PCC, is the founder of Leadership Strategies International (www.leadership-strategies.com). Laura serves as an executive coach, strategic change consultant, conference speaker, and educator who teaches for Pepperdine University and Fielding Graduate University. (Laura@Leadership-Strategies.com)

Kate Hefferon, PhD, lectures in positive psychology at the University of East London. Her areas of interest include existential psychology, optimal experiences, and the psychology of physical activity. (K.Hefferon@uel.ac.uk)

Tony Latimer, MCC, coaches senior leaders across twenty-one countries in Asia Pacific, Europe, and Africa. He is the founder and program designer for the Asia Pacific Corporate Coach Institute. (trainingdirector@acci.sg)

John Leary-Joyce, MA (executive coaching), is dedicated to lifelong learning and personal development. A former Gestalt psychotherapist, John is now executive coach, trainer, and supervisor, and CEO of Academy of Executive Coaching. (John.learyjoyce@aoec.com)

Terrie Lupberger is a Master Certified Coach (MCC) and author. Her work for the last fifteen years has been with executives and experienced coaches, helping them build their leadership presence and maximize their impact and influence. (Terrie@terrielupberger.com)

David Megginson, PhD, is Emeritus Professor of Human Resource Development at Sheffield Business School in Sheffield Hallam University, United Kingdom. Cofounder of EMCC and author of seventeen books on coaching, David researches and challenges taken-for-granted assumptions in the field. (D.F.Megginson@shu.ac.uk)

Edward G. Modell, JD, PCC, Maryland Judiciary Ombudsman, has extensive experience as a conflict management professional, coach, mediator, and facilitator. (edmodell@aol.com)

Mary M. Nash, PhD, PCC, and principal, the Nash Group, LLC, is an organization development professional and coach, specializing in facilitating large-scale organizational change. (mary@thenashgroup.com)

Cinnie Noble, LLM (ADR), ACC, CMed, and founder of CINERGY Coaching, is a lawyer-mediator and coach. She developed the CINERGY model of conflict coaching in 1999 and provides training and coaching worldwide. (cinnie@cinergycoaching.com)

Kathy Norwood, MEd, PCC, educational consultant, trainer, and coach (www.designsforchange.net), trains and coaches educational coaches and leaders and helps establish district coaching models. (kathynorwood@netzero.com)

Linda J. Page, PhD, is a coach, writer, educator, and entrepreneur, and president of Adler Graduate Professional School in Toronto, Canada (www.adler.ca). She presents internationally on neuroscience and executive coach education. (ljpage@adler.ca)

Jonathan Passmore, PhD, is a chartered occupational psychologist and a fellow of the Chartered Institute of Personnel and Development; he is accredited by the Association for Coaching. Jonathan is director of the Coaching Psychology Unit, University of East London, United Kingdom. He has written thirteen books and over fifty papers on coaching. (jonathancpassmore@yahoo.co.uk)

Jenny Rogers is a pioneer of executive coaching in the United Kingdom, with over twenty years of experience in the field. She has a parallel career as a writer and as a teacher of coaching skills internationally. Her many books include *Adults Learning*, in print for more than thirty years though five editions; *Coaching Skills: A Handbook; Facilitating Groups;* and *Developing a Coaching Business.* (Jenny@JennyRogersCoaching.com)

Katrina S. Rogers, PhD, is associate dean for the doctoral program in the School of Human and Organizational Development and the director of the Institute for Social Innovation at Fielding Graduate University. Katrina has a background in international environmental policy and organizational sustainability. (krogers@fielding.edu)

Jennifer Sellers, PCC, is the CEO of Inspired Mastery, a leadership development company, and a faculty member in Fielding Graduate University's Evidence Based Coaching Program. (jen@inspiredmastery.com)

Irene F. Stein, PhD, is a member of the associate core faculty at the University of the Rockies in Colorado Springs, Colorado. Irene develops coaching education and is a graduate student educator and dissertation coach. (irenestein@att.net)

Reinhard Stelter, PhD (psychology), is a full professor of sport and coaching psychology at the University of Copenhagen, and is honorary vice president and accredited member of the Society of Coaching Psychology. (rstelter@ifi.ku.dk)

Chloé Tong, MSc, is a business psychologist at Dove Nest Group, United Kingdom. She previously worked as a research assistant for the Coaching Psychology Unit, University of East London, researching emotional intelligence and its development through coaching interventions in educational settings. (Chloe.tong@dovenest.co.uk)

Karen Tweedie, PCC, is partner at Point Ahead, a consulting and coaching practice dedicated to making Australian organizations the leading places to work for generations to come. Karen was the 2009 president of the International Coach Federation. (karen@pointahead.com.au)

Alison Whybrow, BSc (hons), PhD, is a chartered psychologist with i-coach academy Ltd, London. Alison has had the privilege of contributing significantly to the coaching psychology profession. She is continually delighted by the power of purposeful conversation. (Alison@i-coachacademy.com)

Leni Wildflower, PhD, PCC, is a leading teacher and practitioner of knowledge-based coaching. She envisioned, designed, and launched Fielding Graduate University's Evidence Based Coaching Program, a pioneering blend of theory and skills training. Leni has a private practice in coaching and designs coaching programs and trainings for organizations, corporations, and nonprofits. (leniwildflower@gmail.com)

Carol Wilson runs a global coach training consultancy and is head of accreditation at the Association for Coaching. (carolwilson@performancecoachtraining.com)

NAME INDEX

Brantley, M. E., 335
Braungart, M., 255
Brazzel, M., 173
Brennan, D., 89, 109, 119, 143, 301
Bricklin, S. M., 339
Bridges, W., 93–96, 97, 128, 132, 133–134, 139, 178–179, 182
Briggs, K., 324
Brinkert, R., 114
Britton, K., 339
Brooks, I., 331
Brothers, L., 65–68
Brouwers, A., 333
Brown, A., 337
Brown, S. W., 167–168
Bruner, J., 99, 276, 277
Bryk, A., 212
Buber, M., 81, 100–101, 102, 104
Buckingham, M., 27, 320
Burke, B. L., 91
Burke, D., 334
Burke, K., 272
Burke, M. A., 211, 213, 219–220
Burns, D., 15–16, 19
Burns, J. M., 153
Burr, V., 81, 83, 85, 87–88
Burrus, K., 231, 236–238, 239
Burrus-Barbey, K., 237
Burton, G., 336
Bush, M. W., 153, 175, 331
Butterworth, S., 335
Butwell, J., 332

C

Cameron, K. S, 156, 157
Campbell, D. P., 319–320
Campbell, J., 187, 272
Campion, M. A., 164
Campone, F., 203, 329
Capra, F., 259
Carlson, L. E., 206–207
Carman, J., 226
Carman, N., 226
Carmona, P. E., 203

Carpenter, H. V., 339
Carr, S. C., 336–337
Carroll, D., 228–229
Carroll, J. B., 51
Carson, S. H., 205
Carstensen, L., 224
Caruso, D. R., 54, 59, 323–324
Cattell, R. B., 51, 319
Cavanagh, M. J., 280, 331, 332, 335
Cayer, M., 252
Chaffee, P., 290
Chandler, D. E., 302
Charbonneau, M. A., 331
Check, J. A., 181
Cherney, J., 287
Choong, S., 339
Christian, D., 315
Chung Wei, R., 211
Cissna, K. N., 100
Clancy, A. L., 287, 292, 295
Clandinin, D. J., 272
Clark, D. A., 13
Clark, R. S., 335
Cleary, T., 213, 337
Clegg, S. R., 332
Clifton, D. O., 25, 27, 320
Clinchy, B. M., 39
Cloke, K., 109, 117
Clutterbuck, D., 10, 20, 172, 299
Cobb, J. B., 259
Cober, R. T., 336
Cochran, K., 227
Cogan, M., 214
Cohen, D. S., 182
Cohen, G., 222, 224–225, 227, 228
Cohen, H., 226
Collins, J., 145, 150, 151, 172
Combs, G., 277
Conger, J. A., 18
Connelly, F. M., 272
Conner, D. R., 182
Conway, R. L., 335
Cook-Greuter, S., 302
Cooperrider, D. L, 82, 287, 288, 295

Corley, C. S., 221, 227
Costa, A., 214, 219
Costa, P., 324
Cowan, C., 302
Cox, E., 10, 20, 77, 302, 331, 339
Cozolino, L., 277
Crawshaw, L. A., 336
Creane, V.E.J.R., 330
Cronen, V., 103–104
Crum, T., 117
Csikszentmihalyi, M., 21–22, 26, 27, 128, 136, 139, 188, 199, 202
Cumming, E., 224
Cunningham, C. J., 334
Cunningham, M., 256
Cunningham, W., 256
Curtayne, L., 336
Czigan, T. K., 335

D

Dagley, G., 333
Dalai Lama, 191
Daly, H., 259
Darling-Hammond, L., 211
Dawdy, G. N., 330
De Haan, E., 299, 332
De Shazer, S., 279
Deal, T. E., 156
Dean, B., 22
Dennett, D., 61
Descartes, R., 263
Deutchman, D., 227
Dewey, J., 73, 76
Dexter, E., 212
DiClemente, C. C., 89–90, 97
Dixon, K., 128, 137, 139
Doidge, N., 68, 204
Dole, J., 216
Downey, D., 182
Drake, D. B., 271, 273, 275, 277
Drucker, P., 144, 151
Drum, J., 339
Dryden, W., 16, 205
Duffy, G., 216
DuFour, R., 213
Duijts, S., 334

SUBJECT INDEX

A

Aberdeen Research, 181

Absolutist thinking, 16–17, 280

Abstract conceptualization (AC) stage, 76, 79

Acceptance: of change, 133; as spiritual principle, 191

Accommodator/activist (CE/AE), 78, 79

Accreditation, 300

Achievement-oriented cultures, 234

Action: in GROW model, 283, 284; learning and, 76–77; stage of change, 90

Action research, 216, 287, 337

Active experimentation (AE) stage, 77, 79

Activist style, 78

Activity, in healthy aging, 224–225

Adaptive challenges, 150

Addiction treatment, 90–91, 92, 200–201

Adhocracy culture, 156

Adjourning stage, of group development, 170, 171, 172

Adolescents, coaching impacts on, 337

Adult development: assessment tool for, 325; coach maturity and, 306; coaching models and, 338; gender and, 241–242, 247; sustainable thinking and, 252; theories of, 39–49; transitions and, 93–96

Adult Learner, The (Knowles et al.), 74, 80

Adult learning theories, 73–80

Adult state, 30, 36

Adversity, leadership and, 145

Affection stage, of group development, 170

Affiliation, aging and, 225–227

Affiliative leaders, 147

Affirmations, 92

Afterlife, of speech, 85, 87

Age, identity construction and, 84

Ageless Spirit (Goldman), 228

Aging: "four A" approach to, 223–228; issues of, 43–44, 221–229; new models of, 222–223; resources on, 223; social construction of, 84. *See also* Midlife

Aging Well (Vaillant), 229

Alcoholics Anonymous (AA), 195, 200–201, 202

Alcoholics Anonymous—Big Book, 202

Alexander Technique, 196

All-or-nothing thinking, 15

Alternative dispute resolution (ADR), 111–113, 114

Altruism, 24

American Educational Association, 317

American Management Association, 175

American Psychological Association, 317

Amygdala hijack, 67

Analysis paralysis, 164, 166

Analytic intelligence, 58

Anchoring, 199

Andragogy, 73, 74–75

Anger, 34, 40, 93, 95–96, 132, 134

Anticipatory grief, 132

Anticipatory principle, 290

Anxiety: cognitive behavioral therapy for, 12–13; in conflict situations, 109; Gestalt view of, 6; in groups, 166–167; in transitions, 93, 94, 96, 133, 134

Appreciative Coaching (Orem et al.), 295

Appreciative Inquiry (AI), 261, 287–296

Coach(es) (*continued*)
coaching philosophy of,
306; philosophy- or
discipline-based, 303;
process-based, 303, 305;
research on, 331–332;
supervision of, 304,
308–309, 310, 332, 343;
systemic eclectic,
303–313
Coach assessment centers,
300, 304, 309, 310
Coach development:
maturity model of,
301–313; personal
development and, 309;
personal journey of,
310–311, 312–313;
research on, 331–332; for
systemic eclectic coaching,
312–313
Coach knowledge: of
assessments, 315–317; of
business context, 306–307,
343; for conflict coaching,
111; for educational
coaching, 217; for
narrative coaching,
272–273; for older clients,
225; research on, 331–332;
in sustainability, 256–257;
in systems thinking,
256–257
Coach role: in change
process, 93; in educational
coaching, 215; research
on, 330–331; systems view
of, 126
Coach self-awareness: of
change process, 93; of
gender differences, 246,
247; of language use, 87,
291; maturity and, 302,
306; of mind-body
connection, 265–266;
mindfulness practice for,
207; in philosophy-based
coaching, 303, 305; of
positive emotions,

290–291; of SCARF
reactions, 67–68; of
spiritual and religious
values, 191, 192; in
systemic eclectic coaching,
303–313
"'Coach-Approach' as
Dialogic Discourse, The"
(Stein), 108
Coach-client relationship.
See Coaching relationship
Coaching: assessments in,
315–331; assimilation,
180–182, 183; attacks on,
341–342; career, 129–139;
cognitive, 18–19, 214, 215,
219, 225, 334, 335;
combined with other
development activities,
212–213, 335–336;
components of effective,
298; conflict, 112,
113–117; creative
applications of, 261;
delivery methods of, 331;
educational, 209, 211–220;
ethics of, 113, 276–277,
309, 316; evidence-based,
206, 214; future challenges
in, 341–344; human
potential movement and,
185, 195–202; impacts and
outcomes of, 333–336;
integrative models of, 338;
leadership, 141, 143–152,
177–183, 336, 337; life,
196, 214, 335; mind-sets
of, 302–304, 305;
narrative, 271–278;
ontological, 266–268, 269,
306; organizational
context and, 141, 215,
306–307; peer, 308,
334–335, 336; presence-
based, 208, 339, 343;
psychology and, 1–2, 261,
339; quality in, 297,
299–313, 342–344;
relational, 299; research

on, 297, 329–339;
single-theory models of,
338–339; social context
and, 71; solution-focused,
64, 216, 279–285, 303;
somatic, 265–266, 269;
spirituality and, 187–193;
team, 122, 163–173, 337;
theories specific to,
337–339; workplace issues
for, 155, 175–183
Coaching Across Cultures
(Rosinski), 239
Coaching Continuum,
215–216
*Coaching for Emotional
Intelligence* (Caruso and
Mayer), 59
Coaching for Performance
(Whitmore), 281, 285
*Coaching for
Transformational Change*
(Norwood and Burke),
219–220
Coaching industry, 332
"Coaching Managers in
Multinational Companies"
(Burrus), 239
Coaching relationship:
assessing coach-client fit
for, 311–312; attuned, 67;
boundary management in,
309–311; client-centered
approach to, 5–6;
cocreated meaning in,
99–104; collaborative
approach to, 101, 103,
290; communication in,
99–108; contracting for,
30, 192; cultural
differences and, 235;
gender differences and,
246, 247; importance of,
5–6; inviting others into,
83, 157; mediation and,
113; research on,
331; spirituality and
religion in, 187–193;
trust in, 7

Coaching style, of leadership, 147

Coaching the Team at Work (Clutterbuck), 172

Co-active coaching, 337

Coalitions, in family systems, 121

Code of practice, 309

Coercive leaders, 147, 148

Cognitive ability tests, 52, 55–56, 58

Cognitive behavioral coaching (CBC), 18–19, 225, 334, 335

"Cognitive Behavioral Coaching" (Williams et al.), 20

Cognitive behavioral therapy (CBT), 11–20, 205

Cognitive coaching, 214, 215, 219, 225

Cognitive Coaching (Costa and Garmston), 219

Cognitive distortions, 15–16, 34

Cognitive pessimism, 24–25

Cognitive theory, 12

Cognitive-rational approach, to transformative learning, 75–76

Collaborative, contingent conversations, 66–67

Collaborative language systems, 101, 103

Collaborative relationship: in Appreciative Inquiry, 290; client-centered approach and, 5; in cognitive behavioral therapy, 13; communication and, 101, 102, 103

Collective unconscious, 4, 9, 272

Collectivist cultures, 233, 235

"Combining Passions and Abilities" (Pearce and Pearce), 108

Commitments, competing, 218–219

Communication: coaching models and, 339; conversational styles and, 104–107; family systems and, 121; gender differences in, 244–246, 249, 250; of leaders, 177, 182; narrative skills and, 272, 274–276; nonverbal, 57, 64, 86; social constructionist views of, 85–87, 88, 99–104; theories of, 99–108; in Transactional Analysis, 30. *See also* Conversations; Dialogue; Language

Communities, resilient, 226

Compassion, 191, 192–193, 207, 241–242

Complete Handbook of Coaching, The (Cox et al.), 10, 20

Complexity of thinking, 44–45

Composing a Life (Bateson), 249

Conclusions, jumping to, 15

Concrete experience (CE) stage, 76

Conflict: assessment tools for, 115–116; coaching, 112, 113–117; conversational styles and, 245; dynamics of, 109–111; fear of, 32; in groups, 167, 169, 171; management, 109–117; social constructionist approach to, 86

Conflict Coaching (Noble), 117

Conflict Dynamics Profile (CDP), 115–116

Conflictdynamics.org, 115

Conflicts of interest, 113

Congruency, leader's, 144

Conjunctive faith, 189

Connection: aging and, 225–227, 229; as spiritual principle, 191; women and, 241–242

Conniecorleyphd.com, 223

Consciousness: of choice, 29, 30, 61–63; expanded views of, 9, 10, 39, 47–48, 49. *See also* Human potential movements; Spiritual and religious traditions

Constructivist theory: of adult development, 39, 44–45, 338; in Appreciative Inquiry, 289–290; social constructionism and, 81–88. *See also* Social constructionism

Contemplation stage, 89

Contemplative practices, 190

Context Shifting Worksheet, 19, 20

Continuity theory, 227

Contracting, 30, 192

Control stage, of group development, 170, 171–172

Converger/pragmatist (AC/AE), 78

Conversation(s): about assessment results, 318; coaching mind-sets and types of, 303–304; collaborative, contingent, 66–67; crucial, 110–111; listening to narrative in, 274–277; resources on, 108; social construction in, 291–292. *See also* Dialogue

Conversation, Language, and Possibilities (Anderson), 107

Conversation maps, 212, 214

Conversational styles, 104–107, 108, 244–246, 250

Ecologically intelligent design, 255

Ecology of Commerce, The (Hawken), 257, 259

Economic recession, 341

Education: coaching in, 209, 211–220; reform, 73

Educational approach, in cognitive behavioral therapy, 13–14

Education-world.com, 59

Efficacy, coach, 301, 307

Ego states, 30, 35–36

Elderhostel, 224

Emotional abilities model, 54

Emotional and Social Competency Inventory (ESCI), 321

Emotional Competence Inventory (ECI), 321, 327

Emotional cultures, 233–234

Emotional cutoff or disengagement, 123, 125

Emotional fusion or enmeshment, 123, 124, 125

Emotional intelligence: assessments of, 321, 323–324; capabilities and competencies of, 146–147; coaching applications of, 55–56, 339; coaching impacts on, 336; cultural intelligence and, 232; of leaders, 146–148, 151–152; models of, 54–55; resources on, 59, 88, 151–152

Emotional Intelligence (Goleman), 59, 146

Emotional Quotient Inventory (EQ-i, EQ-360), 321, 327

Emotional reasoning, 15, 24

Emotions: in career transitions, 131, 132; in change process, 95–96, 132, 133, 134, 178–180,

198–199; coach theories on, 331–332; in conflict and conflict management, 109–111, 115, 116; cultural differences in, 233–234; family systems and, 122, 123, 124; focus on positive, 21–24; in group dynamics, 166–167, 168; internal family systems and, 127, 128; leadership and, 145; mind-body connection and, 263–269; principle of positive, 290–291; self-help/human potential approaches to, 197–198; in Transactional Analysis, 30

Empathy: listening with, 5; multicultural, 237–238; self-compassion and, 207; social intelligence and, 56

Encounter groups, 196

Encyclopedia of Positive Psychology, The (Lopez), 27

Ending phase of change, 93–94, 95, 96, 133

Energy field, 300

Enneagram, 325

Enneagraminstitute.com, 325

Entrepreneurship, in older population, 222

Environmental Science (Cunningham and Cunningham), 256, 259

Environmental sustainability, 251–259

Equality, in Transactional Analysis, 29, 30, 32–33

Erhard Seminars Training (est), 196, 197, 202

Esalen Institute, 9, 196

Espoused theories, 159, 161

Essential Ken Wilber, The (Wilber), 49

Est, 196, 197, 202

Ethics, in coaching, 113, 276–277, 309, 316

Ethnorelativism, 236

European Mentoring and Coaching Council, 300–301

EXACT goal setting model, 282–283

Executive Coaching (Lee and Valerio), 182

"Executive Growth Along the Adult Development Curve" (Axelrod), 48

Exercise, 224, 225

Exiles, emotional, 127, 128

Existentialist approaches, 4, 6

Expectations, setting clear, 177–178

Experiential learning, 76–79, 80, 323

F

Failure: leadership and, 150–151; life position of, 32

Faith, stages of, 188–190

Family Healing (Minuchin), 128

Family systems therapy, 119–128

Fear: in change process, 94, 133, 198, 199, 202; of conflict, 32; self-beliefs and, 188

Feedback: client, 312, 330; in performance management, 177–178

Feel the Fear and Do It Anyway (Jeffers), 202

Feeling Good (Burns), 15

Feeling Good Handbook, The (Burns), 19

Fees, coaching, 301

Felt experience, 264

Female Advantage, The (Helgesen), 249

Female Vision, The (Helgesen and Johnson), 249

dynamics of, 166–168,
172, 173; process
perspective on, 7,
166–168; structure of, 164;
task perspective on,
164–166; teams *versus*,
163
Groupthink, 45
GROW model, 77, 281–284,
303
Guided Autobiography, 227
Guilt, 30, 201

H

Hamlet, 10, 90
*Handbook of Improving
Performance in the
Workplace* (Watkins and
Leigh), 183
Happiness, focus on, 21–25
Harvard Negotiation Project,
112
Hay McBer, 147
Haygroup.com, 321, 323
Hbdi.com, 322
Health and wellness: aging
and, 223–229; coaching
impacts on, 335, 339;
social brain and, 67. *See
also* Well-being
Health model framework, 22
*Heart of Change Field Guide,
The* (Cohen), 182
Heller Work, 196
Herrmann Brain Dominance
Instrument (HBDI), 322,
327
Hierarchy, 125, 153, 156,
215, 234, 242, 248
Hierarchy of Needs
(Maslow), 7, 8, 188
High-achieving women,
247–249
Hogan Personality Inventory
(HPI), 322, 327
Hoganassessments.com, 322
Holons, 47–48
How NASA Builds Teams
(Pellerin), 20, 162

How to Be an Adult (Richo),
49
*How to Be an Adult in
Relationships* (Richo),
202
*How We Talk Can Change
the Way We Work* (Kegan
and Lahey), 45, 97
Human potential
movements, 185, 195–202
Humanistic psychology:
mindfulness and, 205;
other therapies related to,
16, 29, 279; principles and
applications of, 3–10;
self-help/human potential
movements and, 195, 196
"Hurry Up" style, 33, 36

I

I and Thou (Buber), 101
IBM, 114, 232
Iceberg of conflict, 109–110,
111
Identity: life-cycle stages
and, 39–44; multiplicity
of, 126–128; narrative,
273–274; personal
brand and, 129, 136–139;
social construction of,
44–45, 83–85, 88, 272,
273–274
Identity crisis, 41
Illness, 223, 225
Illuminated Life, 227
I'm OK, You're OK (Harris),
31–33
"I'm Only Trying to Help
You" game, 35
Image coaching, 138–139
Images of an Organization
(Morgan), 161
Immunity to Change (Kegan
and Lahey), 44, 48, 96, 219
Immunity to Change
process, 45, 48, 96, 97,
218–219
Impact studies, of coaching,
333–336

Improving Performance
(Rummler and Brache),
183
In a Different Voice
(Gilligan), 242, 249
In Midlife (Stein), 49
In Over Our Heads (Kegan),
48
Inclusion stage, of group
development, 170
Indirectness, 106
Individualistic cultures, 233,
235
Individuation, 43
Individuative-reflective faith,
189
Industrial ecology, 254
Injunctions, in Transactional
Analysis, 33, 36
Inner Game of Stress
(Gallwey), 202
Inner Game of Tennis, The
(Gallwey), 198–199
Inner-directed cultures, 235
Innovator's Way, The
(Dunham), 268
Inquiry: Appreciative, 261,
287–296; cycle of, 216
Institute for Corporate
Productivity, 175
Institute for the Study of
Therapeutic Change, 207
Instructional coaching, 214,
215, 219
Instructional Coaching
(Knight), 219
Integral Institute Web site,
48
Integral Life Practices (Wilber
et al.), 49
Integrity, leader's, 144
Integrity-*versus*-despair
stage, 41, 227
Intelligence: cognitive,
51–52, 55–56, 58; cultural/
multicultural, 231–232,
237–238, 339; emotional,
54–56, 59, 146–148,
151–152, 232; multiple,

interviewing to overcome, 90–92; transitions and, 94–95, 97. *See also* Change; Transitions

Resolving Conflicts at Work (Cloke and Goldsmith), 117

Résumé review and coaching, 137–138

Retirement planning, 222

Retooling on the Run (Heller and Surrenda), 265, 267–268

Riding the Waves of Culture (Trompenaars and Hampden-Turner), 239

Riso-Hudson Enneagram Type Indicator (RHETI), 325, 328

Road Scholar, 224

Role-play, 76, 139

Rolfing, 196

Rootlessness, 238

Routledge Companion to International Business Coaching, The (Abbott), 239

S

Satisficing, 164

Saturated Self, The (Gergen), 88

"Saying, Doing and Making" (Holmgren), 108

Scaling questions, 280, 284

SCARF reactions, 67–68

School systems, coaching in, 209, 211–220

Seasons of a Man's Life, The (Levinson), 42–43, 48

Seasons of a Woman's Life, The (Levinson), 42–43

Second Shift, The (Hochschild), 243, 249

Second-shift issues, 244

Secrets of Becoming a Late Bloomer, The (Goldman and Mahler), 228

"See What You Made Me Do" game, 35

Self, multiplicity of, 126–128. *See also* Identity

Self-actualization, 5, 7–8, 9, 10

Self-authoring mind, 44

Self-awareness: activities to develop, 55, 148, 149; destiny and, 293; emotional intelligence and, 55, 146, 147, 148; intrapersonal intelligence and, 53; for leaders, 146, 147, 148, 149; of mind-body connection, 263–269; mindfulness training for, 203–208; of reactions to conflict, 116; for self-esteem, 126; spiritual/religious, 191, 192–193; underlying questions and, 62–63. *See also* Awareness; Coach self-awareness; Self-reflection

Self-destructive behaviors, 127

Self-directed learning, 215–217

Self-efficacy, 18, 46

Self-esteem, 42, 126

Self-help movements, 185, 195–202

Self-judgment. *See* Nonjudgmentalism

Self-leadership, 127

Self-limiting beliefs, 188

Self-management, 146, 147, 148, 310

Self-observation, 16, 206–207

Self-reflection: adult learning and, 79–80; aging and, 227–228; in Appreciative Inquiry, 288–289; in coaching session, 192; developing the capacity for, 45, 46–47; of leaders,

150–151; list making for, 79–80; mindful, 206–207; neuroscience and, 67; of school personnel, 217–219; in spiritual traditions, 190, 192. *See also* Reflection

Self-regulation, 213, 216

Self-Regulation Empowerment Program, 213

Self-reinforcement, 18

Self-Therapy (Earley), 128

Self-transforming mind, 44

Sensitivity training group, 169

Sequential-oriented cultures, 234–235

Serenity Prayer, 201

Shadow director, 306–307

"Should" statements, 15, 16, 30

Silence, 110

Silo thinking, 158

Simultaneity principle, 290

Situational awareness, 56, 57

Situational (social) skills exercises, 56–57

16 Personality Factors (16PF), 319, 327

SMART goal setting model, 282–283

Social brain, 65–68

Social capacities, 55

Social Construction (Gergen and Gergen), 295

Social Construction of Reality, The (Berger and Luckmann), 294–295

Social constructionism: Appreciative Inquiry and, 289–290, 291–292; communication and, 99–104; family systems and, 121; narrative and, 86–87, 272; organizations and, 154; resources on, 87–88, 294–295; theories and applications of, 81–88